D1249042

AN
APPROACH
TO
CHRISTOLOGY

By the same Author

THE NESTORIAN CHURCHES

a concise history of Nestorian Christianity in Asia
from the Persian schism to the Modern Assyrians

Independent Press Ltd.

AN APPROACH TO CHRISTOLOGY

AN INTERPRETATION AND DEVELOPMENT OF
SOME ELEMENTS IN THE METAPHYSIC AND
CHRISTOLOGY OF NESTORIUS AS A WAY OF
APPROACH TO AN ORTHODOX CHRISTOLOGY
COMPATIBLE WITH MODERN THOUGHT

BY

AUBREY R. VINE, M.A., D.D., B.Sc.

LONDON:
INDEPENDENT PRESS LTD.,
MEMORIAL HALL, E.C.4.

First published 1948

TO

MY WIFE

The typography and binding
of this book conform to the
authorized economy standard

Made and printed in Great Britain by
The Camelot Press Ltd., London and Southampton

PREFACE

THERE is no question the answer to which is so fraught with consequence as this: "What think ye of Christ?" If Jesus Christ is but one among the many who have sensed and sought after the highest ultimate realities, then we must certainly study His teaching and attempt to discover what He can contribute to the onward trending of human thought; but He will have no higher claim upon us than Moses, Isaiah, Socrates, Confucius, Mohammed, and many another, all of whom are to be considered but none of whom represents final authority. If, on the other hand, Jesus Christ is in some special and unique sense the revelation of God to man, is indeed in some way God as well as man, then He is the central figure in all history, and to endeavour to understand His teaching, His work and His Person is the most important of all the tasks to which we can commit ourselves.

"What think ye of Christ?" Numerous and diverse though the answers to this question have been, it is important to observe that they nevertheless fall into two main divisions according to the dominant judgment factor in the mind of the answerer. These two dominant judgment factors may be broadly characterized as the rational and the intuitive. There are people whose dominant judgment factor is the rational. They are not willing to accept any element into their scheme of thought unless it accords with the general trend of their deductions from the data of experience. Their approach to life is objective, and they are disinclined to consider matters which seem to them non-factual. Such people are likely to be sceptics: what cannot be fitted into a logical scheme of things must be relegated to the realms of the uncertain and the unknown. On the contrary, those whose dominant factor is the intuitive are anxious to obtain a comprehensive view, and cannot be satisfied unless they possess a concept of things in general into which particulars can be fitted.

It must at once be said that neither the rational nor the intuitive judgment factor is ever found in isolation. It is impossible to build up a view of life based entirely on the data of objective experience without ever formulating hypotheses on those data and, indeed, hypotheses to justify the interpreting of those data. It is equally impossible to build up a view of life based on intuitive postulates without ever considering how the data of experience fit in with those postulates. But there is no doubt that there are types of mind tending towards each of these extremes, of which we may legitimately say that the dominant judgment factors are the rational and the intuitive respectively. The rational type of mind finds satisfaction in working within a field where the problems presented consist in the discovery and correlation of objective data and their marshalling into logical schemes. Many scientific subjects fall into this category, so that the scientific outlook and the rational outlook tend to be identified. The average scientist works in a field which he has reason to believe is logically rigid, and he has two main sources of satisfaction: the discovering of fresh data, and the logical interrelating of data. The former is "scientific discovery", the latter the formulation of "laws". It is an interesting reflection on the structure of the Universe to consider how rigidly logical the various departments of scientific investigation are. There are great areas of knowledge within which there is a most satisfying logicality. If certain assumptions are made, assumptions which most people make without realizing they are assuming anything at all, the contents of the area constitute a logical and coherent system within which the rational or scientific type of mind finds complete mental satisfaction. Such areas of knowledge are found within the purviews of mathematics, mechanics, physics, astronomy, and chemistry. The assumptions are of the type that three dimensional space is not an illusion and that reality is nearly enough as directly understood from the data of human sense perception. Minds of the rational or scientific type may be so engrossed within the area of their chosen interest that the general framework of life does not much interest them, or they may accept such a view of things in general as is customary in their circle. The intuitive mind, on the other hand, may in its extreme form subordinate the data of experience to its own postulates, either ignoring data which it dislikes or inter-preting them in a way which seems unreal or perverse to the rational type of mind.

Fortunately, extreme cases of the rational and the intuitive types are rare, and most of us recognize that our view of life is based on a synthesis of intuition and logical reasoning. However definitely circumscribed and logically coherent our main interests may be—say chemistry and chess, or biology and billiards—most of us need a framework giving us a comprehensive view of life, if only in general outline. A research chemist whose hobby was chess might find that these two things occupied him almost completely and satisfyingly; but he could hardly go through life without a general view of some kind. If he were a Christian theist his general view might be no more than this: "I believe that the Universe was designed and set going by God, and that Jesus Christ is His Son. I accept Him as Master and Saviour, and try to live my life according to His teaching and in the strength of His grace. I am afraid I am not greatly interested in theology, leaving such things to those whose concern they are."

If we call a general view of things a comprehension, it begins to emerge that a comprehension usually includes two main types of constituent. It includes constituents which are rationally connected in coherent systems, and it includes constituents which are held intuitively. No satis-factory comprehension can be based entirely on rationally coherent systems, because such systems can never be more than areas of knowledge. There are always uncertainties of interpretation and aim, of origin and end. All the problems that the philosopher includes under epistemology, ontology and teleology are bound to arise, though they may not be expressed in the philosopher's terms. The comprehension must therefore have, beyond its interrelated or independent rationally coherent systems, a framework of axioms or postulates, which we have described as intuitive. This does not mean that they are irrational as opposed to rational. It means that they are held for reasons other than those following from mental operations conducted on the data of sense experience.

Consider a typical Christian comprehension of the Universe. There will be a framework of postulates: I believe in God, in Jesus Christ His Son, in a purpose for the individual human life. These and similar postulates are not the inevitable results of logical deductions from the data of sense experience. They are held as the faith-reached goal of a number of converging rational paths, as the faith-reached focus of a number of converging rational rays. No path quite reaches the goal, no ray quite reaches the focus. But we believe the goal is there because the paths converge towards it; we believe the focus is there because the rays converge towards it. We believe in God because so many paths converge in that direction: the arguments marshalled as "theistic proofs"; the history and teaching of the Church; religious infection from other people; an inner conviction within ourselves that God is; an experience within ourselves of a power and presence we are convinced is of God. These paths, and others similar to them, converge towards one goal: "There is a God." So it is with all our postulates. They will be considered in some detail later (pp. 208–220 and 228–230), but enough has already been said to prepare the way for the following observations:

(1) No scheme of thought can be based entirely on the data of sense experience and the logical interpretation of those data. It must be assumed, if only tacitly or perhaps even unawares, that the data of sense experience correspond with some kind of reality and that that reality is of an ordered kind. No one can prove either of these assumptions, though without them life is without reason or purpose. These necessary assumptions may be called postulates, and we may define a postulate as a belief, difficult or even impossible of proof, which is held because life is otherwise meaningless to that particular individual or group.

(2) There are, however, many people who dislike accepting postulates. They therefore accept as few as possible and endeavour to build up a comprehension of life on that minimum number of postulates. They are particularly averse to accepting postulates on the ground

that others have accepted them, and have little or no respect for authority, ancient or modern. In theology, such people are likely to be 'liberal'. They do most valuable work in the realms of history and Biblical criticism, and they have contributed very greatly towards the detailed filling in of many areas of knowledge. But in theology proper, and particularly in Christology, they find that their unwillingness to accept postulates compels them to enunciate what may be called a 'reduced'[1] Christology, that is, a Christology which appears to them to be 'rational'—the minimum number of postulates, and the maximum reliance on the power of logical reasoning within and from their areas of knowledge. This type of Christology has been much in evidence during the past century, and we might cite a range of works exemplifying it from D. F. Strauss's *Leben Jesu* published in 1835 to A. Loisy's *Les Origines du Nouveau Testament* published in 1937. Such works must not be lightly set aside as valueless. They have rendered great service in two ways: many areas of knowledge have been explored with meticulous care, and we are the more precisely acquainted with the coherence of the data within those areas and with the type and extent of the deductions we may legitimately make from them; and those holding postulates not held by the liberals have been compelled to examine their own positions, and to make sure that their postulates were not expressed (or interpreted) incompatibly with the ordered contents and the logical consequents of explored areas of knowledge.

(3) The liberal necessarily suffers in one major respect. Holding few postulates, and therefore building within a very open framework, his view of things cannot have finality even as to general shape. He would be quick to admit this, and would say that much is still unknown or inexactly known, and that our quest is to extend the frontiers of knowledge further and further into the hitherto unknown.

(4) On the other hand, there are people who believe

[1] The adjective applied by Sanday to such Christologies in his *Christologies Ancient and Modern*.

that God has not left us to struggle comparatively unaided towards a knowledge of the nature and purpose of the Universe in which we live, and that He has in various ways made known the great fundamental facts. Such people have a much more detailed framework of postulates than have the liberals, and they hold those postulates because to them life would be meaningless without them. This type of person may be called 'conservative', and he tends to hold very tenaciously to tradition and to ancient forms, particularly to the expression of Christian belief in the form characterized as 'dogma'. He does not do so without reasons, and his reasons would probably come under two general headings:

(i) If God were concerned for His world, He would not leave it ignorant concerning Himself, His will and His purpose. It is therefore reasonable to believe that we may expect Him to have made revelation on such matters as man unaided cannot determine. Such revelation is to be looked for in the Bible, the findings of Œcumenical Councils, and in the teaching of the Church.

(ii) If we accept the general corpus of Christian teaching as part of the framework of our view of life, accepting dogmas as postulates, we find that we can build up a view of life which is complete, satisfying, and is verified by experience.

It must of course be admitted that no postulate, and we may regard a dogma as a postulate within the realm of religion or theology, is capable of 'proof', unless we use 'proof' in the obsolescent sense of 'test'. It is very important that we should realize the conditions of our existence. We cannot 'prove' anything that is of ultimate importance, and it is probable that this is no accident. The great ultimates are matters not of proof but of faith, and we reach them by acts of faith. Confirmation follows in various ways, and the 'assurance of faith' may be and often is a far more satisfying and potent factor in the orientation of life than any number of deductions from the data of sense experience.

Nor is it remarkable that this should be so. For the Christian view—and we must to this extent anticipate it in order to state our case—includes faith not merely as an incidental but as a necessary element. The adoption by an individual of the Christian way of life usually follows some such order as this:[1]

(1) The facts and postulates of the Christian faith are presented to him, both as matters of history and dogma and as they affect the life and conduct of those presenting them.

(2) He sees that the arguments for the Christian faith are not of the same type as those to which he is accustomed in the material world. There are no inescapable arguments, nothing he may not reject if he so wills. But he begins to see that there are many lines all leading in one general direction. The records of history, an endeavour to find meaning in the world around him, all that the Church stands for and exemplifies—these and other considerations all point in one direction: that God is, that He has revealed Himself in Jesus Christ His Son, and that life may be lived in dependence on Him and in communion with Him. He begins to see that concurrence in the beliefs and practices of the Church gives a reasonable and satisfying way of life, and recognizes that those beliefs and practices can be fitted in with an intellectually defensible view of life as a whole.

(3) Then comes the great decision, whether reached gradually and by perhaps almost imperceptible stages, or whether reached in one grand moment, when he decides to accept the freely offered grace, decides to make the great venture of faith, and to accept that to which so much has been pointing. This forward step is probably, from God's point of view, the act of greatest significance in any human life, and its significance largely depends upon the fact that it is an act of faith and not of inescapable reasoning. Were it the latter it would merely indicate wisdom in the convert, but not necessarily a response to

[1] Though these paragraphs are phrased objectively, the operation of grace, both previeniently and co-operantly, is of course to be inferred.

the call of truth and beauty and holiness, and not at all a glorious venture.

(4) Having taken this step, he soon finds his venture of faith increasingly justified and verified by experience, and the longer he lives to apply his faith and the more consistently he exercises it, the more convinced he becomes of its truth and the more aware he becomes of the power and presence of God in Christ, both in things in general and in himself in particular. Soon the confidence of faith becomes a far more potent factor in his life than consideration for the apparent realities of the material world: the latter perish, but the former remains. He has a steadily increasing inner assurance, a growing conviction of the truth of the postulates which he has accepted.

Returning to our comparison of the rational and the intuitive types of dominant judgment factor, we now see where the conservative Christian theist finds his place. He accepts the postulates that any reasonable person must accept if life is to have meaning at all—that he exists, that the data of experience give a reliable clue to reality, that there is reason and purpose in the world order. Further, he accepts the postulates of the Christian faith as embodied in the teaching of the Church. Of these postulates he makes a framework, into which all the other data of knowledge and experience must fit. It will also emerge why the conservative has a case more difficult to defend than has the liberal. The liberal has a framework of postulates which no reasonable person is likely to dispute. His framework is the inescapable minimum. In fact, in his case 'foundation of postulates' may be a more apt term than 'framework of postulates'. On his foundation he builds with critical care his superstructure, incorporating areas of knowledge and cautiously building them up towards what he considers to be the inevitable conclusions. These conclusions usually include a reasoned belief in God and the acceptance of Jesus Christ at least as Master and Example. These results are themselves important, for it is a significant and inspiring fact that even those who accept no traditional dogma unless it commends itself to their own painstaking reasoning nevertheless feel their way towards very similar goals. But the conservative has a far more complicated position to defend. He probably accepts most of the postulates accepted by the liberal, and agrees with him in the building into that framework of areas of knowledge. But he also accepts many postulates the liberal does not accept. How is he to justify that acceptance? Let it at once be said that in this matter the demanding of a plain answer to a plain question is a demand almost impossible to satisfy, especially if by 'plain' is also implied 'short'. If we start arguing about each postulate separately, we shall find that our argument necessarily involves many other issues, and we soon realize that our postulates are not separate entities but parts of a system, so interlocked that none is independent, and that each gains support and confirmation from the rest. To answer any one question on matters of faith thoroughly and convincingly really involves giving an outline of our entire view of life, and inviting the questioner to test that view by himself being willing to undergo the experience which confirms and establishes our faith: "If any man will do his will, he shall know of the doctrine."

The liberal view is of necessity continually in flux. Newly discovered data, whether historical or scientific, must be fitted into the scheme, and the liberal believes that he is drawing ever nearer to the goal of ultimate truth, though he may realize that he can never quite reach it. He is nevertheless confident that he is steadily extending the boundaries of knowledge, and consequently speculates with more and more assurance. But what of the conservative? Is his view fixed and final, and are his problems all solved by his act of faith? Do his accepted postulates and dogmas make further mental effort needless? It may be suggested that the acceptance of a dogma is the end of a problem. It is of course to be admitted that the acceptance of a dogma may be all that is necessary for those who feel no need to pursue the matter further. Many a saint has needed no assurance beyond the beliefs he has made his own and proved by experience, confirmed and attested by the illumination and grace of God; many a simple Christian, necessarily busied with many other concerns, has had no inclination to probe into the whys and wherefores of what he has been taught and has accepted. For such the acceptance of a dogma is indeed the end of a problem. To Jesus Christ's own question: "Whom say ye that I am?" (Matt. xvi. 15), simple faith needs no answer other than St. Peter's: "Thou art the Christ, the Son of the living God." That reply, with all its implications accepted, provides sufficient basis for the acknowledgment of Jesus Christ as Pattern, Master, Lord and Saviour, as Messiah and Immanuel.

But there are at least two other types. There is the intellectually curious, who, like Nicodemus, asks: "How can these things be?" Impressed by the uniqueness in history of Jesus Christ, he seeks an explanation of that uniqueness; believing the only explanation to be that Jesus Christ is indeed the Son of God, he wants his belief to form part of a coherent and logical system with the rest of his knowledge; he wants something to satisfy mind as well as heart and soul. Surely there is no reason why he should not seek to envisage as one coherent system the dogmas of his faith and the knowledge gained in other ways of the Universe in which he lives. If he can devise such a coherent system, it may not only represent a closer approach to a general understanding of things, but it will also confirm and strengthen faith in the dogmas, indeed formally accepted, and now seen to be both reasonable and consistent. Then there are those whose privilege and duty it is to expound and defend the dogmas of the Christian faith. Surely they will fulfil their vocation the more effectively if they are not only convinced themselves as to the truth of those things which they believe, but are able to expound them convincingly to others, showing that all things indeed work together, and that the Christian dogmas complete and crown all other knowledge. Those who accept Him as Lord and Saviour are not debarred from seeking to understand in what way and by what means He can be both Son of God and Son of Man, how He can be approached both as our God and our Brother. It may, indeed, be more than permissible to attempt to answer these questions; it may be an urgent duty, as otherwise the ignorant may come to foolish conclusions, and the hostile may suggest answers calculated to destroy faith and belittle its object.

The conservative has therefore to attempt at least three tasks:

(1) Although he accepts his postulates and dogmas, and believes them to be true, he has still the task of endeavouring to discover their full significance and meaning, both in order that he may hold his faith in an intelligent manner, and that he may the better commend it to others.

(2) Although a postulate or dogma may be true, and may have represented at the time of its formulation the utmost that the contemporary mind was able to comprehend, with the advance of knowledge and further exploration in thought it may be that the postulate or dogma can be amplified and extended, so that the truth it enshrines may be comprehended with greater clarity and in more detail. Just as areas of knowledge may be increased both in extent and detail, so may areas of postulation and dogmatism. For instance, we may accept the postulate or dogma that Jesus Christ is the Son of God. We believe this to be true, but the ancient theologians soon found it desirable and necessary to seek further illumination. In what sense is Jesus Christ 'Son' of God? What exactly does 'Son' mean in such a phrase? And how could Jesus Christ's real or apparent manhood be reconciled with His being Son of God? To know that a statement is true is not by any means the same as fully understanding that statement. The conservative may always hope to advance his understanding of the things he believes to be true.

(3) The hardest task confronting the conservative is the reconciliation of dogma with the postulates currently held by his educated contemporaries and with the contents of the various areas of knowledge. This task is necessary for two reasons: no one can hold his convictions with confidence unless he has in his own mind at least the outline of a consistent total view of life in which

those convictions can find a secure and reasonable place; and no one can hope to commend his convictions to others for their acceptance unless he can reasonably relate them to the general corpus of belief held by those others. This is the task to which we shall commit ourselves in the second part of this work, particularly as it bears upon the doctrine of the Person of Jesus Christ.

Our mode of approach must now be indicated. As has already been stated, postulates and dogmas are not capable of direct proof, and it is therefore of little use to argue about them in isolation from one another. The only really useful method is to outline one's entire view of things, giving greater detail where the end in view requires it, and to ask for a judgment on the view as a whole. Thus we should state our postulates, show how from them we build our framework, and show how the various areas of knowledge fit into it. Our hearer or reader may then find the total view convincing and helpful, either finding new light for himself from it or gaining confirmation of what he already believed; or he may reject it altogether; or he may adopt it with slighter or greater modifications. The latter may be the most usual result; and as our best efforts at understanding reality are but shadows of it, none of us need be unduly concerned if others see the shadows slightly longer or deeper, so long as the general shape is the same.

We shall assume, then, that our framework of postulates is a Christian theistic one, and, if such a distinction is pressed, conservative rather than liberal. We shall include among our postulates belief in God the Father, in Jesus Christ His Son, in fact in all those beliefs which were held by the undivided Church of the early centuries and are enshrined in those dogmas which are the common heritage of all who treasure the deep significance of the words Catholic and Orthodox. Those chiefly relevant may be sufficiently indicated by two short quotations, one from the Apostles' Creed: "I believe in God the Father Almighty, Maker of heaven and earth; and in Jesus Christ, His only Son, our Lord"; and one from the Athanasian Creed: "We believe and confess that our Lord Jesus Christ, the Son of

God, is God and Man. God, of the Substance of the Father, begotten before the worlds; and Man, of the Substance of His Mother, born in the world. Perfect God, and perfect Man, of a reasonable soul and human flesh subsisting. Equal to the Father, as touching His Godhead; and inferior to the Father, as touching His Manhood. Who although He be God and Man, yet He is not two, but one Christ. One, not by conversion of the Godhead into flesh, but by assumption of the Manhood into God. One altogether, not by confusion of Substance, but by unity of Person."

Accepting our dogmatic postulates, we have next to interrelate them in a coherent scheme, and to incorporate that scheme into a philosophy acceptable to contemporary thought. That is the difficult task, and it is in attempting that task that heresy has so often originated. If we are committed to a philosophy, we may be tempted to adjust our dogmatic postulates to fit it; or we may attempt to harmonize a philosophy and a theology which are mutually incompatible, and the result will be a system satisfactory to nobody, not even to ourselves. Yet few of us can be content without a comprehensive philosophy.

It is at this point that we should emphasize that theology must be normative to philosophy and not vice versa. We may build up, as there have been built up, any number of philosophies. We may approach the problems of philosophy from a great many different starting points, and our choice of starting point will have a profound effect upon our mode of journeying and possibly on our place of arrival. Those who do not know even the general direction of their destination may explore the areas of knowledge and speculate about frameworks to contain them without making much real progress. But if, as the Christian theist believes, we know the direction of our destination, we are at once in a position to endeavour to find the best path towards it. That is the task of the Christian philosopher. Can he look at life in such a way that all relevant facts are included in his view, and that they are fitted into a general scheme in which the dogmatic postulates have firm and relevant place? If he can do so, his philosophical urge is satisfied and his faith greatly strengthened.

B

Although certain areas of knowledge have been explored with increasing exactitude as the centuries have passed, it is interesting to notice that the main types of philosophical speculation have not undergone any such profound reorientation as have the physical and biological sciences. New philosophies are usually recognizable as ancient ones somewhat revised to accommodate the new shape or enlarged extent of areas of modern knowledge. It may therefore well be that an ancient line of approach, even one that failed in its own time, may set our feet in a profitable direction. A climber may fail to reach the peak he aspires to scale, yet he may have chosen a feasible approach. Others, perhaps better equipped, may follow the same route and succeed. It is for a reason of that kind that this work starts with Nestorius. The present writer, having studied the Bazaar of Heracleides with ordinary care, felt uneasy as to the verdict of history on Nestorius. He therefore made a minute analysis of the Bazaar, and as a result arrived at two conclusions: first, that Nestorius was rightly condemned by his contemporaries, and that their verdict needs no revision; second, that there are nevertheless some most valuable elements in the thought and method of Nestorius which with some revision and extension might provide a way of approach to a solution of the Christological problem.

The first part of this book will therefore be devoted to a careful examination of the metaphysic and Christology of Nestorius. Taking certain ideas and methods of approach from that study, we shall then proceed in the second part to show how an orthodox Christology can be held and understood in harmony with a philosophy tenable in the contemporary world. We shall not endeavour to establish any exact parallels between Nestorius' ideas and a modern interpretation of them, for the second part of the present work is no mere revised Nestorianism. It is very far from Nestorius and his heresy, and the degrees both of indebtedness and departure will be perceived by the careful reader without any interrupting cross-references. Some readers, indeed, may feel inclined to confine their attention to the second part; but we may plead that the first part should not be ignored. Nestorius was condemned, and rightly condemned, as a heretic. He was nevertheless a man of a peculiar and original cast of mind, and approached the problem of Christology on lines distinctively his own. It may be easy to show his place among the Antiochians, and to link him with Diodore and Theodore. But he had within his mind the outline of a metaphysic more rigid and comprehensive than any they ever contemplated, and a view of Christ's Person much more subtly conceived. It may be argued that Nestorius' metaphysic was much too rigid and mechanical and that his Christology leads to a double person. To anticipate our conclusions it may at once be admitted that nothing helpful can be gleaned from the unqualified words of Nestorius himself. We have painstakingly to endeavour to enter his mind, and to set his ideas into order in a way which he himself never did. Some may say that the result is merely a logical system into which the disordered contents of Nestorius' mind have been forced. Even if that is so, the key ideas and the mode of approach are due to Nestorius and the system is derived from him even if not entirely his. It is for this reason that our study starts there. It is as though a great mountain were to be climbed, and Nestorius had endeavoured to climb it by an unusual route. Perhaps he failed to get far, but with better equipment and the help of other climbers we may hope to succeed where he failed. We must at least give him credit for being the pioneer of a new approach. To some it may seem that the echoes of Nestorius in the second part are faint and far; but they are there, even when, to avoid complicating the issue, no attention is called to them.

A return to the mountain analogy may serve to explain the title and limitation of this work. The summit of a mountain is one, but the approaches thereto may be many. So far as we are concerned, the problem of Christology is patently insoluble, if by solution is meant understanding exactly how Godhead and manhood are united in the one Person of Jesus Christ. All our knowledge is mediated, and we can never be certain of the nature of ultimate reality. The best we can do is to formulate systems which may have some resemblance to truth as it really is. If the system survives the test of experience, it is probably in some way parallel with ultimate truth. It is thus with Christology. The best we can do is to endeavour to devise a system which includes logically and reasonably all we believe we know and all we know we believe. The mountain peak is there, whether our route enables us to reach it or not. Even if this approach fails to reach the summit, it may at least give us a closer glimpse of it.

A few remarks may be made concerning the general balance of the second part. The intention is to show how an orthodox Christology can be fitted harmoniously into a modern outlook, and a good deal of space has therefore been devoted to sketching the general view into which the Christology is to be fitted. Though apparently to some extent irrelevant to Christology, this task is really a very necessary one if we are to meet the criticism that theologians and Christologists tend to work in a universe of ideas which is not readily related to general thought. At the same time, undue detail has been avoided, as it is so easy to lose the main threads of an argument if too much extraneous matter is allowed to intrude. For the same reason the second part is not heavily documented. It would not have been difficult to quote authorities and parallels, but it is hardly necessary. As Berguer truly remarks, no good purpose is served by "reopening questions that have been settled in order to settle them again with a great parade of impressive citations."[1] Almost any opinion can be supported by quotations from somewhere, and in the present case it is not so much the separate opinions that are of importance as their conflation into a system and the assessment of that system. But the absence of quotations is not in any way intended to suggest lack of a sense of indebtedness. We are all undischargeably indebted to those who have laboured before us, and throughout this work there is necessarily much dependence on a great company of authors and editors, ancient and modern. Not only references in text and footnotes, but also the bibliography itself must be taken as an indication of the extent of that

[1] *Some Aspects of the Life of Jesus*, p. iii (English trans.).

indebtedness, though necessarily a number of authors are listed from whose opinions the present writer differs; but our convictions are necessarily tested and frequently confirmed by the careful study of those who differ from us. For the sake of consistency almost all authors are cited by surname only; initials are supplied in the bibliography and the index. Special acknowledgment should be made of the greatest single asset for the undertaking of the first part of this work: Driver and Hodgson's translation of the Bazaar into English.[1] The present work may be a partial fulfilment of the hope that their translation might provide "the necessary material" for answering the question "What precisely did Nestorius teach?"[2] Grateful acknowledgment is hereby made of the gracious permission of the editors and their publishers to quote so extensively from it.

I should also like to record my thanks to the Rev. Nathaniel Micklem, D.D., LL.D., Principal of Mansfield College, Oxford, who facilitated my access to certain rare books; to my wife, whose patient assistance as amanuensis so considerably lightened my labours; and to the Senate of the University of London, which has approved this work for the award of the Degree of Doctor of Divinity.

AUBREY R. VINE.

READING.
April, 1948.

[1] *Nestorius: The Bazaar of Heracleides, newly translated from the Syriac* (Clarendon Press, Oxford, 1925).
[2] Op. cit., p. xxxi.

CONTENTS

Part I

THE METAPHYSIC AND CHRISTOLOGY OF NESTORIUS

Part II

AN ORTHODOX CHRISTOLOGY COMPATIBLE WITH MODERN THOUGHT

Appendix

NOTES ON THE BAZAAR

ANALYTICAL TABLE OF CONTENTS

PART I—THE METAPHYSIC AND CHRISTOLOGY OF NESTORIUS

CHAPTER I

CHAPTER II

CHAPTER III

CHAPTER IV

CHAPTER V

CHAPTER VI

CHAPTER VII

PART II—AN ORTHODOX CHRISTOLOGY COMPATIBLE WITH MODERN THOUGHT

CHAPTER I

CHAPTER II

CHAPTER III

CHAPTER IV

CHAPTER V

CHAPTER VI

APPENDIX—NOTES ON THE BAZAAR

PART ONE

THE METAPHYSIC AND CHRISTOLOGY
OF NESTORIUS

CHAPTER I

THE SIGNIFICANCE OF NESTORIUS

THE human mind, aware of its finitude, is nevertheless so constituted that it ever endeavours to comprehend the infinite and, conscious of the veils that conceal reality from it, nevertheless strives to penetrate them. Despite the magnitude of the tasks thus undertaken, there is reason to believe that they are not in vain, and that cumulative human effort is rewarded by progressive human apprehension. It is therefore enlightening to follow the trends of human thought across the centuries. As the areas of knowledge have been enlarged, and as postulated frameworks have been subjected to tests of ever-increasing severity, so has there been ground for confidence that we have drawn steadily nearer to a better understanding of reality. The hitherto unknown is gradually being penetrated, avenues of experiment and speculation are steadily explored, and though the explorer may sometimes find himself in a cul-de-sac, even then he may have profited, if only in being made aware that no advance can be made in that particular direction. It has not been otherwise in philosophy and theology. Many systems of thought and many theological views have been advanced, tested, and rejected. But it is not wise to regard such systems and views as having served no useful purpose. Even acute conflicts of opinion are often seen in the light of later events to have been necessary stages in the clarification of thought: thesis and antithesis, moving towards synthesis. Thus it has seldom happened that such conflicts have left unchanged that which gained dominance. The contribution of that which was rejected may have been quite considerable or very small; it has rarely been completely negligible.

This has definitely been the case in Christology, both in the matter of the formulation of postulates and their crystallization in dogma, and in the setting of dogma in a comprehensive metaphysical system. These two processes have proceeded side by side, and the immense difficulty of the latter task largely accounts for the acuteness of the controversies which have arisen. We must not regard those controversies as sad or valueless incidents in ancient history. We must regard them rather as divinely permitted means whereby the right approach to truth might be the more clearly indicated and the ways of error the more definitely barred. It may be doubted whether catholic orthodoxy would ever have become so carefully and thoroughly defined had it not been for the conflicts with the heresies of the early centuries. It is therefore by no means a useless task to examine those conflicts, for often in them we may find the clues to subsequent clarifications, and even the cause that was defeated may have contributed more than appears on the surface. Thus Athanasius gained dominance over Arius; subsequent thought, however, was influenced, not only by Athanasius, but by the conflict. Similarly, Alexandria and Antioch stand not simply for contrasted Christologies, but for complementary directives in the trend of thought. When this particular opposition reached its climax in the conflict between Cyril and Nestorius, Cyril emerged triumphant and Nestorius was deposed and exiled. Thought moved on, and Cyril and Nestorius were left to their places in history, the one canonized and the other anathematized. But it is not sufficient to say that Alexandria triumphed and that Antioch failed. Granted that Alexandria conserved the postulates, Antioch at least strove after an intellectually satisfying explanation of Christ's Person; and though we may be satisfied that the verdict of history is right and inevitable, there may nevertheless be elements in the teaching of Nestorius which will repay our careful examination. It is the writer's conviction that Nestorius had stumbled upon a mode of approach to the Christological problem which had greater possibilities than could be realized by his methods; and that though his condemnation was necessary, more can be gained from delving into his thought processes than we shall ever gain by regarding him as no more than a mere foil to Cyril.

Until comparatively recently there was one considerable obstacle in the way of an impartial consideration of Nestorius' case: the history of the controversy had come down to us from sources and through channels which were almost without exception opposed to Nestorius. Even those who were confident that the decisions against him were justified none the less wished that his views could be gathered from sources other than the writings or quotations of his enemies. The fact that other sources had existed was attested by Ebedyeshu, metropolitan of Nisibis (*ob.* 1318),[1] and Neander's hope that some of these sources might yet be discovered[2] was fulfilled in 1889. In that year, a Syrian priest named Auscha'nâ obtained for the American Mission at Urmi[3] a copy of a Syriac work now generally known in English as *The Bazaar of Heracleides*. This Syriac manuscript, which had long reposed among the archives of the Nestorian Patriarch at Qudshanis,[4] appeared to be a translation from a Greek original of Nestorius' own apology.[5] Secretly and in haste Auscha'nâ made a copy of this manuscript, and this copy was deposited in the library of the American Mission at Urmi. Owing to the circumstances of its transcription the copy is both incomplete and imperfect.

Though the importance of this discovery was recognized, it was some years before much careful attention was given to it. Interest was shown in the discovery by two members of the Archbishop of Canterbury's Mission at Urmi, the Rev. D. Jenks and the Rev. O. H. Parry, both of whom had copies made; but other duties prevented them from pursuing the implications of the discovery. When, however, Mr. Jenks returned to England in 1899, he placed his copy at the disposal of the Rev. J. F. Bethune-Baker. This manuscript, now reposing at Cambridge and generally known as 'C', was used by Bethune-Baker in the preparation of his book *Nestorius and His Teaching*, published in 1908. It was

[1] Assemani, *Bibliotheca Orientalis*, iii. i. 36.

[2] "This work of Nestorius has unfortunately not come down to us, unless, perhaps, it may be somewhere found in a Syrian translation." Neander, *General History of the Christian Religion and Church* (English trans., 1849), iv. 207.

[3] Urmia, Urmiyah, Ourmiah, anc. Ormia.

[4] Kudshanis, Kotchanès, Kochannes, Kotschanes.

[5] According to Bedjan (see below, p. 34), the Syriac version was made from the original Greek about the middle of the sixth century, and this copy, the only one surviving in either Greek or Syriac, dates from the early part of the twelfth century. It was, unfortunately, badly mutilated during the Kurdish disorders of 1843.

C

not until the publication of this work that the existence of the Bazaar of Heracleides became generally known to English scholars.

Meanwhile, on the initiative of Dr. H. Goussen, a copy had been made for the University of Strasbourg. This manuscript, known as 'S', is mentioned in his *Martyrius-Sahdona's Leben und Werke* (p. 15), which was published in 1897. Brief references were made to it by Dr. Oscar Braun, *Das Buch der Synhados*, p. 97 (1900), by Dr. A. Baumstark, *Oriens Christianus*, vol. iii, p. 517 (1903), and by Dr. F. Loofs, *Nestoriana*, pp. 68–70 (1905). Another copy which should be mentioned is that obtained by Dr. Rendel Harris in 1899. This is now at Harvard University.

But it was not until 1910 that the Syriac text was published in a properly edited form. This was done by the Lazarist Père Paul Bedjan: *Nestorius: Le Livre d'Héraclide de Damas, édité par Paul Bedjan, avec plusieurs appendices.* For his edition Bedjan was able to make use of 'C' and 'S', and he had also been able to obtain an additional copy of the Qudshanis Syriac original, done partly at Van and partly at Qudshanis.[1] This copy is known as 'V', and from the better circumstances of its transcription is of greater value than 'C' or 'S'. Bedjan's text, prepared by a Syriac scholar of such standing and with access to the only available copies of the Qudshanis original, may be regarded as sufficiently definitive. The publication of the Syriac was followed by the publication of two versions, one by Professor F. Nau, *Nestorius: Le Livre d'Héraclide de Damas, traduit en français*, 1910, and the other by Mr. G. R. Driver and the Rev. Leonard Hodgson, *Nestorius: The Bazaar of Heracleides, newly translated from the Syriac*, 1925.

The Bazaar of Heracleides thus became available in Syriac, French and English, and interest in Nestorius received fresh stimulus. Scholars were anxious to discover whether evidence from his own writing would modify the verdict of history or throw fresh light on the circumstances leading up to the Council of Ephesus. It is as well to admit that

[1] "De plus, j'en ai fait venir une troisième du Kurdistan, dont une partie a été faite à Van et l'autre à Kotchanès même sur le fameux manuscrit du partriarche," op. cit., p. ix.

any great hopes or fears in this direction have not been realized. *The Bazaar of Heracleides* is an exasperating work. Its arguments are presented in an unsatisfactory order, important matters are dismissed with too scant reference, unimportant points are unduly elaborated, fundamental concepts are not made clear, repeated assertion is proffered as a substitute for proof. Nevertheless, the impression remains that Nestorius was genuinely confident of the orthodoxy, logic and coherence of his argument, and it is difficult to read and re-read the Bazaar without the conviction growing that something is striving for expression. The book certainly contains many passages which show great acuteness and subtlety of mind; though it has to be admitted that to endeavour to reduce his ideas to an ordered system almost defies ingenuity. It may be disputed whether the task ought to be attempted. Much, however, depends upon attitude and approach. Those who see in the verdict of Œcumenical Councils the guidance of God for His Church will not feel free to question the rightness of Nestorius' condemnation; but that condemnation may have been right for any of a number of reasons of very different kinds. The findings of a Council are not to be regarded as the mere recording of the victory of one set of opinions over another. The findings must mark steps forward in the clarification of doctrine, and such steps must be taken in the right order and with general comprehension. It follows that no acceptable contribution can be made by anyone unable to present that contribution in language generally understandable and within a metaphysical framework comprehensible to contemporary thought, and that ordered doctrinal development must not be interrupted by the introduction before their time of ideas which later might serve a useful purpose.

Agreement that Nestorius' condemnation was just and necessary does not therefore preclude an open-minded approach to the Bazaar. The Bazaar may prove that Nestorius had ideas for which the world at that time was not prepared. He may have had ideas not capable of expression in terms readily understandable by ordinary people, and therefore not suitable for promulgation in doctrine or statement in dogma. He may have had ideas themselves depending on premises not yet firmly established. In any of these cases it would manifestly have been a disaster to the steady onward movement of Christological thought had he been victor. It would, indeed, be permissible to argue that Nestorius deserved condemnation even had his views been right, if he failed to present them in such a way that they should be comprehensible. No good purpose is served by replacing inexplicable mysteries by incomprehensible explanations. At the same time, his thought may have contained something 'born out of due time' which, premature for his own generation, may have value for ours.

An analysis of the views of those who have reconsidered the problem of Nestorius in the light of the Bazaar reveals an interesting distribution of opinion. A number of representative verdicts will now be given, arranged approximately in order of decreasing sympathy with Nestorius. The list has been kept short, but if it were greatly lengthened the range and emphasis would remain much the same.

Among the first to give careful consideration to the evidence was J. F. Bethune-Baker.[1] His approach was frankly sympathetic, as may be seen in his dedication: "Nestorio, illi veritatis divinae indagatori, sive victori seu parum felici viro propositi prae ceteros tenaci, monacho, episcopo, exuli, . . . studia haec . . . dedico." The same spirit inspires his conclusion: "If Nestorius himself did not really 'separate' the natures in the one Person of the Lord, then the way would be smoothed to a real 'union' between his Church and ours. If we both believe that in our Lord Jesus Christ, God and man, Godhead and manhood, while really distinct, were yet brought together, reconciled, united, really, truly, ineffably, indissolubly—has not the time arrived for genuine Christian fellowship, ecclesiastical intercommunion? The age of anathemas is gone. To have realized this will be perhaps the chief merit of the twentieth century of the era of our Lord. If they are willing to cease to pronounce their ancient anathema on Cyril, we shall not surely ask them to disown their early hero Nestorius."[2]

Nevertheless, his careful examination of the evidence

[1] *Nestorius and His Teaching* (1908).   [2] Ibid., p. 211.

does not enable him to go much beyond the assertion that Nestorius was not 'Nestorian'.[1] This conclusion must be generally admitted if by being 'Nestorian' we mean the recognizing in the person of Christ of 'two *kyânê*, two *qnômê*, one *parṣôpâ*',[2] by that understanding 'two φύσεις, two ὑποστάσεις, one πρόσωπον'; and, again, by ὑπόστασις understanding 'person', and by πρόσωπον merely 'presence'. But though Nestorius repeatedly asserts the full humanity and the full divinity of Christ and yet His oneness, Bethune-Baker seems tacitly to recognize that Nestorius gives no clear explanation as to how these apparently mutually incompatible postulates can all be satisfied, except in a unity of πρόσωπον, whatever that tantalizing word may mean.

Friedrich Loofs also approaches the matter sympathetically, but in a rather different manner from Bethune-Baker. Loofs sees in the controversy antitheses irreconcilable in the terms in which they are stated, yet obviously has considerable sympathy with Nestorius. He credits Nestorius with at least a desire to progress in accord with what he thought to be the trend of orthodox doctrine, and a desire to make that doctrine intellectually intelligible. He defends Nestorius against the charge of making the person of Christ a duality, urging that, whether he was approaching the problem from the human or divine side, it was always Nestorius' intention to emphasize the oneness of the person: "The tendency of his Christology to start from the historical Christ and to apply not only the terms Χριστός and κύριος but also the term 'Son of God' only to the historical Lord probably did not come only from his own endeavour to lay stress on the oneness of the historical person of Christ, but must have had a connection with the old tradition which had come down to him. If all this is right Nestorius is justified in his thinking in a higher degree than if he had been shown to be orthodox in the sense of the later orthodoxy; for then he is nearer to the oldest theological tradition

---

[1] Ibid., p. vii and p. 198.

[2] This was the Nestorian formula at least as early as the time of Narses (*ob. circa* 507), as may be seen in his Homilia XI, *De tribus doctoribus græcis: Diodoro, Theodoro et Nestorio.* (Accessible in *Narsai doctoris syri Homiliæ et Carmina* (edited by A. Mingana), i. 181–194.)

and nearer to the N.T. than this later orthodoxy itself."[1]
"All Antiochians, Nestorius included, even when starting
with the Logos endeavoured to make intelligible the
oneness of the person of Christ."[2]

Seeberg appears to hold a somewhat similar view, and
he too feels no small sympathy for Nestorius. He even
goes so far as to say that in the whole history of dogma
no great heretic acquired that name in circumstances so
unfortunate: "Keiner unter den grossen 'Ketzern' der
Dogmengeschichte trägt diesen Namen so zu Unrecht wie
Nestorius."[3]

Sellers, in a careful and well documented survey of the
Alexandrian and Antiochian approaches to the problem of
Christology,[4] regards the schools as complementary rather
than opposed, and regards the controversy between Cyril
and Nestorius as the result of ecclesiastical rivalry and
terminological misunderstanding rather than of difference
in intention and fundamental belief: "So we conclude that,
had Cyril inquired more closely into Nestorius' teaching,
he would have discovered that his opponent was but saying
what he himself was saying—and that in a way which could
give the lie to Eutychianism."[5] While he admits the faults
in Nestorius, he also recognizes the intransigence of Cyril:
"Neither was Cyril the man to allow himself to be mastered
by adverse circumstances: once he had set himself the task
of degrading the upstart see through striking at its new
patriarch who was daring to assert himself, he was
determined to carry it through."[6]

Like Bethune-Baker, Sellers is quite convinced that
Nestorius was not a 'Nestorian': "From all this it seems
clear that Nestorius is hardly deserving of the title
'Nestorian', and that this is a legitimate conclusion is
borne out by statements of his which show that for him
Jesus Christ is very God incarnate. Thus in the *Bazaar* he
denounces those who 'call Christ and the Son [of God]
double in prosôpon as well as in hypostasis—in like manner
as the saints have received the indwelling of God'. Again,

[1] *Nestorius* (1914), p. 126.   [2] Ibid., p. 113.
[3] *Lehrbuch der Dogmengeschichte* (3rd edition, 1923), ii. 220.
[4] *Two Ancient Christologies* (1940).   [5] Ibid., p. 207.
[6] Ibid., p. 220.

in the same work he asks how it can be thought that his doctrine is that there is one Son, who is in the bosom of the Father, and another Son, Christ, 'who is only such as man is', when he directly affirms that[1] the Only-begotten, who is in the bosom of the Father, has expounded unto us God, whom no man has ever seen; and no one else than He who is in the bosom of the Father came and became flesh and dwelt among us.[2] Surely, we could not have a more explicit denial of the Nestorian position than this: for him Jesus Christ is one Person, the Logos made man, whose, since He is God and man, are properties divine and human."[3] Sellers' thesis is that Cyril and Nestorius were approaching the same problem along different lines but with the same fundamental postulates: "However, the point is that here is an illustration of what could happen once the Antiochenes were prepared seriously to inquire into what Cyril was saying, and to take him at his word: Nestorius could claim that he was teaching in the same way. And, as it appears to us, the claim is altogether justifiable."[4] According to Sellers, modern thought can best profit from this ancient controversy by attempting a synthesis of the apparently opposed but really complementary views.

Mackintosh interprets the controversy in its historical context, as a stage in the advance of the definition of doctrine. He sees faults, theological as well as personal, in both Cyril and Nestorius. He also recognizes the sound elements in the views which each was advancing. He emphasizes the great value of the realistic approach of the Antiochian School, and, while admitting Nestorius' lack of skill as a controversialist, doubts whether the charge of dualism against him can be reasonably pressed: "It is indeed a question whether dualism can be charged upon Nestorius in any sense that would not also hold against the Creed of Chalcedon."[5] Mackintosh has no illusions as to Cyril's character: "unscrupulous in his methods, ambitious, proud, and violent";[6] and, agreeing to that extent with Harnack,

---

[1,2] A quotation from Nestorius himself, *The Bazaar of Heracleides*, B. 73 (for the method of page reference, see p. 50).
[3] *Two Ancient Christologies*, p. 164.   [4] Ibid., p. 219.
[5] *The Person of Jesus Christ* (2nd edition, 1913), p. 204 (footnote),
[6] Ibid., p. 205.

points out the monophysite tendency in Cyril's Christology: "One detail of historical importance should be noted. Since the person in the God-man is but the prolongation of the one life of the Eternal Word—not the effect of incarnation— it follows in Cyril's view that Christ's human nature is impersonal (ἀνυπόστατος). This much resembles the theory of Apollinarius, but Cyril escapes the danger, at least verbally, by his emphatic insistence on the completeness of the human nature assumed by the Logos. At the same time, while he does not enter explicitly on the question—even he can still use φύσις and ὑπόστασις as synonyms—Cyril really heads the list of writers who have held that the human nature of Christ possesses no independent personality of its own, and is personal only in the Logos. In itself it is reduced to unconscious and impersonal elements. The step, in a multitude of ways, was a singularly unfortunate one."[1] Mackintosh concludes, however, that Cyril was actuated by the surer religious instincts, and that he realized what were the essentials above all to be conserved: "Nevertheless it is a merit in Cyril not easily to be overestimated, that he strove with such persistence to bring out the living and organic unity of Christ's person. And here he was guided by a genuinely religious interest. 'This school of Greek theology was right,' it has been said, 'in the stress it laid on the closest possible union of God with Man in order that the dynamic power of the Christ-life might operate upon the race whose new Head He is come to be.' "[2]

Cave also views the problem in its broad historic setting, and sees Cyril and Nestorius as representatives of con- verging lines of approach to a solution not yet in clear view, nor perhaps possible in their terms. Cave admits the personal faults of Cyril but recognizes that he was main- taining the dogmatic essentials. On the other hand, he points out that Nestorius was his own worst enemy, and certainly did not hold the views which have since been associated with his name: "Even the fragments of his works,

[1] *The Person of Jesus Christ*, p. 207.

[2] Ibid., p. 207. The words Mackintosh quotes are from an article by J. O. Dykes in the *Expository Times*, xvii. 57 (November, 1905).

which, till recently, were our only source of information, are sufficient to show that he was innocent of many of the errors of which he was accused. There has now been found a great Apologia written by him, just before his death, on the eve of the Council of Chalcedon of A.D. 451. This book makes it clear that the traditional account of Nestorius' teaching owes as much to Cyril's malice as to Nestorius' heresy, and that the condemnation of Nestorius was due less to his false teaching than to his own amazing tactlessness and the clever adroitness of Cyril, his great opponent."[1]

Maclean believes that Nestorius honestly supposed himself to be upholding orthodox doctrine, but considers him to have lacked the ability and equipment for the task. He reckons Nestorius to have been "a very confused thinker" and "a foolish and obstinate man, who did not see the outcome of his own teaching."[2] Maclean quotes with approval the opinion of Socrates (the Church historian), who, "having perused his writings, 'found him to be an ignorant man'; . . . though eloquent, he was not well educated, and did not know the 'ancient expositors'."[2] Maclean gives his verdict thus: "The conclusion, then, which seems most suitable to the evidence is that, while Nestorius was not a consistent and systematic upholder of what we call 'Nestorianism,' yet he sometimes spoke erroneously; and, even if we give him the benefit of the doubt with regard to technical terms, it is difficult to acquit him altogether of a certain amount of heresy, and of a heresy which is particularly dangerous."[2]

Fendt sees the struggle in its time setting, and is convinced that Cyril was in the line of dogmatic orthodoxy. It is obvious, however, that he recognizes that which Antioch and Nestorius were emphasizing. But sympathy for Nestorius must not influence our judgment, and, according to Fendt, it is Cyril to whom the Church is indebted: "The two Patriarchs have long since finished contending. The Egyptian Church is now a waste, and on the reading desk of Saint Sophia lies the Koran. But we honour with deep thankfulness a holy Cyril who has anchored our faith

[1] *The Doctrine of the Person of Christ* (1925), p. 110.
[2] Article, 'Nestorianism', *Encyclopædia of Religion and Ethics*, ix. 331.

in Jesus Christ fast in the depths of eternal Godhead."[1]

Foakes-Jackson recognizes the personal as well as the theological antagonism between Cyril and Nestorius, and evidently has considerable sympathy with Nestorius: "He bore the sufferings of his exile with patience, and the opinions which have covered his name with such infamy were neither originated nor even strongly held by him. It is by the irony of fate that Nestorius is branded with the name of a heresiarch, whilst those who held almost the same views have died in the odour of sanctity. He was a victim to the ecclesiastical politics of his age."[2] However, he considers that it was necessary that Nestorius should be condemned, holding that the triumph of his opinions as generally understood would have been disastrous for the course of Christian theology, and that Cyril in spite of his personal unattractiveness was the sounder theologian: "We are inclined to pronounce him an excellent theologian but a bad man."[3]

Hodgson, who is responsible for the metaphysical and theological comments in Driver and Hodgson's edition, gives Nestorius full credit for his "very gallant and ingenious attempt"[4] to solve the Christological problem; but considers that he was attempting "to solve the problem on the basis of a principle which renders all solution impossible",[5] and that "the '*prosôpic* union' of Nestorius' theory is not strong enough to bear the strain it was designed to meet."[5]

Rucker has investigated the whole problem with meticulous thoroughness. He has endeavoured to comprehend the underlying meanings of Nestorius' terms, and he recognizes that Nestorius was struggling towards something very comprehensive, even if he never reached it.

---

[1] *Die Christologie des Nestorius* (1910), p. 113: "Die beiden Patriarchen haben längst ausgestritten. Die ägyptische Kirche ist nun eine Wüste und auf den Ambonen der Hagia Sophia liegt der Koran. Wir aber ehren mit tiefer Dankbarkeit einen hl. Cyrillus, der unseren Glauben an Jesus Christus unzerreissbar in den Tiefen der ewigen Gottheit verankert hat."

[2] *History of the Christian Church* (6th ed., 1914), p. 461.

[3] Ibid., p. 465.

[4] *Nestorius: The Bazaar of Heracleides, newly translated from the Syriac* (1925), p. 420.

[5] Ibid., p. 419.

Nor does Rucker underestimate either the weight or character of Cyril's relentless opposition. He even suggests that Cyril's concern was as much for ecclesiastical order and authority as for theology, and he recognizes Cyril's callousness and inflexibility: "Und war Cyrill nicht mehr Hierarch als Theolog? Und sein Verständnis für den Standpunkt des Gegners!"[1] Nevertheless, Rucker concludes his exhaustive studies with an uncompromising verdict against Nestorius: Nestorius' doctrine is not Catholic, and Nestorius is irrefutably to be reckoned as a heretic.[2] Junglas (*Die Irrlehre des Nestorius*, 1912) and Pesch (*Nestorius als Irrlehrer*, 1921), as the titles of their works indicate, are also uncompromisingly opposed to Nestorius.

Kidd, in his *History of the Church*, traces the conflict between Cyril and Nestorius and gives a careful analysis of Nestorius' views. His conclusion, however, is definitely against Nestorius, and he supports the findings of the Council of Chalcedon not simply because they are those of an Œcumenical Council, but because in his view they have been confirmed by subsequent history.[3] Kidd is quite definite that Nestorius' theory offered no solution: "Nestorius therefore failed to establish the unity of Christ by his theory of two πρόσωπα—the Word and the human person—making use of each other in a composite Person; and he did not succeed in avoiding the assertion of two persons in Christ, after all. 'The Word of God', he says, 'is the God of Christ': where 'Christ' must necessarily stand not for the composite Person but for the human element in his double being. On the point, then, that, according to Nestorius, for all his efforts to escape the conclusion, there were in Christ two beings and not one Divine Person, Cyril was in the right. He had far greater gifts of theological penetration than Nestorius."[4] He agrees with

---

[1] *Studien zum Concilium Ephesinum* (1934), vol. iv, p. xxvi.
[2] Ibid., iv. 415: "Mit Fug und Recht kann und muss man zu dieser vordringlichen Sichtung dogmatischer Formprobleme und ihrer Formulierung einwenden: 'Katholisch ist dies nicht' "; and iv. 439: "*Nestorius als Irrlehrer*. Dieser eigentliche Titel der Schrift von Pesch (1921) ist unumstösslich, wenn auch der erklärende Untertitel über die theologische Prinzipienfrage viel zu abgestumpft wäre. Denn Nestorius ist ein Häretiker."
[3] *A History of the Church to A.D. 461* (1922), iii. 253.
[4] Ibid., iii. 208.

Bedjan and Nau that even in the light of the Bazaar Nestorius still stands justly condemned.[1]

Tixeront makes a careful analysis of Nestorius' views, and credits him with the intention of being orthodox. He thinks that Nestorius lacked the ability to develop his views on correct lines, and that his error arose from that incapacity. Having given a very fair statement of what he recognizes as correct in Nestorius, Tixeront goes on to say: "Jusqu'ici tout est correct dans cette doctrine de Nestorius, et l'on se demandera donc en quoi consiste son erreur. Elle consiste en ce qu'il explique mal l'unité de personne dans le Christ, et en ce qu'il ne sait pas de cette unité personelle tirer les conséquences nécessaires."[2] Nestorius thus failed to escape the dangers inherent in the Antiochian approach: "En somme, Nestorius restait, avec plus de nuance dans la pensée et de précision dans les termes, dans la voie tracée par Théodore de Mopsueste. Nestorien, on peut dire qu'il l'est moins violemment que Théodore. Il veut conserver les façons de s'exprimer de l'Église; et c'est sincèrement, on doit le croire, qu'il proclame l'unité personelle de Jésus-Christ. Mais de cette unité il n'a pas l'intelligence vraie et profonde: et, dès lors, il ne voit pas non plus les conséquences qu'il en faut tirer pour toute la doctrine de l'incarnation et du salut, non plus que les formules qui s'imposent, ce dogme une fois admis, à la langue théologique."[3] Tixeront emphasizes the importance of preserving the dogmatic postulates as against the advancing of inadequate metaphysical solutions: "Au lieu de construire en quelque sorte artificiellement, comme les antiochiens, l'unité du Christ, le patriarche d'Alexandrie la saisit directement et en a le sens immédiat. Son point de vue est moins métaphysique que religieux."[4] It is exactly here that Cyril was right and Nestorius wrong.

Relton recognizes the necessity of distinguishing between Nestorianism as commonly understood and the actual teaching of Nestorius; but he none the less considers the condemnation of Nestorius to have been inevitable and just:

[1] *A History of the Church to A.D. 461*, iii. 208 (footnote).
[2] *Histoire des Dogmes* (2nd edition), iii. 28.
[3] Ibid., iii. 35.
[4] Ibid., iii. 79.

"He cannot be acquitted of the charges brought against him by the theologians of his time."[1]

There are some, notably Bedjan and Nau, who would go even further in their condemnation of Nestorius. They consider that his condemnation was inevitable and just, and, having scant sympathy with the man himself, reckon that the treatment meted out to him by Cyril was none too harsh. Such a view, advanced by those so familiar with the circumstances of the problem and interested enough to give the world the Syriac text and a French translation, cannot be ignored.

Bedjan is quite convinced that Nestorius was in error,[2] and suggests that he sustained his case through sheer wilfulness.[3] As a Catholic, Bedjan is very opposed to what he considers an obstinate rebellion against authority,[4] and holds that the discovery of the Bazaar only serves to confirm and justify the verdict of history.[5]

Nau recognizes the criticisms which can be levelled against the form and procedure of the Council of Ephesus, but he sees Nestorius as a responsible participant in those far from admirable proceedings rather than simply the victim of them. Nau describes Nestorius as "loquacious, unlettered, mischief-making, despotic, arrogant", and he suggests that, before being too sympathetic towards Nestorius, we should consider what Cyril might have had to say if he could have written a reply to the Bazaar. Even

---

[1] *A Study in Christology* (1934), p. 26.

[2] *Nestorius: Le Livre d'Héraclide de Damas, édité par Paul Bedjan*, p. xiii: "L'étude du présent ouvrage me permet de dire qu'en dépit des précautions qu'il a prises et des négations qu'il accumule on y trouve encore de manière suffisamment claire les erreurs qui l'ont fait condamner."

[3] Ibid., p. xxxviii: "Surtout en lisant le 'Traité d'Héraclide', on voit qu'il connaissait parfaitement les questions, il a résisté sciemment et volontairement; et on ne peut point croire à son innocence quand on lit quelques-unes de ses récriminations ou quelques pièces qu'il rapporte en sa faveur."

[4] Ibid., p. vi: ". . . lui qui, depuis 20 ans, malgré des condamnations réitérées, continuait toujours à réclamer la révision de son jugement!" and p. vii: "Tout porte donc à croire que Nestorius est mort en 450 ou 451, sans se soumettre à l'autorité légitime."

[5] Ibid., p. xxxvii: "Quelle inconséquence! il demande toujours qu'on refasse son procès! on le refait depuis 15 siècles, et tous les siècles l'ont justement condamné comme le condamne de nouveau et sans appel l'apologie que je publie." Also p. xxxviii: "Nestorius est donc un hérétique avéré et justement condamné; et notre temps, comme les temps qui nous ont précédés, ne peut l'excuser."

if everything Nestorius wrote in the Bazaar were taken into account, Nestorius would still justly be condemned as a heretic: "On pourra discuter la forme du concile d'Éphèse, on pourra regretter que le litige n'ait pas été solutionné plus vite et ait duré jusqu'à Chalcédoine, mais ces imperfections tiennent à la nature humaine qui est mauvaise; nous les retrouvons dans tout le cours de l'histoire. Il reste certain que la présente apologie de Nestorius demanderait, comme contrepartie, une apologie de saint Cyrille. Il serait facile de montrer, avec les historiens, que Nestorius était bavard, ignorant, brouillon, despote, orgueilleux. Nous avons enregistré, avec grande complaisance, les louanges qu'il se donne pour le dogme des deux natures, car il est ici un des témoins de la tradition catholique, mais il ne faut pas oublier que *les deux natures entraînent chez lui deux hypostases distinctes et deux personnes (prosôpons) unies en une par simple prêt et échange*. Il est donc certain que, même après la présente apologie, il aurait été condamné comme hérétique. Ce dernier point a été très bien mis en relief, dans la Préface au texte syriaque, par le R. P. Bedjan, avec qui nous sommes ainsi en complet accord."[1]

Sufficient opinions have been quoted, though the list is by no means exhaustive. But, even if its range were considerably extended, its general tenor would remain much the same; the distribution of opinions, from Bethune-Baker at the one extreme to Bedjan and Nau at the other, would not be greatly altered. The majority, with varying degrees of sympathy for his misfortunes, consider that Nestorius was rightly condemned, though the degree of complacency regarding the verdict varies considerably.

It is not easy to dispute this consensus. Quite apart from opinions as to the authority of Œcumenical Councils, it is evident to any student of ecclesiastical history that God has not left His Church undirected, and even if the direction sometimes appears to pass through unworthy and tortuous human channels, there is a steady movement towards the divinely appointed ends. Melancholy reading though the proceedings of the Council of Ephesus may make, it cannot

[1] *Nestorius: Le Livre d'Héraclide de Damas, traduit en français par F. Nau* (1910), p. xxvii.

be doubted that it was necessary that Cyril should triumph and Nestorius fail. Cyril was holding firmly to the irreducible postulates with a splendid instinct which transfigures even his unprepossessing character. Nestorius, on the other hand, was obstinately striving to get others to accept positions which were far from clear definition and correlation even in his own mind. No other verdict was possible, and history has endorsed it. The discovery of the Bazaar, in the opinion of most of those competent to judge, has not brought the verdict into serious question.

Nevertheless, the Bazaar must not be discarded with exasperation or, worse, with pity. There is something here struggling for expression, and the more earnestly we endeavour to disentangle its meaning the more convinced we become that here is something of real value for Christology. Nestorius had neither the ability nor the temperament to make the best of his apology. It is pathetic to recognize that with this opportunity of saying the last word he should have used it so poorly. His matter is ill-arranged, repetitive, ill-proportioned, ill-balanced, and he still dissipates himself and his skill in attack rather than in the careful statement of his own positions. He makes himself a witness for the prosecution in spite of those who would defend him.

There is much in posing the right questions, and that is certainly so in the Nestorian controversy. The question is not whether Nestorius was a heretic. That has been settled long ago. Nor is the question whether he was rightly or wrongly condemned. His condemnation was necessary and inevitable. The question is not whether Nestorius offered a clear, intelligible and valid solution to the Christological problem. He did not. The question is: If Nestorius had been able to set in logical order his metaphysical and Christological ideas, would there have emerged a metaphysic and Christology representing a real contribution to Christian thought?

We shall therefore leave aside the sad and tangled record of the events leading up to the Council of Ephesus, occurring at that Council, and following it; we shall not enter into any discussion as to the characters of Cyril and Nestorius; we shall not concern ourselves with the methods or ethics of their contending; we shall not question on shorter or longer views the findings of the Council. We shall simply endeavour to answer this question: Had Nestorius a real contribution to make to Christological thought?

In order to answer this question we shall limit our consideration to the Bazaar. One reason for so doing is that it is free from the thrust and parry of immediate controversy, which is so liable to lead the contestants into irrelevancies and to force them to adopt or defend positions not of their free choosing. Unless the matter under dispute is clear and simple, which Christology never can be, analysis of a debate is seldom likely to yield a lucid account of the real views of either contestant. Another reason is the fact that the Bazaar was written when the conflict was over. It was written presumably at comparative leisure. It should represent Nestorius' matured and settled views.

The material for our study is readily and conveniently accessible. For the Syriac text we have Bedjan's edition. The text-critical problems are not unduly complicated, and most readers will be satisfied with Bedjan's handling of them. He edits the text with judgment and discretion, and provides apparatus where he deems it necessary. He is conservative in conjectural emendation, and those interested in pursuing such matters further might well start with the suggestions made by Connolly in a valuable article in the *Journal of Theological Studies*, vol. xxvii, pp. 191–200 (January, 1926). Then there are two excellent translations, valuable in their differing ways. That by Nau is competent in itself, and had the great advantage of being prepared in consultation with Bedjan. The style is good, but not to the degree of departing too far from a literal rendering. Where a literal rendering would make the French too inelegant, Nau usually gives a literal translation in a footnote, and there are brief notes on difficult words or sentences.[1] Where there are ambiguities he reproduces them in his translation, in order to avoid "replacing translation by

[1] It should perhaps be mentioned that Rucker quotes Labourt as not being quite satisfied with Nau's translation: ". . . die französische Uebersetzung von Nau, deren Zuverlässigkeit schon Labourt 1911 anzweifelt." (*Studien zum Concilium Ephesinum*, vol. iv, p. xx.)

interpretation".[1] On the contrary, if smoothness in translation from some points of view is to be considered a fault, it is intentionally absent from Driver and Hodgson. This translation professes to provide just what the serious student would wish—a careful literal rendering of the Syriac without regard to elegance of English. These editors state that they "have frequently sacrificed the English to an endeavour to render faithfully the Syriac version, keeping as far as possible the same English word for the corresponding Syriac even at the cost of a certain harshness or awkwardness in many passages; for they have regarded it as their aim not so much to present the reader with their view of what Nestorius said as to enable him to form his own opinion from a careful and accurate version of the Syriac text."[2]

This aim they have certainly endeavoured to achieve, and their translation merits the description 'careful and accurate'. Although the translation was searchingly and competently criticized by Connolly in the article cited above, it is possible to give full weight to all his criticisms and still in general to feel satisfied that Driver and Hodgson have given a reasonably clear rendering where the Syriac is clear and have contented themselves with being vague to the same extent and in the same way where the Syriac is vague. Professor Driver, in a letter dated December 17th, 1947, asks the present writer to call attention to the comments and corrections contained in Connolly's article. While gladly doing so, I would emphasize that Connolly himself, in spite of his criticisms, nevertheless says of Driver and Hodgson's translation: "The reader who has made a study of this volume will be in possession, to an adequate degree, of Nestorius's arguments and of the position taken up by him at the time when he wrote his Apology" (op. cit., p. 192). Again, towards the end of his article, Connolly says:

[1] "Il est probable qu'il existe autant de fautes dans les endroits où nous ne disposons pas du texte original pour corriger le syriaque, nous avons donc laissé subsister l'obscurité de la version syriaque dans les quelques endroits où la suite des idées n'indiquait pas clairement la correction à faire, afin de ne pas remplacer la traduction par une interprétation." (*Nestorius: Le Livre d'Héraclide de Damas, traduit en français par F. Nau*, p. xxv.)

[2] *Nestorius: The Bazaar of Heracleides, newly translated from the Syriac*, p. xvi.

D

"Having now drawn attention to what seem to me the defects of the translation, let me say again that I do not think they are such as to interfere vitally with its value as a presentation of Nestorius's teaching. I would repeat also that the book is a difficult one to translate, as I have reason to know" (ibid., p. 200).

This translation has therefore been used as the basis for our study, partly because it is unlikely that an independent translation of the Syriac would approach Driver's in accuracy, and partly because Driver's translation was made without any metaphysical or theological presuppositions, and the translator was therefore not influenced in his rendering either consciously or unconsciously by a desire to make his rendering accord with any definite scheme of thought. His intentional ambiguities are sufficient proof of this. In those few cases where it may be necessary, reference will be made to the Syriac, to the translation by Nau, to those passages translated in Bethune-Baker,[1] and to the comments and emendations of Connolly in the article mentioned above. All references, however, will be given in accordance with the Syriac page numbering of Bedjan, because this page numbering will serve equally for reference to Bedjan, Driver and Hodgson, and Nau. Driver and Hodgson insert the Syriac page numbers in square brackets at the top of each page, and Nau inserts them in square brackets in his text.[2] Throughout this work all references to the text or to these translations will be given prefixed by a capital B. Thus 'B. 75' means p. 75 in Bedjan's edition of the Syriac text, and the corresponding passages in the translations will readily be found in the manner stated. It is to be noted that Driver and Hodgson and Nau agree in the opinion that at least one section of the Syriac text has been misplaced, the section beginning with the last line on B. 137 and ending with the last line on B. 146. They think that

[1] The identity of Bethune-Baker's "anonymous" Syriacist was not publicly declared until eighteen years after the publication of *Nestorius and His Teaching*. The "anonymous" Syriacist was Connolly, as he admits in the article already cited (op. cit., p. 200). When, as is customary, we refer to 'Bethune-Baker's translation' we therefore imply the translation made for him by Connolly.

[2] For footnote, see p. 55.

this section should be inserted between B. 270 and B. 271, and that is where it will be found in their translations. This must be remembered if difficulty is to be avoided in looking up references from B. 137 to B. 146. Attention is drawn to a few other points on page numbering on pp. 411–412.

As most English readers will probably use Driver and Hodgson's translation, this has helped to a decision in the matter of the rendering of a group of constantly recurring words: οὐσία, φύσις, ὑπόστασις, πρόσωπον, σχῆμα, and their derivatives.[1] To use the Greek forms every time makes both style and typography inelegant. To find English equivalents is almost impossible. I have, therefore, thought it best to follow Driver and Hodgson, and have used *ousia*, *nature*, *hypostasis*, *prosôpon* and *schêma*, with ousias, natures, hypostases, prosôpa and schêmata as plurals, and ousic, natural, hypostatic, prosôpic and schêmatic as the corresponding adjectives. This usage may be open to criticism, but ingenuity would be taxed to find a system completely logical and consistent, and this one seems to provide a workable solution, besides being convenient for those using Driver and Hodgson.

Having resolved to endeavour to discover Nestorius' definitive Christology as enunciated in the Bazaar, difficulty immediately arises as to the method to be employed. As has already been mentioned, Nestorius does not present his case well; and this is not due simply to poor arrangement, needless repetition and lack of proportion, but to far more serious causes. Nestorius does not merely fail to present his case in good logical order; he fails to present parts of it at all. There are many complicated and interdependent chains of reasoning running through the book. Some of the links are well and definitely forged together. This is especially true of the first half of Book I, Part I, where Nestorius displays some particularly brilliant reasoning. The neat way in which his metaphysic disposes of heresies is really admirable, as is his handling of scriptural difficulties: see, for example, B. 26–28, 42–49, 60–63, 68–78.

---

[1] In the Syriac version *ûsiyâ*, *kyânâ*, *qnômâ*, *parṣôpâ*, *eskêmâ*. But it must be remembered that significance attaches not so much to the Syriac words as to the original Greek they represent.

He shows equal adroitness in dealing with the reasonable interpretation of omnipotence (B. 20–21). But in other cases the links seem to be completely absent. Conclusions are sometimes stated before the arguments on which they are based have been given, and in some cases conclusions are assumed on the basis of arguments not stated or even suggested. It is increasingly borne in upon the careful reader that Nestorius had within his mind a complex of ideas to which he never gave clear expression. He uses terms with special connotations,[1] seeming to assume that the reader will understand as clearly as he does how exactly the terms are being used. He fails to give precise definitions,[2] and certain matters are taken for granted without proof and without their being placed into a readily comprehensible general system of thought. The arguments in Book I, Part I, are not really helped by the 'question and answer' method, and it is confusing to have Sophronius playing so many mutually conflicting rôles. Difficulty is occasionally caused by the asking of rhetorical questions to which the answers are not always so obvious as Nestorius apparently thought they should be (e.g., B. 71, 203–204); and it is some-times difficult to tell whether a statement is made seriously or sarcastically (e.g., B. 366). Nor is it always at once clear whether certain statements are meant to represent his own views or those of others (e.g., B. 55–60, 117–120, 126–129). This is especially difficult in cases where the refutation of the view stated is supposed by Nestorius to be self-evident.

It does not take the careful student long to realize that no systematic analysis of the Bazaar, however thorough, will enable him to formulate a coherent and self-consistent Christology. It is of course to be admitted that it is usually undesirable to read more into a writer than he actually writes; but if we apply this principle to the Bazaar it will remain an uncomprehended work. The only way in which it is possible to reduce Nestorius' ideas to a logical coherent system is to read his book and to evolve a tentative meta-physical and Christological system approximately fitting it; to read his book again with that tentative system in mind,

---

[1] E.g., 'in' (see pp. 141–147) and 'he' (see p. 187).
[2] E.g., what did Nestorius understand by *prosôpon*? See pp. 99–108.

to revise the system in the light of the re-reading, and so to continue working backwards and forwards until a system has been evolved which makes it possible to read his book and to understand, as clearly as presumably Nestorius himself did, all its implications, and to find as obvious as he did the shades of meaning to be attached to each word.

The result of this process will be the evolution of a self-consistent metaphysic and Christology. Much of it will be supported and illustrated by Nestorius' own words or their obvious implications. Other parts of it will represent the logical or empirical filling-in of lacunæ left by Nestorius. It is these lacunæ which present at once the irritation and the problem. For it is evident that Nestorius had a clear and definite complex of ideas in his own mind, though he had not the wisdom or the patience to expound it in a systematic manner. People of that type are not uncommon, and sometimes, when another has spoken after them, they will say, "That is exactly what I meant!" This work is an attempt to reduce Nestorius' metaphysic and Christology to a coherent system of which he himself would be able to say, "This is what I meant."

The method is necessarily inductive, and is open to the criticisms inevitably applicable to all inductive methods. The result cannot be described otherwise than as a working hypothesis. It may be possible to construct several working hypotheses to fit any given set of facts. In general, the simplest that will account for all the facts is the most likely to be true, or to represent the closest approximation to the truth. The truth may be more complex than the simplest hypothesis fitting the known facts, but the simplest hypothesis probably does not go beyond the truth, and subsequent discoveries can usually be fitted into a simple hypothesis by a process of amplification of relevant detail. On the other hand, a more complex hypothesis, while possibly nearer the truth, may equally possibly be further from it. It will therefore be our endeavour to construct the simplest metaphysic and Christology which will enable us to read the Bazaar with facility and understanding.

It may at once be said that the reconstruction is far from a simple one; but it is hardly to be anticipated that so

complex a system as the Universe and so complex a problem
as Christology will be soluble in simple terms. If Nestorius
himself had worked out all the implications of his metaphysical assumptions he might have been surprised at the
complexity of the system evolved. We shall not endeavour
to work out all the implications, only so many of them as
are relevant to Christology; but we shall endeavour to
show that the system is powerful and coherent, and offers
a view of the Universe in general and of the problem of
unity in particular which well repays careful consideration.
As we shall endeavour to show by implication in Part II,
there are elements in the thought of Nestorius which provide a helpful mode of approach to the Christological
problem. We discard his heresy, but we are entitled to
develop such of his ideas as are of value.

We thus turn to the first part of our task, the systematization and interpretation of the metaphysic and Christology
of Nestorius. We shall not comment on the merits or
defects of his system, simply expounding it as concisely as
possible in his own terms and their necessary amplifications.
In the second part we shall move onward, seeking an understanding of the same problem in the light of more modern
knowledge. In Part I it should be quite evident to the
careful reader where the reconstruction is based on the
words of Nestorius himself and their obvious implications,
and where lacunæ, in some cases considerable, have had to
be filled by logic, induction, or by the adoption of the
simplest satisfactory hypotheses and their implications. If
the work in Part I were done with complete success, it
might be hoped that, apart from textual obscurities, it
would be possible to read the Bazaar without further difficulty. It has been thought desirable, however, to provide
an Appendix in which are some notes on the general structure of the Bazaar and on passages presenting obscurity or
difficulty. Those approaching the problem of Nestorius and
the Bazaar for the first time might be well advised first to
read Part I with merely sufficient attention to grasp the
general terms of the arguments, then to read through the
Bazaar with the aid of the Appendix, and then to re-read
Part I with critical care.

After due consideration, it has been decided to omit a historical introduction. Presumably no one will be interested in this work who is not familiar with the course of Church History and Christology during the first five centuries, and any such introduction would be to that extent superfluous. Nor has it seemed necessary to give details of the course of the disputings between Cyril and Nestorius, and of the Council of Ephesus. Longer or shorter accounts are so readily available that it is hardly necessary to give yet another summary.[1]

[1] Reference may be made to the footnotes in Chapter II or to the bibliography.

Footnote 2, p. 50: The same method of reference cannot be used, unfortunately, for the passages translated by Bethune-Baker in *Nestorius and His Teaching.* The page numbering of his Syriac copy appears to have followed that of Auscha'nâ's transcription, and each page contains more than half as much again as a page in Bedjan's edition. It may therefore be convenient to give a list of the principal passages translated by Bethune-Baker, with the pages in *Nestorius and His Teaching* where they are found, his Syriac page numbers, and the corresponding Bedjan numbers. Corresponding numbers are placed in the same vertical column.

Nestorius and His Teaching:	141–146	123–138	149–165
Bethune-Baker's Syriac:	27–31	53–63	70–80
Bedjan's Syriac:	42–49	90–110	126–146
Nestorius and His Teaching:	71–77	175–188	6–8
Bethune-Baker's Syriac:	154–159	186–196	279–281
Bedjan's Syriac:	200–208	225–241	376–379
Nestorius and His Teaching:	86–87	168–169	192–195
Bethune-Baker's Syriac:	299–300	314–315	366–370
Bedjan's Syriac:	407–409	431–433	513–518

These are the only passages of any length translated in Bethune-Baker, though there are many short extracts. If it is desired to check these against the Syriac or one of the other translations, difficulty may be experienced in finding the corresponding place. The following list may therefore be of service to any readers who wish to compare Bethune-Baker's translation with the original or with other translations. The first number in each pair is the page number in Bethune-Baker's Syriac copy, and the second number is the corresponding page in Bedjan: 14, 18; 15, 19; 17, 23; 22, 33; 24, 38; 26, 42; 27, 42; 39, 63; 40, 67; 43, 73; 53, 90; 68, 121; 70, 125; 79, 143; 106, 147; 108, 151; 149, 192; 151, 195; 153, 198; 154, 200; 176, 210; 179, 214; 186, 225; 217, 275; 223, 285; 224, 287; 273, 367; 279, 376; 286, 387; 299, 407; 303, 414; 310, 425; 312, 428; 314, 431; 321, 442; 326, 449; 333, 460; 337, 466; 362, 507; 363, 508; 370, 519.

Bethune-Baker's translation reads more easily than Driver and Hodgson's, and is sometimes of value in giving his opinion on the meaning of a difficult passage. But he does not claim that it is a word-for-word rendering, remarking in one of his footnotes (p. 16), "I have endeavoured to give here and elsewhere the exact sense, though not always what is commonly called a 'literal' translation." It must also be remembered that Bethune-Baker had only one copy of the Syriac Text ('C', see p. 33 above), whereas Driver and Hodgson were able to make use of Bedjan's text and apparatus.

CHAPTER II

NESTORIUS AND THE POSTULATES

BEFORE endeavouring to interpret the Christology of Nestorius it is desirable to state the problem as he and his contemporaries saw it, to be aware of the positions reached by their time, and to appreciate the metaphysic with which his Christology had to accord.

The first three centuries of Christian thought on the problem of Christology had culminated in the formulation of the Creed of the Council of Nicæa,[1] which may be regarded as the first really great landmark in the development of precision in orthodox Christology. This creed is notable not for offering a solution, but for affirming certain postulates. It afforded a standard whereby the defects in earlier attempts at solution could be the more readily made manifest and a norm whereby later attempts could be tested. It defines the relationship of Jesus Christ to God the Father, and any orthodox attempt at solving the problem of Christology must accept as a postulate that Jesus Christ is God in the sense conveyed in this creed.

The Creed of Nicæa runs thus: "We believe in one God, the Father Omnipotent, Maker of all things both visible and invisible. And in one Lord Jesus Christ, the Son of God, begotten of the Father, only-begotten, that is, of the essence (οὐσίας) of the Father, God of God, Light of Light, true God of true God, begotten, not made, of the same essence (ὁμοούσιον) as the Father; through whom all things came into being, both in heaven and in earth; who for us men and for our salvation came down and was made flesh, and became man, suffered, and rose again the third day, ascended into the heavens, and is coming to judge the living and the dead. And in the Holy Spirit. But those who say that there was a time when He was not, and before He was begotten He was not, and He came into being from things which are not, or assert the Son of God is from a

[1] The first Œcumenical Council (A.D. 325).

different substance or essence, or is created, changed or altered, the Catholic Church anathematizes."[1]

This creed implies a metaphysic of some complexity, and raises questions as to the precise meanings to be attached to the words οὐσία, ὑπόστασις, and ὁμοούσιος. These matters will be discussed later. The point of immediate importance, however, is this: from the time of the Council of Nicæa any orthodox attempt at solving the problem of Christology must accept the postulate that Jesus Christ is truly God.[2]

The Creed of Nicæa was confirmed by the Council of Constantinople (A.D. 381), the second Œcumenical Council. This Council also approved a modified form submitted by Cyril of Jerusalem. This form, known as the Constantinopolitan Creed, took the place of the Creed of Nicæa in the Eastern Church. It differs little from the Creed of Nicæa in the points dealing with the person of Christ, there being merely a few verbal additions and omissions which do not materially affect its main trends.[3]

Though the Council of Nicæa had established for orthodoxy the postulate that Jesus Christ is truly God, it had left many other questions still unanswered. One of the

---

[1] Πιστεύομεν εἰς ἕνα θεόν, πατέρα παντοκράτορα, πάντων ὁρατῶν τε καὶ ἀοράτων ποιητήν. καὶ εἰς ἕνα κύριον Ἰησοῦν Χριστόν, τὸν υἱὸν τοῦ θεοῦ, γεννηθέντα ἐκ τοῦ πατρὸς μονογενῆ, τουτέστιν ἐκ τῆς οὐσίας τοῦ πατρός, θεὸν ἐκ θεοῦ, φῶς ἐκ φωτός, θεὸν ἀληθινὸν ἐκ θεοῦ ἀληθινοῦ, γεννηθέντα, οὐ ποιηθέντα, ὁμοούσιον τῷ πατρί, δι' οὗ τὰ πάντα ἐγένετο, τά τε ἐν τῷ οὐρανῷ καὶ τὰ ἐν τῇ γῇ. τὸν δι' ἡμᾶς τοὺς ἀνθρώπους καὶ διὰ τὴν ἡμετέραν σωτηρίαν κατελθόντα καὶ σαρκωθέντα, ἐνανθρωπήσαντα, παθόντα, καὶ ἀναστάντα τῇ τρίτῃ ἡμέρᾳ, ἀνελθόντα εἰς οὐρανούς, καὶ ἐρχόμενον κρῖναι ζῶντας καὶ νεκρούς. καὶ εἰς τὸ ἅγιον πνεῦμα. τοὺς δὲ λέγοντας· ἦν ποτε ὅτε οὐκ ἦν, καὶ πρὶν γεννηθῆναι οὐκ ἦν, καὶ ὅτι ἐξ οὐκ ὄντων ἐγένετο, ἢ ἐξ ἑτέρας ὑποστάσεως ἢ οὐσίας φάσκοντας εἶναι, ἢ κτιστὸν ἢ τρεπτὸν ἢ ἀλλοιωτὸν τὸν υἱὸν τοῦ θεοῦ, ἀναθεματίζει ἡ καθολικὴ ἐκκλησία.

[2] The history of the Council of Nicæa may be found in the Church histories and histories of doctrine, e.g. Hefele, Conciliengeschichte (2nd edition), i. 252–443 (or in Clark's English translation, A History of the Christian Councils (2nd edition), i. 231–447) (see note in the bibliography, p. 478), Kidd, History of the Church, ii. 3–68, Seeberg, Lehrbuch der Dogmengeschichte, ii. 20–87, Mackintosh, Person of Jesus Christ, pp. 175–195. Arianism, the precipitating cause of the Council of Nicæa, may be conveniently studied in Gwatkin, Studies of Arianism.

[3] The differences are set out in Briggs, Theological Symbolics, pp. 83–99. It should, however, be noted that Gwatkin (The Arian Controversy, p. 160) regards the Constantinopolitan Creed as a retrogression from Nicæa, particularly noting the omission of the 'key-stone clause' "of the essence of the Father." But the significance or otherwise of this omission depends upon the precise meaning attached to ὁμοούσιον, which is retained.

most theologically important and philosophically difficult
was this: if Jesus Christ is truly God, how can He also be
truly man? This question, with its complex implications,
was brought into urgent prominence by Apollinarius.
Apollinarius, Bishop of Laodicæa (361–377), held a simple
and to himself very satisfying view of the person of Jesus
Christ. Accepting the tripartite theory of the composition
of man as consisting of body, animal soul, and intellect or
spirit (σῶμα, ψυχή, and νοῦς or πνεῦμα), the person of Christ
is fully accounted for by replacing human intellect by the
Logos, the eternally generated Word of God. It was suspected, perhaps definitely known, that he had held this
view for many years, but in 377 he put it bluntly into
writing that the Word took flesh without assuming a
human mind. Basil of Cæsarea, who had for some time
suspected Apollinarius' views, thereafter worked for his
overthrow. He succeeded in getting him condemned by a
Council at Rome in 377 and at Antioch in 379. Finally,
though after Basil's death, the views of Apollinarius were
condemned at the second Œcumenical Council, the Council
of Constantinople (381). This Council confirmed the Creed
of Nicæa and specifically condemned Apollinarianism. The
reason for condemning Apollinarianism is most concisely
stated by Gregory of Nazianzus:[1] "If anyone has trusted in
a man without intellect, he is indeed senseless, and not
worthy to be wholly saved. For that which is unassumed
is unhealed; but that which has been united to God, this
also is saved. If half Adam fell, half also is that which has
been assumed and that which is saved. But if the whole
(Adam fell), he has been united to the whole of Him who
was begotten and is wholly saved. Let them not then
begrudge to us complete salvation, nor equip the Saviour
only with bones and nerves and the portraiture of a man."

From the time of the Council of Constantinople it may

---

[1] Εἴ τις εἰς ἄνουν ἄνθρωπον ἤλπικεν, ἀνόητος ὄντως ἐστὶ, καὶ οὐκ ἄξιος ὅλως
σώζεσθαι. Τὸ γὰρ ἀπρόσληπτον, ἀθεράπευτον· ὃ δὲ ἥνωται τῷ Θεῷ, τοῦτο καὶ
σώζεται. Εἰ ἥμισυς ἔπταισεν ὁ Ἀδὰμ, ἥμισυ καὶ τὸ προσειλημμένον καὶ τὸ
σωζόμενον. Εἰ δὲ ὅλος, ὅλῳ τῷ γεννηθέντι ἥνωται, καὶ ὅλως σώζεται. Μὴ τοίνυν
βασκαινέτωσαν ἡμῖν τῆς παντελοῦς σωτηρίας, μηδὲ ὀστᾶ μόνον, καί νεῦρα καὶ
ζωγραφίαν ἀνθρώπου τῷ Σωτῆρι περιτιθέτωσαν. Epis, CI, 47–51 (Migne,
Patrologia Græco-Latina, xxxvii. 181 C).

therefore be reckoned that the second postulate of orthodox Christology is established: that Jesus Christ is truly man.[1]

There are thus two postulates: Jesus Christ is truly God, and Jesus Christ is truly man. The problem of orthodox Christology is to endeavour to explain how these statements can both be true of one person. The question can be posed in at least three ways: How could God and man be united as one person? How could God, remaining God, become also man? How could man, remaining man, become also God? The next stage in the development of Christological thought resulted from the adoption of the opposite lines of approach indicated by the second and third forms of the question. The Alexandrian School, ever mindful of Christ's deity, and the Antiochian School, never forgetful of Christ's humanity, approached the problem with their distinctive and contrasted attitudes of mind.[2] It was this difference in approach which led to the clash between Cyril and Nestorius, the clash which resulted in victory for Cyril and defeat for Nestorius. Neither doubted the two postulates that Jesus Christ is truly God and that Jesus Christ is truly man. Each recognized in Him one person, but neither thought that the other's views could fulfil all the accepted conditions. The sordid story of the struggle has been told so many times that it need not be repeated here.[3] It raged mainly round the questions of applying the title 'Theotokos' to the Virgin Mary, of applying the name 'God the Word' without qualification to Jesus Christ, and as to whether the divine and human in Jesus Christ were

[1] An account of the Apollinarian controversy and the Council of Constantinople may be found in Hefele, op. cit., i. 727–ii. 33 (English trans., ii. 276–374), Kidd, op. cit., ii. 208–297, Seeberg, op. cit., ii. 170–186, Mackintosh, op. cit., pp. 196–201. For a detailed study of Apollinarianism, see Raven, *Apollinarianism*.

[2] For a careful analysis of the Alexandrian and Antiochian attitudes, see Sellers, *Two Ancient Christologies*.

[3] Vide, e.g., Hefele, op. cit., ii. 141–288 (English trans., iii. 1–156), Kidd, op. cit., iii. 192–276, Seeberg, op. cit., ii. 210–242, Loofs, *Nestorius*, pp. 26–60. (Cyril was born in 376, became Bishop of Alexandria in 412, and died in 444. Nestorius was born in Germanicia near Mount Taurus in Syria, date unknown, was first a monk at the Monastery of Euprepius near Antioch, then a Presbyter at Antioch, became Bishop of Constantinople in 428, was condemned and deposed by the Council of Ephesus in 431, returned to the Monastery of Euprepius, was banished in 435, first to Petra in Arabia then to Oasis in Egypt, and died, still an exile, about 451.)

united hypostatically. But the object of the present work is not an inquiry into their antagonism; it is an endeavour to discover what Nestorius has to contribute to our thought.

It has been seen that the approach to the problem must start from the acceptance of three postulates:

(1) *That Jesus Christ is truly God*

Nestorius explicitly accepts this postulate: "For these reasons, then, and for similar causes, the incarnation of God took place justly: true God by nature and true man by nature" (B. 116). "For no other is called God the Word in the flesh apart from him who is in our own flesh; nor again [is anything else called] the flesh, but it is in the Son, in God the Word: that he should comport himself completely in the nature of men being man, and that he should rise as God being God by nature" (B. 129). Similar statements occur many times, e.g. B. 77, 131, 218.

(2) *That Jesus Christ is truly man*

This also is explicitly stated in many places:

"But in the *ousia* of man [he is] truly man, of the true nature of the true man in which he became incarnate" (B. 30). "He became man in truth, since he had according to nature all [the properties] of a man; he was not the half of a complete [man], that is flesh only, or animal soul, for it is not in this that he became man, in possessing nothing of man except animal bodily frame and soul without reason, but [in possessing] a rational soul and a rational body and a rational life, and not [all these] without reason" (B. 51–52). "Therefore the Evangelists record all those things which in truth show the nature of man, lest on account of the divinity it should not be believed that he was also man" (B. 132). The same assertion is frequently repeated, for example B. 116, 129, 219.

(3) *That Jesus Christ is one person*

This is asserted and implied many times. It is one of several points made in the passage on a king assuming soldierhood:

"As a king, who takes the clothes of soldierhood and is

[so seen], has not become a double king, and as the king exists not apart from him, in that he is in him, and as, further, he is not revered apart from him in whom he is known and whereby men also have known him and have been rescued; so also God used his own *prosôpon* to condescend in poverty and shame even unto the death on the Cross for our salvation" (B. 33).

"In the *prosôpon* then of the divinity is he adored and in no other, and in consequence of this the *prosôpon* is one and the name of the Son [is one]" (B. 34). Later, the matter is dealt with directly, on the basis of John i: "Thou wilt confess aloud with us that there are not two Gods the Words or two Sons or two only begottens, but one" (B. 69). "Does he speak of one God the Word or of two Words? *In the beginning was the Word and the Word was with God and the Word was God. He was in the beginning with God; everything came into being by him and without him came into being nothing whatsoever that came into being.* Concerning whom can these things be said by the Evangelist, except concerning him who is consubstantial [with the Father] and without bodily frame? And this: *In him was life and the life was the light of men and the same light shineth in the darkness and the darkness comprehended it not.* Did he say it of another or of the very same?" (B. 70). "Did the Evangelist speak of another Word or of God the Word, by whom everything came into being, life and the true light, who came unto his own and his own received him not, who gave authority unto those that received him to become the sons of God, [who] were born not of blood nor of the will of the flesh but of God?" (B. 71). See also B. 81, 129, 337.

Nestorius certainly thought that his Christology was in the line of orthodox doctrine, and he equally certainly thought that it was in logical accord with the metaphysical ideas current in his time. It may be doubted, however, whether he can be considered a scholar. Although Socrates is perhaps unduly hard on him, he is probably correct in asserting that Nestorius was not well grounded in the 'ancient expositors': "Being naturally eloquent, he was thought scholarly; but in truth he was uneducated, and deemed it needless to study the books of the ancient expositors. For befogged by his own fluency, he did not accurately pay attention to the ancients, but considered himself master of all."[1] It would appear that this stricture applied equally in the realms of Greek philosophy and of Christian theology.[2] Nestorius was one of those acute and original thinkers who are impatient of the discipline involved in the careful study of the work of others. If, therefore, he is to be understood, he must be approached with few preconceptions.

It will consequently not be profitable to endeavour to sketch the Aristotelian metaphysic as generally accepted in the fourth and fifth centuries; nor will it serve any useful purpose to discuss the history of the terms.[3] Nestorius had his own distinctive approach, and his views will be more readily understood if we investigate them from his own first principles. We shall therefore begin our investigation without preconceptions even as to the use of terms. His own usage will be examined, and the metaphysical framework into which his Christology is to be fitted will be constructed from his own data and their implications.

It is necessary to stress the importance of his distinctive metaphysic. Without a clear understanding of his metaphysical ideas his Christology is incomprehensible. Our first concern will therefore be to elucidate his metaphysic, which has several special features of considerable interest and importance. It is to be regretted that he left so much of it to be implied. There are, however, sufficient clear pointers to enable a coherent system to be constructed, and thereby

---

[1] Socrates, *Historia Ecclesiastica*, Bk. vii, Ch. 32: Φυσικὸς γὰρ εὔλαλος ὢν, πεπαιδεῦσθαι μὲν ἐνομίζετο· τῇ δὲ ἀληθείᾳ, ἀνάγωγος ἦν· καὶ τὰς τῶν παλαιῶν ἑρμηνεύων βίβλους, ἀπηξίου μανθάνειν. Τυφούμενος γὰρ ὑπὸ τῆς εὐγλωττίας, οὐκ ἀκριβῶς προσεῖχε τοῖς παλαιοῖς· ἀλλὰ πάντων κρείττονα ἐνόμιζεν ἑαυτόν. (Accessible in Migne, *Patrologia Græco-Latina*, lxvii. 809 C.)

[2] His surprising ignorance of the history of the term 'Theotokos' is a case in point, to which reference will be found on pp. 451 and 458–459.

[3] Reference may be made to Bethune-Baker, *Introduction to the Early History of Christian Doctrine*, pp. 231–238, to Fortescue, *Lesser Eastern Churches*, pp. 68–70, 84–86, to Bethune-Baker, *The Meaning of Homoousios* (*Texts and Studies*, edited by J. A. Robinson, vol. viii, No. 1), and, for the terms as rendered in Syriac, to Bethune-Baker, *Nestorius and His Teaching*, pp. 212–232. There are also valuable articles in the *Encyclopædia of Religion and Ethics*, especially ix. 326–327 (by Maclean), which gives useful references to sources and authorities.

to provide the necessary framework. It will be the object of the next few chapters to construct that framework, based on what is explicit and implicit in the Bazaar, and to endeavour to build upon the available facts the least elaborate theory which will include them without self-contradiction. Once that framework has been constructed his Christology can be understood and its value assessed.

CHAPTER III

THE UNIVERSE A FLUX OF NATURES

AS has been stated, the metaphysic of Nestorius is based upon the Aristotelian system, though there are important differences. Some of the differences are due to changes in emphasis. Theologians had ceased to be concerned with some of Aristotle's finer points, and, on the other hand, had had to make distinctions necessary for Christian theology which had not been necessary for Aristotle's purposes. But other differences are due to Nestorius' own distinctive viewpoint, and it will be necessary to investigate his metaphysic with great care in order that its peculiarities may not elude us. Although he was not primarily a philosopher, and did not seek to enunciate a complete metaphysic, it is evident that he had a very definite set of guiding principles in his mind, and that he was in no doubt as to their coherence. His concern was Christology; his metaphysic is incidental. It must, however, be reduced to order, so that we may carry in our minds, expressed and systematized, the implied metaphysical presuppositions on which Nestorius based his arguments.

In his view of the Universe Nestorius makes a sharp and fundamental distinction between God, the uncreated Creator, and all things else: "For how can anyone conceive that the Maker, seeing that he is in every way other than that which is made . . ." (B. 40). All things else are created by God: "He who from the beginning was the Word with God was also God the Maker of all; *everything came into being through him and without him also nothing whatever came into being*" (B. 86). God does not create by using or transforming His own substance, nor by any emanation or emission from Himself; God calls created things into being without Himself suffering loss or change: "For in that he is the Maker, he is unchangeable" (B. 40). That which is created is in no way God, nor has ever been in any way

God: "He indeed who changes the divine nature into human nature brings about its suppression, and he who changes human nature into the divine nature makes mock of it and makes of it a nature unmade, in declaring a nature [which is] made unmade, which cannot be" (B. 39). Creation is *ex nihilo*: "For of nothing the maker easily assembles the *ousia*" (B. 39). (Cf. the concept of creation by divine *fiat* in Gen. i, with the recurring formulas: "And God said, Let there be . . .: and there was . . .", and "And God said, Let . . .: and it was so.")

As creation consists in bringing an *ousia* into existence, the connotation of that word must now be considered. The Greek word οὐσία, of which *ousia* is a direct transliteration, is a noun derived through the feminine participle from εἶναι, to be. Its primary meaning would therefore appear to be existence, the state or quality of being. From the time of Plato and Aristotle it has been used to mean the essential being, the essence of any particular thing, the thing in itself absolutely: τὸ τί ἐστι, τὸ τί ἦν εἶναι. οὐσία is the ground of existence of τὸ ὄν, and τὸ ὄν exists in virtue of its οὐσία. *Ousia* is that underlying something without which the object would not be, the ultimate ground of its existence, the thing as it is in itself independently of being known. Underlying what we see and know as a stone, a tree or a man, is that which it is in itself, its ousia. There is an ousia 'stone' existing independently of our knowledge of it, and possessing properties and qualities independent of our interpretation of them, which interpretation may be incomplete or even erroneous. Thus the created Universe consists of a vast complex of ousias, the existence of which provides the basis of the Universe of space and time. The word ousia presents little difficulty, and Nestorius accords with general usage.

Associated with ousia is another word of great importance: *nature*. The properties and qualities of an ousia are included in what is called its *nature*. The word *nature* is used to represent the Greek word φύσις, which is a noun derived from φύειν, which means, transitively, *to produce*, intransitively, *to grow*, *to come into being*. φύσις by derivation and usage thus came to mean the nature, inborn quality,

E

property or constitution of a person or a thing. Thus the nature of an ousia is the sum total of its qualities and properties.[1] Ideally, the full description of the nature of any particular ousia would include everything about it, known and unknown, and would transcend the limits of our knowledge: shape, size, weight, colour, texture, indeed all properties and attributes whatever. The nature of an ousia, completely described, positively identifies the ousia and particularizes all its properties.

It will be evident that the terms ousia and nature are closely correlated. An ousia is manifested by its nature. Indeed, the two are inseparable except in thought. An ousia cannot be perceived or known except as it reveals its nature, and there cannot be a nature, that is, a complex of properties and attributes, without an ousia to give it a ground of existence.

We may link up the two terms by saying that an ousia possesses a nature. An ousia is known by its nature, and without an underlying ousia, a nature could not be. The one is inconceivable without the other. If we could imagine an ousia without a nature, it would be unknowable, because anything by which it could be known would constitute part of its nature. Similarly, we cannot conceive a nature without an ousia, as that would involve phenomena without any kind of reality underlying them. Even illusory phenomena must have some kind of reality underlying them.

Thus the terms ousia and nature are correlative, and, for any given object, the one precisely implies the other. The nature of water, for instance, is the totality of its qualities and properties. Thus we might begin by saying that the nature of water is to be a clear liquid, tasteless and odourless; to possess the property of dissolving certain substances, such as salt and sugar; to solidify to ice at low temperatures,

---

[1] Cf. Loofs, *Nestorius*, p. 66: "Before going further I will make a short remark about the term *nature*, deferring discussion of the term *substance* till later. I can do it by quoting Professor Bethune-Baker. For this scholar is right in saying that the term *nature* at that time meant all the attributes or characteristics attached to a substance and as a whole always associated with it." Bethune-Baker, *Nestorius and His Teaching*, p. 48, says: "To this 'substance' attached all the attributes or characteristics which as a whole were always associated with it, though some of them might characterize other substances as well; and these were called, by a general term, the 'nature' of the thing."

and to turn to steam at high temperatures. If the description were sufficiently lengthy and precise, it would fit nothing but water, so that a full description defines the nature of a given object. The nature of water fully identifies water, and nothing else; and correspondingly, water in itself is a certain something which we call the ousia of water.

This absolute and exclusive correspondence is fundamental: one ousia, one corresponding nature. For, if any ousia were conceived as having two natures, the definitions break down. In such a case the possession of two natures is a property of that ousia, and, therefore, those two natures are, by definition, its nature. The so-called two natures are simply portions of the complete nature, and could only arise from incomplete description. For example, suppose it were said that the ousia water possessed two natures, namely the nature of liquid water, with all its well-known properties, physical and chemical, and the nature of ice, a hard solid, differing in many respects, particularly physically, from liquid water. Might it not be argued that here is an ousia with two natures? The reply is that the nature of water is one, not two, and we must include these two states, liquid and solid, in our description of the one nature. We must say that it is the nature of water to be a clear liquid with certain properties at ordinary temperatures, and to be a hard solid with certain properties at low temperatures.

Similarly, one particular nature cannot belong to two ousias, for by definition the ousia is the underlying reality evidenced by the nature. If, therefore, we imagined two ousias to underlie one nature, the two ousias are, by definition, the ousia of that nature, and there would be no means of discriminating them. Any definite ousia has its corresponding nature, and while it remains that ousia it can have no other; and a particular nature is ascribable to one particular ousia, and to one only. The absolute correspondence of an ousia and its nature, and vice versa, is fundamental to the metaphysic of Nestorius: "For things which are changed from their first *ousia* possess only that nature into which they have been changed" (B. 25). We may take it that the concepts of ousia and nature were very definite in Nestorius' mind, and their absolute interdependence is fundamental to his reasoning. Neither ousia nor nature is conceivable without the other, nor can an ousia possess any other nature than its own, nor can a nature be ascribed to any ousia other than that from which it derives its definition.

A single simple object, therefore, is definable as a certain ousia with a certain nature; it is inconceivable without both. Both expressions are sometimes used, e.g.: "For human nature is definite, and [the things] which he possesses who is man in *ousia* and in nature ought to be his who comes to be in the nature of man neither more nor less" (B. 53). But in that the terms exactly imply each other, they are often used as though they were interchangeable, or as though either implied both. To speak of a certain ousia, say the ousia of water, carries with it the idea of the corresponding nature; and to speak of a certain nature, say the nature of water, carries with it the idea of the corresponding underlying ousia. Although, therefore, to express both underlying reality and totality of properties both the terms ousia and nature are really required, the expressions 'the ousia water' and 'the nature water' would ordinarily be taken to mean 'the ousia and corresponding nature known as water'. This somewhat loose use of the terms ousia and nature is frequent in many writers, Nestorius among them; see, for example, such passages as B. 25, 30, 40, 117. It is, however, usually easy to see precisely what is meant, that is, whether ousia and nature are being used strictly, or whether either is being used instead of the full expression 'ousia and corresponding nature'. Throughout this work the same usage will inevitably be followed, and it will usually be quite obvious whether the words are being used rigidly, or to convey the complete idea 'ousia and corresponding nature'. It is natural to use 'ousia' when the thing itself is the concept principally in mind, and 'nature' when it is thought of primarily in relation to its properties.[1]

[1] Cf. Bethune-Baker, who says that natures "could be spoken of almost as if they were real existences in themselves. This however was only a loose mode of speech—the reality was always the 'substance' to which the nature belonged. The 'nature' was not conceived of as being the 'substance', nor the 'substance' as being the 'nature'. 'It' was not 'it's nature', nor was it's nature 'it'. It was usually, no doubt, quite enough to speak of the 'nature'. It was the more popular term and expressed all that was wanted" (*Nestorius and His Teaching*, p. 48).

From these general ideas it is necessary to advance to finer distinctions. God, directly or indirectly, is the creator of all ousias and natures. As He creates them, so they are, and they cannot of themselves become anything else. This is fundamental in the thought of Nestorius: "For the definition and circumscription of all nature is that in which it has to be" (B. 56). This is a very important definition, and involves the following views of the material world:

All things, which exist by virtue of their created ousias, possess natures appropriate to those ousias. No ousia comes into existence except by God's act; nor can it cease to be, be changed, divided or become part of some other ousia except by God's act. The ousia and its nature are precisely determined by the kind of ousia God has created and by the nature appropriate to that ousia: "For human nature is definite, and [the things] which he possesses who is man in *ousia* and in nature ought to be his who comes to be in the nature of man neither more nor less; since the [properties] of the nature are definite" (B. 53). The nature is described by a complete catalogue of properties, which necessarily includes limitations as well as powers. One limitation common to all created natures is their inability to escape from that nature by their own act or will: "For the definition and circumscription of all nature is that in which it has to be" (B. 56). "From a punishment which lies in his nature there is no escape" (B. 13). "For he, who is composed of [one] nature, of necessity adheres in the nature to all the nature's own properties" (B. 125). Cf. also B. 135.

This rigid definition involves a proper understanding of the creative and directive activity of God. His creative activity consists in calling ousias into existence *ex nihilo*. His directive activity consists in willing ousias to cease to be (extinction), to be changed (transformation), to be divided (disintegration), or to become part of some other ousia (integration). This directive activity can be special, when it may be described as a miracle, or it may be effected through those laws which God has made operative in His Universe. Thus sugar becomes carbon and steam if it is sufficiently heated. To divide the ousia sugar in this way into the ousias carbon and steam is not an act of sugar or of man, but of God. God's relevant law is that, at a certain temperature and pressure, the ousia sugar ceases to exist, and is divided into the ousias carbon and steam. Man cannot make this happen. All man can do is to provide the conditions in which God's law operates: God effects the decomposition through His laws. All chemical reactions come under this heading: they take place, whether decompositions, combinations or interactions, by acts of God— God acting through His regular laws—and all man can do is to place the ousias concerned in the appropriate conditions. No man can cause hydrogen and oxygen to combine. But if a mixture of the gases is raised to a certain temperature, God will combine them. It will thus be seen that changes of ousia fall into a well ordered scheme. The usual types of change are integration and disintegration. These, if of normally experienced types, are due to God's acts through His regular laws. If of types not normally experienced, they are due to God acting in a special way, and are described as miracles, as also are all cases of creation, extinction or transformation.

All created ousias, therefore, have a definite beginning and a definite end. They come into being by an act of God, and they cease to be by an act of God. They may begin by creation *ex nihilo*, or more normally, by integration or disintegration of previously existing ousias. No ousia, inanimate or animate, can assemble or decompose itself, nor can man assemble or decompose an ousia, except, as already explained, by bringing about the conditions in which God's laws will act.

It may be useful for clearness and reference to enumerate the modes of origin and end of created ousias:

I. Origin of ousias

(i) Creation ex nihilo

This was the method whereby God brought the material Universe into existence: "God said, Let there be . . .: and there was . . .". "For of nothing the maker easily assembles the *ousia*" (B. 39). Having thus created all the material constituting the Universe, God ceased to use this method as a regular procedure, except possibly for the creation of human souls. Although within the normal powers of God, creations *ex nihilo* later than the initial acts of creation are quite exceptional, and would be described as miracles.[1] From one point of view the accord with experience of the law of the conservation of matter is simply a confirmation of the fact that God now seldom or never either creates *ex nihilo* or destroys that which He has created.[2]

(ii) Transformation of ousias

God, who creates and can destroy, can obviously and consequently transform; for, even if by no other method, God could transform one ousia into another by the simultaneous destruction of the first and creation of the second: "For of nothing the maker easily assembles the *ousia* and makes the *ousia* which is made by change of that which is made" (B. 39). Such transformations are not God's normal procedure, and would be classed as miracles. Examples are the transformation of the waters of the Nile (B. 25–26), which is discussed on pp. 84–86, and the transformation of Lot's wife into a pillar of salt (B. 24–25) (see p. 424).

It may be observed that it is a matter of indifference whether an ousia comes into existence by creation or transformation, and, in the latter case, it is evident that the transformed ousia must not be thought of as retaining any relation to that from which it has been derived: "For things which are changed from their first *ousia* possess only that nature into which they have been changed" (B. 25).

The mode of transformation of one ousia into another is unimportant, but perhaps the most intellectually satisfying concept of the procedure would be to suppose a

[1] E.g. the miracle of the loaves and fishes (Mark vi. 35–44).

[2] Modern physics has given us a more comprehensive understanding of the realities behind this 'law', and it now has to be stated in more circumspect terms than formerly. Possibly a closer approximation to truth would be to state that the totality of matter plus energy in the Universe remains constant: "Thus the three major conservation laws, those of the conservation of matter, mass and energy, reduce to one. One simple fundamental entity which may take many forms, matter and radiation in particular, is conserved through all changes; the sum total of this entity forms the whole activity of the universe, which does not change its total quantity" (Jeans, *The Mysterious Universe*, p. 73).

break-down into *hylê* of the ousia to be transformed, and the formation of the new ousia from this hylê (see pp. 88–91). This would presuppose some kind of equivalence in the amount of hylê composing each ousia. It is interesting to observe that in almost all cases of transformation it seems reasonable to suppose that there is such an equivalence. It would appear to be so, for example, in the cases of the transformation of the waters of the Nile, Moses' Rod, Lot's wife, and the water into wine. But it is very important to observe that in no case is there to be supposed to exist any kind of communication or relation between the ousia which was and that into which it has been transformed: "And it is of no importance that, as I have said, the *ousia* of man issues from a stone or from earth or from the seed of man, for that which is from a former *ousia* is changed into the nature which it has become" (B. 25). (Cf. B. 39, 55.)

(iii) Integration of ousias

A new ousia can arise by the combination of two or more other ousias. It is to be carefully observed that in this case the ousia brought into existence has its beginning from the moment of integration or combination, and the ousia thus formed is not to be regarded as merely a totality or conglomerate of the ousias entering into combination to form it. It is an ousia distinct and defined, distinguished and defined by its own corresponding nature, which nature is no mere total or conglomerate of the natures of the ousias entering into the composition of the new ousia. This is illustrated abundantly in chemistry. Sugar, for example, is an ousia with a corresponding nature, whose characteristics are well known. A description of its nature would include particulars as to its crystalline form, solubility, sweetness, and its various other physical and chemical properties. It is well known that the ousia of sugar is an integration of the ousias of carbon, hydrogen and oxygen—a black amorphous solid and two colourless gases. But we cannot think of the ousia of sugar as a mere mixture or association of these ousias, nor is its nature in any way a totalling, averaging or resultant of those of its constituents. When sugar is formed, directly or indirectly by the integration of its constituent elements, the former ousias cease to exist as such and a new ousia with its correspondent nature has commenced its existence.

The most important example of an ousia formed by integration is that of man. Man is regarded as tripartite: body, soul, and spirit or intellect (σῶμα, ψυχή, and πνεῦμα or νοῦς). The ousia of any particular man is to be regarded as the integration of the three ousias, body, animal soul and spirit. But the ousia of man is something very different in its nature from the mere totalling of the three ousias. The body by itself would have no feeling, no activity, no possibility of vital process, indeed not even the ability to continue unchanged as such. Animal soul, whatever that may be, can hardly be conceived apart from a body, unless as energy or life-force. Spirit apart from body or animal soul is conceivable, but would maintain contact with its environment through some means very different from a material body, and would, presumably, be impassible at least physically, that is, to whatever extent we regard suffering as correlated with the nervous system of a material body. But when the ousias body, animal soul and spirit are combined into the ousia living man, the resultant has properties different from those of any of its constituents taken separately, and is in no way a mere resultant of them: "The soul and the body[1] are bound [together] in one nature and [the soul] suffers sensibly the sufferings of the body whether it will or not, even though it has not of itself [the means] to accept them in that it has not a body in which to suffer" (B. 13). "The soul and the body are combined in one nature, and by natural force the soul naturally suffers the sufferings of the body, and the body the sufferings of the soul" (B. 49). Cf. B. 54, 55.

(iv) Disintegration of ousias

Two or more ousias can come into existence by the disintegration of another ousia. For example, if sugar is heated to a certain temperature, it disintegrates ultimately into steam and carbon. In such a case the ousias steam and

[1] Although Nestorius accepted the tripartite view of man ("The body and the soul and the intelligence are the completion of the nature of man" (B. 51)), he often drops into the more obvious dichotomy.

carbon have come into existence by the disintegration of the ousia sugar.

(v) Reintegration of ousias

For the sake of completeness we should mention the possibility of ousias originating by the disintegration of two or more ousias, and the immediate reintegration of the disintegrated ousias in some other manner. This is a very familiar process in chemistry, and is known as double decomposition. To take a very simple example: if caustic soda is brought into intimate contact with hydrochloric acid, the caustic soda presumably disintegrates into sodium and a hydroxide radicle, and the hydrochloric acid into hydrogen and chlorine, whereupon the sodium and chlorine integrate into sodium chloride, and the hydrogen and the hydroxide radical into water. This is expressed chemically by the reaction $NaOH + HCl \rightarrow NaCl + H_2O$.

II. End of ousias

(i) Destruction of ousias

This corresponds with creation *ex nihilo* and represents special action by God. It would always be classed as miracle and is quite exceptional. (By destruction is meant the ceasing to exist of an ousia not simply as such, but in such a way that nothing of that which it was continues to exist in any form or manner. The word 'destruction' as commonly used usually signifies the end of an ousia as such, but does not necessarily preclude the continuance of its hylê[1] in some other form or forms. For example, if a piece of paper is 'destroyed' by fire, what has really happened is that the ousia paper has disintegrated into the ousias steam, carbon dioxide, ash and whatever other decomposition products may arise.)

(ii) Transformation of ousias

Just as a new ousia can come into existence by the transformation of a formerly existing one, so also the formerly existing one comes to an end at the moment of transformation.

[1] See pp. 88–91.

(iii) Integration of ousias

When a new ousia arises by integration from two or more other ousias, at the moment of integration those other ousias cease to exist as such.

(iv) Disintegration of ousias

When new ousias arise by the disintegration of another ousia, at the moment of disintegration that other ousia ceases to exist as such.

(v) Reintegration of ousias

When two or more ousias reintegrate, and two or more ousias thus come into existence, at the moment of reintegration the former ousias cease to exist as such.

It is important to observe that all these methods whereby an ousia is brought into existence or has its existence terminated are acts of God either by miracle or by the operation of His laws, the 'laws of nature'. Apart from God no ousia can come into existence, change or terminate. It is absolutely bound by its nature: "For the definition and circumscription of all nature is that in which it has to be" (B. 56).

So far our discussion has envisaged the ousias and corresponding natures of definite objects, and there is no difficulty in forming the concept of the ousia and nature of an object such as a stone, a vase or an animal. The underlying ousia may be simple or complex. It may, in modern terms, be a single element, as in the case of the ousia of a lump of pure iron; it may be a particular chemical compound, as in the case of a lump of pure white marble (calcium carbonate, $CaCO_3$); or it may be a highly complex organism made up of a number of correlated members ("For as the body is one, and hath many members, and all the members of that one body, being many, are one body" (1 Cor. xii. 12)), such as a plant, animal or man. But whether the object is simple, complex or a highly developed organism, the underlying ousia is to be regarded as a unity dissoluble only by

God, using miracle or His laws; the nature is definite and inescapable. No nature can make or unmake itself; man cannot make or unmake a nature except by observance of God's laws. Man cannot make or unmake himself except by observance of God's laws. It is to be noted that the process of making or unmaking may be irreversible if God's laws so determine. For example, many natures can be disintegrated if man brings about the necessary conditions of temperature or physical stress. A metal rod or a piece of wood is a natural unit, and may be converted into two or more fresh natural units by force, as by fracture or the use of a saw. It is interesting to notice that one characteristic of interference with natural unities is man's absolute dependence on the laws of God, and sometimes reintegration of a disintegrated natural unity is not humanly possible. A piece of wood may be sawn in half, but it cannot be joined as it was before. Similarly a plant can be disintegrated by heat or by pulling it to pieces, and here again is a case in which man cannot bring about reintegration. ('Pulling to pieces' superficially may appear to be the voluntary act of man. From the point of view of man's nature that is so. His nature includes the ability to pull certain things to pieces; but the possibility of the application of that ability depends upon the nature of the object on which he operates. If the nature of that object includes disruptibility on the application of certain stresses, the application of those stresses, however applied, will cause that disruption, and the end of that nature as such. The nature is ended by disintegration because the properties of the nature, as ordained by God, include disruption under a certain stress.) Inability to bring about reintegration always applies to what are, in modern terms, called organisms; but while illustrating the utter dependence of the Universe on the will and acts of God, this fact must not be regarded as a criterion of natural unity. Some natural unities when disintegrated cannot normally be reintegrated; but if, like many others, for example most chemical compounds, they can be so reintegrated, it would only be in accordance with an act or law of God.

Similarly, man can neither make nor unmake himself. His nature is a unity determined by God, which is integrated by observance of God's laws. Its disintegration is also in accordance with God's laws, which determine when the ousia 'living man' shall break down into the ousias 'soulless and spiritless body, disembodied animal soul, and disembodied spirit'. Man can voluntarily place himself in circumstances in which his own disintegration will come about—hence the possibility of suicide. But the disintegration cannot be otherwise than in accordance with the laws of God for the disintegration of the ousia 'living man'; and, so far as man is concerned, the action is irreversible.

It will be evident that, in the Nestorian metaphysic, at any particular moment the Universe consists of a complex of natural units, ousias with their corresponding natures. Any particular ousia is to be regarded as a unit, a natural unit, because it cannot depart from its nature except by the act or law of God. The unity of a particular ousia is of an ultimate fundamental kind, and is very clearly envisaged as being so by Nestorius. A natural unit is definite, precise and circumscribed. It has a definite beginning and a definite end. A natural unit may, as we have seen, come into existence in various ways. If it comes into existence by the integration of two previously existing natural units, those two natural units have become, by integration, one natural unit. This process may, for clarity, be called natural unification. The two natures which have thus become one, thus ceasing to exist as individual natures, are said to be in natural union. Finally, the state of a natural unit is natural unity. It would be convenient if a clear discrimination could be kept in the use of the words unit, unification, union and unity: by natural unification two natural units may enter into natural union and become a new natural unit possessing the attribute of natural unity. To accord with general usage, however, we shall frequently use 'unity' where 'unit' would be preferable. But it will always be obvious whether unity is being used in the abstract or concrete sense.

It is now desirable to introduce qualifying terms whereby we may describe, with some exactitude, the precise limits of the words ousia or nature in any given context. Generally, we have in mind the ousia and nature of some definite object: a man, a tree, a rock, a piece of metal. This may be qualified as a particular ousia. In such a case the ousia is that underlying this particular definite object, and the nature is that of the same particular definite object. This is the basic type and corresponds with the πρώτη οὐσία of Aristotle. This we shall discriminate when necessary as particular ousia.

But the term ousia is often used in a general sense, to indicate the fact that objects of an exactly similar kind must be supposed to possess exactly similar ousias. A number of blocks of iron, for example, exist by virtue of the existence of their underlying ousias; and we cannot but imagine that these ousias are precisely similar in nature. We therefore readily form the generalized concept 'ousia of iron', as that which underlies each and every piece of iron. To this type of generalized concept Aristotle applied the term δευτέρα οὐσία, to which we shall usually refer as general ousia. As we only know particular ousias, the idea of a general ousia is necessarily an abstraction of thought, unless we extend it to mean the totality of that type of ousia. But trying to visualize the totality of all the iron ousia in the Universe is rather different from holding the concept in our minds that there is a kind of ousia that we recognize in any piece of iron. Nestorius does not trouble to distinguish between particular, general or total ousia, but it is usually quite easy to see whether the word ousia in any given context is to be taken in the particular, general or total sense. However, as the force of Christological arguments often depends on this concept of general ousias, it is one which must be borne constantly in mind. To complete the classification it may be useful to add the term collective ousia, which is of service when dealing with a large number of particular ousias in one conglomeration, such as powders, granules, gases or liquids.

Precisely the same distinctions apply to natures. All that has been said concerning particular, general, total and collective ousias applies equally to natures. There is the particular nature revealing a particular ousia, and there is the general nature characterizing all examples of a general ousia. We shall in the same way, when necessary, refer to particular, general, total or collective natures, though it will usually be obvious which is meant without a qualifying adjective.

It will thus be seen that, according to the Nestorian metaphysic, the present Universe was called into being by act of God, by the fiats of creation; that in this way a primordial complex of ousias with corresponding natures was called into being, and that all subsequent events have depended on their mutual interaction in accordance with acts of God, normally through His laws, exceptionally through His direct interference. We thus envisage the material world as comprising a complex of natures in a continual state of mutual flux, a flux maintained by the interaction of the natures with one another and by their reactions to their general circumstances. Material natures are, for example, greatly influenced by changes of temperature and pressure, and by the application of mechanical force. Changes of temperature and pressure bring about many of the effects on natures which are classed as chemical and physical changes, and mechanical force is often the cause of the division of one nature into two or more new natures. In this flux of natures there are continual endings and continual beginnings. Each nature, each natural unit, has its beginning and its end, and the duration of a particular nature may be anything from the fraction of a second to millenniums. Generally a nature begins by integration from some previously existing natures and ends by disintegration into other natures, which thus have their beginning.

If the metaphysic is to be made completely coherent, there are a number of difficulties of detail which must be considered. These difficulties are not vital to the main lines of Nestorius' thought and argument, but they must be clarified if only as a test of the validity of this view of the Universe. While it must be admitted that the metaphysic of ousia and nature, completely worked out, must be a somewhat complicated one, it must be remembered that the Universe itself is very complicated, and it is hardly to be expected that it will be explicable in terms of a simple metaphysic. Without going into full and needless detail, it will be sufficient to indicate the lines along which the metaphysic could be completely explicated. Difficulties will arise in delimiting the ousias and natures of unorganized bodies. An animal, or even a plant, is a more obviously defined unit than a volume of gas, a portion of liquid, or an amorphous powder. Where do we look for the circumscription of the particular natures in such cases? It is here that the concepts of particular, collective, general and total ousias and natures are useful, and, although a rigid analysis of all cases might involve some very close discrimination, it is not difficult to see that such discrimination would be well within the compass of the Nestorian metaphysic. In order to give indications of the line of approach, the following observations may be made:

1. *Gases.* In modern terms it might be best in the case of a gas to regard the separate molecules as the units: a volume of gas is a collection of a large number of particular ousias, each with its own nature. All are identical, and so it is easy to regard the gas as a collective ousia and nature. The concept of the ousia and nature of any particular gas is thus easy to form, though the precise following through of processes and reactions in which a gas might be involved is obviously not simple, and would involve careful discrimination in the use of the words particular, collective and general.

2. *Liquids.* The case of a liquid is somewhat similar. Each molecule might be regarded as a particular ousia. Any given volume of water may be regarded as having, for convenience of reasoning, a collective ousia and nature which is the totality of the individual ousias and natures; and, perhaps in such cases, most useful of all, we have the concept of the general ousia and nature of any particular kind of liquid.

3. *Change of state.* The existence of any particular ousia in the state of gas, liquid or solid, is, in general, dependent on conditions of temperature and pressure. Unless it decomposes before the appropriate temperature is reached, on being heated a solid normally reaches a temperature at which it melts, and on further heating reaches a temperature at which it becomes a gas. If we started with a solid, easily recognized as a particular nature, on melting and vaporization

we obviously meet difficulties arising from the application of the word 'particular'. These difficulties are real, but they are not insuperable.

As the object of the Nestorian metaphysic is the solution of problems involving the interrelation and union of unities readily recognizable as particular, it is irrelevant to work out a complete metaphysic dealing with inanimate unorganized natures. But such a metaphysic could, undoubtedly, be elaborated. In the case of homogeneous unorganized substances it may be that the right concept is that of total ousia and nature. There is an ousia and nature 'water' manifesting itself wherever and in whatever circumstances water is found. Any mass of water, large or small, whether as gas (steam), liquid (water), or solid (ice), is ousia of water and has the nature of water. Similar observations apply to amorphous solids or powders. In most cases it may be best to think in terms of total ousia and so to apply general concepts to particular cases. If a given case is to be followed through, we might regard each lump or grain as a particular natural unit. The application of force in pulverization could terminate the existence of that particular natural unit and bring into existence a number of particular natural units of the same kind but smaller. On the contrary, pressure, fusion or recrystallization might cause a number of smaller units to become one larger unit.

The second group of difficulties arises in relation to what are now called organized bodies. These difficulties are the reverse of those dealt with above. They do not arise from difficulty in particularizing the general, but in defining a continuity which, at first sight, would appear rigidly to be a flux of natures. At any given moment it is easy to imagine the ousia of a plant, animal or man, for the ousia is the totality of that absolutely existing which is the ground of the being of the particular object under consideration. Similarly, experience and observation enable us to form a sufficiently clear idea of the nature. At any instant, therefore, the ousia and nature of an organism present no conceptual difficulties. When we are thinking specifically of a nature at any particular instant, the adjective 'instantaneous' may be applied, though it will usually be obvious

F

whether it is applicable or not. But organized life is in a continual state of flux. Ordinary life processes necessarily involve gradual, but none the less real, changes in ousia, and consequently in nature. These changes may be scarcely perceptible over short periods. The organism to-day is not usually perceptibly different from the same organism yesterday. But over longer periods the differences may be quite apparent. The old animal differs obviously in ousia and nature from that which it was when young. It is manifestly incompatible with the concepts already formulated to have to regard the life of an organism as a flux of similar but yet different natures. There is a continuity. How can this continuity be reconciled with a coherent and rigid metaphysic of ousia and nature?

Let us endeavour to describe the general duration cycle of an organized unit. There is its inception or integration, its flux of life process, and finally its disintegration. Its inception is usually the result of the integration of previously existing ousias. Generally, perhaps, the moment of integration may be fixed as that of the union of gametes. A new nature has thus come into being possessing the properties assigned to it by God. These properties include the potentialities of its subsequent life history: growth, maturity, decline, and ultimate disintegration. Such a nature is a continuity from its integration to its disintegration, although, at particular instants, an analysis of the ousia and nature would produce different results. There is, nevertheless, a very definite continuity; the nature has its beginning and end, and between those terminal points it is a continuity and a unity. At any moment there is ἡ νῦν φύσις, but there is also ἡ ἀεὶ φύσις. It may be useful to distinguish this by the adjective 'durative'. Thus the durative ousia and nature of an organism are the continuity in unity of its successive instantaneous ousias and natures.

It is recognized that the above paragraphs do not completely work out a metaphysic of the Universe as a flux of natures, but it is hoped that sufficient has been said to demonstrate that such a metaphysic could be elaborated logically and coherently.

We now proceed to state a number of propositions on

ousias and natures. They arise from the considerations set out in this chapter, and have a direct bearing on the Christological problem:

1. *The real and true existence of any object depends upon the real and true existence of the appropriate ousia with its corresponding nature.* Nothing really and truly is unless the ousia of that thing is. The expression "a thing in its ousia" simply means "a thing existing because there is a basis for its existence." A thing apart from its ousia is unthinkable, as, in the last resort, the ousia is the thing. Nothing can be what it is supposed to be unless there exists the ousia which enables it to be what it is.

2. *There is an absolute correspondence between an ousia and its nature.* An ousia without a nature would be unknowable, and a nature without ousia would have no basis in which its properties could cohere. For purposes of thought we may be able to separate ousia and nature, but in actuality they are inseparable. A real object is ultimately an ousia and is knowable as a nature, but the ideas of ousia and nature are only differing approaches to the same ultimate reality. It is, therefore, evident that any particular ousia has its own particular nature and can have no other; otherwise, all logical definition breaks down. Similarly, any particular nature has its basis of existence in some particular corresponding ousia and in no other. One ousia cannot have two or more natures, for, by definition, its nature is its totality of properties; if one ousia were supposed to have two or more natures, in reality its nature would simply be a summation of the supposed two or more natures. Similarly, one nature cannot be based on more than one ousia. For, if it be supposed that any particular nature has the basis of its existence in two or more ousias, by definition those two or more ousias constitute the basis of its existence, that is, its ousia. The supposed two or more ousias are, therefore, simply parts of the one ousia. 'One ousia, one nature' is therefore absolutely fundamental.

It is obvious that a nature may be far from simple; similarly an ousia may be highly complex. The singleness and unity of an ousia is not to be thought of in physical analytical terms. The ousia of an animal, for example, is

highly complex, and, from some points of view, for example
its original integration and final disintegration, is obviously
analysable into other ousias; but, while these other ousias
are integrated into this one natural unity, they are themselves integrated into one ousia. They cannot, except by
an act of God, become other than one self-consistent
coherent ousia.

3. *A transformed ousia is that into which it has been transformed, and is nothing else.* It has no more relationship in
ousia or nature with that from which it has been transformed than if it had been directly created. Only God can
transform one ousia into another, and, after such a change,
the ousia is what it has become. After such a change the
ousia is what it has become, and is in no sense whatever
what it was. It is as though what it had been had never
been. That is, no changed ousia can be thought of as both
what it was and what it has become, even if God were to
keep changing it backwards and forwards from one to
the other.

This idea is of some importance; we have to recognize
both the ability of God to transform one ousia into another,
and the fact that such a transformation does not establish
any relationship between the two ousias, that originally
existing and that into which it is transformed. It is the same
as if the first had been destroyed and the second newly
created *ex nihilo*: "For of nothing the maker easily assembles
the *ousia* and makes the *ousia* which is made by change of
that which is made" (B. 39).

This divine power is well illustrated in the case of the
water of the Nile during the plagues of Egypt. It would
appear that Sophronius thought that the water was only
turned into blood so far as the Egyptians were concerned,
while the Hebrews were able to use it as water: "For the
staff of Moses, when it became truly a serpent, was a serpent
as well as a staff; and the waters of the Nile, which became
blood, became the nature of blood as well as of water. The
ousia was the same although it was changed and for this
reason the children of Israel used water which had become
blood as the nature of the water, and Moses [used] a
serpent as a staff, in that it was truly both of them. For

God sustains natures as he will" (B. 25–26). This is not definitely stated in the record (Exod. vii. 14–25), but it may perhaps be legitimately deduced from the wording of verses 18, 21 and 24, which suggest that it was only the Egyptians who suffered. Nestorius is willing to concede this point, for his metaphysic gives a simple explanation: God changed the ousia water into the ousia blood, and then changed the ousia blood into the ousia water, repeating this transformation just as circumstances necessitated. Presumably all the waters of Egypt were first changed into the ousia blood, and so remained until a Hebrew drew some, in which case the ousia blood was changed to the ousia water. If what a Hebrew drew was water, and what an Egyptian drew was blood, no further explanation is needed beyond God changing the ousias as required: "There were then two *ousias*; for the water which was taken by the Hebrews was blood and water and that which was taken by the Egyptians was both in the same way. But if the former was only water and the latter only blood, then they were afterwards changed; for when they were taken, those which were taken were changed and further were something else, namely that which they became. How then is it not seen that that which it became by nature is by all means that which it has become and nothing else?" (B. 26).[1]

But God's use of this power must not be thought of as in any way affecting the fundamental correspondence of an ousia and its nature. If God changes one ousia into another, there must also be a corresponding change of nature, and after the change the ousia is only what it has become; in

[1] As this is a passage of some importance, it should be remarked that Connolly is not satisfied with Driver and Hodgson's rendering of it, and would translate thus: "For then there would be the two ousias, when those waters which were taken up by the Hebrews were blood and water, or those which were taken up by the Egyptians were both in like manner. But if those were water only and these only blood, and they were afterwards changed—for when they were taken up those which were taken up were changed, and they were (no) more anything else except that which they became: how then do not the same things appear in these things (sc. in the Christological discussion) (namely) that he who becomes (something) by nature is by all means that which he has become by nature, and not anything else?" Connolly substantiates his version in detail, and we admit his correctness; but his revision of the passage has no effect on the main arguments we have been stating. Connolly's version and notes may be seen in the *Journal of Theological Studies*, vol. xxvii, p. 195 (January, 1926).

relation to the transformed ousia, what it was formerly is as though it had never been. When, for example, God changes ousia blood into ousia water, there must of necessity be a corresponding change of nature blood into nature water. For just as ousia blood implies nature blood, so ousia water implies nature water, and if God changes the ousia, it only possesses the nature corresponding to the ousia into which it has been changed: "For he who becomes man from stone or from earth is the nature of man, in that he truly has become man, and not the nature of stone or of earth; and that which has become a pillar of salt from a human body is only the nature of whatever it has become. For things which are changed from their first *ousia* possess only that nature into which they have been changed" (B. 25). "And it is of no importance that, as I have said, the *ousia* of man issues from a stone or from earth or from the seed of man, for that which is from a former *ousia* is changed into the nature which it has become" (B. 25). If God changes an ousia, it is in no sense the ousia it was formerly, nor can it retain anything of its former nature.

4. *An ousia cannot change or add to its nature.* For any property revealed by the ousia, or any potentiality realized, is by definition part of its nature. In particular, no ousia can include within its nature the nature of any other ousia, because that other nature is the totality of properties possessed by a certain ousia, and totality includes restriction as well as power. For suppose that a nature included another nature; if it demonstrated that part of its nature which enabled it to be that other nature, the process would be irreversible, since it would have become something which is a totality, and would be restricted to that other totality other than the totality which is its own nature. This idea is of great importance: "For the definition and circumscription of all nature is that in which it has to be" (B. 56).

5. *The result of the combination of ousias with their corresponding natures into a new ousia with its corresponding nature is the formation of one ousia with its corresponding nature, which is to be regarded as a distinct unity just as though it had been newly created, and is not to be regarded as in any way still containing the original*

combining ousias or natures as such. While it is impossible to think of the new ousia as other than some kind of mingling or combining of the two ousias from which it was formed, it must, nevertheless, be thought of as a unity, one ousia, and not as a mere mixture or juxtaposition. On the other hand, it will be more obvious that the new nature is by no means a mere sum or average of the combining natures, in that experience shows how different the nature of a compound is from the natures of its constituents; that is to say, when two ousias combine to form a new ousia, their separate natures are replaced by a new nature, the nature appropriate to the new ousia.[1] Chemistry will provide abundant examples of this fact. The nature of water is obviously a very different thing from the natures of hydrogen and oxygen, though its ousia is necessarily to be regarded as some kind of combining or mixing of the ousias of hydrogen and oxygen. This principle is of very important application in considering the nature of man. Regarding man as tripartite—body, animal soul, and spirit, two things are evident: First, man's nature being a complex or compound of these three, although a natural unity is not a simple entity; for the ousia underlying that unity is highly complex, comprising everything which composes the material body and whatever may underlie soul and spirit. Second, the complex has very different properties from those of its constituents considered separately. The nature of a body without life is very different from the nature of the same body when incorporated into the nature of a living man. When the three constituents body, soul and spirit are combined into a living man, the body has a power of continuance which, without soul and spirit, it does not possess. By itself, the nature of a body would be to decompose, that is, to break down into simpler natures. Similarly, the nature of a spirit is profoundly modified if it is in natural union with a body. For example, a spirit is presumably insensitive to physical pain or other physical sensations; but in natural union with the body the spirit shares the sensations which are mediated through the body: "The soul and the body are bound [together] in one nature and [the soul] suffers

[1] Cf. B. 236: "Natural union is a second creation."

sensibly the sufferings of the body whether it will or not, even though it has not of itself [the means] to accept them in that it has not a body in which to suffer" (B. 13).

Brief reference must be made to a term which Nestorius seldom uses—the word ὕλη (*hylê*). In contrast with his very definite views on ousia and nature, Nestorius' ideas about *hylê* are never clearly stated. So far as the few references reveal, it would seem that Nestorius thought of hylê as the material basis of an ousia regarded characterlessly. Thus to think of the ousia of a lump of iron is to endeavour to conceive that underlying something by virtue of which the iron exists, that which the lump of iron is in itself. Different objects have their differing ousias, but it is almost impossible to avoid the idea that these different ousias have something in common: that the basis of all material ousias must be some common 'stuff', which God, God alone, can cause to take the character and nature of any particular ousia He wishes. This common 'stuff' is thought of as hylê. The Greek word ὕλη originally meant 'wood', whether as forest, tree or timber. Then the word tended to be used more particularly for wood when felled and cut, or broken up, wood as a material. Next it began to be applied to material in general, whether wood, metal or stone, so that the way was prepared for Aristotle's adoption of the word ὕλη to mean matter in general.

Nestorius' usage seems to accord broadly with Aristotle's. We may regard hylê as the prime matter, the raw material, out of which an ousia is made. We must not, however, envisage creation in two stages—making of hylê and the shaping of the hylê into some particular ousia. What we have to envisage is the creation of hylê with the character of some particular ousia with its corresponding nature. Created ousias share the characteristic of being composed of hylê, though no one but God could resolve an ousia into hylê or compose hylê into an ousia. Indeed, hylê in and of itself is inconceivable; for, if hylê as such could be known, it would by definition be an ousia, and what was known of it would be its nature. Hylê thus corresponds with our idea of matter. We cannot think of matter except in some form— iron, wood, stone; but we nevertheless think of these things

as having something in common, which we call matter. It is
of no consequence whether we think of matter as something
into which these things iron, wood, stone can be broken
down, or as the ground of reality underlying them all. In
the former case, hylê bears some kind of analogy to the
protons and electrons of which modern physics considers
all matter to consist;[1] in the latter, it corresponds nearly
enough with the vague, useful idea we have in mind in
such phrases as "the world of matter". The concept of the
common hylê of created ousias has a bearing on the transformation of ousias (pp. 71–72). It is logical to suppose that
God's act in transforming one ousia into another consists
of breaking down the first ousia into hylê and re-forming
the hylê into the second ousia, just as we might conceive
a substance being broken down into protons and electrons,
and those protons and electrons being reassembled as some
other substance.

Nestorius only refers to hylê about six times. One reference is non-technical, just as we may talk of 'matter for
debate': "It is not he who provides matter for blas-
phemy . . ." (B. 270). Two references presumably refer to
hylê as matter of the created Universe, the hylê underlying
created ousias: "Together with this [there is] another
absurdity which they predicate in limiting God himself by
the necessity of nature and ascribing, as the Manichæans,
to *hylê* such might that it drags after it by authority and its
own force whosoever receives it" (B. 124). Here hylê
obviously means matter in general. The same emphasis
occurs in the sentence: "Why does he lead us astray with
the birth of a material flesh, with which God the Word was
formed, and why have unconvincing and incredible fables
been fabricated?" (B. 259). The expression 'material flesh',
literally 'flesh of hylê', is used to emphasize the ordinary
reality of the flesh; it is flesh whose ousia is of the hylê of
ordinary created things.

If it is supposed that created ousias have underlying
them the common hylê of created matter, is it to be supposed, if only for logical consistency, that the ousia of the
Godhead has underlying it a corresponding hylê, the basis

[1] Jeans, *The Mysterious Universe*, p. 52.

of the eternal and uncreated? It must be pointed out that, as the Godhead is not only eternal but unchangeable (see pp. 121–122), its ousia can neither be conceived of as being originated from anything, broken down into anything or transformed into anything, so that its hylê can hardly be discriminated from the ousia itself. It would only be in fallacious arguments, or in their reductio ad absurdum, that any processes involving the hylê of Godhead could be contemplated. For example, Nestorius quotes Theophilus as saying: "For he took not a body of an *hylê* precious and heavenly and came among us, but of clay" (B. 353). This is in refutation of the idea that God could have transformed the 'hylê precious and heavenly' of His own ousia into the ousia of some kind of body, presumably visible and quasi-material, even if not of an ousia of created material hylê. It will be seen that the sentence does not necessarily involve the possibility of any actual transformation of divine hylê.

A somewhat similar case is a sentence used in refuting one of Sophronius' arguments: "Therefore, if thou sayest that he became the nature of the flesh from the former *hylê* of the nature of God, he possesses that *ousia* which he has become without having been [it]" (B. 25). On the whole sentence see pp. 424–425. With regard to hylê, the case is as in the quotation from Theophilus. It is a mere supposition inconceivable if we accept the attributes ascribed to the Godhead.

The only other case likewise arises from the refutation of an erroneous suggestion: "Therefore in that they do not allow the flesh to remain in its own *ousia*, they resemble the Manichæans by destroying the *ousia* of the flesh, but diverge from them in that they say that God was altogether in the *hylê* of the flesh" (B. 36). The altogether impossible idea to which Nestorius is here referring is the idea that the ousia of the flesh, breaking down into hylê, could re-form as ousia of God, such ousia of God still being regarded as composed of hylê of the ousia of flesh. Any such idea overlooks the fundamental proposition that "a transformed ousia is that into which it has been transformed and is nothing else" (p. 84), so that even if there were continuity through the hylê it would be of no significance. But the more fundamental consideration is to realize that in any case the hylê of God and the hylê of created ousias are two things absolutely apart. Hylê of God is conceivable, though as we have already seen it is of necessity indiscriminable, except for conceptual distinction, from His ousia, and is certainly in no way to be regarded as able to enter into any kind of transformations or actions involving the hylê of created ousias.

It will thus be seen that hylê is a term only significant in relation to material things, in reference to which it means matter in the sense already explained. If, for the sake of logical consistency, we care to suppose divine hylê underlying divine ousia, just as material hylê underlies created ousias, there is no objection, though the concept, unlike the concept of material hylê, has no significance for metaphysical analysis.

CHAPTER IV

SYNTAX AND PROSÔPON

IN the previous chapter it has been seen that the Universe is primarily to be regarded as a flux of natures. The basic units are natural unities. In general there is little difficulty in defining them when they are what we should now call organic unities such as plants, animals, or men. There is rather more difficulty in considering inanimate objects, and in such cases the concept of general natures is very useful. To work out a complete metaphysic of the Universe as a flux of natural unities would be perhaps difficult and complicated, but the difficulties are by no means insuperable. From the point of view of Nestorius, however, the concept of natural unity is of major significance as it affects organic unities, and in such cases the definition of a nature as 'that in which it has to be' is obviously applicable.

Although the concept of natural unity is of such fundamental importance, a complete understanding of the Universe is not possible in terms of natural unities only. There are unities of other kinds, and as Nestorius' solution of the Christological problem depends on the concept of a unity other than a natural one, it is now necessary to determine whether there are other types of union which can produce what may, in any true sense, be described as unities. A complete classification of the possible kinds of unity would be a difficult task, and for our present purpose unnecessary. There is, however, one type of unity which covers a very wide and relevant range. Its subdivisions will be found to include not only the Nestorian solution but also most of the types of solution which are unsatisfactory. It is unfortunate that Nestorius never systematized his ideas to the point of reaching this general concept which would have been so invaluable for the elucidation of his ideas, for we shall be able to unravel his thought with much more assurance and certainty once this general type has been defined.[1]

[1] Nestorius' nearest approach to this concept is to be found in his passages on craftsman and instrument, B. 333, 341–342, 359 (see pp. 465–467).

The idea may be approached by considering man's ability to produce what we regard as unities. Man can produce articles of two main types. By observing the necessary conditions, the laws of God, he can produce natural unities: for example, a metal casting, a glass vase, a wooden rod. The making or unmaking of these articles is absolutely conditioned by the laws of God: their natures, natural unities, have their definite beginnings and their definite ends. On the other hand, man can make articles which must without doubt be regarded as unities of some kind, by assembling natural unities into complexes, complexes which are certainly unities from the point of view of appearance, purpose or function. A clock, for example, is made by assembling together a very great number of separate natural unities. In being screwed or bolted together, the separate pieces remain in their natures, the continuity of their natural existence is not broken. Yet obviously a clock is some kind of unity, though equally obviously it is a complex built up from very many still continuing natural unities. It has a unity of appearance, purpose and function. So indeed have natural unities, but the great distinction between a clock and a natural unity is that the natural unities which have been brought together to form the clock have retained their identity and continuity, unlike natural unities which come together to form a new natural unity by natural union, in which case they lose both identity and continuity. A clock, then, is an example of a unity, real but not natural, its prime characteristic being the fact that it is composed of natural unities, arranged, ordered or assembled together, but not ousically and naturally combined. It will be convenient to apply to such a unity the adjective 'syntactic' (σύνταξις, a putting together in order, arranging, a drawing up in order, array, arrangement), and just as we commonly call a natural unity a nature, so we may call a syntactic unity a *syntax*.

It will at once be seen what a large range is covered by this concept. Things which consist of separable parts come into this category, which thus includes machines, fabrics, books and the great majority of manufactured articles. The general characteristics of syntactic unities are that the natural unities of which they are composed are readily discernible and that they can be taken to pieces or put together again without their components leaving their natures.

Man can himself enter into syntactic unions and thus constitute himself a component in syntactic unities. Immediately a man is clothed or making use of an instrument, he becomes an element in a syntactic unity. Nudus homo is a natural unity. But immediately we regard a man as arrayed or equipped for a rank or a function, he becomes part of a syntactic unity. A king in his royal robes is a syntactic unity; so is a soldier armed for battle; so is an artificer equipped with his tools.

In the case of a syntactic unity, part of which is a man, one very obvious characteristic is the ability of the man to make and unmake, to enter and leave, the syntactic unity. This large and important class of unions into which man may enter may be called voluntary unions, and the unities so formed may be called voluntary unities. It will thus be seen that there is a very sharp line between a natural unity brought about by natural union, in which the combining ousias constitute one new ousia, and in which the combining natures constitute one new nature, and a voluntary unity in which the combining ousias and natures remain as those ousias and in their own natures, their unity being a union of association and function.

Two broad classes of unities can thus be distinguished: natural unities which are brought about by acts of God, and syntactic unities which are brought about by the volition of some animate being other than God. A syntactic unity is necessarily composed of natural unities, and the syntax may further be described as imposed or voluntary according as whether the elements in the syntax are completely controlled by the will of an external agent, or the agent itself enters of its own free will into the syntax. The former type, imposed syntactic unity, includes all articles made by the assembly of parts. The latter type, voluntary syntactic unity, includes all cases in which a free agent enters into a syntax on his own volition. It will be evident that any syntax composed of inanimate natures is necessarily an imposed syntactic unity, whereas a syntactic unity composed of an

inanimate nature or natures together with an animate nature
or natures, may be imposed or voluntary according as
whether the animate nature, or natures, has entered the
syntax on its own volition or by the will of some other
animate nature. Thus a man arrayed according to his own
wishes comprises with his raiment a voluntary syntactic
unity, whereas a horse caparisoned is in an imposed syntactic unity with his trappings. It is also evident that the
adjective 'voluntary' can only apply to the animate elements
in a syntax, and the same syntax may contain both elements
entering it voluntarily and elements on which it has been
imposed. When applied to a syntactic unity, it is therefore
necessary to bear in mind that the adjective 'voluntary'
only refers to the element or elements which are animate,
or to some of them.

The metaphysical analysis of a syntax consists in discriminating the natures of which it is composed and deciding
in the case of each of those natures whether their entry into
the syntax was by imposition or their own volition. To
describe a syntax as an imposed syntactic unity implies that
all the elements composing it were brought into syntactic
unity by a will outside themselves. To describe a syntax as
a voluntary syntactic unity implies that at least one element
therein has entered the syntax voluntarily, though it must
be remembered that the syntax may contain other elements
in the syntax by imposition.

It thus emerges that while the adjective 'imposed' applies
to all natural unions, in that they are acts of God, it may or
may not apply to any or all of the elements in a syntactic
union. On the other hand, the adjective 'voluntary' can
never be applied to a natural union, for all natural unions
are acts of God; but the adjective 'voluntary' may apply to
some or all of the elements entering a syntactic union, and,
with an understanding of the elements to which it does and
does not refer, may be applied to the syntax itself.

Nestorius, unfortunately, never arrived at the concept of
syntax as compared with nature. But the concept of syntax
clears the way to a logical understanding of Nestorius'
expression 'voluntary union'. It is at once clear that a
voluntary union cannot in any circumstances be a natural

union, and a voluntary unity cannot be a natural unity. This Nestorius intuitively recognized, and many of these distinctions emerge in the following passage: "If then they say that it is the *ousia* of the Father and of the Son and of the Holy Spirit united by a natural union, this is not a natural union with the flesh but a voluntary, since they are united for the use of the *prosôpon* and not of the nature; since [those things] which are united in one nature are not united voluntarily but by the power of the Creator, who combines them and brings them to a fusion in such a way that whatever is not of and belongs not to each of them obtains it in virtue of a natural and not a voluntary union, by which it has been united in one nature. By whom then are these united in nature? It is evident that that which has been united has been so [united] by the creator of the nature. If anyone says that anything is united of itself, I do not suppose that it is right; for when the natures are united in the *ousias* in one nature, it possesses also a certain kind of change of *ousia* and it is necessary that that nature which has been united should be bound in virtue of an equality of nature and not by the will. . . . The natures indeed which are united voluntarily acquire the union with a view to [forming] not one nature but a voluntary union of the *prosôpon* of the dispensation. If then they say that the union of the natures resulted in one nature, even though we ourselves should concede to them that it took place voluntarily, yet, after it took place, the union existed not voluntarily in that the natures have acquired it. And it suffers as being united, whether it will or not, and accepts the sufferings of that nature to which it has been united, since it is defined by it" (B. 54–56). The contrast is also definitely stated in this passage: "Then there has not been an *hypostatic* and natural but a voluntary union with the body and with the rational and intelligent soul which are united *hypostatically* and naturally in the nature of the man. But the union of God the Word with these is neither *hypostatic* nor natural but voluntary, as consisting in a property of the will and not of the nature. For the things which are united by the natural *hypostasis* have a natural and not a voluntary quality" (B. 262).

Nestorius' expression 'voluntary union' thus necessarily means 'voluntary syntactic union', and the distinction between syntactic union and natural union must be borne constantly in mind.

There are, however, also similarities of a very close kind, which must both be recognized and discriminated. Underlying any one nature is one corresponding ousia. Underlying a syntactic unity is the totality of the ousias underlying its component natures. They are not ousically combined in that their corresponding natures are not naturally combined (see pp. 86–88); yet because they are in a syntactic unity, we must regard them as having some kind of mutual interdependence. It may be useful to regard the totality of the associated ousias underlying the constituent natures of a syntactic unity as constituting the quasi-ousia of that syntactic unity. Similarly, by definition, a syntactic unity is not a nature, but it has a complex of qualities and properties, which may conveniently be termed its quasi-nature; its quasi-nature is the resultant of the interrelations of its constituent natures.

It will be evident that a syntactic unity has properties dependent upon its constituting natures, and it will be equally evident that a syntactic unity may possess attributes not within the nature of its constituents taken separately or collectively. For example, a man using a tool constitutes a syntactic unity, and this syntactic unity has powers which neither the man nor the tool possesses except in association with the other. A man using a saw comprises a syntactic unity able to saw through wood. Ability to saw wood is not in the nature of man as such (nudus homo), nor is it in the nature of an unactuated saw. The nature of a man includes the ability to use instruments and to enter into syntactic union with them, and the nature of an instrument includes the possibility of being used by an agent; but in each case the potentiality can only be realized in a syntactic unity.

It may be useful to enumerate some of the differences between a syntactic unity and a natural unity:

1. A natural unity is brought about by an act of God, who is responsible directly or through His laws for the

G

integration and disintegration of all natures. They can neither come into being nor depart from their natures without His fiat, explicit or implicit. On the other hand, a syntactic unity can be integrated or disintegrated by the volition of an animate nature, usually man.

2. In a natural union there is often a profound difference between the separate natures coming into the union and the resultant nature. This is illustrated abundantly in chemistry. Carbon and sulphur are very different from carbon bisulphide, the result of their natural union. But there is not always such a profound difference, and it must not be thought that an obvious change of this kind is a necessary criterion of natural union; in many cases the two originating natures in a natural union may be clearly discriminated. For example, the organs of a body are in natural union, but they are readily discriminable, though they cannot be separated and reunited by the act of man alone. On the other hand, in a syntactic union the constituent natures always retain their obvious individuality. Each part of a clock is readily recognized for what it is, and has not lost its recognizable individuality by entering into a syntactic union.

3. In a natural union the combined ousias acquire a nature which may differ profoundly from the separate natures of the original ousias; but in a syntactic unity, the quasi-nature is readily deducible from the known natures of the constituents, although by their association they are able to display powers which in separation they could not.

4. The disintegration of a nature affects the whole nature in that it ceases to exist as such; but the disintegration of a syntactic unity does not affect the separate natures of which it is composed.

The four contrasts set out above indicate the main distinctions between natural and syntactic union. Though of interest and value, it is not necessary to work out the further implications of the concept of syntax, as the main positions so far as they affect Christology have already been established.

The analysis of reality in terms of ousia and nature is completely descriptive, and to regard the Universe as a flux of natural unities is a powerful and comprehensive concept. If in addition we recognize the ability of natures to be associated in syntaxes, we have a view of the Universe both as established by the fiats of God and affected by the volition of animate natures. But this approach leaves out of account the continuity of manifested purposiveness revealed in an animate organized nature. An animal or man exhibits something which, in modern terms, we should describe by words such as purpose, character or individuality. These qualities are made manifest by appearance and action. In our thought we tend to separate personality and its manifestation; but in the thought of Nestorius there is no such separation. He envisages what we should call individuality and the manifestation of it in appearance and action as one entity. This one entity is πρόσωπον.

It is now necessary to discover what exactly Nestorius implied when he used the word πρόσωπον. Its history is interesting, and is admirably summarized in Driver and Hodgson's edition of *The Bazaar*.[1] But however instructive the history of a word may be, the final criterion is usage. This is particularly true in the case of a word which an author uses with a nuance of his own. Any Greek lexicon will tell us that πρόσωπον means face, front, mask, character, person; only the usage of Nestorius himself can tell us just how much he understood by the word. We shall endeavour to set out an understanding of πρόσωπον (*prosôpon*) which seems to fit the arguments, explicit and implicit, of the Bazaar. In general, we may say that for Nestorius *prosôpon* appears to mean the self-revelation and self-manifestation of an individual particular natural unity. It reveals what the thing is, and includes the presentation of itself. The word equally implies what we should call the underlying individuality and the manifestation of that individuality. Each of these two aspects must carry equal stress. To describe prosôpon as manifesting individuality places too much stress on the idea of individuality, while to describe prosôpon as self-manifestation places too much stress on the idea of the objective manifestation. With this caveat,

[1] *Nestorius: The Bazaar of Heracleides, newly translated from the Syriac*, pp. 402–410.

self-manifestation may perhaps be the best general rendering.

Prosôpon thus signifies the self-manifestation of a particular natural unity. It necessarily has its ground of reality in the ousia of the natural unity, and is within its nature. Just as there can be no ousia without a nature, nor a nature without an ousia, so also no ousia and nature can be without prosôpon. Prosôpon is, therefore, as necessary a term in the metaphysical analysis of an entity as ousia and nature, and interdepends with them as do they with one another. Ousia, nature and prosôpon are interdepending analytical elements in the reality: ousia is that which it is in itself, independently of being known, the ground of its existence, τὸ τί ἐστι; nature is the totality of its properties and qualities, both effective and restrictive, and completely describes τὸ ὄν in all circumstances, actual and potential; prosôpon is the manifestation of τὸ ὄν regarded, in modern terms, both as objective to a beholder and as definitive of the actual state and condition of τὸ ὄν within the range of its nature.

Our ideas regarding prosôpon must not be unduly coloured by our concept of person or personality, and prosôpon must certainly not be translated by either of these words without careful circumscription.[1] Prosôpon must be looked upon as indissolubly correlative with ousia and nature. It is another aspect of total reality, and is inconceivable without an underlying ousia, and is inconceivable except as the manifestation of a nature.[2]

As in the case of nature, prosôpon has two aspects. There is the prosôpon at any given instant, τὸ νῦν πρόσωπον, which we may call the instantaneous prosôpon; this, in general, is the manifestation of the ousia appropriate to the circumstances; and there is τὸ ἀεὶ πρόνωπον, which represents the continuity of the prosôpon, and may be called the durative prosôpon; this represents the unity in continuity

[1] For footnote, see p. 120.

[2] Cf. Loofs, Nestorius, p. 78: "Nestorius as an adherent of the Antiochian school could as little realise a really existing nature without πρόσωπον as without ὑπόστασις, for the whole of the characteristics which make the nature must, in his opinion, as necessarily have a form of appearance, i.e. a πρόσωπον, as a real being by which they are borne, i.e. an ὑπόστασις."

4 0473

of the prosôpon, just as durative nature represents the unity in continuity of a nature.

The word prosôpon, unlike the word person, can be applied to an inanimate object, though it is obviously evident that the concept is primarily relevant to an animate nature, and that certain restrictions are necessarily implied if the term is applied to an inanimate nature. These restrictions will emerge, but it may be convenient to distinguish in thought, if not always in expression, between an inanimate prosôpon and an animate prosôpon.

From one point of view, prosôpon is revelation of nature as circumscribed by circumstances, and, in the case of an animate willing nature, by its own volition. No nature can express all of itself simultaneously, and many potentialities are mutually exclusive as simultaneities. Although, in one sense, a durative prosôpon is a continuity, it may show remarkable differences and abrupt changes. This will be seen in the case of an animate prosôpon by changes of mood and action; in the case of an inanimate prosôpon, changing physical conditions may impose changes on the form and character of the prosôpon. For example, the nature of the ousia water includes the properties of being steam at high temperatures, liquid water at ordinary temperatures, and ice at low temperatures. At ordinary temperatures, the prosôpon of water is a clear mobile liquid with certain well-known characteristics, whereas at temperatures below freezing point the prosôpon of water is a hard brittle transparent solid. In such a case as this it is obviously the instantaneous prosôpa which are under consideration. This distinction will not be continually remarked on, but it must be constantly borne in mind. Nestorius illustrates this in his refutation of Sophronius in the matter of the nature of water: "Things which have no distinction in nature and are distinguished are distinct in the *prosôpon*" (B. 22). Liquid water and ice, for example, have no distinction in nature, but are distinct in prosôpon.

This illustration from the nature of water brings out an important point. The prosôpon in which a nature appears is not arbitrary or accidental, but is governed by very definite conditions, the description of which belongs to the nature of the object. For example, at a pressure of 760 mm. of mercury and a temperature of 16° C., the ousia water cannot appear otherwise than as the prosôpon liquid water, and at the same pressure and a temperature of −16° C., the ousia of water cannot appear otherwise than as the prosôpon ice.

The prosôpon of an animate nature is complicated by the fact that its nature includes the ability to express itself by the imposition of syntactic union on other natures and the voluntary entry into syntactic unities itself, and as the prosôpon is the self-manifestation of the nature, these complications must be taken into account. The prosôpon of an animate nature may entirely arise from that nature. The prosôpon of an animal is usually entirely based in its own ousia and nature. Such a prosôpon may be called an autogenous prosôpon, in that the ousia is manifesting itself in its nature without making use of anything other than itself. This is the case in almost all inanimate prosôpa.

But if an animate nature uses its power to enter into syntactic union, there are some interesting and important complications. Just as the continuity of its durative nature is not broken by entering into syntactic unions, so also there is unbroken continuity in its durative prosôpon. While, however, the syntax continues, the prosôpon of the animate nature—its self-manifestation—may be profoundly modified by the composition of the syntax, and may include elements arising from ousias other than its own. The durative nature of a king, for example, is an unbroken continuity during his life-time, and so also is his durative prosôpon. His entry into and departure from a series of syntaxes causes no discontinuity in either his nature or his prosôpon. But though there is continuity of durative prosôpon, the instantaneous prosôpon varies with the king's moods and actions, and with his syntaxes. Only when the king is nudus homo is his prosôpon autogenous, that is, the manifestation of himself by no means other than those arising from his own ousia and nature. But when he enters into a syntactic unity this simplicity no longer obtains. He has now become part of a syntactic unity, which so far as the king is concerned is a voluntary syntactic unity, and so far as his clothing or equipment is concerned is an imposed syntactic unity. This syntax has its quasi-ousia, which is simply the totality of the ousias of its constituents, and its quasi-nature, which is the resultant of the inter-relation of the natures of its constituents. At the same time the constituent ousias and natures continue as such, because they are only associated in syntactic union, not ousically and naturally combined into a new ousia and nature.

In regard to the prosôpa, however, there is a less simple result. A syntax, quite logically, must be regarded as having a quasi-prosôpon, corresponding with its quasi-ousia and quasi-nature, of which it is the manifestation. In an imposed syntactic union this covers the whole of the ground; the constituent ousias, with their proper natures and prosôpa, remain. They are in syntactic union with one another, and the syntax thus formed has its quasi-ousia, quasi-nature, and quasi-prosôpon. If, however, the syntax includes a voluntary element, there is a further complication; for not only do the ousia and nature of the voluntary element continue uninterrupted, as also does the continuity of its prosôpon; but it is evident that the prosôpon of the voluntary element—its self-manifestation—is no longer arising simply from its own ousia. The voluntary element is express-ing itself through the syntax as a whole, so that the quasi-prosôpon of the syntax is actually also the prosôpon of the voluntary element in it. Thus the prosôpon of a king arrayed and equipped is the totality of the manner and means of his manifestation of himself, and includes not only all that he is in his own ousia and nature, but also all that of which he is making use by entering into voluntary syntactic union. The king's prosôpon is, in short, the quasi-prosôpon of the syntax. In such circumstances the king's prosôpon is not entirely based on his own ousia, and, in distinction from cases in which it is so based, when we describe the prosôpon as autogenous, we may distinguish it by describing it as allogenous. An allogenous prosôpon is the self-manifestation of an ousia and nature, the said ousia and nature making use of other ousias and natures for its self-manifestation, so that the prosôpon is indeed the self-manifestation of that ousia and nature, but contains elements not within its own ousia and nature, of which it is making use by entering into voluntary syntactic union.

We thus arrive at a very comprehensive analysis of the course run by an animate nature. It has its inception and its end, and between those two bounds there is continuity of ousia, nature and prosôpon. All three undergo changes, so that we need to speak of the instantaneous ousia, nature and prosôpon, when we are considering them as they are at any instant, and the durative ousia, nature and prosôpon, when we are considering them as continuities. Further, an animate nature may voluntarily enter into syntactic unions, in which the continuity of its durative ousia, nature and prosôpon is not broken; but its prosôpon is then for the time being allogenous. In the case of ousia and nature, we need to be able in every case to recognize whether we are using the words to mean instantaneous or durative ousia or nature (and, of course, particular, collective, total or general), and in the case of prosôpon we have in addition to recognize whether it is autogenous or allogenous. Ability to do this is of great value in following Nestorius' arguments. Nestorius never made these distinctions, but they no doubt rested implicitly in his own mind, for without them many of his arguments are incomprehensible, whereas with them they are quite clear.

It is easier to explain what prosôpon means than to give any short and satisfactory definition of it. If a short definition is required, we may perhaps adapt the ending of one of Nestorius' own sentences, and define prosôpon as "that which makes known the ousia" (B. 231: ". . . the prosôpon [makes known] the *ousia*"). This is similar to Loof's short definition, that according to Nestorius "everything had its πρόσωπον, that is its appearance, its kind of being seen and judged" (*Nestorius*, p. 77).

But conciseness may be obtained at the sacrifice of completeness. No short definition meets the case, and we can hardly say less than this: that a prosôpon is the manifestation and evidence of a particular ousia; it arises by the power of the nature of the ousia, and its basis is either in the ousia itself (an autogenous prosôpon), or is partly or wholly in other ousias of which the particular ousia is by its nature able to make use (an allogenous prosôpon). Further, we may regard the prosôpon at some particular instant (instantaneous prosôpon), or in its changing continuity (durative prosôpon).

To make use of a geometrical analogy, we might say that the nature of an ousia could be depicted as an area representing the totality of the powers and characteristics of the ousia, which like any given area necessarily both includes and excludes; and that the prosôpon of the ousia is the actualization, regarded both absolutely and objectively, of some particular part or parts of that nature. The instantaneous prosôpon at any moment might be represented by a shaded area in the totality of the nature (not all of which can ever be actualized at once), and the durative prosôpon would then be represented by the flux (expansion, contraction and movement) of that area.

Bearing in mind the interrelationship of ousia, nature and prosôpon, a few preliminary observations can be made as to prosôpic union and prosôpic unity:

(1) As a prosôpon is the manifestation of an ousia according to its nature, there is the same necessary correspondence between an ousia and nature and its prosôpon as between an ousia and its nature. There can be no prosôpon without an underlying ousia to give it a ground of existence, and the prosôpon of an ousia is as necessarily related to it as is its nature.

(2) Just as union of ousias necessarily involves union of natures, so that an ousic unity is necessarily also a natural unity, so also union of ousias and natures involves union of prosôpa, and an ousic unity is necessarily both a natural unity and a prosôpic unity.

(3) In an imposed syntactic unity all the parts retain their own ousias, natures and prosôpa. Syntactic union being neither ousic nor natural is also not prosôpic. The syntax, having a quasi-ousia and quasi-nature, has also only a quasi-prosôpon.

(4) In a voluntary syntactic unity all the parts retain their own ousias, natures and prosôpa. Syntactic union being neither ousic nor natural is also not prosôpic. The syntax, having a quasi-ousia and quasi-nature, has also only

a quasi-prosôpon. But as regards the voluntary element, a most important fact emerges with regard to its durative prosôpon: the syntax has arisen by the will of the voluntary element, that is, by the exercise of a power of its nature; the syntax is therefore the manifestation and expression of that voluntary element, that is, its prosôpon, its allogenous prosôpon. It follows that the quasi-prosôpon of a voluntary syntactic unity is also the allogenous prosôpon of the voluntary element in the syntax.

(5) If a voluntary syntactic unity includes more than one voluntary element, the syntax is the allogenous prosôpon of each of those voluntary elements. For example, we can imagine a syntax consisting of two men using a two-handled saw. The syntax includes on the one hand the two men, for whom entry into the syntactic unity is voluntary, and on the other hand the saw and their clothing, inanimate objects as to which the syntax is imposed. The men, the saw and the separate items of clothing all retain their own ousias, natures and prosôpa. In the case of the inanimate objects their prosôpa remain, as always, autogenous. But in the case of each of the two men their prosôpa are, while the syntax continues, allogenous. Each man is manifesting himself by his entry into and activity in the syntax. His durative prosôpon, which is continually varying, is for the time being an allogenous prosôpon, comprising his clothing, the saw, and his fellow workman. When he puts down his end of the saw, the syntax comes to an end, and his allogenous prosôpon is himself as clothed and comporting himself in whatever way he may choose. If he strips and bathes, his prosôpon then becomes autogenous. It thus emerges that a voluntary syntax containing voluntary elements has the quasi-prosôpon of the syntax, and is also the allogenous prosôpon of each voluntary element. It must, however, be remarked that each of the two men retains his own ousia and nature. The men are not ousically or naturally united. Nor are they prosôpically united. They are not a prosôpic unity. Each includes the other in his own allogenous prosôpon, which in each case is the quasi-prosôpon of the syntax, and is made up of a number of autogenous prosôpa. Looked at from the point of view of continuity,

each man's durative prosôpon (and a durative prosôpon passes through a series of phases both autogenous and allogenous) includes temporarily a phase when its prosôpon is the quasi-prosôpon of the syntax. For each, it is an allogenous prosôpon, and, objectively analysed, has the same constituents. But there is this important difference: for each, the autogenous element is himself, while the other is one of the allogenous constituents. It may be clearly envisaged thus: the durative prosôpon of an animate nature may be likened to a continuous cable, beginning at birth and ending at death. If this cable be regarded as made up of strands, we may liken one of the strands to the autogenous element in the prosôpon. This will continue unbroken (even if changing) through the nature's duration; other strands will be wound with it from time to time and for varying periods. These represent the allogenous elements in the prosôpon at any period, short or long. They twist into the cable, and twist out of it again. While in, they are part of the cable, which, while they are in it, is an allogenous prosôpon of the nature. They leave it, but the autogenous strand continues to twine itself in due course with various other allogenous elements. Nudus homo is the continuing strand in the durative prosôpon of homo, and his durative prosôpon alternates between autogenousness and allogenousness as he puts on and discards clothes, or picks up and discards implements. The cable may contain many or few strands, and each strand may continue for a long or short time—a pen held for ten minutes or a ring worn continually for fifty years. But one strand goes continuously through, and on its continuity depends the continuity of the nature and of the prosôpon. That strand is the autogenous prosôpon itself when the nature's prosôpon is autogenous, and it is the autogenous element in the prosôpon when the prosôpon is allogenous.

The case of two voluntary elements in the same syntax, having the same allogenous prosôpon, thus becomes simple. For the time being it is one cable. But from the point of view of one of them the continuity depends on one particular strand, while from the point of view of the other it depends on another particular strand.

This, incidentally, brings out very clearly the fact that prosôpon and person are quite different concepts. A syntactic unity has a quasi-prosôpon which may be the allogenous prosôpon of each of two voluntary elements in the syntax. From our point of view there are two distinct persons all the time. Nor is it altogether correct to say that the autogenous strand in the cable of durative prosôpon is the person. It is best to recognize that the concepts are different, patiently to follow through the Nestorian metaphysic to its logical conclusion, and to see whether that conclusion is satisfying.

What has been said above will be found of particular value in elucidating many otherwise obscure passages, such as B. 80, 81, 84, 94, 101, 252, 143, 305, 361, 425.

Mention must be made of another frequently recurring word, σχῆμα (*schêma*). This is a noun derived from the aorist root of ἔχειν, to have, hold, possess, and has a large number of direct, derived and idiomatic meanings: bearing, manner, form, shape, outward appearance, figure, show, pretence, plan, scheme. But in Nestorius the primary meaning is almost invariably "outward appearance", though with shades of meaning which it is important to detect.

Starting with the idea of schêma as "outward appearance", and remembering that the prosôpon of any particular ousia is its self-manifestation, both as the revelation of its individuality and as seen and known objectively, it is evident that schêma is necessarily an element in prosôpon, except in those cases where the prosôpon is invisible.[1] We may therefore rightly speak of the schêma of a prosôpon, by which we mean its outward appearance as presented to and interpreted by a beholder. But whereas prosôpon is a real element in the analysis of a particular object, being the presentation and manifestation of the ousia according to the powers of its nature, schêma, outward appearance, is only one of the means whereby the prosôpon may be understood, and taken by itself may be incomplete or even misleading. For example, we might take three cubes of

[1] E.g., the prosôpon of a colourless gas, of a discarnate spirit, or the autogenous prosôpon of God (see p. 126). The prosôpon of anything invisible is known by its effects on senses other than sight, and by its effects on other objects.

exactly the same size. The first might be solid and of pure gold, the second might be hollow, but of pure gold, the third might be solid silver, plated with gold. In schêma the three cubes would be identical, and judging by schêma only we should say of each: "This has the schêma of a cube of gold." But if we investigated the cubes by other methods, such as weighing or cutting, we should find that their prosôpa were different, for the prosôpon is the self-manifestation, and is revealed in many ways besides mere schêma. Schêma is thus an incomplete guide to reality. Skilfully made waxworks have often been mistaken for real persons. They present the schêmata of people, but in reality their prosôpa are those of waxworks, which is soon discovered by touch or closer observation. Every visible prosôpon has its schêma, but the schêma may or may not be a true aid to the identification and understanding of the prosôpon.

The word schêma can therefore be applied to an appearance which is a true revelation of a prosôpon, to an appearance which is accidentally or intentionally misleading, or to an appearance considered simply as such, without further deductions. In every case it can be rightly translated 'appearance', and if we prefix in thought the adjective 'mere', we safeguard ourselves against deducing too much from it: it may be true or false, complete or partial.

Nestorius uses the word with exactly these shades of implied meaning, and it is usually easy to see whether it is being used colourlessly, to mean appearance as such, without implied deductions as to truth or deceit; or whether the appearance is to be taken as a true element in prosôpon; or whether the appearance is deceptive. A few examples of each usage may be given:

(1) Appearance as such, without implied deductions:

B. 30–31: "As a king in the *schêma* of a soldier comports himself as a soldier and not as a king, he is clad in the manner of a soldier against whatsoever has need of correction, and it is said that in everything he is [so] clad, in that he has become the *schêma* of one soldier, even that which clothes all the soldiers."

B. 84: "And he is both God and man, and the likeness of God in condescension and in *kenôsis* and in *schêma*, [and] the likeness of the flesh as man."

B. 88: "As God appeared and spoke unto Adam in *schêma*, and as it was none other, so will God be [seen] of all men."

(2) Appearance as a true element in prosôpon:

B. 88: "So will God be [seen] of all men in the natural *schêma* which has been created, that is, that of the flesh."

B. 89: "Man indeed is known by the human *prosôpon*, that is, by the *schêma* of the body and by the likeness."

B. 441: "But the quality, however, is not the nature of the *ousia* but either the *schêma* of the *ousia* or of the nature or of [that which is] not *ousia* or a view in mere idea only expressed concerning the natures."

(3) Appearance which is deceptive, mere appearance:

B. 36: "These indeed are distinct from the Manichæans in that they confess truly that the flesh is of our own nature and that it is not the *schêma* of the flesh but the nature of the flesh."

B. 120: "But if the things which were commanded had been possible to do and had not been observed, justly would Satan have been condemned; for, when he could obey, he obeyed not but rose up against God by means of the *schêma* of a man and slandered God before man as jealous, and man before God as ungrateful."

B. 270: "For indeed [in that case] he would not have been of man, but of God the Word would he have been, and [that] in such wise as to make use of the *schêma* of a man but not of the *ousia* of a man."

The third usage is by far the most frequent, so that it is always advisable to prefix the adjective 'mere', at least in thought, when translating schêma as 'appearance'. We thus accept a caveat, to judge whether the word is descriptive of an appearance which is a true and informative element in a prosôpon, revealing an ousia according to its nature; or whether the schêma is liable to mislead us into believing it to reveal some prosôpon other than that which we should at first sight suppose.

In consequence of this tendency for the word schêma to be used in a derogatory sense, it is frequently applied in a vague and general way to anything which may not really be what it appears to be. Here again "mere appearance" is a satisfactory translation. A few examples of this usage may be given:

B. 207: "And if you all leave it unconfuted and if there was none among you capable of confuting it, utter [this] absurd question, examine it, although you are judges [only] in *schêma*."

B. 258–259: "And supposing that he is a Manichæan, you will bear witness in his favour that, in that he suffered impassibly, he suffered in *schêma*."

B. 298: "The things of Christ are neither folly nor fiction. He did nothing in *schêma*, in hungering and thirsting and fearing."

When used in the strict sense, to describe the actual appearance of a prosôpon, it is obvious that whether the schêma reveals or deceives, it must be a revelation of some reality, some ousia. There cannot be a schêma without a prosôpon of which it is an element, any more than there can be a prosôpon without an ousia and nature.

A schêma, therefore, true or false, necessarily has its basis in some ousia. If there is no deception, and the ousia in question is being objectively manifested in the completest possible manner in the given circumstances, the schêma is a true element in its prosôpon, namely its external visual appearance. If there is deception, intentional or accidental, the prosôpon presents a schêma which is intended, or is liable, to be mistaken for the schêma of some other prosôpon. But the schêma must be an element in some prosôpon and must arise from some ousia. A statue at a distance may be mistaken for a living man. It presents the schêma of a man, but its schêma is actually an element in its own prosôpon, that of the ousia of carved wood or sculptured marble as the case may be.

It is to be noticed that we have been able to describe the

Nestorian analysis of a particular object without using the word ὑπόστασις (*hypostasis*). This omission is significant, as it throws light on the failure of Nestorius and Cyril to understand one another. To Nestorius, *hypostasis* was an almost unnecessary word, apart from its special use in the doctrine of the Trinity. Unless we examine his usage very minutely, we may conclude that for Nestorius hypostasis is simply ousia. In fact, in all cases except those involving the doctrine of the Trinity, we may, without affecting the sense or the arguments, replace hypostasis by ousia, and where both are used side by side, we can simply omit the word hypostasis.

Nevertheless, there are reasons why Nestorius has to use the word. Quite obviously, he has to use it in answering the arguments of opponents who used it. But there are also cases in which Nestorius uses the word by his own preference.

We have seen (p. 65) that ousia, derived from εἶναι, to be, had come to stand for the essence of any particular thing, that underlying something without which an object could not be. The very derivation tended to keep the emphasis on the idea of existence: οὐσία accounts for τὸ ὄν. ὑπόστασις, on the other hand, was a noun derived from the verb ὑφιστέναι, the primary meaning of which is to place under, set under, stand under; ὑπόστασις hence primarily means a standing under, that which stands under, and its derived meanings, both concrete and abstract, logically follow: base, prop, support, groundwork, subject-matter, quality, substance, essence. As a metaphysical term, hypostasis thus came to signify that which stands under any particular object as presented to the senses, the reality behind the phenomenon: that which is perceived is perceived because there is something underlying it, something giving it a ground of existence. This concept is fundamentally the same as the concept of ousia; but whereas the word ousia emphasizes the reality of the existence of the thing itself, the word hypostasis emphasizes the reality of the particular basis of that which appears.

Until usage made a distinction in significance, ousia and hypostasis were therefore synonymous, being words of different derivation describing the same thing—the ground of an existence. Even so, the influence of derivation would sometimes suggest the suitability in a given context of the one word rather than the other.[1] This is occasionally so in Nestorius, and though he generally preferred ousia, there are contexts where hypostasis evidently seemed to him more appropriate.

These considerations enable us to account for almost every instance. It may be convenient to give examples of Nestorius' usage under a number of headings:

(1) Hypostasis used in exactly the same sense as ousia, and only used by Nestorius because he was replying to the arguments of opponents who had used the same word:

B. 23: "And the Manichæans also have taken [these opinions] from them and say that the change of likeness resulted in a *schéma* without *hypostasis*."

B. 149–150: "For in that he disputed against the Anomœans, [saying] that the Son is consubstantial with God the Father, and against Photinus and Paul, [saying] that he is by nature and *hypostasis* homoousian with the Father, unwittingly he was accounted as [one of] the orthodox."

B. 237–238: "And he who can create everything, that is, God, will be the nature of the union, and it is not the *hypostasis* of the humanity which is known [to be] animal in nature, as even the body without the soul is not animal in its own *hypostasis*, but by the construction of the natural union it is its [property] to be animal. If it is so, it is also through God [the property] of man to be animal, but it is not his [property through] his own *hypostasis* and his nature, but through the *hypostatic* union which establishes one nature."

[1] Cf. Bethune-Baker, *Nestorius and His Teaching*, p. 47: "To express any kind of real existence two terms were in common use among Greek thinkers, viz. *ousia* and *hypostasis*: the former the noun of the verb 'to be' ('being'), the latter the noun of a verb of similar sense 'to subsist' or 'to exist' ('subsistence', 'existence'). Subtle shades of difference of meaning may be detected in these two terms; but in practical use they were synonymous, and Greek writers who well knew the values of words declared them to be so."

H

These examples illustrate the principal reason why Nestorius felt any need to use the word hypostasis: that he might deal with his opponents' arguments in what he considered the same terms. That it is usually used by him with no real distinction from ousia is evident in the above and many other passages, e.g., B. 64, 67, 264, 265, 302.

(2) Hypostasis used in preference to ousia in cases where emphasis was desired on the root meaning, "that which underlies":

B. 22: "But [to be distinguished] by the *prosôpon* without nature is a *schêma* without *hypostasis* in another *schêma*."

B. 81: "Therefore has he said 'the likeness' and 'the name' which it has taken, which indicates a *prosôpon* as of one; and this same name and *prosôpon* make the two of them to be understood; and the distinction of nature, one *hypostasis* and one *prosôpon*, is theirs, the one being known by the other and the other by the one, so that the one is by adoption what the other is by nature and the other is with the one in the body."

B. 291: "I say not . . . that the [properties] of the flesh were taken upon God without [their] *hypostasis*."

(3) Hypostasis used in preference to ousia in cases where emphasis rested on the idea of a particular individual existence. There is enough internal evidence in the Bazaar to suggest that although ousia, as already explained, could be readily understood in a particular, general, or total sense (see pp. 77–78), hypostasis tended to be restricted to use in the particular sense. A tendency in usage is often the beginning of a discrimination. Nestorius cannot be said (except in Trinitarian use) to have passed beyond tendency, but he certainly seems to prefer to restrict hypostasis to signify a particular ousia, and most often he restricts it to an animate ousia. The beginnings of a discrimination may be sensed, but it must not be pressed: in Nestorius, ousia can always replace hypostasis (except in Trinitarian use); but hypostasis cannot always appropriately replace ousia. Hypostasis can certainly always replace ousia when it is

particular.[1] We must not, however, generalize to the extent of saying that for Nestorius hypostasis is particular ousia, even if it often appears to amount to that in his usage. The following examples illustrate hypostasis (or hypostatic) used where reference is to a particular ousia:

B. 125: "Therefore the words of the Divine Scriptures befit not Christ in any other manner than this; but as we have examined and found, all refer not to the union of the nature but to the natural and *hypostatic prosôpon*."

B. 239: "When he speaks as from his own *prosôpon*, [he does so] by one *prosôpon* which appertains to the union of the natures and not to one *hypostasis* or [one] nature."

B. 304: "Neither of them is known without *prosôpon* and without *hypostasis* in the diversities of the natures."

(4) There are some important cases where hypostasis and ousia are used together. These cases are very significant, and must be accounted for if the essential identity of hypostasis and ousia in the Nestorian metaphysic is to be maintained. They fall into two classes:

(i) Both words are used, redundantly, for emphasis. Either can be omitted without affecting the sense:

---

[1] Cf. Loofs, *Nestorius*, pp. 70–71: "Originally ὑπόστασις is a synonym of οὐσία, if this latter is understood in the sense of real being; both words then may be translated by *substance*. As synonymous with οὐσια the term ὑπόστασις appears in the Nicene Creed, because the *Logos* here is deduced ἐκ τῆς οὐσίας τοῦ πατρός, and the assertion is anathematised, that he was ἐξ ἑτέρας οὐσίας ἢ ὑποστάσεως. And Athanasius said even about the end of his life: ἡ ὑπόστασις οὐσία ἐστι καὶ οὐδὲν ἄλλο σημαινόμενον ἔχει ἢ αὐτὸ τὸ ὄν. Αὐτὸ τὸ ὄν, *the being itself*—that is the meaning of ὑπόστασις. The term means τὸ ὑποκείμενον, as Aristotle said, the ultimate reality which is the bearer of all the attributes which are called the *nature* of a thing, the *substance* in the sense in which the earlier philosophy, that of the middle ages included, made use of this term and which was afterwards criticised by Locke and Hume. The term οὐσία could also be used in a generic sense and then received a meaning similar to *kind* or *nature*, but ὑπόστασις means only that which οὐσία could mean in addition to its other meaning, viz., a single and really existing being, whether material or immaterial." Also Webb, *God and Personality*, pp. 41–42: "Thus it is that ὑπόστασις comes into use as a philosophical term, often equivalent to οὐσία, which for Aristotle is most properly used of the concrete individual of a certain kind; but of Aristotle's two notes of real being, its *intelligible character* and its *concrete independence*, emphasizing the latter, as οὐσία emphasized the former."

B. 240: "Everything suffers not in the same way, neither light nor air nor fire, nor the animals which are in the waters nor the animals which are on the dry land, nor birds nor bodily frames nor souls nor angels nor demons, but they are passible indeed in *ousia* and in *hypostasis*."

B. 265: "Eternally [exists] the Father, eternally the Son, eternally the Holy Spirit; but the flesh which was made flesh, which was of the Holy Spirit and of the Virgin Mary, exists not eternally, but there was when it was not; and it is of another *ousia* and of another nature and of another *hypostasis*, [to wit, of that] of men, and not of the *ousia* of God the Father."

(ii) Both words are used because it is desired to emphasize both aspects of the same reality: that which exists in itself (ousia) is the underlying basis (hypostasis) of that which appears:

B. 215: "In that thou hast said that he made for himself all the properties, so then God the Word was born of things which were not, because his flesh was [formed] of things which were not, unless thou darest to say that the flesh itself has eternally existed and sayest that God the Word was of another *hypostasis* and another *ousia*, and not of that of the Father but of that of which the flesh was, and [that] God the Word is changeable and corruptible on account of his flesh which is therein."

B. 316: "In so far as they are distinguished in the *prosôpon*, although they are not distinguished in nature but remain always in their being, we say that the Son is adored with the Father and with the Holy Spirit, in order that we may not, like Sabellius, make the *prosôpa* without *hypostasis* and without *ousia*."

(5) There are just a few very interesting cases in which the incipient distinction between hypostasis and ousia begins to emerge even in Nestorius. In all these cases the distinction seems to depend on the tendency to use hypostasis as particular ousia, the ousia underlying some particular object, and the corresponding tendency to use ousia in a more

general sense: as though it were convenient to think of
ousia in general but hypostasis in particular. Let us consider
three examples:

"But in name alone he has a body, without *hypostasis*
and without activity; and for this reason thou callest him
man as something superfluous only in word and in name,
in that thou art not content to predicate the *ousia* and
activity of man or the existence of two natures, each of
them with properties and *hypostases* and *ousia*" (B. 291).
Here each word is used twice. At the first mention, hypostasis has reference to a particular case. We could quite
well substitute "without its own particular ousia." Ousia,
on the other hand, refers to man in general, and we could
say "thou art not content to predicate the (general) ousia
and activity (generally characteristic) of man." Finally, the
two words come together: ". . . each of them with properties
and hypostases and ousia." The distinction is made clear by
the difference in number: each nature has its own hypostasis, each particular nature has its own particular ousia
underlying it; but each nature is characterized, as all natures
must be, by being based on ousia of some sort. The distinction is faint, but becoming definite enough to justify
both words being used; the addition of the words "and
ousia" emphasizes the necessity of bearing in mind that
every individual existence has its ground reality, as if to
say: ". . . two natures, each of them with properties and
their own particular ousias, both of them of course being
necessarily based on ousia of some sort."

"It is not indeed that one *ousia* without *hypostasis* should
be conceived, as if by union into one *ousia* and there were
no *prosôpon* of one *ousia*" (B. 305). Here again the same
distinction enables us to understand what is meant: "It is
not indeed that one of the ousias should be conceived
unparticularized, as if one of the ousias were held in sub-
servient union by the other, without its own means of
self-manifestation (prosôpon)."

"And he indeed who would hinder the saying of 'two
natures' and 'him who is adored with it' would suppress
[the saying] that 'the humanity and the divinity exist in
ousia and in *hypostasis*', even as has been our argument

also concerning the Trinity, as also Gregory says" (B. 317). Both the humanity and divinity exist in a real manner—they have ousia underlying them; and each is particularized.

It will be seen later that this slight distinction provides sufficient basis, even in the Nestorian metaphysic, for contemplating "three hypostases in the one ousia of the Godhead."

(6) In spite of the distinctions indicated above, it must be emphasized that to Nestorius hypostasis and ousia always represented the same aspect of reality: the ground of a real existence. Even if emphasis on the mode of approach to the same reality varies, thus suggesting one or the other as the more appropriate word, and even if he sensed that hypostasis was perhaps more applicable to a particular ousia, especially if animate, and ousia to the general or total, it cannot be too definitely realized that for Nestorius no hypostasis (except in the Trinity) is anything but an ousia, and it is always possible to say 'this ousia' instead of 'this hypostasis'. It follows that, for Nestorius, hypostatic union is exactly the same thing as ousic union. As ousic union necessarily involves natural union (see pp. 86–88), and is simply a different aspect of the same event, so hypostatic union necessarily involves natural union. Indeed, 'ousic and natural union' and 'hypostatic and natural union' are synonymous. To Nestorius, hypostatic union, ousic union and natural union represent the same fact. He could not conceive any meaning in 'hypostatic union' other than 'hypostatic and natural union'. This accounts to a very great degree for the failure of Nestorius and Cyril to understand one another.

Examples may be given where Nestorius uses 'hypostatic and natural union' (or 'natural and hypostatic union') to mean exactly 'ousic and natural union':

B. 261: "Let it be [granted] that he is united to the soul and to the body and to the intelligence; but if it is an *hypostatic* and natural union, thou effectest an addition and not a diminution and thou avoidest a diminution of the sufferings of the body in such wise as to make subject unto the sufferings of many sufferings him who is consubstantial with him who is impassible."

B. 405: "There is then need to state the meaning, according to which the *hypostatic* and the natural union of God and the natural birth from a woman is excluded."

B. 133: "For they suppress all these things through the natural and *hypostatic* union and they take everything which is in his nature and attribute them naturally unto God the Word."

B. 238: "For he received as a result of the construction of [all] creation by the Father and by the Son and by the Holy Spirit to become man, but to become the only-begotten Son he received from the union with God the Word, for it belonged not unto his own nature nor did it lie in the natural and *hypostatic* union."

In other instances 'hypostatic union' is used by itself, but in these cases also the meaning, to Nestorius, is exactly 'ousic and natural union':

B. 140: "When he speaks against the *ousia* of God, he refers all the human qualities to the nature of God the Word by the *hypostatic* union, so that he suffers in natural sensibility all human sufferings."

B. 226: "Why dost thou wish that there should be an *hypostatic* union, which makes us neither understand that there is [in the union] the *ousia* of man nor understand [that he is] man in nature but God the Word in nature, that is, God who is not in nature what he is in his nature through the *hypostatic* union, wherein there are no distinctions and definitions of the various [elements]."

B. 237: "If thou thus predicatest the *hypostatic* union of the nature, thou sayest, as the Arians, that it is natural and not voluntary, because he suffered with a natural passibility. He suffered as a result of the natural union, for the sufferings of the soul are the sufferings of the body in the natural composition."

B. 261: "For you give him the things which make [men] passible because of the *hypostatic* union, since he is united in a natural composition, so as to suffer without his will the sufferings of the body and of the soul and of the intelligence and [since] he is united in *ousia* and in nature, as the soul in the body endures of necessity the sufferings of the soul and of the body."

Footnote 1, *p.* 100: It is perhaps a defect in the passages translated in Bethune-Baker's *Nestorius and His Teaching* that parṣôpâ (πρόσωπον) is uniformly rendered 'person', though Bethune-Baker was of course aware of the subtle differences in the ideas underlying prosôpon and person. It seems better to avoid any tendency to associate ideas and, like Driver and Hodgson, simply to transliterate πρόσωπον into prosôpon. Loofs (*Nestorius*, pp. 76–77) may be quoted on this point: "First, it must be emphasised that πρόσωπον is for Nestorius not the same as what we call *person*. For our notion of *person* the main thing is the oneness of the subject or of the internal self. We can, therefore, use the term *person* only for rational beings or at least those living beings, in which—as in the case of the higher animals—we see some analogy to human thinking, feeling and willing. For Nestorius, who in this respect was influenced by the manner of speaking common at that time, the main thing in his notion of πρόσωπον, according to the etymology of the word and to the earlier history of its meaning, was the external undivided appearance. He was, therefore, able to call a bishop preaching from the pulpit *the* πρόσωπον *of the church* (because the church appeared in him) and to say that Christ had exhibited in himself *the* πρόσωπον *of the human nature as being sinless*. In his opinion, I believe, everything had its πρόσωπον, that is its appearance, its kind of being seen and judged. In not a few places in Nestorius, it is true, the meaning of πρόσωπον coincides with our understanding of the term *person*, e.g. 'Cyril's πρόσωπον' means Cyril, 'these πρόσωπα' means these persons, and εἷς καὶ ὁ αὐτός and ἓν πρόσωπον may be used alternately. Nevertheless, before we go further, I must lay stress on the fact that the notion of πρόσωπον in Nestorius grew upon another soil and, therefore, had a wider application than our term *person*."

CHAPTER V

GOD stands in distinction from His Universe, as well as in relation to it. Nestorius has God's distinction from the Universe very much in mind—"The Maker . . . is in every way other than that which is made" (B. 40)—and the attributes of God are defined in such a way that this distinction is emphasized. God possesses attributes which humanity lacks completely, possesses powers in fulness which humanity possesses only partially, and is free from the limitations which circumscribe humanity. It may be well to enumerate the attributes constantly and consistently applied to God:

(1) God is eternal, which of necessity implies that He is uncreated (unmade), and immortal.

That God is eternal, uncreated and unmade is implied throughout the following passage, the whole argument of which hinges on these attributes: "But there are no means whereby the *ousia* which was should cease to be nor whereby that which was made should become unmade, nor again [are there any means whereby] that which is not should become an eternal nature and be with the eternal; nor again whereby a nature which was not should come into being nor whereby that which is not eternal should become eternal either by a change of nature or by confusion or by mixture; or whereby from the *ousia* of the eternal [should come into being] that which is not eternally. For either by mixture or by confusion of the two *ousias* a change of ousia took place [making] for one nature which should result from the mixture of both of them; or one *ousia* of them was changed into the other. It is not possible that the unmade [should become] made and the eternal temporary and the temporary eternal and that the created [should become] uncreated by nature; that that which is uncreated and which has not come into being and is eternal should thereby become made and temporary, as if it became part of a nature made and temporary; nor that there should come forth a nature unmade and eternal from a nature made and temporary to become an *ousia* unmade and eternal" (B. 39–40).

That God is immortal is stated in B. 258: ". . . him who is impassible and immortal and the maker of all created things", and in B. 318: "I have said that God is incorruptible and immortal and the quickener of all."

(2) God is the maker of all created things, whereby a fundamental distinction exists between Himself and all things else.

B. 258: ". . . him who is impassible and immortal and the maker of all created things." B. 318: "God is incorruptible and immortal and the quickener of all." B. 40: "The Maker . . . is in every way other than that which is made."

(3) God is unchangeable, and therefore incorruptible.

B. 40: "For in that he is the Maker, he is unchangeable." B. 41: "For in so far as he is God he is unchangeable." B. 318: "God is incorruptible."

(4) God is without needs, and therefore impassible.

That God is without needs is implied in the description of Arianism on B. 12: "The Arians confess that he is half God and half man of soulless body and of created divinity; deeming him inferior to men in saying that there is not a soul in him and again deeming him inferior also to God in saying that he is not uncreate and without needs." Impassibility is attributed to God on B. 258: ". . . him who is impassible and immortal and the maker of all created things." It is implied in B. 11, 12, 50 and 54.

(5) God is omnipotent.

"For it appertains to God to be able to effect everything" (B. 20).

(6) God is infinite, and therefore omnipresent and incomprehensible.

B. 73: "He has expounded unto us what he is in the bosom of his Father—it being evident that he has not explained the infinity and the incomprehensibility of the *ousia*." B. 76: "God by his nature is invisible and incomprehensible."

(7) God is invisible.

B. 73: "And consequently the only begotten who is in the bosom of his Father has expounded unto us God whom no one has ever seen." B. 76: "God by his nature is invisible."

This complex of qualities is included within the nature of God, and there are obvious potential difficulties inherent in such a complex; but Nestorius always applies and expects others to apply a sturdy common sense in the use of terms and definitions, and does not allow the unreasonable or unbalanced pressing of the definition of any part of a complex to dislocate the coherence of the complex regarded as a whole. God cannot have defects arising from His qualities; the above enumerated attributes must be interpreted in mutual relationship, and none of them must be interpreted in isolation from the others in such a way as to lead to absurdities.

This attitude is characteristic of Nestorius; unfortunately, he often expects his readers instinctively to comprehend fine distinctions which are quite obvious to himself. For example, the attribute of omnipotence must not lead us to suppose that God would do things contrary to the general character of His nature. Omnipotence means ability to do all things, but it does not mean that God would do all things which He is able to do, and we must not imagine God doing anything contrary to the general character of His nature; nor can we imagine Him doing anything which would impair Himself. Nestorius makes this clear in disposing of one of Sophronius' arguments. Sophronius says: "It appertains to the omnipotent and infinite nature to be able to do everything; by its will then all other things are limited while it is not limited by anything, and it, as God, can do what cannot be [done] by any one else. For it cannot be [created] by a nature or a cause greater than itself, by which it possesses [the property] of being and of not being God" (B. 14); and: "For he who says 'God in truth' attributes to him the [quality] of being able [to do] everything; for everything that he wishes he does. He wished indeed to become flesh and he became flesh, not the *schêma* of the flesh but the nature of the flesh, that is truly flesh" (B. 19). To this Nestorius replies: "In truth hast thou spoken, and we ought not to dispute what has been said in truth; for indeed [thou hast said] that God is all-powerful and does all that he wishes. And because of this his *ousia* became not flesh, for that which becomes flesh in its nature ceases to be able to do everything, in that it is flesh and not God. For it appertains to God to be able to effect everything, and not to the flesh; for it cannot do everything that it wishes. But in remaining God he wills not everything nor again does he wish not to become God so as to make himself not to be God. For he is God in that he exists always and can do everything that he wishes, and not in that he is able to make himself not to be God; for he into whose *ousia* the nature of the flesh has entered makes himself not to be God, and further cannot do everything that he wishes" (B. 20). There is nothing God could not do, but there are many things He would not do. Again, there may be things contrary to logical possibility: "But it is impossible that [he should make] that which is unmade and that which was not from that which was" (B. 39).

The qualities attributed to God have certain consequences in our understanding of and definition of His ousia, nature and prosôpon. All ousias as such are unknowable, but they are revealed, more or less completely, through their natures as manifested in their instantaneous and durative prosôpa. In the case of God, His ousia is unknowable, and His nature, being infinite and eternal, can only be partially revealed in a Universe which is finite and temporal. It will thus be seen that there is a fundamental and unbridgeable difference between the ousia and nature of God and all other ousias and natures. In particular:

1. The ousia and nature of God, being eternal and unchangeable, cannot be created, transformed or annihilated.

2. The ousia and nature of God cannot take part in integrations or disintegrations; that is to say, God can never enter into ousic or natural union. For, if we were to suppose Him to do so, we could only deem the result to be the virtual annihilation of the other ousia and nature, since nothing can be added to the ousia and nature of God, which is infinite and without needs, and we cannot suppose His nature to accept any imposed limitations.

3. The definition of the ousia of God need not be different from the definition of any other ousia: it is simply that which underlies the existence of God—God as He is in Himself absolutely. The ousia of God cannot be further defined or known. But the definition of the nature of God evidently cannot be the same as that of other natures: "For the definition and circumscription of all nature is that in which it has to be" (B. 56). God being infinite and omnipotent cannot be subjected to circumscription or compulsion. The application of the term 'nature' in the case of God must, therefore, take a somewhat different connotation from its application in the case of all things else. All created natures are circumscribed and compelled by the nature they have been given, whereas God, eternal and infinite, is what He is, without compulsion or necessity, and His nature is dependent on nothing other than Himself: "Together with this [there is] another absurdity which they predicate in limiting God himself by the necessity of nature" (B. 124). The description of God's nature, if fully known, would be the description of what God is, not of what He has to be. In the case of God, therefore, we may define His nature as 'that in which He is', as opposed, in the case of any other nature, to 'that in which it has to be'. It will be seen that this definition of the nature of God not only discriminates it from all other natures, but also accounts for the impossibility of the nature of God entering into natural union with any other nature. Natural union produces a new nature, a natural unity, which, if it is other than the nature of God, is a circumscribed and compelled nature. It is inconceivable that God should thus relinquish any of His attributes, for, to that extent, He would thus cease to be God. If, on the other hand, the new nature, resulting from

the natural union of the nature of God and any other nature, retained all the attributes of the nature of God, the other nature would virtually have ceased to exist, so that the so-called union would be nothing but the annihilation of the other nature.

The prosôpon of God cannot be fully considered until we have considered the problem of the Trinity, but a few preliminary observations may be made:

1. The autogenous prosôpon of God, whether instantaneous or durative, cannot be in any way analogous to the autogenous prosôpa of other natures. In that God is by His nature invisible, His autogenous prosôpon would be invisible: "No man hath seen God at any time" (John i. 18). All that can be said of the autogenous prosôpon of God is that it would be the self-manifestation of God in His qualities, and our acknowledgment of them: "Man indeed is known by the human *prosôpon*, that is, by the *schêma* of the body and by the likeness, but God by the name which is more excellent than all names and by the adoration of all creation and by the confession [of him] as God" (B. 89).

2. On the other hand, God can quite easily manifest Himself by allogenous prosôpa. God can create any instrument He wishes: "For of nothing the maker easily assembles the *ousia*" (B. 39), and can use this instrument as His allogenous prosôpon. Thus one of the unique powers of God is the ability to produce an allogenous prosôpon without using any formerly existing ousia. When the purpose of the allogenous prosôpon has been served, He can presumably destroy it, resolving it into that nothingness from which it was created. This gives a satisfactory explanation of all types of theophany, whether the prosôpon is of human schêma or otherwise. It will thus be clear what meaning is to be attached to such expressions as "This is God", or "It was the Lord". The phenomena referred to may have been visible and may have been entirely due to God, and truly revealing Him; but, obviously, no visible phenomena could arise directly from the ousia of God. They could only arise by God revealing Himself in allogenous prosôpa. Examples abound in the Old Testament:

for example, the Pillar of Cloud by day, the Pillar of Fire by night, the Burning Bush, the Voice heard by Samuel. All these are self-manifestations of God through allogenous prosôpa, presenting the schêmata of the visible elements in the various syntaxes: "And wherein he took the *schêma* of a man or of fire, it is said that God appeared or that one saw God; and in another place, that *God gave the law*, and again: *by means of the angels the law was given*. They are not lies nor further are they contradictory one to another; it is not that he calls the angels God nor again that an angel calls himself God; but, because he appeared by means of the angels, both are truly said, both that God appeared by means of the angels in the fire of a bush and that by means of it God appeared unto him" (B. 77).

3. It is also possible for God to make use of a man as His allogenous prosôpon. This is one way of approach to the mechanism of prophecy. God by omnipotence or by the willing submission of the prophet makes use of the prophet as His allogenous prosôpon. It is this fact which justifies a prophet saying, "Thus saith the Lord".

4. In that ousic and natural union involves prosôpic union (see p. 105), and as God cannot enter into natural unions, it follows that He cannot enter into a prosôpic union of the type underlaid by a natural union. There may, however, be other types of prosôpic union.

All the above assumes the unity of God, but Nestorius must find place in his metaphysic for a doctrine of the Trinity. In order to remain consistent in his rigid method of analysis in terms of ousia and nature, and at the same time to remain orthodox, Nestorius was bound to postulate that the Godhead was one ousia with one corresponding nature. This postulate is one of Nestorius' fundamentals, and God must always be thought of as one ousia and nature. However the Trinity is to be defined, there must be no breaking of the homogeneity of the divine ousia and nature: that is inviolable, and however we may think of God the Father, God the Son and God the Holy Ghost, we must not think of Them as differing one from the other in ousia or nature.

Nestorius emphasizes this in many passages. As to oneness of ousia: "If then God the Word, who is consubstantial with the Father and the Holy Spirit . . ." (B. 54). As to oneness of nature: "What after all is the nature in this natural union which you predicate? Is it that of the Father and of the Son and of the Holy Spirit, an impassible nature, immortal, eternal and without needs?" (B. 54). As to oneness of both ousia and nature: "But they are not one thing and another but one only in *ousia* and in nature, without divisions, without separation, without distinction in all the things which appertain by nature" (B. 143).

All the qualities of Godhead are consequently to be ascribed to every member of the Trinity, as there can be no discrimination of the qualities and powers of the same ousia and nature. The attributes of God (pp. 121–123) are illustrated by quotations referring to God alone, without discrimination as Father, Son or Holy Spirit. But quotations could be given for almost all these attributes showing that Nestorius ascribes them in exactly the same manner to each member of the Trinity separately. For example: "What after all is the nature in this natural union which you predicate? Is it that of the Father and of the Son and of the Holy Spirit, an impassible nature, immortal, eternal and without needs?" (B. 54); "Or, by granting that in nature naturally, by a passible sensibility, he accepted sufferings, you evacuate him of impassibility and of immortality, and of being consubstantial with the Father, because he acquired a change of nature, seeing that [the Son] accepts and [the Father] accepts not [these sufferings]. Or if he had not had one change of *ousia* in his nature, while that of the Father and the Holy Spirit was without needs and accepted neither suffering nor death, he would have been deprived of being God in that he was not in everything of an *ousia* without needs" (B. 57–58); "I have kept without blemish the faith of the three hundred and eighteen who were assembled at Nicæa, saying that God the Word is unchangeable [and] immortal, that he is continuously that which he is in the eternity of the Father. He was not [formed] of things which existed not nor of any other *hypostasis*, and there was not when he was not. Eternally [exists] the Father, eternally the Son, eternally the Holy Spirit" (B. 265). To the Nestorian metaphysic this homogeneity of the ousia and nature of the Trinity is axiomatic, and it is obvious that insistence on this point is bound to present great difficulties in considering the person of Jesus Christ. If God is eternal, uncreated, unmade, immortal, unchangeable, incorruptible, without needs, impassible, omnipotent, infinite, incomprehensible and invisible, how could Jesus Christ be God?

The Nestorian emphasis on the oneness of the ousia and nature of God makes the concept of any but a Sabellian Trinity very difficult. Obviously, God could reveal Himself by means of allogenous prosôpa, and indeed has done so. But to reduce such prosôpa to three classes and to imagine that the three classes constitute the Trinity is mere Sabellianism. Manifestations of God such as the theophanies in the Old Testament would thus be classed as prosôpa of God the Father. The durative prosôpon of Jesus Christ would be classed as a prosôpon of God the Word, and manifestations such as the Dove at the Baptism, the rushing wind at Pentecost, and God's power working through the Church and the Saints, would be classed as prosôpa of the Holy Spirit. Nestorius not being primarily concerned with the problem of the Trinity does not give any clear exposition of his views. It can only be said that he is equally insistent on the unity of God and on a real Trinity as opposed to Sabellianism: "Although they are not distinguished in nature but remain always in their being, we say that the Son is adored with the Father and with the Holy Spirit, in order that we may not, like Sabellius, make the *prosôpa* without *hypostasis* and without *ousia*" (B. 316). Cf. also B. 64. He uses the word ousia only for the common essence of the Godhead, and he uses the words prosôpon and hypostasis in connection with the three constituents of the Trinity. But, as do others, he uses the words with a necessarily different significance from that which he attaches to them when using them in other connections.

This difference must be recognized and allowed for. Whenever the words prosôpon and hypostasis are used, we

I

must determine whether their ordinary connotation applies, or whether the special connotation applicable to the Trinity is indicated.

As we have already seen, in ordinary usage Nestorius makes ousia and hypostasis practically synonymous. But he concurs in the already established convention whereby the one ousia of God is supposed to comprise three hypostases. When, as so often, Nestorius expects us to grasp ideas he never troubles to explicate, we must by trial and error devise a coherent scheme to fit what slender data he gives. A view of the Trinity, in keeping with the Nestorian metaphysic, with necessary special provisions to meet the special peculiarities of the problem, would be somewhat as follows:

The Godhead is one ousia with one corresponding nature. This one ousia and nature represents the totality of all that is God, and is self-consistent and indiscriminable. But the multiplicity of the divine activity involves not only successive exercising of the powers and functions of the divine nature, but also concurrent exercisings. It has been seen that a man's nature includes powers which can be exercised successively but not simultaneously. But God, for the fulfilment of His divine purposes and for the inner harmony of His divine being, needs simultaneously to function in parts of His nature which, in ordinary cases, would represent successive phases. Thus there is always in the Godhead creative and sustaining impulse; there is always the urge to bring into willing harmony with Himself that to which He has given volition; there is always a surging forth of Himself in aiding power to those who will respond thereto. These phases of the divine nature are not successive: they co-exist, and to those three phases it is necessary to apply some distinguishing term. We could think of three ousias working in the closest harmony with one another. But that would be tritheism. We could think of one ousia assuming the successive phases as and when desired. But that would be Sabellianism. In terms of the Nestorian metaphysic, Sabellianism means that God, of one ousia and nature, manifests Himself, from time to time, in a series of allogenous prosôpa, which, according to that part of His

nature which He is exercising, may be called God the
Father, God the Son and God the Holy Spirit.

To avoid these opposed errors, tritheism and Sabellianism, we may suppose that the divine ousia, one and
indiscriminable, must, both for its outer functioning and
its inner harmony, always maintain within itself three complementary phases of its nature. These three phases may
be characterized as creative, redemptive, and directive—
not that the terms need be exhaustively significant. Within
the one ousia, these three phases of its nature simultaneously
co-exist. The ousia of God is one, but the ousia exists in
three simultaneous phases. Each phase has as its basis
ousia of God, and it is a matter of indifference what ousia
of God, for all divine ousia is one. We can always discriminate the phase, but the ousia is not ousia of the phase,
it is ousia of God. Yet the phase is the manifestation of the
ousia of God, and possesses all the powers and qualities of
God. If we could isolate a phase at a given moment of time,
it would be ousia of God in that part of the divine nature
represented by that phase. But the ousia is not special to
the phase: it is ousia of God; nor is the phase special to the
ousia: the same ousia can equally subsist in the other phases.
What can such a phase be called? If the phases were directly
perceptible, we could call them simultaneously existing
prosôpa of the one ousia. But the members of the Trinity
are not directly perceptible to man: an allogenous prosôpon
is necessary. So if the three phases are to be styled prosôpa,
it must be with a special connotation; the term prosôpon
would have to mean the autogenous element in the durative
prosôpon proper to the phase and providing the continuity
of the durative prosôpon, whether, instantaneously or for
a given period, autogenous or allogenous. The allogenous
prosôpa of God as creator and sustainer of the Universe,
for example, presuppose divine ousia in the creative phase;
the allogenous prosôpon "Dove", on the other hand, presupposes the divine ousia in the directive phase. The continuity of each phase is due to the autogenous element in
its durative prosôpon. The continuity is actual, and is in
fact co-continuous with the durative prosôpon of that phase
of the divine ousia; using, if we wish, the analogy of strands

and cable (cf. pp. 107–108), the strand of continuity is the autogenous element in the durative prosôpon, and the other strands are the various other elements in the durative prosôpon when it has become for a period allogenous. With this in mind, a real and special sense attaches to the term prosôpon as applied to the Trinity. Each of these prosôpa has its existence in the ousia of God, and each prosôpon has ousia of God in a certain phase underlying it. That is, ousia of God is hypostatic (in the root sense of 'underlying') to each phase, or each phase has as its hypostasis ousia of God. We thus arrive at the rationale of applying the term hypostasis to the continuity of each phase: there are three hypostases corresponding to the three prosôpa, but there is one ousia.[1] The terms have an obvious slight difference in connotation; hypostasis emphasizes the continuity of the ousia underlying a particular phase—it is the ousia for the time being in that phase; prosôpon emphasizes the continuity of the ability of the phase to become manifest, a potential ability when the prosôpon is autogenous, a realized ability when the prosôpon is allogenous.[2]

These concepts of hypostasis and prosôpon as applied to the Trinity make it clear how confusion arose between Nestorius and Cyril. We have already seen that, in ordinary usage, Nestorius makes ousia and hypostasis almost synonymous, and only in Trinitarian use would he recognize a hypostasis definable otherwise than as an ousia, usually a particular ousia. Using the word in relation to the Trinity, for Nestorius it would mean the autogenous element in one of the three durative prosôpa of the Trinity, each

---

[1] We may see a parallel but developed view of the Trinity in another Antiochian, Theodoret of Cyrus, who, unlike Nestorius, formulated his teaching on this subject. Theodoret's views are admirably summarized by Sellers in the course of an article in the *Journal of Theological Studies*, vol. xlvi, No. 183–4 (July–October, 1945), in which he demonstrates that the *Expositio Rectæ Fidei* formerly attributed to Justin Martyr is really a work of Theodoret of Cyrus. Sellers says (pp. 148–149): "After an introductory chapter, the author" (i.e., Theodoret) "affirms that there is one God, made known in the Father, the Son, and the Holy Spirit (c. ii), and that their difference is seen in their 'manner of subsisting' (ὁ τρόπος τῆς ὑπάρξεως), the terms Ἀγέννητον, Γεννητόν, and Ἐκπορευτόν referring, not to the divine ousia, which is signified by the name 'God', but to the three hypostases, which, while possessing sameness of essence, differ in this way (c. iii)."

[2] For footnote, see p. 147.

prosôpon necessarily having divine ousia in one of its simultaneously existing phases hypostatic to it; in any case the word would need comprehending in a special sense. To Nestorius prosôpon would seem more appropriate than hypostasis, though he concurred in the use of the word hypostasis, tacitly recognizing its special connotation. Cyril, on the other hand, used the term hypostasis to describe any one member of the Trinity, in so doing placing emphasis on particularity and individuality rather than upon the concept of ousia. This difference in concept is most significant. For Nestorius hypostasis, even when applied to the Trinity, means primarily ousia—the ousia hypostatic to a particular prosôpon. He is willing to call a member of the Trinity a hypostasis, but he prefers prosôpon. Each word, however, must be understood in the special sense—the Trinity comprises three prosôpa or hypostases, by which we mean that the ousia of the Trinity exists in three complementary simultaneous phases, each of which manifests itself as it desires in appropriate allogenous prosôpa. The continuity of each phase depends on the autogenous element in the durative prosôpon, and that autogenous element is necessarily ousia of God, the ousia of God which happens at the moment to be hypostatic to the particular phase. If we know what we mean, we may call the phases either prosôpa or hypostases; but it is fairly evident why prosôpon seemed to Nestorius the more appropriate word: the emphasis is on the continuity of phase and manifestation rather than on the ousia.

There was a moment when Nestorius glimpsed hope of mutual understanding. In regard to the Trinity, did Cyril after all really mean by hypostasis what Nestorius meant by prosôpon? "Dost thou wish to regard a *hypostasis* as a *prosôpon*, as we speak of one *ousia* of the divinity and three *hypostases* and understand *prosôpa* by *hypostases*? Thou callest therefore the *prosôpic* union *hypostatic*" (B. 229). But the hope soon faded: "Yet" (that is, according to Cyril) "the union was not of the *prosôpa* but of the natures. For 'diverse are the natures which have come into a true union, yet from both of them [is formed] one Christ' " (ibid.). This, of course, dispels any hope of reconciliation along such lines,

for if Cyril posited true union of the natures, that is, presumably, natural union, it would involve hypostatic union
in the sense of ousic and natural union, not hypostatic
union in the sense of prosôpic union. It is therefore to be
concluded that Cyril did not mean by hypostasis what
Nestorius meant by prosôpon, even with regard to the
Trinity.

In a consistent Nestorian metaphysic we may refer to the
Trinity as three prosôpa or three hypostases, but only if
we bear in mind the special connotation of the terms. We
may think of the manifestations of God as necessarily
underlaid by ousia in its phases, and thus think primarily of
the manifestations as hypostases; or we may think of the
ousia in its phases manifesting itself, and thus think primarily of the manifestations as prosôpa. Thus in the Trinity,
and the Trinity only, we admit three hypostases in one
ousia; and in the Trinity, and the Trinity only, we admit
three prosôpa which are not objective unless allogenous.

Nestorius never troubled to define his terms, but an
examination of the relevant passages shows that they can
be consistently interpreted by applying the concepts set out
in the above paragraphs. Some passages may now be quoted
showing his use of the terms and illustrating their interdependence.

Consider B. 316: "In so far as they are distinguished in
the *prosôpon*, although they are not distinguished in nature
but remain always in their being, we say that the Son is
adored with the Father and with the Holy Spirit, in order
that we may not, like Sabellius, make the *prosôpa* without
hypostasis and without *ousia*. For he who would suppress
[the saying] that the Son is adored with the Father suppresses [the saying] that the Son exists in *hypostasis*." This
passage implies the oneness of the ousia and nature of God,
"they are not distinguished in nature but remain always in
their being"; recognizes the distinction in prosôpon, "they
are distinguished in the *prosôpon*"; and goes on to imply
that each prosôpon has both hypostasis and ousia, "that we
may not, like Sabellius, make the *prosôpa* without *hypostasis*
and without *ousia*." The implication of each word is here
to be recognized; each prosôpon is underlaid by ousia of

God, ousia of God hypostatic to the phase revealed by that prosôpon. The prosôpon has an underlying ousia, and, still more particularly, an underlying hypostasis: the ousia implies God, but the hypostasis implies some one member of the Trinity. The next sentence is significant in that it brings out the distinction between the use of prosôpon and hypostasis as applied to the Trinity: "For he who would suppress [the saying] that the Son is adored with the Father suppresses [the saying] that the Son exists in *hypostasis*." If the Father and the Son were nothing more than prosôpa of the same ousia, their adoration would be one. But though there is only one ousia, the distinction between Father and Son is more than merely prosôpic: the ousia, though one, is ever hypostatic to the three prosôpa, so that Father and Son are distinct in prosôpon and hypostasis, understanding hypostasis in the special sense applicable to the Trinity. Distinguishing the hypostases, the Trinity is not completely contemplated unless all three hypostases are included in the adoration: we worship God in one ousia; but in contemplating God as Father or Son, we are contemplating one hypostasis, and if we contemplate hypostases, to worship God we must adore the Son with the Father (and the Holy Ghost), that in the three hypostases we may adore the totality of the ousia of Godhead. Nevertheless, each hypostasis is God, with all the powers and attributes of God in its ousia; the existence of the three hypostases involves no limitations to the ousia. Any divine prosôpon is a prosôpon of the ousia of God, as well as a prosôpon of a hypostasis of God. The distinction, indeed, is in the mode of approach: we worship the totality of Godhead when we worship Christ as God. But if we worship Christ consciously contemplating Him as God redemptive, we are contemplating the ousia as in that hypostasis, and though the hypostasis is of the ousia, the ousia subsists in the three hypostases, and its totality can only be contemplated when we include all three hypostases in our thought.

The terms prosôpon and hypostasis are brought into interesting parallel in B. 326. Nestorius quotes with approval that the members of the Trinity are "distinct only in the *prosôpa*", and goes on to say that "the division lies only in the *hypostases.*" There is no difficulty here when it is borne in mind that the objective distinction of the prosôpa depends on the one ousia in simultaneous phases hypostatic to each prosôpon: each prosôpon corresponds with one hypostasis; and as only prosôpa are directly perceptible, the distinction is only in the prosôpa; and as each prosôpon is simply the revelation of each corresponding hypostasis, the division is only in the hypostases.

When no exact distinctions are called for, Nestorius usually prefers the term prosôpon for distinguishing the members of the Trinity: "In the Trinity, [there is] there one *ousia* of three *prosôpa*, but three *prosôpa* of one *ousia*" (B. 342); "The *prosôpon* is one thing and the *ousia* another, even as [it is] in respect to the Father and the Son, [who are] one thing and another indeed in the *prosôpon* but not one thing and another in the divinity" (B. 361); "Thus [it is] that God is indicative of the nature but the Father and the Son and the Holy Spirit of the *prosôpa*. For this reason the divinity indeed [is] one but the *prosôpa* three; for God is Father and God Son and God Holy Spirit" (B. 425). The next sentence, "The *prosôpa* are not without *ousia*", is anti-Sabellian, and in this context means that each prosôpon has ousia of God hypostatic to it in particular.

Though Nestorius prefers to use prosôpon of the members of the Trinity, the term hypostasis presents no difficulty, as he quotes with approval passages in which it is used: "It is not indeed as though one divinity were divided, but the Divine Scripture, for the proof and the likeness of the Trinity proves that [there is] one power and that it is distinguished for each single one of the *hypostases*" (B. 335). "One divinity" implies one ousia; "one power" implies one nature; "distinguished for each single one of the *hypostases*" implies the distinction in the prosôpa of the simultaneously existing ousic phases, each of which is hypostatic to a particular prosôpon. This is the concept underlying the use of the term hypostasis in the special Trinitarian sense, and accounts for hypostasis being preferred in cases where the emphasis is on the reality of the underlying ousia, the divine ousia hypostatic to some one particular member of the Trinity. This exact use occurs in the following sentences, which are quoted with approval by Nestorius: "He is the Word in nature and in *hypostasis*" (B. 149); "He is by nature and *hypostasis* homoousian with the Father" (B. 150).

Nevertheless, Nestorius certainly prefers the term prosôpon. There are advantages and disadvantages in the use of each term. If we use hypostasis, we think primarily of the ousia, and cannot particularize it without thinking of the corresponding durative prosôpon: it is 'ousia of God hypostatic to one of the phases, manifesting through a durative prosôpon', it being remembered that the durative prosôpon is only objectively perceptible when allogenous. If we use prosôpon, we think primarily of the manifestation, realizing that the manifestation is based on ousia of God in one of its three phases: the objectivity of the prosôpon is due to allogenous elements, while its continuity is due to the durative autogenous element, which is ousia of God hypostatic to the durative prosôpon. Either term is permissible if used with understanding, though there are slight differences in emphasis when one is used rather than the other. In some contexts the one term may be preferable and in other contexts the other. But as with ousia and nature, the reality is one; whether we use prosôpa or hypostases of the members of the Trinity we mean 'the manifestation of the Godhead in three simultaneous and mutually complementary phases, each phase revealing itself in a durative prosôpon only objectively perceptible when allogenous, and each phase underlaid by ousia of God hypostatic to it in particular'. Though we know that a Trinitarian hypostasis underlies the prosôpon by which any member of the Trinity reveals Himself, our immediate understanding is of the prosôpon, not of the hypostasis. So though we may speak in terms of hypostasis, our thought, unless consciously metaphysical, is in terms of prosôpon: "We speak of one *ousia* of the divinity and three *hypostases* and" (for all practical thinking) "understand *prosôpa* by *hypostases*" (B. 229).

It is now desirable to consider the precise meaning attached by Nestorius to the word ὁμοούσιος (*homoousian*, 'the same in *ousia*'), as applied to Christ being *homoousian* with

God on the one hand and with man on the other. Bethune-Baker's valuable study of this word[1] provides a useful background, but as with so many other words Nestorius' usage is not quite in line with that of others, and it is his usage we must understand if we are to follow his arguments.

Just as the ousia and nature of God need careful definition in view of their infinity, so that the definitions applicable to other ousias and natures need modification when applied to the ousia and nature of God, so also the word homoousian cannot be defined in exactly the same way when applied to God as when applied to things other than God.

In the case of things other than God, the concept of total or general ousia is useful. All particular ousias which would have to be included in arriving at the total ousia of that type, or all particular ousias which could be classified under the same general type, can truly be said to be homoousian one to another. Thus all lumps of pure iron are homoousian to one another, because the total ousia 'iron' would include them all; alternatively, they are all examples of the general ousia 'iron'. Again, any two men are homoousian to one another, because the total ousia 'all men who have ever lived or will live' includes them both; alternatively, they are both examples of the general ousia 'man'. Jesus Christ must be truly man in such manner that He can be truly described as homoousian to all mankind.

But in the case of God, the nature of His ousia includes the attributes of infinity, omnipotence, and being maker of all, so that no other ousia could possibly be homoousian to it: otherwise there would be two Gods, each of whom was infinite, omnipotent, and maker of all, which is unthinkable. In the case of God, therefore, the word homoousian applies, and applies only, to the consistency and continuity of His own ousia as manifesting itself in time and space, in infinity and eternity. God experienced in one place or time is a revelation of the same ousia as God experienced in some other place or time: the ousia of God is one and indiscriminable. God, in all times and in all places, is homoousian with Himself. The unity and continuity of all that

[1] *The Meaning of Homoousios* (*Texts and Studies*, edited by J. A. Robinson, vol. viii, No. 1).

is God is implied in anything which can be said to be homoousian with Him. It follows that nothing can be homoousian with God except Himself, so that to say that Jesus Christ is homoousian with God the Father is simply to say that Jesus Christ is God. It is important to recognize that the idea of unbroken continuity is prominently in Nestorius' mind. The divine ousia in Jesus Christ is unbrokenly continuous with all else that is ousia of Godhead. There never was and never could be any detachment or separation: "Now for those who predicate the union in a change there follows in any case an addition in *ousia* as well as in *prosôpon*. The *ousia* indeed, which became flesh out of God the Word, was added to the Trinity, and it is evident that this *prosôpon* is a part detached and that it is conceived in detachment; or it became the nature of the flesh [emanating] from the *ousia* of God the Word in detachment, an addition took place . . ." (B. 34). The point is that 'ousia of God the Word in detachment' is no longer simply 'ousia of God the Word': it has become a distinct ousia, necessarily lacking many of the attributes of the ousia of God, such as infinity, and if it were to return to God the Word it would constitute an addition. The same idea underlies B. 67: "Since then there is only one divinity and lordship and authority and knowledge and opinion and power of God the Father and of the Son, by means of whom everything came from the Father and without whom nothing at all which has come into being came into being, for what reason does he apply only to God the Word *he became flesh*, not *he made the flesh* but *The Word became* flesh, even he who was with God? And said he not of God the Father *he who is with the Father*? For *he became* and *he made* both belong unto him, since they make no division." 'One divinity and lordship and authority and knowledge and opinion and power of God the Father and of the Son' signifies one nature and ousia; 'they make no division' implies continuity of the ousia. For the hypostases of the Trinity to be homoousian to one another, their continuity and mutual interrelationship in the same ousia must be maintained. As applied to the hypostases of the Trinity, the word 'homoousian' implies that the common ousia underlying all the hypostases is one and the same, uniform, continuous and indiscriminable. The divine ousia underlying, hypostatic to, the prosôpon of God the Father is continuous with and indiscriminable from the divine ousia underlying, hypostatic to, the prosôpon of God the Word. God the Father and God the Word and God the Holy Ghost are homoousian to one another, and Jesus Christ, God the Word incarnate, is therefore homoousian with God the Father. We may if we wish picture the one divine ousia as ebbing and flowing among the three hypostases, just as we might imagine the water in a pump-operated fountain, some always rising, some falling, some in the pool. The same water, the same states, the states always existent, the water always existent, water always underlying the states, but indiscriminable portions of the same water underlying each particular state. Analogies are dangerous and liable to mislead, and must not be pressed. The points are: the ousia is one and continuous, unbroken and indiscriminable; it exists in the three hypostases, but no portion of ousia is special to any one hypostasis: the ousia is ousia of God, whose nature demands for its inner harmony and outward expression three mutually responding coexisting phases, the three hypostases with their corresponding prosôpa. Except in the Trinity, hypostasis (in the Nestorian metaphysic) is the same as ousia, one ousia has its one corresponding nature and the nature is revealed in its prosôpon, which in its duration passes through various phases, autogenous and (in the case of an animate nature) allogenous. But in the Trinity we have to use the term in a special sense, recognizing one ousia with three simultaneous prosôpa, the ousia hypostatic to each prosôpon being termed the corresponding hypostasis, and each prosôpon having its own phases, autogenous and allogenous.

It should perhaps be remarked that God being infinite is not limited as to His prosôpa, except according to His own will. So that while we admit the three hypostases with their corresponding prosôpa, we have to recognize that the prosôpa are not well definable and finite like other prosôpa. The durative prosôpon of God the Father is the continuity of His self-manifestation, and at any moment the instantaneous prosôpon of God the Father is the totality of His self-manifestation at that moment. The prosôpon includes what He is as God the Father, the autogenous element necessarily and always present in His prosôpon; for an allogenous prosôpon must contain an autogenous element arising from its own ousia functioning according to its nature, which element provides the unbroken continuity of the prosôpon —its durative hypostasis, its durative ousia. But on account of His infinity and omnipotence, God the Father can manifest Himself, if He so wishes, simultaneously in two or more allogenous prosôpa—theophanies—so that the instantaneous prosôpon of God the Father is the totality of His self-manifestation at that moment, which may include a number of allogenous prosôpa. This is another important matter in which the nature of the ousia of God involves modification in our understanding of terms; but the modifications are all such as logically arise from the attributes of God and the infinity of His ousia and nature.

God's attribute of being infinite, and therefore omnipresent, involves a clear understanding of the meaning of the word 'in'. This word occurs in many passages of great moment in Driver and Hodgson's translation of *The Bazaar*, just as 'dans' or 'en' occurs on the corresponding pages in Nau. In each case the translators are in the great majority of instances thus rendering the Syriac preposition ܒ ('b'). But ܒ in the Syriac is itself a translation of whatever was written in the original Greek, and while in perhaps the majority of cases this may have been ἐν, this is by no means true in all instances. Syriac is poor in prepositions, and those in common use consequently have to cover a wide general and idiomatic use. The difficulty of translating ܒ will be seen by reference to Payne Smith's "Thesaurus Syriacus",[1] which gives an admirable analysis of its main uses. He summarizes the usages under eight main headings: (1) de loco in quo aliquid est vel esse cogitatur, (2) de rebus inter se conjunctis, sive societate, sive tempore, (3) de moto in locum, (4) de statu et conditione in qua aliquis vel aliquid versatur, aliquidve facit, tum externa, tum interna, (5) de ratione et instrumento, cujus ope aliquid perficitur, (6) de

[1] i. 429–432.

causa, (7) de pretio, et causa materiali, (8) de causa finali. He adds instances of rarer and more exceptional uses.), then, may have to serve to indicate meanings differentiated in Latin by the following prepositions: in with the ablative or accusative, cum, inter, secundum, per, ob, propter, a (ab), coram. Cases may even be quoted where the Latin equivalent would seem to be de, contra or e (ex). A corresponding Greek list would give ἐν, εἰς, σύν, μετά with the genitive, κατά with the accusative, διά with the accusative or genitive, πρός with the dative, or even περί with the genitive, πρός with the accusative, or ἐκ (ἐξ). We must be cautious in endeavouring to simplify the problem. Nestle, for example, states that) means 'in, von Ort, Zeit, Zustand, Ursache, Instrument' ('in, of place, time, circumstance, reason, instrument').[1] It is perhaps better to keep in mind the main meanings as in, with and by, remembering that they are to be interpreted somewhat widely.

However, it must not escape us that) in the Bazaar is not the word of Nestorius, but of his translator. In the great majority of cases Nestorius no doubt originally wrote ἐν, though the other possibilities must not be overlooked. But ἐν itself is a word of wider meaning than either the Latin or English in or the French dans or en. Although in the latest edition of Liddell and Scott's Greek-English Lexicon[2] an attempt is made to classify the meanings of ἐν under the radical senses of in of place and motion (in and into), so that ἐν can be classified as in of (1) place, (2) state, condition, position, (3) instrument, means, manner, (4) time, (5) number, it still remains true that both in English equivalent and in concept ἐν may convey meanings as varied as within, upon, at, by, amongst, with, by means of, as to. So that even when it can certainly be assumed that Nestorius used ἐν, there is often difficulty in sensing the precise shade of meaning he attached to it. One thing can be 'in' another in many different senses, as Nestorius himself indicates: "For the [words] He is and He dwelt are of necessity to be confessed and interpreted by us according to the will of God. God indeed is in all creatures; for in

---

[1] Nestle, Syriac Grammar (English translation by R. S. Kennedy), p. 139.
[2] New edition, 1940, revised by H. S. Jones and R. McKenzie, i. 551-552.

him we are and thereby is it defined that, although thus he is verily in all, he is said to have dwelt in some men; but in regard to others it is even said that he is not their God. And it is not said that he dwelt in all men in like manner, but according to his love; in some of us it is said that he only dwelt in a composition as in a house, as in the believers, while in others, although he is acting, yet [he acts] not in like manner but to a greater or less degree; in others as in all the apostles and in others as in the prophets and in others as in teachers and in others according to the division of gifts. In this one and in that and in another he dwells, and he acts also in all; and all of them are not equal to all nor like one another, but [all are] according to the love of him who dwells in them" (B. 82). Nestorius thus recognizes that 'in' can imply many differing degrees of mutual relation, from mere conspatiality to natural unification. We may conveniently recognize at least four degrees of increasing closeness of relationship indicated by 'in':

(1) 'In' with reference to general circumstances, which may be rendered '*in (circumstantially)*'.

This meaning is illustrated in the following examples: "He was revealed in the things of men" (B. 30). (This sentence occurs in a context of great interest as to the word 'in', and will be considered shortly.) "In a human manner of life" (B. 118). "In moral life" and "In the manner of life of man" (B. 140). (In this case also the context is considered below.)

(2) 'In' with reference to mere conspatiality: two things sharing what may be regarded as the same defined portion of space, usually in such a manner that the one may be regarded as spatially contained by the other, or that the two may be regarded as intertwined or intermingled within the same space, though without either natural or syntactic unification. This may be rendered '*in (spatially)*'. God, being infinite and omnipresent, is of course in all things in this manner. In the case of human beings, this inevitable conspatiality with God may vary in degree from unawareness or indifference on the human side to loving communion in all degrees from rare occasionalness to complete self-surrender. There is a definite line, though perhaps difficult

to define, where, from God's side, conspatial communion
with a human subject passes into use, voluntarily on both
sides, of the human subject as His allogenous prosôpon,
the case then becoming as under (3) below.

The following examples illustrate the use of 'in' spatially:
"For he who dwells [in anything] is far removed from that
in which he dwells and accepts neither the nature nor the
name of that wherein he dwells" (B. 51). "God indeed is in
all creatures; for in him we are and thereby it is defined
that, although thus he is verily in all, he is said to have
dwelt in some men; but in regard to others it is even said
that he is not their God" (B. 82). "In some of us it is said
that he only dwelt in a composition as in a house" (B. 82).

(3) 'In' with reference to the interrelation of the constituents of a syntax, which may with most generality be
rendered '*in (syntactically)*'. In the case of an animate being
entering voluntarily into a syntax, the quasi-prosôpon of
the syntax thus becoming for the time being the allogenous
prosôpon of the animate being, it is evidently further true
that the animate being is in the syntax voluntarily and
prosôpically. In that an animate being when its prosôpon
is autogenous is prosôpically in its own nature, and can
be truly said to be voluntarily in circumstances and spaces,
it is not advisable to use the terms 'in (prosôpically)' and
'in (voluntarily)' without linking them with some other
qualifying adverb.

The following examples illustrate the use of 'in' syntactically. In many of the cases voluntarily and prosôpically
are also implied: "So he became incarnate in one man for
all men who are of the [same] nature, since he was in their
nature, and in it he spoke to all men, as if he spoke in his
own nature" (B. 31). ('He' is God the Word. The first three
cases show 'in' meaning 'in syntactically, voluntarily and
prosôpically', whereas the fourth case is simply 'in naturally'
(see (4) below).) "He took his own *prosôpon* and not another,
not for distinction but for the union of his own *prosôpon*
and that in which he became incarnate" (B. 34). "As he
knows our nature he has expounded unto us in our
very nature that which none of mankind has ever seen"
(B. 73-74). "It is not, in fact, wonderful and worthy of

praise that God the Word became in the body and observed all the observances of the soul and of the body" (B. 123–124). (In the very next sentence 'in' is used naturally: "For if he had not remained in his nature above the nature of the body or of the soul or of the intelligence, he would surely have been required [to do so], since the rational soul also sufficed to observe the commandments.") "I made known in every way that God the Word was made man and that God the Word was at the same time in the humanity, in that Christ was made man in it" (B. 210–211). (God the Word was in the humanity syntactically, voluntarily and prosôpically; Christ was in the humanity naturally in that He was man and syntactically in that He was God.)

(4) 'In' with reference to the definition and circumscription of an ousia by its own nature, or with reference to the definition and circumscription imposed upon anything entering into a natural union. To describe an ousia or hypostasis as 'in its nature' implies its imposed and inescapable properties; to describe anything 'in natural union' implies its subjection to the conditions of the natural unit into which it has become integrated. This is the most rigid and precise use of 'in', and may be rendered '*in (naturally)*'. Owing to the necessary correspondence of an ousia with its nature, 'in ousically' does not differ in significance from 'in naturally'. Except in Trinitarian usage 'in hypostatically' is the same as 'in ousically', and therefore the same as 'in naturally'. Usually we shall use 'in (naturally)'. In the case of God, we must bear in mind any consequences of the fact that His nature is that in which He is, not that in which He has to be (see p. 125). This usage is very frequent, and the following are merely typical examples: "For the definition and circumscription of all nature is that in which it has to be" (B. 56). "Or, by granting that in nature naturally, by a passible sensibility, he accepted sufferings, you evacuate him of impassibility and of immortality" (B. 57–58). "He might support the sufferings of the body and of the soul and of the intelligence in a natural union which would have united the nature" (B. 124). "For the Son of God the Father is by nature consubstantial with the Father and that which the Father is in his nature the Son

K

also is" (B. 143). "Now God the Word is not of them both in *ousia*, nor again is God the Word in flesh, nor is God the Word of two nor is God the Word two natures" (B. 215).

'In' is used in many other senses, including many idiomatic phrases; but the four senses distinguished above are those which have a bearing on the metaphysical and Christological problems, and are therefore to be carefully identified in the appropriate contexts. Many passages are apparently meaningless or even self-contradictory unless we have sufficiently entered into Nestorius' thought to be able to know in every case the sense in which 'in' is used.

A few typical passages may be given with the meanings of 'in' indicated:

[1] "But in" (naturally) "the *ousia* of man [he is] truly man, of the true nature of the true man in" (syntactically, voluntarily and prosôpically) "which he became incarnate altogether for all and which he made his *prosôpon*, and he was revealed in" (circumstantially) "the things of men in comporting himself in" (syntactically, voluntarily and prosôpically in so far as God the Word was ousia and nature of Godhead, naturally in so far as the allogenous prosôpon of God the Word, with which He identified Himself in ways which will be considered later, was of the ousia and nature of manhood) "the nature of man, being God in" (syntactically, voluntarily and prosôpically) "human nature" (B. 30).

"The *ousia* of the divinity remains and suffers not when it is in" (syntactically, voluntarily and prosôpically) "the *ousia* of the flesh, and the flesh again remains in" (naturally) "the *ousia* of the flesh when it is in" (syntactically and voluntarily) "the nature and in" (syntactically, voluntarily and prosôpically) "the *prosôpon* of the divinity; for the body is one and both of them [are] one Son. For no other is called God the Word in" (prosôpically) "the flesh apart from him who is in" (syntactically, voluntarily and prosôpically in so far as God the Word was ousia and nature

---

[1] This passage is also obscure owing to Nestorius' undefined use of 'he'. (See p. 187.) The passage is explained with reference to both 'in' and 'he' on pp. 427–428.

of Godhead, naturally in so far as the allogenous prosôpon of God the Word was of the ousia and nature of manhood) "our own flesh; nor again [is anything else called] the flesh, but it is in" (prosôpically) "the Son, in" (prosôpically) "God the Word: that he should comport himself completely in" (naturally in so far as the allogenous prosôpon was of the ousia and nature of manhood) "the nature of men being man, and that he should rise as God being God by nature" (B. 129).

"For I rebuked him for not having confessed that Christ is God, but because he did not say that Christ was man whole in" (probably merely 'as to', but interpretable as 'naturally') "nature and in" (circumstantially, or perhaps merely 'as to') "moral life and that God the Word became not the nature of man but in" (syntactically, voluntarily and prosôpically) "the nature and in" (circumstantially) "the manner of life of man, in such wise that God the Word became both of them in" (syntactically, voluntarily and prosôpically in so far as God the Word was ousia and nature of Godhead, naturally in so far as the allogenous prosôpon of God the Word was of the ousia and nature of manhood) "nature" (B. 140). This passage is of special interest as indicating the necessity of understanding the precise force of 'in' in various contexts. Nestorius would have expected this to be obvious, but in the above passage the sentence "God the Word became not the nature of man but in the nature" is only comprehensible when we appreciate that 'in the nature' cannot possibly mean 'in the nature naturally', but must mean 'in the nature syntactically, voluntarily and prosôpically'.

There are many other passages where similar methods of analysis must be applied. If the above examples are followed, there should not be undue difficulty.

Footnote 2, p. 132: The statement on pp. 130–132 may be compared with the concise summary of orthodox Trinitarian doctrine given by Fulton, *Encyclopædia of Religion and Ethics*, xii. 459–460: "There are then (as the statement may run) three Persons (Hypostases) or real distinctions in the unity of the divine Nature or Substance, which is Love. The Persons are co-equal, inasmuch as in each of them the divine Nature is one and undivided, and by each the collective divine attributes are shared. As a 'person' in Trinitarian usage is more than a mere aspect of being, being a real ground of experience and function, each divine Person, while less than a separate individuality, possesses His own hypostatic character or characteristic property (ἰδιώτης). The hypostatic characters of the Persons may be viewed from an internal and an external standpoint, *i.e.* with reference to the inner constitution of the Godhead or to the Godhead as related to the cosmos or world of manifestation. Viewed *ab intra*, the hypostatic character of the Father is ingeneration (ἀγεννησία), of the Son filiation, of the Spirit procession; wherefore, 'the Father is of none, neither begotten nor proceeding; the Son is eternally begotten of the Father; the Holy Ghost eternally proceeding from the Father and the Son.' Viewed *ab extra* (for Love functions externally as well as internally, is centrifugal as well as centripetal), the hypostatic character of the Father is made manifest in creation, whereby a world is provided for beings who should be capable of experiencing fellowship with the divine Love; the hypostatic character of the Son in redemption, whereby the alienating power of sin is overcome; and the hypostatic character of the Spirit in sanctification, whereby human nature is quickened and renewed and shaped to the divine likeness. Yet, while this is said, as there is no separation in the unity of the Godhead, so the one God is manifested in the threefold work of creation, redemption, and sanctification; moreover, each of the Persons as sharing the divine attributes is active in the threefold work, if with varying stress of function."

CHAPTER VI

IT is now possible to approach the Christological problem in terms conformable with the metaphysic outlined in the preceding four chapters. It has already been seen (pp. 60–61) that Nestorius accepted the three postulates which by his time were recognized as fundamental to orthodox Christology: that Jesus Christ was truly God, that He was also truly man, and that He was one person. If Jesus Christ is truly God, He must be ousia of God, with the corresponding divine nature, manifesting through a prosôpon necessarily allogenous, and appropriate to the hypostasis of the Trinity underlying that prosôpon. If Jesus Christ is truly man, He must be ousia of man; that ousia will have the corresponding nature, and will manifest itself by an appropriate prosôpon, which in its duration will pass through phases autogenous and allogenous. How can Jesus Christ be truly God and truly man, and yet one?

Before considering Nestorius' solution, it is relevant to observe how effectively his metaphysic disposes of the principal types of invalid attempt at solving the problem. The first part of the Bazaar is devoted to this purpose, and his method of classifying heresies is set out on pp. 414–416. As there remarked, except when concerned with the immediate controversy with Cyril, he preferred to deal in general principles rather than with the views of particular individuals: "We wish to decline to [give] the names of their chiefs, so as not to prolong our discussion nor to be found to have omitted any point in the inquiry by first becoming entangled in [questions of] names" (B. 14). This facilitates the transposition of the views of others into the terms of his own metaphysic without the risk of being charged with misinterpreting them, and at the same time permits him to make his own classification. There is no need to give a detailed analysis of heresies at this point. It will be sufficient to indicate how they may be disposed of under several broad headings, with references to the appropriate sections of the Bazaar.[1]

I. Those who do not accept the postulates:

(i) Those who do not believe that Jesus Christ was God: the heathen, the Jews, the Paulinians (I. i. 1–2, 4) (B. 11–12); (I. i. 51–53 (second paragraph)) (B. 63–66).

(ii) Those who do not believe that Jesus Christ was man; they accept Him as God, and consider His humanity a mere schêma or His body a mere instrument: the Manichæans and others (I. i. 3) (B. 11–12); (I. ii. 1, 5) (B. 126–128).

(iii) Those who do not believe that God the Word and Jesus Christ were one; they think that there were two Sons, a heavenly, God the Word, and an earthly, Jesus Christ (I. i. 53 (second half of third paragraph)) (B. 67).

II. Those who suppose that God became man by exercising the powers of His own nature: that His ousia included the ousia of manhood, or that His nature included the nature of manhood, or that He could change His ousia into the ousia of manhood while remaining in His own nature, or that He could change His nature into the nature of manhood while remaining in His own ousia, or that He could change part of His own ousia and nature into the ousia and nature of manhood, or that He could change part of His own ousia into the ousia of manhood, or that He could change part of His own nature into the nature of manhood, or that by some combination or variation of these changes He could become man without taking to Himself in any way any ousia and nature other than His own. This category includes a great many variants, many of which are dealt with explicitly or implicitly in I. i. 10–30 (B. 14–34), I. i. 37 (B. 40–41), and I. ii. 2 (B. 126).

However presented, all such views are readily disposed of by the application of the principles of the Nestorian metaphysic, particularly those enunciated in the fundamental propositions on ousia and nature which are set out

[1] It is sometimes convenient to give references by Book, Part and Section numbers, as well as by page numbers. Thus I. ii. 3 means Book I, Part II, section 3.

on pp. 83–88, and by taking into account the special properties of the ousia and nature of God (see pp. 124–126).

III. Those who suppose that God, or something of God, entered into ousic and natural union with man, or something of man:

(i) Those who suppose that the Godhead in Christ was passible because of the union, that the manhood was soulless in that it was animated only by Godhead, and that the union was ousic and natural: the Arians (I. i. 5) (B. 12–13), (I. ii. 3) (B. 127).

(ii) Those who suppose that God the Word ousically and naturally united Himself with a human body or with a human body and animal soul: the Apollinarians and others (I. i. 42) (B. 49–52), (I. ii. 4) (B. 127).

(iii) Those who suppose that God the Word ousically and naturally united Himself with complete manhood. Some suppose that the union is of the ousias (I. i. 31–34) (B. 35–38), (I. ii. 6) (B. 128), some that it is of the natures (I. i. 42 (second half of second paragraph)) (B. 51–52), some, notably Cyril, that it is hypostatic (B. 132–137, 225–240).

According to the Nestorian metaphysic, all these views are the same. Ousic union is necessarily natural union, because ousia and nature are inseparably correlative; and hypostatic union, for Nestorius, is exactly the same thing as ousic union (see p. 118), for hypostasis is simply ousia, except in Trinitarian usage, where it is ousia in a certain phase (see pp. 130–133). All such views fail to fulfil the conditions of the problem, for ousic, natural or hypostatic union—all of which are the same thing—would result in the formation of a new ousia and nature, a new hypostasis, which would have ceased to be either of its constituents (see pp. 86–88). Besides, the ousia and nature of Godhead, which includes its three hypostases, cannot be supposed to enter into ousic, natural or hypostatic union with any other ousia (see p. 125).

The necessary rejection of all these types of solution indicates the great difficulty of the problem which Nestorius set himself: Jesus Christ must possess complete and ousically and naturally uncombined ousia and nature of God, must possess complete and ousically and naturally uncombined ousia and nature of man, and must be one.

Ousic and natural union, which for Nestorius includes hypostatic union, is not a possible solution. Then let us tentatively consider syntactic union. God the Word could enter into syntactic union with the man Jesus, thus forming a syntactic unity. The union would certainly be voluntary on the part of God the Word and might be so on the part of the man Jesus. If this syntactic unity were called Christ, it is obvious that Christ would be a syntactic unity having a quasi-ousia (ousia of God and ousia of man), a quasi-nature (the natures of man and God interacting), and a quasi-prosôpon (God the Word revealing Himself through the syntax). The dominating nature is that of God the Word, whence it follows that the quasi-prosôpon of the syntax is an allogenous prosôpon of God the Word, and is part of His durative prosôpon. The prosôpon of the man in the syntax is subordinated, so that the prosôpon of the man Jesus is in its own nature only and is autogenous. This, of course, is exactly a theophany and would make Christ simply the prophet Jesus, having his part in a syntactic unity which was an allogenous prosôpon of God, and aware of his own subordinated prosôpon as a mere element in that syntax, presumably willingly.

The above is a concise description, in terms of the Nestorian metaphysic, of what is usually understood by Nestorianism. It can scarcely be wondered at that his views were misunderstood and given this interpretation. So many of his own statements, unless comprehended within the complex of his metaphysic, which for the most part he leaves us to deduce, would lead one to suppose that this kind of duality was actually in his mind. For instance, when Sophronius charges Nestorius with this very view, Nestorius' immediate reply does little to clear matters. Sophronius says: "But, further, you lay down that God did [this] by means of an intermediary" (B. 28). Nestorius replies: "But, O admirable man, it remains to compare the things which have been said by thee, [namely] that he appeared to us in his own nature without an intermediary.

For what reason then hast thou said that he became the nature of man while remaining God? For he who appeared in his nature had no need to become another *ousia* in which to appear. If he appeared in his own, then thou sayest an impossible thing, that he was a mediator for him[self]. For *a mediator is not of one, but God is one*, and consequently he cannot be God but the mediator of God" (I. i. 24) (B. 28). A similar conclusion would be drawn from a sentence in I. i. 27 (B. 30): "But in the *ousia* of man [he is] truly man, of the true nature of the true man in which he became incarnate."

Although Nestorius, as we shall see, did not hold any such crude and simple view, this kind of syntax may nevertheless be regarded as the first step towards a Christology conformable with the Nestorian metaphysic. It is evidently far from being a solution, but it does fulfil certain very important conditions: there is no impairment of the ousia or nature of God the Word, the man Jesus is a complete and perfect man, Christ is an objective unity. The obvious objections are that the objective unity of Christ by no means implies a real unity of God the Word and the man Jesus, and that although the union is voluntary from the side of God the Word, the man Jesus would seem to be a forced instrument with little or no will of his own. The second objection might be disposed of by postulating that the union was vóluntary on both sides: that the man Jesus was voluntarily in the syntax with God the Word, just as God the Word voluntarily chose to use him as His allogenous prosôpon, and that the voluntary union could be broken by either side. But though this disposes of the second objection, it only intensifies the first.

Keeping in mind the idea of voluntary syntactic union as a first step in the direction of solving the problem, it must now be seen how Nestorius overcomes the difficulties involved. It will be best to consider how the characteristics of Jesus Christ differ from those of an ordinary syntax, and to see whether those differences establish His real unity while leaving the integrity of His Godhead and manhood unimpaired,

I. *The genesis of Jesus Christ*

Nestorius' views on the incarnation are usefully prefaced by a reference to his passage on the king assuming the schêma of soldierhood (I. i. 27–29) (B. 30–34). This passage is considered on pp. 429–432. It is of present importance to notice what is required for a king to become a soldier: he must lay aside his royal apparel and put on the clothing and equipment of a soldier, and he must lay aside the powers and privileges of kingship and accept the conditions and limitations of a soldier's life. There is nothing to prevent him doing these things, for he has the power to divest himself both of raiment and dignity and to assume the clothing and status of a soldier. Having done that, nothing else is required, for he lacks nothing which a soldier possesses: he has a body with the same physical powers, and presumably has the ability to do all that a soldier has to do. Further, as Nestorius emphasizes, a king could become a soldier with any degree of thoroughness from mere masquerading in the clothing and equipment of soldierhood to complete permanent self-lowering of himself to the condition of soldierhood, though it would always be possible for him to reassert his kingship. In none of these circumstances is there any duality: "A king, who takes the clothes of soldierhood and is [so seen], has not become a double king" (B. 33). It is also to be noted that although the king could at any moment lay aside his assumed soldierhood and reassert his kingship, to do so before his purpose in assuming soldierhood had been achieved would be a confession of weakness and failure.

Reference must next be made to the creation of Adam. There is a significant difference between the creation of Adam and the creation of all things else. The two accounts of the creation of man (Gen. i. 27 and Gen. ii. 7) would anciently have been regarded as supplementary rather than alternative, and the latter would have been considered the more circumstantial. That being so, this difference emerges: in the case of all things else, God created by simple fiat: "God said, Let there be, . . .: and there was . . ." (Gen. i. 3), or "God said, Let . . .: and it was so" (Gen. i. 6–7, 9, 11, 14–15, 24). But in the case of man (Gen. ii. 7), there are two stages: first, the transformation of the ousia and nature of some of the dust of the ground into the ousia and nature of man as an animal mechanism; second, the infusion into that animal mechanism of that which made it a living soul, a completed man. It is evident that God is thought of as acting in some special way for the creation of man. Even though we must never forget the fundamental distinction between the ousia and nature of God and the ousia and nature of all things else, there is evidently some special place to be allocated to that which makes an animal mechanism into a living soul. If only for distinction, God does not see fit to call man into existence by mere fiat. Given, therefore, the animal mechanism of man, its becoming a living soul depends on this special act of God. There was a moment, the moment of generation, when the existence of the first man was momentarily linked with that of God Himself, when the vitalizing inbreathing was at once the vivification of Adam and a present act of God. During that moment of generation the vivifying power going forth and entering in was both God's and Adam's.

All, therefore, that the animal mechanism needs in order to become a complete and living man is the divine inbreathing, the divine vivification. This act performed, God withdrew Himself, and Adam became a separate entity. Now Christ is the second Adam, and however spirits subsequent to Adam's are derived, whether by traducianism or creatianism, the cases of Adam and Jesus Christ are those in which we are to seek analogy. God, then, instead of allowing the normal later procedure to operate, returned in the case of Christ to the method used in the case of Adam. He simultaneously caused to originate and directly vivified that which came into being in utero Virginis. But instead of vivifying it and then withdrawing Himself, which would preserve a parallel with the case of Adam, He remained permanently as at the moment of vivification, "when the existence of the first man was momentarily linked with that of God Himself, when the vitalizing inbreathing was at once the vivification of Adam and a present act of God." If God, or, to particularize the hypostasis, God the Word, chose so to remain, He would have entered into a relationship concerning which we may make the following observations:

(1) While He so remained, the animal mechanism which He had thus vivified would have everything it needed to make it a living man, for it had received that vivifying power which constituted the animal mechanism a living man. Indeed, it would be a living man, for if He at any moment withdrew as He did from Adam, a separate living man would remain.

(2) If He withdrew, He could do so in either of two ways: as in the case of Adam, leaving in Adam the vivifying power He had given; or He could withdraw without releasing from Himself the vivifying power by which the animal mechanism was being vivified, but which had never left Himself because He had remained in that which He was vivifying.

(3) If He withdrew as in the case of Adam, a man Jesus would have begun His separate existence. If He withdrew without releasing from Himself the vivifying power, He would leave a spiritless animal mechanism, which would either be at once dead, or, horrible to contemplate, a living animal body without spirit or intelligence.

Meaning can now be attached to the expression "potentially separate man Jesus". There never was a separate man Jesus, separate, that is, from God the Word. But if at any time God the Word had withdrawn Himself from that with which He had associated Himself, as He immediately did from Adam, a separate man Jesus would have at once come into existence.

That Nestorius must have thought of the Incarnation like this is indicated by a number of passages. That concerning the king and the schêma of soldierhood has already been mentioned. As to the completion of the animal mechanism to living manhood by the vivifying act of God: "The temple is passible, not God the impassible who has quickened the passible temple" (B. 317). "I called the temple passible and not God the quickener of the temple which has suffered" (B. 318). As to the parallel between the

first and second Adam, and the implication of the vivification of Jesus by a comparable direct act: ". . . the incarnation
of God who in him is what God was in the first man"
(B. 87). Further, Nestorius is very emphatic that this unceas-
ing union in vivification began at the very moment of the
commencement of the existence of the animal mechanism:
"He who from the womb was son by union" (B. 132–133).
"The union took place with its very creation" (B. 419).
The most significant passage is that in I. i. 64 (B. 87):
". . . in such wise as not originally to be man but at the
same time Man-God by the incarnation of God who in
him is what God was in the first man." This emphasizes
that there was never a separately existing man Jesus[1] even
in utero—"not originally to be man but at the same time
Man-God"—and that the parallel of His generation is with
Adam—". . . God who in him is what God was in the
first man." If Nestorius had troubled to explicate the ideas
in this sentence, he might have anticipated the concept of
enhypostasia.

It thus begins to emerge how we may hope to avoid the
admission of two personalities in Jesus Christ. We cannot
conceive that the syntactic union of God the Word with
a perfect man could produce anything other than a duality;
but it is not so difficult to conceive God the Word vivifying
and remaining with the animal mechanism of humanity in
such wise that if He withdrew there would be a perfect
man remaining. That is, Christ is not God the Word plus
the man Jesus; such an addition never took place: Christ is
God the Word plus what would have become the man
Jesus if God the Word had withdrawn. The idea of the
"potentially separate man Jesus" is an important one.

II. Disintegration of the syntax

It has been seen that we may regard the genesis of Jesus
Christ as the continuing voluntary syntactic union of God
the Word with the animal mechanism which He had vivified,
in such wise that if He withdrew Himself there would have

---

[1] This is probably also the significance of the otherwise difficult sentence
on B. 350: "For the man, who, as not united, was not what he is by nature,
[namely] man, is called God through that which is united." See p. 466.

come into existence a separate man Jesus. The ties uniting God the Word and the potentially separate man Jesus are not ousic and natural, but syntactic, for the nature of God the Word cannot be circumscribed, and He could at any time have withdrawn Himself from the syntax. On His side the union is evidently voluntary. But it is not equally obviously so in the case of the manhood, and this aspect of the matter can best be contemplated by considering how the syntax might have disintegrated.

First we must recognize that the problem is unique, and that God was doing something quite unlike anything He had ever done before or would, presumably, ever do again. In the Incarnation His nature interacted as intimately with another nature as was possible; indeed, we may say that God wished to come as near to natural union with humanity as the self-consistency of His own nature permitted. It must not be overlooked that the continuity and initiative are God's, not man's. God, then, God the Word, wishing to 'become man', united Himself syntactically with the animal mechanism of manhood, in such a way that if He withdrew Himself He would leave a complete and separate man. We must face what this means in terms of the Nestorian metaphysic. It means that God the Word had entered into what would in the case of any other nature have been a natural union, for during the continuance of the syntax the manhood was complete and a natural unity: the body and animal soul of Jesus were inescapably united with that which completed them into the nature of manhood, even though that was still in and of God the Word. The only fact preventing the union of the body, animal soul and that which completed the manhood being a natural unity was the fact that that which completed the manhood was within God the Word, and therefore beyond the circumscribing power of ordinary nature. Otherwise, that which completed the manhood would have been in natural union with the body and the animal soul; indeed, from the side of the body and soul, from the side of any but God, it was in natural union with them. The bonds of the syntax were therefore of a unique kind, and the syntax could have disintegrated in any of three ways:

(1) God the Word could have withdrawn Himself without releasing from Himself the vivifying power which completed the manhood. He would thus have left derelict the mere animal mechanism. This would have been to admit the failure of His venture in incarnation, and the abandonment of the allogenous prosôpon He had assumed. It would be as if a king had adopted the schêma of soldierhood for a certain purpose, had found the purpose difficult or irksome to fulfil, and had returned to his royal dignity with his object unattained. So far as the manhood was concerned, such an end to the syntax would have been a miraculous dissolution, as death ordinarily comes about not by the withdrawal of the vivifying power, but by a defect in the animal mechanism rendering impossible the continuance in natural union of body, soul and spirit. God the Word did not do this, but He could have done so had He wished: "But that God the Word is so voluntarily and not by force: *I have authority over my life, that I should lay it down and I have authority to take it again*" (B. 125).

(2) God the Word could have withdrawn Himself leaving the vivifying power with the body and animal soul. This, as already seen, would have brought the potentially separate man Jesus into separate independent existence. In what circumstances can we suppose that such a possibility might have eventuated? It must be recalled that the Incarnation meant that the hypostasis of God the Word was in voluntary syntactic union with that which, with His own vivifying power, completed manhood. Through that voluntary syntactic union He acquired an allogenous prosôpon, by which He became known and in which He experienced. In that His vivifying power, still with Himself, was also, from any side but His own, in natural union with body and animal soul, He was able through that part of Himself to realize the interests, the urges and the passions of humanity. This we know He did, "For we have not an high priest which cannot be touched with the feeling of our infirmities; but was in all points tempted like as we are" (Heb. iv. 15). Quite obviously, while He remained God the Word,

although He was aware of all these urges and passions, He could not yield to them, for that would have been contrary to His own nature, and we must say 'was aware' of them rather than 'suffered' from them, in that He was in His nature impassible. But He was certainly aware that the body to which He had united Himself both suffered and thrilled. Hence, though in that sense tempted, He remained without sin: "In all points tempted like as we are, yet without sin" (Heb. iv. 15).

In order to pursue the matter to its logical conclusion, it is now necessary to contemplate an awful possibility: suppose that God the Word, experiencing through this linkage with humanity the urges and passions of human nature, as admittedly He did, had availed Himself of the opportunity of fulfilling these for the first time sensuously apprehended urges. This supposition, terrible though it may seem, makes very real the consciousness of humanity in Jesus Christ and the actuality of His struggle with sin. The temptation in the wilderness was a real presentation of real possibilities: He realized what the attractions were, though He did not yield to them. But although reason and piety alike revolt at the contemplation of such possibilities, it is necessary to consider what would have happened had He yielded to any temptation. The act of yielding would have involved schism in the ousia and nature of Godhead itself. The ousia and nature of Godhead is impassible and without needs, and therefore cannot be thought of as sinning, for sin is an attempt to fulfil a real or imagined need without regard to the will of God. God the Word, therefore, if He wished to yield to temptation through the syntax, would have had to relinquish His status as a hypostasis of the Godhead, depart from that part of His nature which pertained to the ousia and nature of Godhead, and cling with what attributes might remain to the body and animal soul through which the realization of sin was possible. There would be an awful schism in the Godhead: part of the divine ousia and nature would have separated off, and would have chosen to remain in union with a body and animal soul, in so doing surrendering such attributes of

Godhead as would have made sin impossible. Subtraction from infinity leaves infinity unchanged, so Godhead would have continued with all its qualities. But what had once been part of Godhead would now be the νοῦς or πνεῦμα in a human being, having taken the irrevocable step of self-alienation from divinity and acceptance of the circumscriptions of a non-divine nature. Godhead in one of its hypostases would have suffered schism. We might call such a disaster schizohypostasia.

The concept of this dreadful possibility is a logical consequence of an interpretation of the Nestorian metaphysic and Christology, and is of real value in reference to the explanation of the reality of the human temptation of Jesus Christ. Just as there was always the potentially separate man Jesus, so there was always for God the Word potential schizohypostasia. This is a very significant implication of Nestorian Christology, in that it emphasizes, in a way which perhaps no other Christological theory has ever done, the reality of the tension within Jesus Christ Himself, a tension which we cannot conceive as ever being in real danger of ending in failure, although the reality of the tension is not thereby diminished. Frangibility may be posited without actual fear of fracture. From the Birth to the Cross there was always the potentiality of the syntax ending in schizohypostasia. If it had happened, it would have emerged that Godhead, unable to resist the temptations and tensions to which it had submitted its own creatures, had suffered internal schism in an attempt both to continue as Godhead and to experience as sinful man.

(3) The only other way in which the syntax could have disintegrated would have been by natural disintegration of the nature of that part of the syntax which, had it existed separately, would have constituted the man Jesus: that is, ordinary death of the natural human component of the syntax. If God the Word endured in the syntactic union until this disintegration, He would thereafter be again God the Word without self-limitation in the syntax. God the Word did so endure, and the very significant facts emerge that the total duration of the natural life of

L

the potentially separate man Jesus was spent in syntactic union with God the Word, and that God the Word remained self-limited to the syntax during the total period of the existence of the potentially separate man Jesus.

III. *Stability of the syntax*

It is now possible to consider the nature and significance of the bonds uniting divinity and humanity in the syntax Jesus Christ. By the hypotheses of the Nestorian metaphysic as applicable to the conditions of the Christological problem, the union cannot be deemed ousic, natural or hypostatic. Nestorius is, however, anxious to establish that the bonds are as strong and significant as is possible without their being actually natural. The union is:

(1) *Syntactic*. This adjective must be retained in order to keep it clearly before us that the union is not ousic and natural.

(2) *Voluntary*. In that God the Word cannot be bound by any nature other than His own, and seeing that even His own nature is that in which He is rather than that in which He has to be (see p. 125), the union is necessarily a voluntary one so far as He is concerned. As already seen, He could have withdrawn from the union at any time either by dereliction of the animal mechanism or by schizohypostasia leaving the separate man Jesus. In that either of these modes of departure from the syntax would have been tantamount to an admission of failure and weakness on the part of God the Word, they are unthinkable. That is, we cannot and dare not suppose that God the Word, having entered into voluntary syntactic union with manhood, would have departed from that union until His purpose had been achieved. The union is therefore as firm as a natural one, but we do not call it a natural one in that God the Word could have departed from it had He wished, though it is unthinkable to suppose that He would in any circumstances have so wished.

But can we truly say that the union was voluntary in so far as the manhood was concerned? It is to be recalled that the manhood was a complete human nature, being the natural union of a body, animal soul and that supplied by but never separated from God the Word which completed the animal mechanism into a living man, in such wise that if God the Word had withdrawn Himself, leaving it, there would have remained a separately existing man. It is also to be recalled that that from God the Word which completed the manhood was in natural union with body and animal soul so far as they and any but God were concerned, but, being still of God the Word, was not in natural union with the body and animal soul so far as He was concerned: He was free, but the body and animal soul were circumscribed by human nature. The manhood, therefore, was in the circumscription of a defined nature from the point of view of any but God, and, further, was an entity by means of which God the Word could and did experience sensuously. It was open to Him, as that sensuously experiencing entity, to break away from Godhead by schizohypostasia as already explained, and thus become free to satisfy worldly ambition or any other sinful human urge. In that sense the manhood was free, and its union with Godhead voluntary. It will be noticed that this approach gives a solution possibly as satisfactory as the dilemmas presented by the problem permit. How could there be voluntary union from two sides without two personalities? Only by positing one personality experiencing two sets of urges, and positing the possibility of that personality dividing. Nestorius, unfortunately, never clarified his thought beyond emphasizing his postulates—true God, true man, true unity—and emphasizing none the less the reality of temptation in the manhood. But the logical development of his ideas leads to the concepts of enhypostasia, the manhood as the potentially but never actually separate man Jesus, and potential schizohypostasia.

It may here be remarked that Nestorius is very definite on the reality of the human experience and temptation in the manhood. It is to be noted that Nestorius, assuming that his reader will have accepted and agreed that the unity is real and unbroken—"Thou wilt confess aloud with us that there are not two Gods the Words or two Sons or two only begottens, but one" (B. 69)—nevertheless keeps writing of 'the man'[1] and 'he',[2] for which we must mentally

[1] See, for example, B. 47, 84, 131, 273, 305, 350.   [2] Cf. p. 187.

supply 'the potentially separate man Jesus' or 'God the Word in so far as by schizohypostasia He could have become only man'. Three typical passages may be quoted:

"But, although he had all those things which appertain unto our nature, anger and concupiscence and thoughts, and although also they increased with the progress and increase of every age [in his life], he stood firm in thoughts of obedience" (B. 92).

"As he moved among all men, where all the commandments surrounded him on all sides and showed him the strength of disobedience, he comported himself valiantly in the midst of them all, in that he used nothing special or extraordinary for his support, but he made use, as all men, of those very things which are common so that it should not be supposed that through observance of these things he was preserved from sin and that without them he could not be preserved" (B. 93).

"Therefore the Evangelists record all those things which in truth show the nature of man, lest on account of the divinity it should not be believed that he was also man nor be believed together with this that it was he who was affirmed by the promises. Therefore the Blessed Mary was recorded as a woman who was betrothed to a man, of whom he has written both his name and his race and his trade and his place, in order that there might be nothing to raise a doubt leading to disbelief that she was a woman. Therefore also [he wrote] of his low estate and with all these things also of the annunciation of his conception and of his birth and of the manger, to make known him who was born together with her who bore him, that it might be affirmed that he is truly man, of [his] sleeping in the manger, of the swathing in swaddling bands such as are natural to infants, of the offerings which were offered for him for his progress, of his increase in stature and in wisdom with God and with men, of his manner of life in the world, of his observances, of his submission, of the prayers which he prayed, of all his fulfilment of the law, of the baptism and of the saying which was said of him, that he who from the womb was son by union was the Son, of the witness to the observance of the customs, of the word of the Father, of the appearance of the Holy Spirit, of his dispensation with all zeal on our behalf, not in illusion nor in the *schêma* of a man but in the human nature [formed] of the body of a man and a rational soul which thinks and reflects in the nature of men, that it may have everything which is in the nature of man without being deprived of the union with God the Word" (B. 131–132).

Although from the metaphysical viewpoint it may be sufficient to describe the bonds of the syntax as syntactic and voluntary, Nestorius rightly felt that soteriology demanded a linkage of the divinity and humanity of an additional and different kind. Hence he emphasizes that God and man in Christ were also linked by love, adoption and acknowledgment, so that God would be unwilling to break the bonds not simply because to do so would be to admit His own defeat and failure, but also because He wished to link manhood to Himself by ties the more precious because uncompelled and the more binding because arising from the volition of His own nature rather than from the compulsion of any other nature, which would not in any case be possible. The reciprocity of these bonds as from Godhead to manhood on the one hand and from manhood to Godhead on the other is of the same kind as in the case of the voluntariness of the union. But the emphasis is on Godhead loving, adopting and acknowledging manhood to a greater degree than the converse. Nestorius is anxious to emphasize these ties, as a few typical quotations will show. To resume, then, the union is:

(3) *Of love.* "Nor are the things which are to be distinguished the one from the other in the *prosôpon* distinct in love, for they are conceived of his *prosôpon* in the love and the will of God in that he took the flesh" (B. 80).

". . . the two natures which are distinct in *ousia* but are united by love" (B. 81).

(4) *Of adoption.* "And since he became [flesh] and sojourned among us, he has drawn to himself the very flesh for [the purpose of] the adoption as for his own *prosôpon*, which is in both of them, in that on the one hand [there is] the *ousia* of God, but on the other the flesh by the union and the adoption; in such wise that the flesh, which

is flesh by nature, is also Son by the union and the adoption of the *prosôpon*" (B. 78).

"But since he became flesh in taking the flesh, he was named after both of them in both of them, but as though he were one in both of them, not [in both] in nature, but in the one indeed in nature but in the other in *prosôpon* by adoption as well as by revelation" (B. 79).

"The one is by adoption what the other is by nature" (B. 81).

(5) *Of acknowledgment.* "Those who become sons by adoption and by acknowledgment [become the sons] of him of whom they are born not by flesh nor by blood but by the will and the love of him who has no bodily frame but has become their body by adoption and by love and by acknowledgment like a father" (B. 71–72).

"He will be their flesh by the taking of the flesh and he will make it [his] by adoption and he will acknowledge it is his body by adoption" (B. 72).

IV. *Quasi-ousia and quasi-nature of the syntax*

The quasi-ousia of the syntax consists of the syntactically united but ousically separate ousias of God and man. The ousia of God is that hypostatic to God the Word and the ousia of man is that of the potentially separate man Jesus, an ousia complete and nature-bound from every point of view but God's, for whom in any case no nature is binding. It is of no significance that this ousia was never otherwise than in syntactic, voluntary, loving, adoptive, acknowledged union with God the Word, or that the third element in it (intelligence or spirit, the other two being body and animal soul) was never separate from God the Word: ". . . in such wise as not originally to be man but at the same time Man-God by the incarnation of God who in him is what God was in the first man" (B. 87); for the cardinal fact remains that had God the Word withdrawn Himself by schizo-hypostasia there would have remained the separate and complete man Jesus. While the syntax endured there were the two ousias, united indeed by special ties of a kind we cannot imagine being broken, yet never ousically united: "The *ousias* remain without change" (B. 33).

The quasi-nature of the syntax consists of the interacting natures of Godhead and manhood. All interactings of natures involve consequential modifications in the method and degree of the ability of each nature to express itself, these modifications taking the form both of extensions and restrictions. Thus a man in syntactic union with a diving suit has accepted certain extensions—he can move and work under water; but he has also accepted certain restrictions—he cannot successfully run or jump in competition with a man not in such a syntax. Similar consequential modifications are necessarily involved when the natures of God and man are syntactically united in the quasi-nature of the syntax Jesus Christ. These consequences fall for consideration under two main headings:

(1) The effect of the syntax on the expression of the nature of God. How can the divine nature fully express itself through such a syntax, and how can we avoid positing restrictions on divinity?

(2) The effect of the syntax on the expression of the nature of man. How can human nature express itself with independence of will when syntactically united with the divine?

To take these in turn:

(1) The effect of the syntax on the expression of the nature of God.

The divine nature cannot be limited or controlled by anything other than itself: "It appertains to the omnipotent and infinite nature to be able to do everything; by its will then all other things are limited while it is not limited by anything" (B. 14). (Although said by Sophrónius this is common ground.) How, then, can God the Word accept the necessary limitations even of a syntax? Nestorius evades this difficulty by accepting the idea of kenosis: "And he is both God and man, and the likeness of God in condescension and in *kenôsis* and in *schêma*, [and] the likeness of the flesh as man; and the man is by exaltation what God is, through the name which is above all names. Consequently in the *kenôsis* he humbled himself *unto death, even death upon the cross*, in that he made use of the *prosôpon* of him who died and was crucified as his own *prosôpon*, and in his own *prosôpon* he made use of the things which appertained unto him who died and was crucified and was exalted" (B. 84–85). In terms conformable with the Nestorian metaphysic, the kenosis means this: God the Word, wishing to reveal Himself through the syntax Jesus Christ, decides to limit Himself to that range of His nature which can make its self-manifestation and self-expression through the syntax. It is His own act of choice and will. He is not limited to or by the nature of that with which He has entered into syntactic union; He has self-limited Himself voluntarily to that range of His nature within which the syntax can function, but He could at any moment reassert Himself and leave the syntax, by dereliction or by schizohypostasia. His only limitation is voluntary self-limitation. The nature of the limitation, in the somewhat mechanical terms of the Nestorian metaphysic, may be likened to acceptance of limited instead of limitless equipment, to use for the time being the physical and mental equipment of a man instead of the infinity of Godhead. The idea is not difficult to grasp, though explanations and analogies need very circumspect handling.[1]

(2) The effect of the syntax on the expression of the nature of man.

The problem in the case of the manifestation of the manhood is almost the reverse of that in the case of the Godhead. In the case of the Godhead we ask: "How can Godhead restrict itself to a syntax of a limited kind?" In the case of the manhood we ask: "How can manhood be real manhood when it has the guiding and volitional power of God acting syntactically with it?" Nestorius, as already seen, emphasizes the reality of the experiences and temptations of the humanity (pp. 163–165), but duality is avoided by stressing the fact that the will of the humanity was in complete accord with the will of God. It could be expressed thus: God the Word, in so far as He had become man in completing the manhood of the potentially separate man

---

[1] The problem is given useful short discussion in Mackintosh, *Person of Jesus Christ*, pp. 463–486, or by Loofs in *Encyclopædia of Religion and Ethics*, vii. 680–687.

Jesus, and in so far as He realized through that syntax into which He had entered the feelings, urges and temptations of manhood, fully appreciated the human approach and attitude toward life, and realized the various alternatives. Realizing all this, and being aware of the results of sin in the world around, He had one consuming desire: to fulfil the will of God, and to resist all sensuously appreciated urges in other directions. God the Word, therefore, who by schizohypostasia could have yielded to self-fulfilment on levels contrary to His divine nature, or by dereliction could have given up the struggle, chose rather to retain unity of will both as God and potential man. Thus can be poised the delicate balance between two wills and personalities on the one hand and unreal temptation and choice on the other. This, a matter in which careful phrasing is necessary, is dealt with by Nestorius at some length but with little exactitude. It is the main theme of I. i. 67–72 (B. 90–97), and there are other references to it. But from all of them we should gain little light unless we had entered by devious ways fairly fully into Nestorius' unexpressed ideas. As so often, much hinges on the meaning of 'he'.[1] Sometimes 'he' means God the Word as in His own nature, sometimes God the Word as in the syntax Jesus Christ, sometimes God the Word as aware of the potential existence of the separate man Jesus. A few examples may be quoted to show how Nestorius emphasized both the accord of wills and the reality of the struggle. In almost all these passages 'he' means 'God the Word as aware of the potential existence of the separate man Jesus'.

"For, as the image of God, he ought to have kept himself for God without spot and without blemish, and that by willing what God wills, since he had the *prosôpon* of God. For [to have] the *prosôpon* of God is to will what God wills, whose *prosôpon* he has" (B. 87).

"And consequently he took the likeness of a servant, a humble likeness, a likeness which had lost the likeness of God, not for honour nor for glory nor for adoration nor again for authority, although indeed he was the Son, but for the obedience which it should observe in the

[1] See p. 187.

prosôpon of the Son according to the purpose of God;
since it had the purpose of the latter and not its own nor
anything that it wished, but that which God the Word
wished. For this is the likeness of God, to have neither
purpose nor will of its own but that of him whose *prosôpon*
and likeness it has" (B. 90–91).

"But, although he had all those things which appertain
unto our nature, anger and concupiscence and thoughts,
and although also they increased with the progress and
increase of every age [in his life], he stood firm in thoughts
of obedience. . . . Now in all the primary commandments
his inclination [was] towards obedience, but not in the others,
in order that it might not be supposed that he was able to
conquer on account of their easiness; nor again in obedience
made he use of those wherein there was attraction in honour
and power and glory, but of those which in misery and
poverty and contempt and weakness could offend the
thoughts of obedience, those also wherein there was no
attraction to obedience but rather to remissness and to
negligence, and in nothing was he helped; but for this only
was he anxious, to obey God, and he loved that which
God willed" (B. 92–93).

"As he moved among all men, where all the commandments surrounded him on all sides and showed him the
strength of disobedience, he comported himself valiantly in
the midst of them all, in that he used nothing special or
extraordinary for his support, but he made use, as all men,
of those very things which are common so that it should
not be supposed that through observance of these things
he was preserved from sin and that without them he could
not be preserved" (B. 93).

"He raised up his very soul unto God, conforming
that which was according to his will to the will of God"
(B. 96).

"Because then he condescended in every thing inscrutably
with an incomparable condescension, there was further
demonstrated one purpose, one will, one intelligence,
indistinguishable and indivisible as in one" (B. 102).

"And because also the *prosôpon* of the one is the other's
and that of the other the one's, and the one [comes] from

the other and the other from the one, the will belongs to each one of them" (B. 239).

V. Quasi-prosôpon of the syntax

The quasi-prosôpon of the syntax in the case of a voluntary syntactic unity which includes a dominating animate nature is necessarily identical with the allogenous prosôpon of that dominating animate nature (see pp. 102–104). In the case of the syntax Jesus Christ the dominating animate nature is God the Word. Jesus Christ, then, is the allogenous prosôpon of God the Word, and holds a place in the continuity of His durative prosôpon. Indeed, during the duration of the syntax Jesus Christ, God the Word remained continuously in that syntax, so that for that entire period His prosôpon was an allogenous prosôpon, the quasi-prosôpon of the syntax Jesus Christ. Jesus Christ, therefore, may be regarded as a syntax with a quasi-prosôpon, or as the allogenous prosôpon of God the Word during a certain period. Anything or anyone of which God the Word made use as an allogenous prosôpon would similarly be a syntax with a quasi-prosôpon which was also the allogenous prosôpon of God the Word; this is the mechanism of theophany (see pp. 126–127). But in the case of Jesus Christ there is another and unique factor: ordinarily, the compelled elements in a syntax retain their own prosôpa (see pp. 105–107); it is only the dominating animate nature which can claim the whole system as its prosôpon, its allogenous prosôpon. In the syntax Jesus Christ, however, the allogenous part from the point of view of God the Word is the potentially separate man Jesus. That potentially separate man Jesus, who God the Word was conscious that by schizohypostasia He could become, was not merely in syntactic, but also, because God the Word experiencing as man so wished, in perfect voluntary, loving, adoptive, acknowledged union with God the Word as Godhead, so that the syntax was also his complete self-manifestation and expression, his prosôpon, his autogenous prosôpon. It thus emerges that the quasi-prosôpon of the syntax is identically the autogenous prosôpon of the potentially separate man Jesus and the allogenous prosôpon of God the Word.

Further, excepting God the Word, the elements of the syntax never existed apart from it: the whole duration of the potentially separate man Jesus was spent in the syntax. Thus there was never any act of syntactic or prosôpic union: the other elements in the syntax came into being simultaneously with incorporation into the syntax, "in such wise as not originally to be man but at the same time Man-God by the incarnation of God who in him is what God was in the first man" (B. 87). Similarly there was never a separate prosôpon of the potentially separate man Jesus: it never existed except as the allogenous prosôpon of God the Word.[1] Using the words strictly (see p. 77), there was never actually a prosôpic unification, for the prosôpa were never separate. There was a prosôpic unity, theoretically discriminable into the autogenous prosôpon of God the Word and the autogenous prosôpon of the separate man Jesus; but actually the prosôpon of the man Jesus was never otherwise than in syntax with God the Word, and never other than His allogenous prosôpon, and similarly, during the duration of Jesus Christ God the Word was never apart from the syntax so named. Jesus Christ was a prosôpic unit, one prosôpon, which was at the same time the allogenous prosôpon of God the Word, the autogenous prosôpon of the potentially separate man Jesus, and the quasi-prosôpon of the syntax. These prosôpa were never separate, which makes this syntax unlike any other.

There are these reciprocities:

(1) God the Word takes as His (allogenous) prosôpon the (autogenous) prosôpon of the (potentially separate) man Jesus, and completely restricts Himself thereto. Jesus Christ is God the Word in His (allogenous) prosôpon, and during the duration of Jesus Christ there is no God the Word apart from Jesus Christ: "For no other is called God the Word in the flesh apart from him who is in our own flesh" (B. 129).

(2) The (potentially separate) man Jesus accepts as the directive element in his prosôpon the will of God the Word, so that his prosôpon is completely the (allogenous) prosôpon of God the Word and nothing else. Jesus Christ

---

[1] "Christ exists not apart from God the Word" (B. 254).

is an autogenous prosôpon of manhood, but during its
entire duration is at the same time the (allogenous) prosôpon
of God the Word: "For, as the image of God, he ought to
have kept himself for God without spot and without
blemish, and that by willing what God wills, since he had
the *prosôpon* of God. For [to have] the *prosôpon* of God
is to will what God wills, whose *prosôpon* he has" (B. 87).
"For he was living not for himself but for him whose
prosôpon he was, and he kept the *prosôpon* without blemish
and without scar and thereby gave victory to the nature"
(B. 94).

There is only one prosôpon, which is alike and at once
the (allogenous) prosôpon of God the Word, the (autogenous) prosôpon of the (potentially separate) man Jesus,
and the (quasi) prosôpon of (the syntax) Jesus Christ. The
same prosôpon can be described from three points of view,
but it is one prosôpon, was never more than one prosôpon
and did not come to unity by unification from prosôpa
previously existent. Whether we regard Jesus Christ as the
prosôpon of God the Word, the prosôpon of Jesus Christ,
or the prosôpon of ideal manhood, it is one and only one
reality that we contemplate: God the Word manifesting
Himself in self-limitation in true manhood. Even if for
convenience of discussion we refer to two prosôpa, it is
really one and the same: ". . . one *prosôpon* without division;
the one is the other and the other is the one, while the other
and the one remain" (B. 96). "The *prosôpon* of the one is
the other's and that of the other the one's, and the one
[comes] from the other and the other from the one" (B. 239).
"All the [properties] of God the Word whose nature is
impassible and is immortal and eternal, and all the [proper-
ties] of the humanity, which are a nature mortal and passible
and created, and those of the union and of the incarnation
since the womb and since the incarnation—are referred to
one *prosôpon*, to that common *prosôpon* of our Lord Jesus
Christ" (B. 249–250). Nestorius reiterates the fact that there
is only one prosôpon time and again; see, for example,
B. 34, 85, 129, 143, 144, 210, 214, 230, 233, 252, 266, 281,
288, 305, 341.

It has thus been seen how the Incarnation is to be thought

of in terms of the Nestorian metaphysic: the durative prosôpon of God the Word, manifestation and expression of
the durative nature of the ousia of Godhead hypostatic to
God the Word, includes the period during which He
entered into voluntary syntactic union with and vivified
that which, had the act of vivification been momentary as
in Adam instead of continuing, would have constituted
the separate man Jesus. He maintained that voluntary syntactic union throughout the whole of the duration of the
potentially separate man Jesus, and during that period
there was unbroken continuity in the durative prosôpon of
God the Word. Like all animate prosôpa, the prosôpon
of God the Word in its duration has passed through many
periods both autogenous and allogenous. But there was
this unique and special feature in the period of thirty or
forty years during which His allogenous prosôpon was the
syntax Jesus Christ: that which He took to Himself to complete His allogenous prosôpon had no separate existence as
a prosôpic entity before, during, or after that period. There
was never any separate prosôpon other than that of God
the Word: the entire duration of the non-autogenous
element in His prosôpon during that period was spent in
His prosôpon, so that there was never a prosôpon other
than His. It was therefore a prosôpic unity of a unique and
special kind, and the separate ousias and natures of Godhead and manhood were united not merely prosôpically,
but in a prosôpic unity whose constituents had never had
separate prosôpa.

Does such a view of the Incarnation satisfy the conditions? It will be well to review the conditions to be
satisfied, and to make the necessary observations.

(1) Jesus Christ is truly God.

Jesus Christ is certainly truly God, for the very words
'Jesus Christ' describe nothing other than a precise period
in the durative prosôpon of God the Word, that period in
His durative prosôpon when He had made Himself a voluntary, syntactic, prosôpic, loving, adoptive, acknowledging
unity with that which, united with His own vivifying power
could have constituted, but never did actually so constitute,
a separately existent man. We truly say of Jesus Christ:

"This is God." Not indeed God in His ousia and nature alone, in an autogenous prosôpon, for in His own ousia and nature He is invisible and unknowable; but God, the hypostasis of Godhead 'God the Word', manifesting Himself in an allogenous prosôpon which was His by ties as close as they could be made without being ousic and natural, ties not merely voluntary and syntactic but prosôpic, loving, adoptive, and acknowledged. "Christ himself—who is also God, and none other than God the Word, consubstantial—is God" (B. 218-219).

(2) Jesus Christ is truly man.

The terms of the Christological problem are such that they must be interpreted with due mutual reference, for otherwise the problem is patently insoluble. If to be God means to be God and nothing at all but God in Himself absolutely, and if to be man means to be man and in no way anything else, Jesus Christ cannot possibly be both God and man. If, again, it were granted that Jesus Christ could in some way be both God and man, yet it were demanded that the Godhead and manhood should be complete and entirely separate, then a real unity would be impossible. It may be submitted that the Nestorian metaphysic leads to a solution as satisfactory as the conditions of the problem allow. Jesus Christ is truly man in that He has all that a true man has: body, animal soul, and vivifying power derived from God, that vivifying power which completed Adam from an animal mechanism into a 'living soul'. Though that vivifying power did not leave God the Word, and though the awareness in the manhood was that of God the Word, if God the Word had, experiencing as man, wished to yield to the urges and temptations of manhood, which He fully realized, He could by schizohypostasia have brought into existence a true and separate man. The manhood is as real and separate as the conditions of the problem allow, and, if we know precisely what we mean, we may say: "Jesus Christ is truly man." He was born as we are, lived as we do, died as we do. He knew all the urges and temptations of our nature, bodily, mental and spiritual. Nestorius, as already seen, emphasizes this repeatedly (see pp. 168-170). Through Christ we may truly say, "God knows what it is to be man": "He comported himself with sublime obedience in our things, that is, in things human and weak, in such wise that he possessed not any authority or superiority; he was persecuted and beaten and fearful [with] the fear that terrifies all men; and he had not as the birds and as the beasts a place to lay his head. He went from place to place and was bruised and constrained in every way, for the sake of our obedience. He was not constrained by anyone, but he fulfilled [everything] and taught with all zeal, and he endured all temptations" (B. 98–99).

(3) Jesus Christ is truly one.

Before, during and since the Incarnation, there has been unbroken continuity in the durative prosôpon of God the Word. At the Incarnation that durative prosôpon passed into a phase wherein it made use, as its allogenous prosôpon, of the then coming into being nature of the potentially separate man Jesus. This syntactic union persisted throughout the total duration of the potentially separate man Jesus. Apart from God the Word, Jesus never was, and while Jesus was, apart from Him God the Word was not. In modern terms, there was only one personality, that of God the Word, subjecting Himself in the Incarnation to stresses within His own being which, if yielded to, would have led to schizohypostasia and the coming into existence of a separate man Jesus.

It may be useful to return to the analogy of a stranded cable (see pp. 107–108): From eternity to eternity runs the strand of continuity, the autogenous element in the prosôpon of God the Word. This autogenous element is that ousia of Godhead which is hypostatic to the phase of Godhead distinguished as God the Word. That phase, that hypostasis, always and continuously exists, though it is a matter of indifference what ousia of Godhead actually underlies the hypostasis, as the ousia of Godhead is one and indiscriminable. Thus the strand of continuity is the hypostasis God the Word. The durative prosôpon of God the Word is the self-manifestation, revelation and expression of this hypostasis, the prosôpon including both the self, the manifestation, and the means of manifestation. In Himself, or as related to the other hypostases in the Trinity, His prosôpon, His autogenous prosôpon, is His hypostasis as revealed in the power of its ousia and nature solely. But throughout the ages His durative prosôpon has passed through phases when it has for longer or shorter periods been allogenous, using for its self-revelation syntaxes, the other elements in which were in some cases created by fiat ex nihilo ad hoc, and in other cases were other exist-ences already in being, animate or inanimate. Such non-autogenous strands in His durative prosôpon may be regarded as twisting in with the autogenous element in His prosôpon, and so constituting His allogenous prosôpon for the time being. Now for thirty or forty years His durative prosôpon maintained an allogenous phase, during which ousia and nature of manhood (in the sense already precisely explained) constituted a continuing allogenous element in His allogenous prosôpon. (There were of course other allogenous elements from time to time—clothing, tools, implements.) This continuing allogenous element came into being already in union (voluntary, syntactic, prosôpic, loving, adoptive, acknowledged) with His hypostasis and so remained until the natural end of this allogenous element, the natural end of death, when the ousia and nature of manhood disintegrated into body, animal soul, and spirit, the latter being the vivifying power of God, which, had it left the body and animal soul before that natural end, would have left the animal mechanism derelict, or, if it had separated from Godhead and kept to the body and animal soul, would have brought into existence a separate man Jesus.

The significant point is that during the duration of Jesus Christ the cable is one, and that the continuing non-autogenous element in it, the ousia and nature of manhood, was never separate from it and never apart from it, never existed before union with it, and never existed after separa-tion from it: "Christ exists not apart from God the Word" (B. 293). (It is of no significance that the body and animal soul were integrated from other ousias and natures and broke down after death into other ousias and natures. What they were before they became the ousia and nature of His humanity and what they became afterwards is a matter of indifference—see pp. 86–87.) The 'personality', from our point of view, was that of God the Word, and the personality of the manhood was potential—that which would have arisen by schizohypostasia in God the Word had His purpose failed. This comes to very much the same idea as enhypostasia, but perhaps has the advantage of making the struggle more real and the temptation an actual conflict. The unity is not ousic and natural, nor hypostatic in Nestorius' use of the term. It is prosôpic, in the very special senses which have been described: "The natures remain in their properties, and there is one *prosôpon* without separation and without distinction, having made them its own for the *prosôpon*" (B. 266).

(4) Jesus Christ, though truly one, experienced in both natures.

The Nestorian Christology readily provides for a communicatio idiomatum. God the Word, vivifying the manhood, knew what it was to experience as man, and the manhood, retaining accord with Godhead, knew what it was to feel and fulfil the will of God:

"So also in manliness and in authority and in ordering of life and in judgement, as in all things, he was associated with God indivisibly as if each thing were in one by the distinguishing and by the choice of them both, so that he possessed nothing human of his own in human things, but the will of God became his own will, when he was made firm in the actions and sufferings of the nature. Thus also, in things divine, nothing is his own apart from the human humiliation; but, while remaining God in all things, [he is] that which the man was by nature in sufferings, even in impassibility" (B. 102–103).

"The divinity has obtained a likeness by the *ousia* of the humanity and the humanity has obtained a likeness by the *ousia* of the divinity, so that there is one *prosôpon* of the union and so that the [properties] of the humanity belong unto God the Word and those of the divinity unto the humanity wherein it was made man [and so that] they were closely united unto one and the same with a view to the dispensation on our behalf" (B. 266–267).

"In all the things which are the divinity in *ousia*, in them exists the humanity in honour, not by another honour but by the same as that of him who took the *prosôpon*: the humanity making use of the *prosôpon* of the divinity and the divinity of the *prosôpon* of the humanity, since for this it has been taken and for this he has taken it" (B. 289).

(5) Jesus Christ was really tempted, and the struggle within Him was real.

All the urges and desires of humanity were mediated through bodily perception and appetite to that which completed the humanity, which was itself still in one with God the Word. God the Word could at any moment have relieved Himself of the awareness of these urges and desires by dereliction of the animal mechanism, or could have indulged them by schizohypostasia and the bringing into existence of a separate man Jesus. He did not do either of these things, and in so far as the postulates concerning Godhead allow it, we may say that God the Word was aware of stress and temptation, though in His own ousia and nature impassible: "He had all those things that appertain unto our nature, anger and concupiscence and thoughts" (B. 92).

(6) Jesus Christ truly died.

God the Word endured in the syntax until the natural disintegration of the human part of it by death on the Cross. The human part of the syntax disintegrated in exactly the same way as any other human nature would have disintegrated: external conditions made the continuance of the human nature in the syntax impossible, so that it broke down into inanimate body, disembodied animal soul, and discarnate spirit. God the Word, who was vivifying the human nature by power not leaving Himself, was not indeed subject to the nature, but He endured in it just as though He were so subject. He therefore knew by experience how body, animal soul, and spirit, naturally disintegrate. That of Himself which vivified the potentially separate man Jesus continued so to do from the moment of His conception to the moment of His death. If by death we mean the experience of the disintegration of human nature into its constituents, God the Word in Jesus Christ truly died. That God the Word should have endured in unity with the humanity till death was indeed the supreme proof of the strength of the ties of love, adoption and acknowledgment by which He held the humanity to Himself, in bonds so much the stronger and more gracious because not merely voluntary, syntactic and prosôpic, and so much the more glorious and effectual than if they had been ousic and natural: "The likeness of this servant served him altogether as he wished; but he wished [it to be] according to what appertained to the nature, not only that he should obey his own *prosôpon* for himself, so that there might be no doubt concerning him, that he is the Son of God, but also that he might comport himself on our behalf and die for our salvation" (B. 102).

(7) Jesus Christ was able to make true atonement between God and man.

For our present purpose the doctrine of the Atonement only concerns us in so far as it presupposes the fulfilment of certain conditions in any view of the person of Christ which is to be regarded as orthodox. In so far as these conditions include that Jesus Christ must be truly God, truly man, truly one, that He must have truly suffered and truly died, it has already been seen that the Nestorian Christology may claim to fulfil the conditions.

In addition, Nestorius seems to contemplate the Atonement as proceeding according to a logical sequence, the successive steps in which are fully comprehensible in the terms of his Christology:

(i) There is a great gulf between God and humanity.

"In God the Word in fact there is not anything whereby he and we should be of one, or whereby we should be called sons in his likeness, that for this [reason] we should become his brothers, in that we have no reason for such a likeness, as those who are brothers and of one father; nor further that we should become his sons, because we do not participate in the same *ousia*" (B. 46–47).

(ii) To bridge this gulf a mediator is needed.

It is assumed as an axiom by both Nestorius and Sophronius that God cannot, in His own ousia and nature solely, bring about atonement between Himself and humanity. Nestorius says: "If he appeared in his own, then thou sayest an impossible thing, that he was a mediator for him[self]. For *a mediator is not of one, but God is one*" (B. 28–29). Sophronius says: "Because in fact God by his nature is invisible and incomprehensible, he must have some mediator, through whom to provide these things" (B. 76).

(iii) The mediator must be God and man and one, that in Himself He may establish a unity between Godhead and humanity.

It has already been seen that Nestorius agreed in accepting that Jesus Christ was God, man and one (see pp. 60–61 and 174–178). He also recognized that these conditions were essential for a real atonement: "Even as it must have been fitting that our renewal also should take place through the Maker of [our] nature, through him who also originally formed us and made us from the earth, he who took the body and made it in his likeness and constituted it in his *prosôpon* in everything as his own in the honour and glory of God, made use of the nature of the Divinity on the one hand and of the *prosôpon* of the Son on the other" (B. 86). Thus Jesus Christ fulfilled the double condition: "He indeed was the Maker of all, the law-giver, without king, the glory, the honour and the power; he was also the second man with qualities complete and whole" (B. 87–88). "For these reasons, then, and for similar causes, the incarnation of God took place justly: true God by nature and true man by nature" (B. 116). As He is both God and man, we, by consubstantiality with His humanity, are brought into union with Him who is God: "We are his body and consubstantial with him, in that we are that which is also the *ousia* of his body" (B. 49).

(iv) God the Word therefore adopts the flesh, human nature, uniting it with Himself by all possible bonds, and having thus adopted human nature makes possible the adoption of humanity by God.

This is stated, with variations of phrasing, about five times on B. 71 and 72. It is put concisely at the end of section 54 (B. 71): "As they have received him as being God, who has become [their] kin-by-adoption, and as they have acknowledged that he is their God who has made everything and who has come unto his own, so also he has made them his kin-by-adoption and has acknowledged them to be the sons of God, as sons who have entered into sonship but who possess not the nature." This is amplified in the first part of the following section (I. i. 55, B. 72), from which these extracts are taken: "Those who become sons by adoption and by acknowledgement [become the sons] of him of whom they are born not by flesh nor by blood but by the will and the love of him who has no bodily frame but has become their body by adoption and by love and by acknowledgment like a father; so also God the Word who has come into his own has given authority unto those who have received him and confessed him and believed in his name." "Thus therefore he who came into his own and was received gave to those who believed in his name authority to become the sons of God, and he will be their flesh by the taking of the flesh and he will make it [his] by adoption and he will acknowledge it as his body by adoption." "As those who have received him have become voluntarily by reception the natural[1] [sons] of God, so also he, in that he received the flesh and sojourned in it, became their flesh by adoption and not by change of *ousia*." Thus it comes about that "to those who received him and believed in his name he gave authority to become the sons of God" (B. 77–78).

(v) God the Word in Jesus Christ by obedience even unto death redeems the human nature which He has adopted, thus gaining the victory first for Himself and then for us.

God the Word in Jesus Christ sought in all things to be obedient and submissive to God (that is, to be consistent with His own divine nature): "He comported himself with sublime obedience in our things" (B. 98–99). "It was preferable to him that the will of God should be done and not that of the flesh" (B. 96). He carried this submission even to death on the Cross: "And he prostrated himself to such a degree that his own creation in its nature was not in honour nor in glory but in contempt and in abasement and in all humiliation unto death upon the cross; he humiliated

[1] On the word 'natural' in this quotation, see p. 442.

himself unto death, even death upon the cross; there is nothing more scorned than death" (B. 89). "And he possessed as a supreme honour *obedience unto death, even death upon the cross,* and he showed unto Satan and unto every principality and unto every authority that the cause of honour is rather obedience abounding and not disobedience unto God" (B. 100). In this way He gained the victory, first for Himself: "And because there remained only death to be [endured] for defeat and victory, he endured this also after everything so as to have won the victory even over it, utterly annihilating it" (B. 106); and then, consequently, for us: "Because in fact he took this [likeness] in order to abolish the guilt of the first man and in order to give to his nature the former image which he had lost through his guilt" (B. 91). "In this very hope he obtained also obedience and immeasurable love, not that he might obtain victory for himself but that he might secure the exaction of our own [ransom] and conquer not only for himself but also for all men" (B. 107). "As then to him who has conquered and been victorious in all things there has been given in return for the honour of his victory authority to preach and to announce the hope of the kingdom of heaven, saying: *Be of good cheer; I have conquered the world; now is the judgement of this world, now is the prince of this world condemned, and I, when I shall be raised up from the earth, shall draw all men toward me*" (B. 97).

(vi) Thus by virtue of the common nature, humanity, we are redeemed and united (given kinship) with God.

"But *Christ is the head of all* and in him are we bound together; but also God is the head of Christ, for whom, as he is for us the head and the *prosôpon,* is God so also his head and his *prosôpon* in his incarnation. Therefore we have received from him to become the sons of God" (B. 83). "But because he stablished his own image in all temptations perfectly and without failing and without falling short in anything, he comported himself on our behalf, being zealous to rescue us captives from the violence of the tyrant and to draw us towards him and to make all of us the sons of his own kingdom, the associates and the heirs and the sons of God" (B. 97–98).

(vii) Thus Satan was foiled, and though God allowed him still to assault humanity, victory can always be obtained by those who avail themselves of the victory won by Christ, and final joy and glory will be theirs.

This is the main theme, though dealt with somewhat discursively, of I. i. 78–87 (B. 104–116): Christ in His obedience even unto death conquered not only death but also Satan: "Because there remained only death to be [endured] for defeat and victory, he endured this also after every thing so as to have won the victory even over it, utterly annihilating it. And two things he wrought thereby: he defeated Satan and he took away from him all hope of disobedience" (B. 106–107). Hence "humanity has conquered and Satan has been defeated" (B. 108). But God still allowed Satan to assault humanity: "All this time of long-suffering has been given unto him, and it is given unto him until the day of judgement to do whatever he will" (B. 115). Victory, however, can always be obtained by those who avail themselves of the victory won by Christ, for "he has shown that his incarnation was a universal dispensation for all those who have been accounted equal with him in one purpose and in one persuasion, to stand against the enemy of them all, whom he has driven out and whose authority he has suppressed" (B. 109). "In the same way as the defeat of Adam caused the defeat of all men, so also the victory of the former[1] made all victorious" (B. 107–108). Finally, through Christ we shall enter into joy and glory everlasting: "And after this, seeing that everything has been well [done], we shall be in the joy of the world to come, having no cause [to fear] deprivation thereof nor that we shall have further need of instruction" (B. 116).

A digression must be made at this point on one of Nestorius' most irritating characteristics: on the one hand, his own use of unqualified and undefined terms, expecting his readers to sense the nuances as exactly as he himself does; on the other hand, his unwillingness or inability to make the same allowance for others. We have already seen how we have to understand the shades of meaning in

[1] Jesus Christ.

various contexts of 'in' (pp. 141–147), and 'prosôpon' (pp. 99–108). It is now necessary to remark on his use of 'God the Word', 'Christ', 'the man', and 'he'. For precision, we must distinguish:

(1) God the Word as in His own nature solely, one of the three eternally existing hypostases of the Godhead, of divine ousia and nature, unknowable by man except as He reveals Himself in allogenous prosôpa. For distinction we might convey this concept by 'God the Word in Himself' or 'God the Word as such'.

(2) God the Word during the period when He was revealing Himself as Jesus Christ, using in His allogenous prosôpon the potentially separate man Jesus, uniting humanity to Himself by love, acknowledgment and adoption, determining to remain in that union until the natural disintegration of the allogenous part of His prosôpon. God the Word during that period may correctly be described as 'Jesus Christ', 'Christ', 'Lord', or 'Son'. For precision we might use the expression 'God the Word as Jesus Christ'.

(3) The potentially separate man Jesus. This never-separate entity, even if described as 'the man', 'Jesus', or 'the humanity', must always be thought of with emphasis on 'potentially'. It might be best to use the term 'the manhood', understanding by that 'the potentially separate man Jesus'.

If we have perfectly clear ideas as to the connotation of 'God the Word as such', 'God the Word as Jesus Christ', and 'the manhood', there will be no need to use the full and exact expressions every time. Nor will it usually be open to objection to use 'God the Word' to mean either 'God the Word as such' or 'God the Word as Jesus Christ'. Exact expression can become very tedious.

Nestorius had a very great desire to keep clear distinction not only in thought but in expression between 'God the Word as such' and 'God the Word as Jesus Christ'. He desired to keep 'God the Word' to mean 'God the Word as such', and he desired that 'God the Word as Jesus Christ' should not be referred to simply as 'God the Word', but as 'Christ', 'Lord', 'Son', or some similar title. He harps on this point wearisomely. He had it firmly in mind that in using 'God the Word' to describe Jesus Christ, Cyril was somehow implying hypostatic union and denying the human nature in Christ. The greater part of Book II, Part I, is taken up in circling round the same points: Nestorius insists that the union of Godhead and manhood in Christ was prosôpic, not hypostatic; that the two natures remained, and that the Virgin Mary was mother of the humanity, and only by careful definition to be described as 'Theotokos'; and absurdly anxious lest to call Jesus Christ 'God the Word' should imply hypostatic union and the abolition of the human nature in Him. Thus we shall find the attack on the idea of hypostatic union carried on passim on B. 133–137, 225–240, 257–270, 405; the objection to Jesus Christ being described simply as 'God the Word' passim on B. 201–204, 211–225, 245–270, 141–146, 271–363, 404–459; his views on 'Theotokos' on B. 151–152, 220, 255–256, 271–281, 405. All these passages are in Book II, Part I, except B. 133–137, which is the closing portion of Book I, Part II, and B. 151–152, which is near the beginning of Book I, Part III.

In reference to Christ, Nestorius emphasized that 'God the Word' signified the divine ousia and nature in the prosôpic unity. He did himself a disservice by this emphasis, as it lent colour to the charge of dualism, of which we do not believe he was guilty. He should have recognized, and probably did, that 'God the Word' could be used quite legitimately and understandably to mean 'God the Word as Jesus Christ', and that no one could possibly misunderstand the usage. But he attacks Cyril time and again for using 'God the Word' where Nestorius would have used 'Christ'.

His objection to 'Theotokos' is exactly parallel. If Jesus Christ was God the Word—as He was—then the Virgin Mary was 'Theotokos'. Nestorius knew quite well in what way Jesus Christ was God the Word, and he knew quite well in what way the Virgin Mary was 'Theotokos'. But he obstinately preferred to call God the Word as Jesus Christ 'Christ' rather than 'God the Word', and consequently Mary 'Christotokos' rather than 'Theotokos'. This matter is dealt with on pp. 450–452 and 458–459. On the other hand, in closely reasoned arguments it is sometimes necessary to make exact distinctions between 'God the Word as such', 'God the Word in Jesus Christ', and 'the potentially separate man Jesus'. Here emerges Nestorius' antithetic fault: in such arguments he will persist in using simply 'he'. As Bethune-Baker remarks with regard to Nestorius' use of pronouns, so often "it is difficult to assign them to their proper subjects."[1] This is a grave matter when the whole coherence of an argument may depend on knowing whether 'he' means 'God the Word as such', 'God the Word in Jesus Christ', 'God the Word as conscious of Himself as united with humanity', or 'the potentially separate man Jesus'. These distinctions must have been in Nestorius' mind if only subconsciously, and they must assuredly be in ours if certain passages are to make sense. As in the case of the use of 'in', we have to enter his mind to understand his arguments. Examples may be found on B. 30, 32–34, 84, 87, 90–93, 96, 102, 214–215, 252. A few are worked out in the notes (e.g. B. 30 on pp. 249–250, B. 84 on p. 275), but once the general principles are understood the matter is not unduly difficult. Nevertheless, it is irritating to read page after page in which Nestorius attacks others for inexactitude of expression, while he himself was guilty of exactly the same inexactitude in the use of 'in', 'prosôpon', and 'he'.

[1] *Nestorius and His Teaching*, p. 126.

CHAPTER VII

SUMMARY AND ESTIMATE

IN the preceding chapters an endeavour has been made to reduce the ideas of Nestorius to an ordered system. As was stated in the Preface, it is not possible to do so without filling in certain lacunæ in his arguments, deducing the precise significance of terms he does not define, and classifying the modes of usage of certain words which he uses with shades of meaning which he no doubt considered self-evident from the contexts. But the reduction to order is not impossible, and if the reconstruction set out in the preceding chapters is tentatively accepted, it is believed that the Bazaar can be read from beginning to end with complete understanding.

If, however, we are asked to give a brief summary of Nestorius' views, we begin to understand why they were never accepted. It is not possible, even by the most careful selection, to gather together a series of quotations from the Bazaar which, without explanation or linkage, will give a coherent and connected account of his view of the Incarnation. Any such series of quotations would contain gaps and ambiguities, and assertions in place of reasoned proofs. Probably the best summary statement in his own terms is that to be found in Book I, Part II, section 7 (B. 128–133), from which two important sections should be quoted:

"But others[1] say of the incarnation of our Lord [that it was in] an animate flesh in[2] a rational and intelligent soul, complete in its nature and in its might and in its natural activities, and not in *schêma* nor in a change of *ousia* nor again for the natural completion of the nature of the body and of the soul, or of the intelligence, or [that it was] mingled into one nature out of two of them or that they were changed from the one into the other, or that [it took place] for the completion of the natural activities in such

[1] I.e., Nestorius himself.
[2] On the meanings of 'in' in this passage, see p. 449.

wise that the flesh should not act in its own nature; but
[it was in] one *prosôpon* of both natures, both of them
maintaining the properties of their own natures; and the
ousia of the divinity remains and suffers not when it is in
the *ousia* of the flesh, and the flesh again remains in the
ousia of the flesh when it is in the nature and in the *prosôpon*
of the divinity; for the body is one and both of them [are]
one Son. For no other is called God the Word in the flesh
apart from him who is in our own flesh; nor again [is anything else called] the flesh, but it is in the Son, in God the
Word: that he should comport himself completely in the
nature of men being man, and that he should rise as God
being God by nature, that he in consequence of sinlessness
and of having observed [the commandments] should be
delivered to death for our salvation, that he might preserve
the likeness of his own image. In order then to become
so, he took not for [his] likeness *a name which is more
excellent than all names*[1] that the nature of men might be
exalted; for the honour and exaltation has not been given
to an *ousia* which henceforward is not of man but of God
the Word. Our own nature has been honoured in another
nature and not in our own nature; for the exaltation of
our own nature to *a name which is more excellent than all
names*[2] belongs generally to that nature which is the exaltation of one who remains in his own *ousia* and can be that
which is in the *ousia* of God the Word; this in fact is properly
the exaltation, like which there is not [any other]"
(B. 128–129).

"Therefore he[3] said *he humiliated himself*[4] in reference
to a voluntary union, the incarnation and the kind of
humiliation which he showed when *he took the likeness
of a servant*,[5] and again that which took place resulted in
a voluntary and not a natural [union]; in *schêma* he was
found as a man,[6] not in *ousia*; for in the likeness of God
[was] the likeness of the servant. The likeness of God was
in *schêma* as a man, for God was in his own *ousia*, in such
wise that it was conceived also as an humiliation in him
that he took the likeness of a servant, and as an exaltation

[1] Phil. ii. 9.   [2] Ibid., 9.   [3] St. Paul.   [4] Phil. ii. 8.
[5] Ibid., 7.   [6] Ibid., 8.

in the likeness of the servant that it took *a name which is more excellent than all names*,[1] and [so that] it was not conceived as a change of *ousia* either into an *ousia* or into a natural composition of one nature, but as being a voluntary [union], as [being] one in humiliation and in exaltation; for that of nature is passible and changeable, since it is a nature created and made, not uncreated nor unmade nor unchangeable nor immutable" (B. 131).

How could the ordinary reader be expected to gain any very clear ideas from the above passages unless he had first painstakingly investigated the shades of meaning to be attached to 'in', and had grasped Nestorius' connotation of the highly specialized yet unexplained word 'prosôpon'? No wonder Maclean describes these passages as "hopelessly confused"![2] Though we may eventually feel confident that we have grasped Nestorius' meaning, he might have saved us much labour by explaining his views in more detail: more proof and less assertion, more defence and less attack.

If a summary is to be given, it would have to be in some such terms as these:

(1) God, the uncreated Creator, has caused all things else to come into being. He has done this without loss or change to His own being, which remains unchanged. He creates by divine fiat, and created things come into existence ex nihilo. The Uncreated and the created thus stand in sharp contradistinction. Underlying the existence of God is the divine ousia, the properties and attributes of which constitute the divine nature. Underlying the existence of any individual created thing is its appropriate ousia, the properties and attributes of which constitute its nature (pp. 64–69).

(2) The ousia of God is unchangeable and His nature is infinite. He is not subject to any circumscriptions. But all other ousias have their beginnings and their endings, and their natures are precise and limited. They cannot escape from their natures, which define and circumscribe them (pp. 121–126, 69–70).

(3) Having created ex nihilo the ousias which in the

[1] Phil. ii. 9.
[2] Article "Nestorianism", *Encyclopædia of Religion and Ethics*, ix. 329.

beginning constituted the present material Universe, God made provision for change and development by ordaining laws for the interaction of ousias, so that in certain circumstances an ousia would break down into other different ousias, or ousias would combine to form a new and different ousia. These changes depend entirely on the will of God, acting specially or through His laws, and the existence of an ousia as such is to be reckoned from the time of its origin to the time of its end; it is not to be reckoned as in any way connected with that from which it may have been derived (pp. 70–79, 82–88).

(4) An ousia is known by the exercise of the powers and the manifestation of the attributes of its nature. It cannot exercise all its powers and manifest all its attributes simultaneously. At any given moment an ousia is exercising certain of its powers and manifesting certain of its attributes —presenting itself in a certain way. This self-presentation, this self-manifestation, this instantaneous cross-section of the existence of the ousia, is its instantaneous prosôpon. It includes the ousia in itself, and the mode and method of its manifestation. At any instant an ousia has a prosôpon just as inevitably as it has a nature. Ousia, nature and prosôpon are necessarily correlated, and are aspects of one reality: an ousia without nature would have no powers or attributes to manifest, and without prosôpon there would be no manifestation of the powers and attributes; a nature without an underlying ousia would postulate phenomena without basis, as would a prosôpon without an ousia with a nature to give rise to it. Objectively, we see and appreciate prosôpa; but we know that the prosôpon is the manifestation of an ousia, and we know that the mode and method of the manifestation depend on its nature (pp. 98–100).

(5) At any moment an ousia manifests itself by its instantaneous prosôpon, which depends on what powers of its nature it is exercising. But there is a continuity in the existence of an ousia, and there is a continuity in the succession of its instantaneous prosôpa. This continuity is the durative prosôpon of the ousia, which begins with the beginning of the existence of the ousia and ends with

the end of the existence of the ousia. A durative prosôpon is the continuity of the manifestation of an existence, and implies that existence and its nature (pp. 100–101).

(6) An ousia having volition, an animate ousia, is able to make use of other ousias. These other ousias are thus brought into the mode and manner of the self-presentation of the animate ousia, and therefore constitute part of its prosôpon. A man clothed and using a saw presents himself to eye, ear and understanding in a certain way. This presentation is his instantaneous prosôpon, and this instantaneous prosôpon is part of a phase, long or short, in his durative prosôpon. The prosôpon reveals the man's nature, though for its expression it includes not simply the ousia of the man himself, but also the ousias of his articles of clothing and of the saw. The whole presentation is his prosôpon, but it includes ousias other than his own. It may be termed an allogenous prosôpon, as opposed to a prosôpon based entirely on its own ousia, which may be termed autogenous (pp. 102–104).

(7) Hence an animate ousia manifests itself as a durative prosôpon, which passes through phases autogenous and allogenous. But even the allogenous phases always imply and reveal the ousia itself, which is the basis of the continuity (p. 104).

(8) God, of one ousia and nature, unlike other ousias, which can only manifest themselves in one durative prosôpon, though that prosôpon may pass through many phases autogenous or allogenous, manifests Himself in three simultaneous and complementary phases, so that He has three simultaneous prosôpa. These prosôpa are all based on the one ousia of God and all possess the one divine nature. But as they exist continually, there exist unique distinctions within the Godhead, for these prosôpa are implicit in His inner harmony as well as explicit in His outer functioning. To indicate that the three prosôpa are more than three modes of manifestation of the same ousia (Sabellianism) and at the same time not the manifestation of three separate ousias (tritheism), the three prosôpa are also referred to as hypostases (though hypostasis is normally synonymous with ousia), it thus being understood

that there are three simultaneously existing prosôpa of the Godhead, to each of which ousia of Godhead is directly and simultaneously hypostatic (pp. 127–141).

(9) One of these prosôpa or hypostases (prosôpon bearing more particular reference to the manifestation and hypostasis to the underlying ousia, but both implying the same total reality), distinguished as God the Word, is the hypostasis of Godhead through which the divine urge to redeem His creation is expressed (pp. 130–132).

(10) God the Word, wishing to become man, that He might experience as man, reveal Godhead to mankind, and by obedience unto death redeem mankind and make atonement between God and man, made use of a potentially complete and separate man as part of His prosôpon for a certain period. He thus had an allogenous prosôpon, consisting of Himself and of the potentially complete and separate man as His instrument (pp. 155–157).

(11) But He did not use the potentially separate man as a mere dwelling or instrument. He so loved mankind that He determined that He would attach Himself as closely as was possible to the potentially separate man whom He had taken into His prosôpon. Being divine ousia, He could not enter into ousic union with the potentially separate man; but He united Himself with him as completely as was otherwise possible, by ties of love, acknowledgment and adoption, determining to stay in that voluntary union with him until the natural duration of the potential man ended in death (pp. 162–166).

(12) By uniting Himself with the potentially separate man from the moment of the latter's inception in utero Virginis, and maintaining that union until the dissolution of the human nature by death on the Cross, He established and maintained a union of an unexampled kind: the total duration of the existence of the potentially separate man was spent as part of the allogenous prosôpon of God the Word, and during the existence of the potentially separate man God the Word had no prosôpon other than the allogenous prosôpon of which the potentially separate man was part (pp. 154–157).

(13) Further, God the Word self-limited Himself to the

N

powers and modes of self-expression of the potentially separate man, so that during the existence of the potentially separate man His prosôpon was the potentially separate man (pp. 167–168, 171–174).

(14) God the Word brought the potentially separate man into existence in such a way that He was never separate from Him, and the vivifying power which made the manhood complete had both entered into association with the body and animal soul of the potentially separate man and had remained with God the Word, in such a way that had any but ousia of Godhead been involved the union would have been ousic and natural (pp. 154–161).

(15) God the Word thus consciously experienced in human nature, and, though in His ousia impassible, yet realized what human urges were and what human stresses meant. He therefore felt and experienced exactly as a man does, and so far as the manhood was concerned, He had consciously to school and discipline Himself to conform with the will of Himself as God. If, dreadful to contemplate, He had wished to yield to the sensuously apprehended urges of humanity, to sin, He would only have needed to discard the attributes of the divine nature which made Him one with Godhead, and cleave to the body and animal soul of manhood with that of Himself which would complete it into a separate man. This would have been schizo-hypostasia, a rending of the divine hypostasis by failure to withstand the internal stresses caused by His own venture, and the emergence of Himself fallen into rebellion against His own will and law (pp. 157–165, 178–179).

(16) If for lack of a better term we call this union of Godhead and manhood prosôpic, we may claim that in this prosôpic union God the Word united Himself with manhood, in such a way that the durative prosôpon of God the Word during the period of union was a real unity, was truly God, and was truly man (pp. 174–178).

The above is almost too lengthy to be called a summary, but it can hardly be further abbreviated. Indeed, it would not be readily comprehensible or properly understood by anyone who had not read the preceding chapters, and the writer feels that it is not an adequate statement; and that brings us to a secondary but not unimportant criticism of the Nestorian Christology: it is incapable of being expressed clearly and at the same time concisely. Explanations may be inevitably involved, but a formula for general acceptance must be clear and concise. Nestorius never succeeded in giving a clear and concise statement of what he really meant by prosôpic union, and it is not easy for us to do it for him.

We should, however, recognize that there are elements in the Nestorian metaphysic and Christology which are of real value, and which we may well carry forward, perhaps considerably modified, in our further thinking. Consider, for instance, Nestorius' approach to a discrimination of the two natures in Jesus Christ: (1) Jesus Christ was God in that He was the (allogenous) prosôpon of God the Word, who during the existence of Jesus Christ had no other prosôpon, and God the Word is God in that His ousia and nature is ousia and nature of God, an ousia and nature one and indiscriminable. When we say "Jesus Christ is God" we know exactly what we mean, and we know that it is true: in Him is God revealed, through a prosôpon as completely revealing of Godhead to mankind as is possible. (It must be remembered that an allogenous prosôpon necessarily includes the ousia of that of which it is the self-manifestation, though it includes other elements also.) (2) Jesus Christ was man in that He had a body and animal soul just as we have, and a centre of consciousness and will (a νοῦς or πνεῦμα), capable of feeling our urges and stresses, capable, as we are, of sinfully yielding to those urges. Had He so yielded, He would have become a man and nothing more. As He did not yield, the centre of consciousness and will remained in Him who was giving it, God the Word. (3) Jesus Christ was one, because there was never any centre of consciousness and will other than God the Word, who experienced in two natures, that of His own divine ousia and that of the ousia of humanity which He Himself completed.

It may at once be remarked that the weakest point in this interpretation is the establishment of the true manhood of Jesus Christ. But it must be recognized that any greater emphasis on the manhood leads to a dualism, to "Nestorianism" as commonly understood. It must never be forgotten that the Incarnation consisted in God becoming man, not man becoming God, nor God and man uniting. Unless the terms of the problem are pressed to the point of impossibility of fulfilment (see pp. 174–176), the writer fails to see how God could 'become' man (within the meaning of the rigid ancient terms) more completely than as explained by the Nestorian Christology as here clarified. It has to be remembered that the continuity is God the Word: before the birth at Bethlehem, there was God the Word; during the earthly life of Jesus Christ there was God the Word manifesting Himself through that which He was completing into true manhood and which He had joined to Himself by all ties other than natural; after the earthly life of Jesus Christ was over, God the Word continued as a prosôpon, a hypostasis, of the Trinity, though in honoured remembrance of the period when He was in prosôpic union with His adopted humanity, it is still right and fitting to call Him Jesus Christ. God the Word always was, is and will be; Jesus Christ names the period in the duration of God the Word when He adopted humanity as His prosôpon; the man Jesus never existed as a separate entity, though he would have done had the purpose of God the Word failed.

If we adopt Nestorius' terms, and help ourselves to use them with accuracy and understanding by using the adjectives instantaneous and durative, autogenous and allogenous, especially in relation to the word prosôpon, we may develop from his a Christology at once orthodox and powerful, which fits all the scriptural references by enabling us to know the precise way in which to interpret any given phrase.

As the purpose of this part of our work is the interpretation of Nestorius as nearly as possible in his own terms, it is perhaps inadvisable to attempt to make any brief transcript of his views into modern idiom. That would involve consideration of many debatable matters which are outside our present intention, and we consider it better to leave Nestorius in his own terms. Part II will represent our approach to the problem in modern terms, and it is not useful to go over similar ground twice. Sufficient to say that the writer believes that the ancient categories of thought still have value as an approach to reality. Though they are admittedly liable to lead to a rigid and mechanical metaphysic, properly understood they nevertheless provide a normative framework. If a modern view cannot be translated intelligibly and logically (with of course inevitable adjustments and qualifications) into the ancient terms, it is probably false or unduly vague. Correspondingly, a view expressed in the ancient terms should without undue difficulty admit of restatement in terms conformable with modern science and philosophy, possibly with great gain and a desirable loss of rigidity. The significance of this statement will emerge in the first chapter of Part II.

For example, though at first sight the Nestorian metaphysic may seem far from modern ideas as to the nature and behaviour of matter, properly understood it emphasizes an aspect of reality which is valuable and significant. The modern physicist or chemist can gain a humbler and truer view of the behaviour of the physical world by realizing that all action is by God's law: each organism, each compound, each electron, has a divinely appointed nature "in which it has to be" (B. 56). No man can make things act otherwise than as God's laws allow. We may know more than the ancients about each thing's ousia and nature. But it is still true that every existence is based on the totality of that which underlies it—and why not name that totality its ousia?—and that every existence has definite powers and properties—and why not call them its nature?—and that every existence manifests itself in a changing continuity—and why not call that changing continuity its durative prosôpon?

We are therefore of the opinion that there is real value even to-day in making an endeavour to understand Nestorius' outlook and in trying to discover the positions towards which he was striving. Whether or not the problem was solvable in the terms in which it was then approached, which some doubt,[1] it must nevertheless be recognized that the more rigid metaphysic and the more consciously space-

[1] E.g., Cave: "The problem raised was possibly insoluble. Certainly it could not be solved by the categories of ancient thought, and the supposed solution at Chalcedon was no solution, but only a preservation of the problem." (*The Doctrine of the Person of Christ*, p. 104.)

temporal framework of the Conciliar period led to an exactitude of expression which may serve as a check and a corrective to the somewhat changed emphasis of more recent approaches, in which there is sometimes danger that a feeling after intangible ultimates may result in loss of touch with the normative standards of objective reality. For it must surely be recognized that anything ultimately true must, in so far as it can be objectively contemplated, fit harmoniously in suitably comparable terms into a Universe only directly perceivable as objectively apparently real. That is to say, ultimate truth may be very different from objective apparent reality, but a self-consistent interpretation of a set of phenomena in terms of the latter is at least probably in some way in parallel correspondence with the former. Applying this to Christology, it may be submitted that however unlike ultimate reality may be to any image of it expressible in terms apparently real to beings for whom reality is apparently a space-time continuum, an interpretation of reality consistent and satisfactory within the terms of a space-time continuum is prima facie more likely to be in parallel correspondence with the truth than one that is not thus consistent. We thus conclude that the terms of the Conciliar Christology still have a normative value.[1] If a modern view cannot be translated into terms rendering it interpretable within the framework provided by the Conciliar metaphysic, there is a probability that the view is too vague, generalized and inexact to be a real contribution to constructive thought. Correspondingly, a solution of the problem in terms of the Conciliar metaphysic may be transposable, possibly with great gain, into more modern terms. The object of this part of our work has been to enunciate, as clearly as may be, Nestorius' metaphysic and Christology in his own terms and their necessary amplifications; and in the next part it may be found that the attempt to do this has enabled us to make what we hope may prove a valid and helpful approach to the same problem in categories consistent with modern thought modes.

[1] As Sanday so well remarks concerning the Christologists of the early centuries, "It is not for us to blame them; and least of all, to blame them before we have got a coherent and consistent theory of our own that we can substitute for theirs." (*Christologies Ancient and Modern*, p. 55.)

Before leaving this part, a word should be said in answer to a criticism that will surely arise in many minds: "Why all this attention to Nestorius? Why not rather give attention to the teaching of Cyril?" It must at once be said that a careful analysis and development of Cyril's views would lead to a Christology of undoubted and definite orthodoxy; for Cyril, quite rightly, was more concerned with the answer than with the argument. He knew that Jesus Christ had two natures, and he knew that Jesus Christ was one Person. "Two natures, one hypostasis" simply asserted those facts. If the definition of hypostasis as particular ousia does not fit that statement, then hypostasis must be re-defined! Cyril was right, and it is well to recognize that Nestorius was obstinately foolish in making so much of the point that hypostatic union was necessarily natural union. It was—if hypostasis was ousia. But if we retain Nestorius' rigid ideas of ousia and nature, and recognize that for Cyril hypostasis means something more like dura-tive prosôpon, we shall surely be very near a reconciliation of the two positions. As to the casus belli, 'Theotokos', we have scarcely needed to mention it. It is only relevant—apart from a right and natural desire to honour her whom God chose to be the mother of His humanity—as a test of the clarity of our Christological views, and what little needs to be said about it will be found in the notes on pp. 623–625.

Furthermore, it may be noted that the Nestorian Christ-ology as here interpreted is not inconsistent with modern statements of the orthodox position. For example, if we wish for a statement on the exact relation of Jesus Christ to Godhead, we might quote Nolloth:

"In the statement, Christ is God, the subject and the predicate are not identical. We can predicate Godhead of Christ: but we cannot invert the statement and say, God is Christ. In other words, the Godhead is a term of greater content than Christ. When we say that He is God, we do not exhaust the conception of Godhead."[1]

How lucidly this same idea is expressed in terms of the Nestorian Christology! There is one ousia and nature of Godhead, one and indiscriminable, manifesting itself in

[1] *The Person of Our Lord and Recent Thought*, p. 328.

three durative prosôpa, to each of which ousia and nature of Godhead is hypostatic: one of those durative prosôpa, God the Word, manifested Himself for a period as the allogenous prosôpon Jesus Christ. Thus Jesus Christ was truly God, in that He was the (allogenous) prosôpon of God the Word, a Trinitarian prosôpon to which ousia of Godhead was hypostatic. But the totality of Godhead includes all three prosôpa, which together include everything to which ousia and nature of Godhead is hypostatic.

Again, we may quote a typical statement of the way in which God the Word self-limited Himself in order to make manhood His only mode of self-expression during His duration as Jesus Christ: "The assumption of a continuous act of Self-limitation on the part of the Word meets all the demands of Scripture, and gives us considerable assistance in conceiving the character of the Incarnation of the Eternal Son. We have in such an act of Self-restraint on the part of the Logos no depotentiation of His powers, no Self-paralysis, no ceasing of the Second Person of the Blessed Trinity from His Trinitarian functions; but, on the contrary, a profound manifestation of His essential Deity in a continuous act of Self-sacrifice which is carried over into His glorified existence and which, therefore, eternally secures the verity of His Manhood."[1] In Nestorian terms, we should simply say that God the Word, wishing to live and experience as man, voluntarily restricted Himself during a certain period to self-manifestation and self-expression through an allogenous prosôpon whose limitations were those of manhood. In that the experiences remained with God the Word after the actual period of self-restriction as Jesus Christ, we may certainly agree that its significance "is carried over into His glorified existence and . . ., therefore, eternally secures the verity of His Manhood." The permissibility, perhaps even the inevitability, of the idea of the voluntary self-limitation of God the Word is confirmed by the implications of Iverach's concept of perfect self-consciousness: "The conception of a perfect self-consciousness consists in the fact that it is in possession of itself, and can set the bounds of its own experience. Self-knowledge,

[1] La Touche, *The Person of Christ in Modern Thought*, p. 389.

self-reverence, self-control—in these, and not in finitude or infinitude, lies the conception of a perfect selfhood."[1]

As to the assumption of perfect manhood, we may quote as an example the words of Grensted: "In Jesus the Second Person of the Blessed Trinity, the Word, the Only-begotten Son of God, took whole and complete manhood, of the substance or personal being of His Mother. Thus as man He is perfectly the expression of God."[2] In Nestorian terms, we say that God the Word entered into voluntary, loving, acknowledged, adoptive, prosôpic union with a human body and animal soul, which He completed into whole manhood by the vivifying power going forth from Himself, which similarly vivified the first Adam, but in this case was never separated from Himself, so that it was at once the completing of the manhood and still in Himself. The substance of His body certainly had its inception and first development in and from the substance of His mother, and the unification took place within her.

As to the completing of the manhood by the vivifying power of God the Word, that power being at once the completing of the manhood and still in Himself, we may quote a close parallel from Relton: "The Divine Logos, prior to the Incarnation, already possessed everything needful to enable Him to live a truly human life. . . . His advent, therefore, in the flesh brought to the human nature He assumed, not an alien element such as would render a truly human life for the God-Man an impossibility, but just that which alone could make the life of Christ in every stage of its growth and development a truly and perfectly human life. The Divine Logos was capable of being the Ego, not only of His Divine but also of His human Nature."[3]

Finally, we can apply the test of the Definition of Chalcedon.[4] If we regard this as the ultimate criterion for a Christology expressed in the terms developed and used

---

[1] Article "Consciousness", *Encyclopædia of Religion and Ethics*, iv. 57.
[2] *The Person of Christ*, p. 246.   [3] *A Study in Christology*, pp. 226–227.
[4] The fourth Œcumenical Council met at Chalcedon in 451. Its most important result was the formulation of a Definition of the Faith, usually referred to as the Definition of Chalcedon or the Chalcedonian Definition. A general account of the Council may be found in Kidd, *A History of the Church*, iii. 311–339.

during the first five centuries of the Christian era, we may see whether we can read and understand that Definition the better for having endeavoured to unravel the thought processes of Nestorius. The Definition says:[1] "Following therefore the holy Fathers, we all with one voice teach to confess one and the same Son, our Lord Jesus Christ, the same perfect in Godhead and the same perfect in manhood, the same truly God and truly man of a reasonable soul and body, consubstantial with the Father as to the Godhead and the same consubstantial with us as to the manhood, like unto us in all things except sin; before the ages begotten of the Father as to the Godhead, and the same in the last days, for us and for our salvation, of Mary the Virgin the God-bearer as to the manhood, one and the same Christ, Son, Lord, Only-begotten, acknowledged in[2] two natures, unconfusedly, immutably, indivisibly, inseparably; the distinction of the natures by no means being taken away by the union, but rather the peculiarity of each nature being preserved and concurring in one prosôpon and one hypostasis, not parted or divided into two prosôpa, but one and the same Son and Only-begotten, God the Word, the Lord Jesus Christ; according as the prophets taught concerning Him from the beginning, and as the Lord Jesus Christ Himself taught us, and as the Creed of the Fathers has delivered to us."

Would Nestorius have been willing to subscribe to this Definition? Fisher thinks so: "Notwithstanding the deference paid by the Chalcedon Fathers to Cyril's teaching, Nestorius might have signed the Creed, including the title 'Theotocos,' as it was qualified by the words appended to it."[3] But though he might have accepted θεοτόκος qualified by κατὰ τὴν ἀνθρωπότητα, it is more than likely that he would still have boggled at μίαν ὑπόστασιν. Though it is almost certain that he died before the Definition of

---

[1] For footnote 1, see p. 203.

[2] It is disputed whether the preposition should be 'in' or 'of' (ἐν or ἐκ). Without entering into a discussion on the matter, it may be remarked that ἐν is the more generally accepted reading (e.g., by Gieseler, Hefele, Seeberg, Kidd, Bethune-Baker, Mackintosh, Curtis, Foakes-Jackson), but ἐκ is held to be original by Baur, Dorner, Briggs, and Relton.

[3] *History of Christian Doctrine*, pp. 155–156.

Chalcedon was formulated, and was spared the humiliation of knowing that yet another Council had condemned him, for our purpose the anathematizing of Nestorius and the condemnation of what was thought to be his doctrine is not relevant. The question relevant for us is: does what Nestorius was striving to express help us to comprehend the Definition? Surely it does. If we read the Definition through, bearing in mind the Nestorian Christology as we have interpreted it, we shall find it glowing with a new lucidity. Only the word hypostasis will give us any concern. But if we remember that Nestorius was wrong in identifying it with a particular ousia in its nature and that Cyril was right in regarding it as the criterion of unity of person in something like our way of understanding such unity, even that difficulty disappears. Jesus Christ was one hypostasis, if by hypostasis we understand something very akin to durative animate prosôpon.

The first part of our inquiry is ended, and although it does not lead us to wish to reverse the ancient decisions against Nestorius, it may at least have shown us that he had something to contribute to our thought. If we have shown that there is a way of interpreting that contribution coherently and unambiguously, making clear what Nestorius may have had in mind though he never clearly expressed it, then something may have been done to help us in our further thinking. Thus we may have mitigated the sadness of his fate by giving a patient and unbiassed hearing to a voice from the dust of the desert.

Footnote 1, *p.* 202: Ἑπόμενοι τοίνυν τοῖς ἁγίοις πατράσιν ἕνα καὶ τὸν αὐτὸν ὁμολογεῖν υἱὸν τὸν κύριον ἡμῶν Ἰησοῦν Χριστὸν συμφώνως ἅπαντες ἐκδιδάσκομεν, τέλειον τὸν αὐτὸν ἐν θεότητι καὶ τέλειον τὸν αὐτὸν ἐν ἀνθρωπότητι, θεὸν ἀληθῶς καὶ ἄνθρωπον ἀληθῶς τὸν αὐτόν, ἐκ ψυχῆς λογικῆς καὶ σώματος, ὁμοούσιον τῷ πατρὶ κατὰ τὴν θεότητα καὶ ὁμοούσιον τὸν αὐτὸν ἡμῖν κατὰ τὴν ἀνθρωπότητα, κατὰ πάντα ὅμοιον ἡμῖν χωρὶς ἁμαρτίας· πρὸ αἰώνων μὲν ἐκ τοῦ πατρὸς γεννηθέντα κατὰ τὴν θεότητα, ἐπ' ἐσχάτων δὲ τῶν ἡμερῶν τὸν αὐτὸν δι' ἡμᾶς καὶ διὰ τὴν ἡμετέραν σωτηρίαν ἐκ Μαρίας τῆς παρθένου τῆς θεοτόκου κατὰ τὴν ἀνθρωπότητα, ἕνα καὶ τὸν αὐτὸν χριστόν, υἱόν, κύριον, μονογενῆ, ἐν (*v. l.* ἐκ) δύο φύσεσιν ἀσυγχύτως, ἀτρέπτως, ἀδιαιρέτως, ἀχωρίστως γνωριζόμενον· οὐδαμοῦ τῆς τῶν φύσεων διαφορᾶς ἀνῃρημένης διὰ τὴν ἕνωσιν, σωζομένης δὲ μᾶλλον τῆς ἰδιότητος ἑκατέρας φύσεως καὶ εἰς ἓν πρόσωπον καὶ μίαν ὑπόστασιν συντρεχούσης, οὐκ εἰς δύο πρόσωπα μεριζόμενον ἢ διαιρούμενον ἀλλ' ἕνα καὶ τὸν αὐτὸν υἱὸν καὶ μονογενῆ, θεὸν λόγον, κύριον Ἰησοῦν χριστόν· καθάπερ ἄνωθεν οἱ προφῆται περὶ αὐτοῦ, καὶ αὐτὸς ἡμᾶς ὁ κύριος Ἰησοῦς χριστὸς ἐξεπαίδευσε, καὶ τὸ τῶν πατέρων ἡμῖν παραδέδωκε σύμβολον.

PART TWO

AN ORTHODOX CHRISTOLOGY COMPATIBLE WITH MODERN THOUGHT

CHAPTER I

"For we walk by faith, not by sight."
2 COR. v. 7.

WHEN we come forward from the realms of ancient thought to our own times and endeavour to state an orthodox Christology in modern terms, we find that our first difficulty is to formulate a coherent metaphysical framework within which to set our Christology. The difficulties of Nestorius and his contemporaries arose partly from the rigidity of their metaphysics; ours arise from a situation quite the reverse. The increase of scientific knowledge, the greater rigour in philosophical speculation, the awareness of the hazy and unexplored hinterland to every area of investigation, these and other factors have combined to make it very difficult for us to hold a comprehensive view of things which can claim any great degree of rigidity or finality or can hope to gain any considerable measure of general acceptance. It was never more true that there are as many philosophies as philosophers. At one extreme the rationalist must realize that there are many things not dreamed of in his philosophy, and at the other extreme the dogmatist must feel uneasy in reflecting how uncertainly his dogmas fit in with the general attitude. We live in a period when the formulation of a comprehensive metaphysic presents grave problems. This inevitably has an effect on our theology in general and on our Christology in particular; and though it may be difficult at this juncture to construct a metaphysic, and to set in it a Christology, with any hope of gaining a considerable measure of general acceptance, the attempt may perhaps be made with some degree of usefulness if we avoid undue rigidity. There are many matters on which it is at present premature to give even a provisional judgment, and even if we must have some opinions on them we may be wise to admit that the opinions are only tentative. We may find it best to leave certain questions unanswered, or perhaps to indicate alternative possible answers.

We shall now endeavour to outline a mode of approach to a metaphysical system. It must be emphasized that many modes of approach are possible. It is only claimed that this one is reasonable, and may lead us to a metaphysic of a kind suitable to present conditions, in that it is not unduly rigid, allows for modifications and developments, and recognizes its own uncertainties. The mode of approach is not self-evident, and it is not to be supposed that anyone would consciously make his approach along these lines at a first endeavour. But the best course for a road through difficult territory is not found at the first attempt. There is need for preliminary surveying and the consideration of alternatives; and it may later be recognized that the finished road is the best way through the territory, or at least one practicable way through. Starting from the most elemental of all facts, the living individual's awareness of his own existence, we may endeavour to progress to a comprehensive view of reality in its totality.

The living individual is aware of what is going on in his own mind, and postulates his own existence: "Cogito, ergo sum."[1] He next discriminates between that which is himself and that which is other than himself. He thus postulates a distinction between himself and other things. He next assumes that he and these other things are real: he postulates reality. It may safely be asserted that the great majority of individuals would answer with a decided affirmative if asked whether they were convinced of their own existence, of a distinction between themselves and other things, and of the reality of themselves and other things. Yet these three convictions are by no means easy to prove. Most ordinary people would not attempt to prove them. They would assert that they are self-evident, and that life does not make sense otherwise. This may give us a clue to the place of postulates in our scheme of things: a postulate is the statement of a belief which is difficult or perhaps impossible of proof, but which is held because the individual holding it is convinced of its truth and regards belief

[1] René Descartes.

in it as necessary if his view of life is to have meaning and purpose. It is evident that a postulate is a personal matter. We cannot argue anyone else into believing in our postulates. We may so present our reasons for believing in them that they will believe in them too, but the decision to accept the postulates is free and personal. My postulates are the things I believe because without those beliefs life would cease to have meaning and purpose for me. Someone else may hold other postulates. Is there, then, no criterion as to the validity or otherwise of postulates? There certainly is, but that cannot be considered at this stage. Sufficient at present to say that a postulate is a belief, difficult or perhaps impossible of proof, which an individual holds because life is otherwise without meaning and purpose for him.

The average individual, as already stated, accepts at least these three postulates: the postulate of his own existence; the postulate of discrimination, that he is distinct from other things and they from him; and the postulate of reality, that he and those other things are real. Although philosophers do and must discuss the problems implicit in these postulates, anyone not holding them would in ordinary life be regarded as peculiar or unbalanced. These three postulates provide sufficient basis for intelligent living, and there are many persons of low type who do not proceed much beyond them. They take life and the Universe for granted, and live empirically and pragmatically. They are just not interested in God, immortality, or the structure of the Universe: "Nobody really knows anything about these things, and I don't worry my head about them." It should perhaps be remarked that these postulates are held, at any rate in the first instance, in a general and ill-defined manner. We can postulate our own existence without having much idea of what that existence comprises. We can postulate our distinction from other things without defining the boundary. Is my hand part of 'me' or of the 'not-me'? If it is cut off, I am still surely 'I'. And what about my body as a whole? If it came to an end would 'I' end with it? There is no need to answer these questions in order to hold quite confidently the postulate that I am distinct from other things. If pressed, the primitive person would say: "I know

o

that I exist, and that I am not other things. What you call 'the real me' is linked up in some way with my body, though I know I could lose a good many 'bits and pieces' and still be 'I'. Whether 'I' goes on after I die, nobody knows, and I don't worry about things like that." We can also postulate reality without being at all sure what we understand by it. By postulating, or agreeing, that he and other things are real, the ordinary person simply means real as opposed to illusory: "Of course that's a red ball. Can't I see it is? What else could it be?" He would agree that matter exists independently of his own thought.

These three postulates are implicit even in the behaviour of an animal, and we may call them the postulates of animal life. Most intelligent human beings accept a further postulate, the postulate of rationality: that there must be order and purpose in the Universe, that the general scheme of things is definite and logical. This postulate has far-reaching consequences, for, taken together, the postulates of reality and rationality provide the starting point for an ordered view of life and the Universe, and they determine the mode of approach to the problem of the individual's consciousness of his own existence and of that same individual's awareness of other existences. If his own existence is real and rational, the individual feels justified in placing reliance on what may be called the subjective aspect of reality: his own centre of existence, whatever precisely it may be, is real; his thoughts are valid processes for dealing with real data; his convictions are to be relied upon unless they are definitely disproved or proved untenable—and even then the decision to reject or revise them is his own. If other existences are real and rational, the individual feels justified in believing that objective reality provides reliable data for his thought processes, and that he need not doubt that there is a real and true connection between things as they really are and things as he thinks about them.

By an analogy which the postulates of reality and rationality seem to justify, the individual, conscious of his own existence, concludes that other individuals exist in a similar way. There thus emerges the first great dichotomy in looking at the Universe: there are a number of intelligent individual existences like my own, and there is a great mass of 'material'. Recognizing that the individual is essentially something other than his material body, which we conclude on the analogy of our own self-existence, and calling that essential something mind or soul or spirit, the Universe falls into two great divisions, which may be called mind and matter, or the spiritual and the material. Having made this division, a very significant difference emerges: postulating reality and rationality, and therefore assuming the reliability of the data gathered from observation of and experience in the material world, it is found that what may be called objective reality abundantly justifies our postulates. We find great groups of facts and happenings that can be brought into orderly systems, and in this way we are able to link up great tracts of observation and experience into 'subjects'. The contents of these 'subjects' constitute areas of 'knowledge', which areas may be defined as ordered systems deduced from the data gathered from observation and experience of some aspect or part of the material world. Each separate datum is a piece of 'information'. It is a prima facie confirmation of the postulates of reality and rationality to remark how satisfyingly self-consistent the various areas of knowledge are. Indeed, there is frequently an urge in the student of a particular area to reduce his chosen "subject" to an exact science, by which he means that all the data to do with it are to be marshalled into a neat, logical and comprehensive system. There will of course be lacunæ, but he would not doubt that the same principles would apply in those unexplored areas as apply in those he has explored in detail. Chemistry, for example, is the name of the 'subject' under which we set out all we know concerning the various forms of matter and the way in which they react on one another. It justifies our postulate of rationality, and under the heading 'chemistry' a great tract of knowledge is brought into systematic and satisfying order. The facts of chemistry are so amenable to ordered investigation that we consider that this is an area of real knowledge. But let it be remembered that the facts of chemistry depend on the validity of our postulates of discrimination, reality and rationality. Unless we accepted the postulate of discrimination, we should be unable to believe that anything was real except our thoughts and imaginings; unless we accepted the postulate of reality, we should believe that all is illusory; unless we accepted the postulate of rationality, we should believe that everything is by chance and meaningless, or capricious and even sinister. But the ever accumulating mass of coherent scientific data is a very cogent confirmation of the truth of these postulates. Mathematics, mechanics, astronomy, physics, chemistry, are so beautifully self-coherent that those who study them feel no doubt as to the truth of the postulates of reality and rationality. To them a chemical reaction illustrates reality and rationality magnificently. So it does, and though these postulates may need modifying, there is evidently something at least parallel with ultimate truth in them.

In the realm of the subjective, however, far more difficult problems are presented. In the world of objective reality, once we have accepted the postulates of reality and rationality there is no more anxiety as to framework. That is why so many people find great satisfaction in an objective subject (mathematics, chemistry, history, literature), while they feel a revulsion from subjects such as psychology, philosophy, and theology. It must be admitted that the postulates of reality and rationality are amazingly confirmed in the realm of the exact sciences. Within his own realm, the scientist moves with an assurance very different from that of the psychologist or philosopher. It is interesting also to observe that where such subjects (exact sciences) approach the 'framework' problems, some students experience an unwillingness to proceed. There are mathematicians who recoil from the study of infinity (as approached mathematically), and physicists who recoil from atomic physics. Compared with the philosopher, the exact scientist feels that he works in a factual and certain realm, though he should never forget that he is postulating a reality and rationality which he cannot prove, and that without a large postulated framework to contain himself, his subject, and all else, self, subject, and all else would be meaningless.

But the philosopher has no such satisfyingly precise realm

in which to work. His struggle has barely begun when he postulates reality and rationality. Souls—if there are any—cannot be tested in eudiometers, and spiritual energy—if there is such—cannot be measured on an ammeter. He has to go on building with postulates, making as coherent a system as he can, the truth or error of which can only be tested by its own self-coherence and by the way in which it fits in with the general scheme of things. Like the scientist, the philosopher or theologian postulates reality and rationality, though perhaps with certain reservations considered superfluous by the scientist. Unlike the scientist, he does not find that his material after that is factual. He has to go on making postulates; but let this be emphasized: unless he can build up a satisfactory scheme, life for the scientist and himself alike is steeped in gloom and purposelessness. As a matter of fact, almost every scientist and ordinary man has a philosophical scheme, however simple and whatever he may call it. Otherwise his exact knowledge is a mere disjunctum membrum. Similarly, it is well that the philosopher should have exact and detailed acquaintance with at least one branch of objective knowledge, in order that he may realize that he does not live in a Universe of generalizations.

We must now consider the trend of postulation needed if problems to do with mind and spirit are to be pursued further. Just as life can be lived without postulating even rationality, so life can be lived, and is lived by many, without postulating anything further about mind and spirit: "Animals and men are alike machines working by natural processes akin to those discoverable in physics and chemistry, and further speculation is futile." But the great majority of thinking people make a further postulate, which to them seems necessarily to follow the postulate of rationality—the postulate of moral order: that we believe that we and others like us do not live in vain; that there is a purpose for the existence of ourselves and of the Universe; that values are conserved; and that when the present Universe has run its course, that course will have been justified.

Up to this point most thinking people of most periods and types would be in agreement, not necessarily, of course, in these terms, but to this effect. They hold, at any rate implicitly, the primary personal postulates of self-existence, discrimination of self from not-self, and reality. They further postulate rationality and moral order in the Universe. With these postulates and the data of experience it appears to be possible to build up a comprehensive view of life and the Universe as a whole, and another postulate usually follows: that it is possible so to do. This may be called the postulate of synthesis: that it is possible to formulate a comprehensive view of the Universe as a whole, pervaded by rationality and moral purpose.

It is now important to consider the nature and content of such a view. It will contain three main elements, which we may call postulates, areas of knowledge, and hypotheses. Something must be said concerning each of these main elements.

Postulates

It has already been seen that we cannot even begin to think reasonably, consecutively and constructively unless we assume certain postulates: our own existence, our discrimination from other things, that we and those other things are real (not in the sense of opposed to ideal but as opposed to illusory), that we live in a rational order, that it is also a moral order, and that a synthesis of these postulates and the data of experience is possible. It must be admitted, indeed emphasized, that these postulates are difficult or even impossible to prove. Those who hold them hold them because without them life has no meaning or purpose for them. A postulate is, to its holder, very fundamental. The framework of our view of life is composed of our postulates. Everything else is fitted into that framework. It is thus that faith triumphs even over hard experience and principle over its apparent negation. If our postulates fail us, life loses its meaning; and thus it is that a serious disturbance of a person's postulates may involve a mental upheaval which may not be resolved for months or years while they seek fresh postulates in which to believe, a descent into listlessness or pessimism, or actual mental unbalance. The above sentence implies that postulates are not unalterable. This is so, and the philosopher should hold a further postulate about all his postulates: that a postulate is the noetic[1] expression of an intuition concerning ontic[2] reality. This ensures a safeguard, a hope of progress, and a defence against pessimism. Ontic reality is beyond us. We must admit that we are incapable of comprehending things as they actually are in themselves or to God. Our finite and space-time-matter confined minds inevitably have a finite and space-time-matter conditioned view of things. This view may be characterized as a noetic view, and all our views and judgments are conditioned by the fact that they are held and operated upon by our type of mind. Our judgments, views, opinions and experiences are noetic, and may or may not exactly correspond with ontic reality. Indeed, the more we think and study, the more we see the need for another postulate—the postulate of real correspondence: that although ontic reality is beyond our experience and comprehension, and can only be interpreted by us in noetic terms and modes, we nevertheless believe that our noetic understanding of ontic reality is in no way essentially erroneous; that there is a true parallel, a real correspondence, between things as they really are and things as we can comprehend them. For example, if we see three balls, one red, one blue, and one yellow, placed so that each of them is one foot from each of the other two on a billiard table, we may well suspect that in ontic reality the balls are not smooth solid spheres, that red, blue and yellow are merely our interpretations of an ontic reality quite different from our idea of colour, and that "one foot" as a measure of distance, indeed distance itself, has no meaning outside a space-time continuum. We may nevertheless feel convinced that there is a reality which we interpret as a solid sphere, that difference in colour does correspond with a real difference of some kind, and that what we interpret as mutual relationship in space does correspond with some kind of mutual relationship. That is, noetic interpretation is in real correspondence with ontic reality. Things may be interpreted to us by our senses and

---

[1] νοητός, held in the mind, interpreted by the mind.
[2] τὸ ὄν, that which actually is.

through the space-time continuum in complex and incomprehensible ways, but we are not being fundamentally deceived and misled. This is the postulate of real correspondence between noetic understanding and ontic reality. Since then all our postulates are noetic expressions of what we believe to be ontic reality, we shall not be seriously disturbed if we find that they need restatement or subdivision. It is not that our conviction concerning the underlying ontic reality has changed, but that we are aware that our noetic expression of it is capable of better or fuller statement.

It has already been stated that the disturbance of postulates is a very serious matter, especially for people of uncomplex minds. It is like removing a pillar. The fewer the pillars, the greater the danger of collapse of the building they support if one is removed. But as we plunge further and further into philosophical and theological problems we find that our thought structure needs more and more postulates. The more we sense of ontic reality the more we need to express what we believe, and we can only do so in postulates which are noetic expressions and therefore capable of improvement. Is there no finality, then, in the matter of postulates? There is not; but postulates are not all equally vital to our sanity. We could keep sane, hopeful and purposeful if our only postulates were those of reality, rationality, and moral order. Those pillars, so to speak, might support the roof of a mean building, merely enough to shelter us. But if the structure of our thought is larger and more detailed, a mere three pillars will not suffice. We must also postulate the existence of God, and not His existence only, but that He is good, omnipotent, omniscient, and eternal; that He sent Jesus Christ His Son into this world to reveal His will and purpose and to offer us salvation from sin and death; that we have spirits destined for eternal life; and many more such postulates.

It is now time to return to a matter hinted at but not dealt with. How can we be sure about our postulates? How do we defend or justify them? It has been said that we hold them because life is otherwise meaningless for us, that they are difficult or impossible of proof, and that they are noetic and not ontic. All that is true. To take the first question: how can we be sure about our postulates? As regards the primary postulates of intelligent man, our own existence, our discrimination from other things, reality, rationality, and moral order, the following must suffice, or we shall be occupying too much space with problems not germane to our main purpose: we believe these things because we feel innately and intuitively that we must; life and the Universe do not make sense if we think otherwise; and the consensus of opinion of the great majority of intelligent people confirms our conviction. We can advance many arguments in support of these postulates. But we do not hold them as the result of argument. We hold them because life has no meaning otherwise, and all our experience supports our conviction.[1]

As regards our further postulates, we hold them because they seem to us to follow on from the postulates of reality, rationality and moral order, because they fit in with and accord with our knowledge of life and the world, our experience and observation, our knowledge of history, what we believe to have been revealed to mankind or to special individuals or groups, and what we believe has been revealed or confirmed to us personally. From our postulates, our knowledge, and our speculations, we build up a comprehensive view of things, and if it seems coherent and reasonable, and stands the test of time and experience, we believe in it, and that, in effect, is our faith and philosophy. A great part of the structure consists of postulates. Many of these we share with other people, and it encourages us to know that they think as we do and hold the same convictions. To anyone who does not hold some of our postulates we can only say: "These are among my postulates, and I believe them because all the data of my life and experience, what I have learned and read, what I have felt and experienced, lead me to believe them to be true." (Instead of

[1] A very similar position is maintained by Farrer, who says that one of his objects in writing *Finite and Infinite* was "to show how far down in our common thinking the question of faith enters. This is not to use faith in the sense appropriated to revealed theology, but as it is an act correlative with those highly important but yet not undeniable intuitions which mould our practical thought" (op. cit., p. vi).

'true' some of us might prefer to say 'a noetic expression in real correspondence with ontic reality'.) We could further ask them to consider our view of things, our faith and philosophy as a whole, and to judge whether it gave a reasonable and acceptable interpretation of the Universe. The significant distinction should be observed between a postulate and a 'fact'. Granted certain postulates, say reality and rationality, a 'fact' can be proved from other 'facts': twelve pence make a shilling; twenty shillings make a pound; therefore two hundred and forty pence make a pound. That is a 'fact', and, the data being given, is of universal and inevitable acceptance. Such arguments proceed thus: "Because . . ., therefore . . ." But it is not wise to argue that way concerning postulates. It is better to say: "I believe . . .; and my reasons for doing so are . . ." Actually, our belief in our postulates is due to a convergence of many lines of approach, some of which may be expressible in the form of logical arguments and others may not be so expressible. We may take, as a very important example, belief in God. Belief in God is a postulate. Most of us say "I believe in God" with the utmost conviction, for this postulate is one of the main pillars in the structure of our view of things. But we do not hold this postulate as a 'fact' within a specified field of knowledge. Fundamentally, we hold this postulate because without it life would not make sense for us; and that is because:

(1) We were brought up to believe in God, and the weight of opinion of those whom we have most loved and respected has greatly influenced us to accept their belief.

(2) This belief has been bound up with our whole approach to life and our understanding of it. It has 'fitted', and has made life purposeful and reasonable.

(3) Our study of history, especially Biblical history, and the teaching of the Church have confirmed our belief. We feel that the facts of history and the fact of the Church give great and potent support to our belief.

(4) Our study of science and the natural order seems to support the idea of a God who planned, created and sustains the Universe.

(5) If of a studious turn of mind, we may have studied the so-called 'theistic proofs', and they have confirmed us in our beliefs by making us realize that logic and reasonableness point in the same direction.

(6) We have had moments of ecstasy or illumination at Holy Communion, in private prayer, or at some other time, when we have felt an overwhelming inner conviction of God's power and presence.

These six reasons are merely typical; they are not exhaustive. Each individual believer would probably produce a different list, even if the differences were mostly in emphasis and order or in the mode of expression. But none of these headings, nor any other, could *make* anyone believe in God. They are not 'proofs' in the sense that we can prove to any intelligent person that two triangles are congruent if two sides and the included angle of the one are equal to the two sides and the included angle of the other. It is useless to think that we can say: "Because . . ., therefore there is a God." We should say: "I believe in God; and my reasons for doing so are as follows: . . . Further, if you will consider my view of life and the Universe as a whole, which includes this belief, I think you will find it reasonable and satisfying. To me, without belief in God life does not make sense. With that belief, life is purposeful, challenging, and worth while." In that way, and only in that way, may we induce anyone to decide to make belief in God one of his postulates.

The framework, then, of our philosophy is necessarily a group of postulates. If they are few and simple, our philosophy will be simple, and perhaps true so far as it goes. But if we seek a fuller and deeper understanding of life, our postulates will be many and some of them complex. In that case, we have to bear in mind a number of warnings:

(1) We must realize that our postulates are the framework of *our* view of life, without which life would not make sense to us. Then we must be very careful to see to it that we do not elevate ill-informed or ill-digested opinions into postulates. If we do, we shall be in danger

of receiving the damaging shock that inevitably comes to anyone whose postulates prove false.

(2) We must see to it that our postulates are mutually consistent. It is amazing how inconsistent are the postulates some people hold simultaneously. Sooner or later the inconsistency will be made evident, and there follows the shock of readjustment.

(3) We should avoid undue multiplication of postulates. Let such as we hold be held with deep conviction, supported by (not resulting from) the best reasoning of which we are capable and tested in every way we can devise. We shall thus have a firm and abiding framework for our philosophy.

Knowledge

If, explicitly or implicitly, we have accepted the postulates of reality and rationality, we are forthwith able to systematize vast tracts of information and thus constitute them into areas of knowledge. We shall do this with all the more assurance and sense of certainty if we have not gone so far as to worry ourselves with the considerations that make it necessary to postulate real correspondence between noetic interpretation and ontic reality. To most people bricks and planks, houses and trees, are real, and that's all there is to it. But even including the postulate of real correspondence, there is an indubitable satisfaction in exploring and systematizing these areas. They are realms in which the material consists of 'facts', and we find that these facts can be marshalled, sorted, arranged and developed in all sorts of ways and that they fall into well ordered schemes. There are many such realms, many of which overlap and interlock. For convenience we give names to certain areas of knowledge—mathematics, physics, geography, history, philology. We can, as it were, thus obtain great blocks of certain and detailed 'knowledge' to fit into our general scheme of things. But it is of the utmost importance to remember that such blocks of knowledge, however extensive, do not provide a framework. They must, on the other hand, be fitted into a framework, otherwise they are mere disjecta membra. The scientist, the historian, the philologist, however extensive and self-consistent their fields, must have their postulates, if only that the Universe is real and rational. Unless each of them can at least say, "I believe the Universe is real and rational", himself and his knowledge are alike meaningless and illusory. Knowledge, therefore, is a proper word to apply to detailed or general information concerning a certain area or areas of observation and experience, which may provide us with a great block to fit into our general view of things, and may indeed provide material for the formulation and support of our postulates, or for their reformulation or rejection. Knowledge is invaluable as a check on our postulates, and we do well to reject any postulate which does not accord with knowledge. But the framework is more important than any block within it.

We thus envisage a philosophy of life as a framework of postulates, into which blocks of knowledge may be fitted. Perhaps a helpful analogy is a steel-framed house; the framing consists of steel, and the filling of planks of various shapes and sizes. Without the framing the filling lacks stability and plan. So does knowledge without postulates. But if we were given the filling in the form of great blocks or sections, we should suspect our framework had been wrongly put together if the sections would not fit into it. We must thus see to it that our postulates can contain our knowledge. If they do not, they probably need modification.

If our primary concern is some branch of knowledge, we find our satisfaction in exploring or systematizing that field or some part of it, and we realize that our field fits into a greater framework, the importance of which we may recognize, though it does not interest us to the same extent as our field. If our primary concern is the general view of things—philosophy and theology—we are anxious to construct a sound framework of postulates, and to verify that the various systematized fields of knowledge fit harmoniously into our framework. We need not be, indeed we cannot be, specialists in all the fields, but we must at least know where and how they fit into the framework and their relevance to it.

Hypotheses

We might wish that with a set of well chosen postulates we should be able to construct a framework into which all knowledge would fit, and that we should thus have a complete philosophy of life and the Universe. This wish, however, is not possible of fulfilment. There are many matters concerning which we neither have knowledge nor the ability to form a precise postulate; and in any case we need to remember the postulate of real correspondence, which has both an optimistic and a depressive side: optimistic, in that we believe that our noetic concepts have a real correspondence with ontic reality; depressive, in that we have every reason to believe that in many matters our noetic concepts are a very faint, even if reliable, image of ontic reality. There are therefore matters concerning which we have no knowledge and concerning which we cannot frame confident postulates. Yet we are loath to leave lacunæ in our scheme of things. We feel that we must link our postulates with our knowledge, and that we must fill in the lacunæ. It is therefore legitimate, even necessary, to complete our scheme with hypotheses, even with alternative hypotheses, so long as we recognize where knowledge ends and speculation begins and that our speculations are not to be elevated into postulates. We hold our postulates because life is meaningless without them, because they are necessary for the making of a framework to contain all we know and sense. Knowledge fits into that framework, and fills a great part of it. But there are gaps, and it is very difficult to keep an open and unspeculating mind, perhaps even undesirable to do so. We are therefore entitled to speculate in the region between our knowledge and our postulates. The ground covered by hypotheses may later be covered by knowledge, or by postulates of which we can feel confidently assured. This has happened often enough in the past. Almost every scientist speculates beyond the field of his actual knowledge. Some of these speculations are eventually proved to be correct; some are eventually proved to be incorrect.[1] It is not otherwise in philosophy and theology. In certain matters it is legitimate to speculate,

[1] For footnote, see p. 226.

and the speculations are eventually either rejected by an accumulation of evidence against their tenability or confidence in them attains such a degree that the speculation is accepted as a postulate. It has justified its place in the framework, and we may become increasingly convinced that it is a necessary element in the framework.

It may be objected that reality is definite, so that the building into the framework of fresh postulates is not reasonable. If the postulate is necessary for a right view, how could the view have been right without it? The answer is best made on the analogy on a building. If we suppose that ontic reality is comparable with a Gothic cathedral of grey stone, and that we are endeavouring to make a model of it, which will be at least a noetic interpretation of ontic reality, it may readily be supposed that our material is of three kinds: buttresses and arches of concrete which we could not make, but which we could place into position: these are our postulates. We cannot make (prove) them, but when they are placed into position we are confident that they represent the grey stone buttresses and arches of the cathedral. Then there might be a supply of bricks and mortar with which we could fill in the bays and erect the walls. This we proudly erect brick by brick—our systematized knowledge—the brickwork of systematized knowledge corresponding with the stonework of the ontic reality behind the noetically interpreted phenomena of the material part of the Universe. Then there might be parts of the cathedral of whose nature and design we were completely ignorant. In our model the best we could do would be to put in some matchboarding or plaster and say: "Something must be here, but we don't know what, so we have put in this matchboarding for the time being. Maybe later we shall find a concrete arch that goes in here (a postulate), or maybe the brickwork may come up to here (knowledge); but perhaps this is a part we shall never know about until we see the glorious ontic reality itself. If so, our matchboarding must remain a monument to our ignorance. But we will not pretend it (hypothesis) is either concrete or brick (postulate or knowledge)."

Thus our scheme of things, our metaphysic, will contain

three elements: our postulates, our knowledge, and our hypotheses. We shall be wise to keep our postulates as few and fundamental as possible, and to make sure that they are mutually consistent. We shall do well to make our knowledge as wide as possible and to be quite sure where it passes over into speculation. We shall be wise to speculate as conservatively as possible: a plain glass window is a better speculative substitute for an unknown stained glass one than a stained glass window of quite different design. We must avoid fanciful speculation.

The construction of a metaphysic is therefore a fourfold task:

(1) We must state our postulates and give our reasons for believing in them.

(2) We must show that present knowledge fits consistently into our scheme.

(3) We must fill the gaps with reasonable hypotheses.

(4) We must present our scheme as a coherent and consecutive whole.

The first of these tasks is so tremendous that it is best not to attempt it, particularly if our objective is the presenting of a metaphysic as a whole. When we state a particular postulate, the average person will in most cases either accept or reject it at once, his mind having been made up long before; or he will hesitate a little, especially if the postulate is beyond the degree of detail he has hitherto reached in the construction of his noetic model of ontic reality, and he will then almost instinctively reject or accept it according to whether it fits harmoniously with his already held postulates or not. We shall therefore in due course state our postulates. Most of them are common stock to Christian philosophers and theologians, and a massive literature could be cited giving sound and convincing reasons (not 'proofs') for holding these postulates. We would only ask the reader tentatively to accept them until he has read the scheme as a coherent whole. If the whole scheme seems coherent and convincing, that is surely a good reason for accepting the postulates.

The second task is not difficult. We need to know the

general shape and nature of the various fields of knowledge and how they fit into our scheme. We leave the detailed surveying of each field to the appropriate specialist, conceding his mastership in his own field, but not as to where and how it fits into a general scheme. No philosopher or theologian, as such, has any right to give opinions on the details inside a given field of knowledge, unless he is competent in that field as such. Similarly, no scientist or historian, as such, has any right to give opinions on the way his field fits into the general scheme of things, unless he is competent in philosophy and theology as well as in his own subject.

The third task needs approaching with the utmost care, and we do well to let it be very clear when we are speculating. We may legitimately give alternatives, and we must always be prepared for advancing knowledge to fill in the area of our speculation, perhaps in a very different way. It is very much wiser to speculate and know that we are doing so than to formulate rigid and premature postulates in areas where uncertainty should be recognized.

The fourth task is the most useful. Instead of endeavouring to build up a scheme piece by piece, getting lost in argument as to why we believe this and reject that, we may do better to set out the scheme as a whole. It may then be assessed as a whole, and this is particularly important where postulates are involved. Indeed, a postulate is held because it fits in with our general view of things, so that the arguments in support of any one postulate really involve our whole philosophy of life.[1] For example, to answer the question "Why do you believe in God?" really involves setting out one's whole philosophy of life. So we may as well set out our philosophy and ask whether our postulates commend themselves to others or not. Such a setting out may serve two purposes. Those already holding the same postulates may feel that they now hold them more securely and confidently and in better mutual relation with each other and with general knowledge; and some who did not

---

[1] Cf. Emmet, *The Nature of Metaphysical Thinking*, p. 76: "Truth then must be sought in the coherence of an idea with other ideas, whereby it becomes a more developed systematic idea."

previously hold the same postulates may recognize their claim and make them their own, feeling that life makes better sense with them than without them.

The primary objective of this work is to state an orthodox Christology in terms compatible with modern thought. It will now be seen that this task resolves itself into two parts: a statement of postulates for an orthodox Christology; and the presentation of a general scheme into which these postulates and the rest of our knowledge can fit, if speculative completion is necessary indicating of what kind it should be. It is hoped that the result of this endeavour will be that those already holding an orthodox Christology will feel their conviction has been strengthened, and that some whose minds are still open may feel how cogent are the claims for the postulates some of us already hold and may be led to adopt them for themselves.

Footnote 1, *p.* 222: For example, Sir Humphry Davy, noting the resemblance in chemical properties between soda and potash and metallic oxides, formed the opinion that soda and potash, which had formerly been regarded as elements, must really be the oxides of hitherto unisolated metals. Following up his supposition, in 1807 he succeeded in substantiating his view, by obtaining the metals sodium and potassium by the electrolysis of fused soda and potash. Naturally, not every scientist has his speculations proved correct in his own lifetime. We may mention William Prout, who in 1816 advanced what is known as "Prout's hypothesis". He supposed that all the other elements were derived from hydrogen by some process of condensation. Although the theory was speculatively attractive, for nearly eighty years few chemists felt able to support it, because the atomic weights of the elements, instead of being whole multiples of that of hydrogen, contained awkward fractions—not merely halves or quarters, which might have been allowed for by supposing that hydrogen itself consisted of two or even four units of 'protyle'. Thus J. S. Stas (1813–1891), a noted Belgian chemist, made extremely careful determinations of a number of atomic weights in order to test Prout's hypothesis and decided against it. With hydrogen as unity, among his results were chlorine, $35 \cdot 368$, silver, $107 \cdot 66$, lead, $206 \cdot 396$. It may be remarked that modern methods of atomic weight determination would not sufficiently have altered his figures to affect his conclusions. Nevertheless, since the beginning of the present century evidence has been accumulating which shows that Prout was substantially correct. The ordinary hydrogen atom consists of a relatively heavy centre known as a proton and a relatively light 'planet' known as an electron. The atoms of all the other elements consist of relatively heavy centres made up of definite numbers of protons, with definite numbers of electrons associated with or around them. But the atomic weights are not whole numbers for two reasons: it is now known that the weight of a number of protons depends on their mode of grouping as well as on their actual number; and because most elements are mixtures of isotopes (see pp. 246–247) containing differing numbers of protons.

On the other hand, many speculations are eventually proved erroneous. Thus Sir Isaac Newton believed that light consisted of streams of rapidly moving minute solid particles (*Opticks*, 4th edition, 1750); but in 1850 J. B. L. Foucault, as a result of a series of experiments which we need not describe here, conclusively disposed of Newton's view. As E. Edser says, "From the moment of the completion of Foucault's experiment, the corpuscular theory became untenable" (*Light for Students*, p. 235). Or we might mention the "phlogiston theory" controversy of the late seventeenth century. Becher and Stahl supposed that combustion consisted in the escape of phlogiston from the burning substance. Such a theory well fits the burning of such substances as wood, coal or sulphur. But, as Boyle and Hooke pointed out, many substances gained in weight on being burned (e.g., combustible metals), so that phlogiston would in some cases have positive and in other cases negative weight. The theory was therefore abandoned.

CHAPTER II

THE MATERIAL UNIVERSE

"Through faith we understand that the worlds were framed by the word of God, so that things which are seen were not made of things which do appear."

HEB. XI. 3.

IN the previous chapter it was shown that a metaphysic must contain three elements: postulates, knowledge, and hypotheses, and it was explained what each of these terms is to be understood to cover. It was also stated that the presentation would be of the scheme as a whole, so that it could be evaluated as a whole, and not by arguing each part. Although in that way it would soon emerge what were the writer's postulates, what he regarded as knowledge, and what he regarded as speculation, it will probably be helpful to state without comment the main postulates herein accepted. Those who agree with them will start with that much in common; those who do not agree with some of them will be able to suspend judgment until they have considered the scheme as a whole. The postulates which the writer deems necessary for a complete and balanced view of life in accordance with his own knowledge, experience, conviction, and intuition, are as follows:

I believe:

    I. That I exist.

    II. That I can distinguish myself from other existences.

    III. That myself and those other existences are real.

    IV. That the scheme of things in general is rational.

    V. That there is a moral order, so that my own life and the lives of others have purpose and value, that there are real and ultimate standards of right and wrong, and that one of the chief ends of life is to find that purpose, to appreciate values and standards, to choose the highest, and to bring myself into accord with them.

    VI. That all knowledge and experience can be brought into a reasonable and harmonious scheme, enabling life and the Universe to be contemplated as a comprehensive and coherent whole.

VII. That ontic reality is beyond human comprehension, but that our minds are capable of forming an impression of it which is in real correspondence with it. We see through a glass darkly, but we are not fundamentally deceived. (From this it follows that all our postulates are noetic impressions of our intuitions concerning ontic reality.)

VIII. That I myself, all other sentient beings, and the Universe as a whole, owe our existence to the will and purpose of an antecedent and eternal Being, God, whom I believe to be supremely perfect.

IX. That God has revealed Himself for me and for all men in various ways, most especially in Jesus Christ His Son.

X. That God not only created but sustains the Universe, and that He is actively concerned in it; and I therefore believe that there are certain matters on which human decisions have not been reached without divine overruling, and I therefore accept as postulates those declarations concerning the Christian faith which are universally accepted by Christians who claim to be truly Catholic and Orthodox. In particular, and as specially relevant to our present purpose, I accept as postulates the following statements concerning the relationship of God to Jesus Christ:

"I believe in God the Father Almighty, Maker of heaven and earth; and in Jesus Christ, His only Son, our Lord" (Apostles' Creed).

"We believe and confess that our Lord Jesus Christ, the Son of God, is God and Man. God, of the Substance of the Father, begotten before the worlds; and Man, of the Substance of His Mother, born in the world. Perfect God, and perfect Man, of a reasonable soul and human flesh subsisting. Equal to the Father, as touching His Godhead; and inferior to the Father, as touching His Manhood. Who although He be God and Man, yet He is not two, but one Christ. One, not by conversion of the Godhead into flesh, but by assumption of the Manhood into God. One altogether, not by confusion of Substance, but by unity of Person" (Athanasian Creed).

The above list of postulates is not by any means exhaustive. In fact, our postulates are a system rather than a set of statements, and their mutual coherence as a framework is analogous to the mutual coherence of a specific area of knowledge. It is also very important to bear constantly in mind the great significance of the postulate numbered VII. This postulate is normative to almost all the other postulates, and acts to a great extent as a buffer against the shock of change. Instead of having to abandon a postulate that has perhaps been stated too rigidly, we are able to retain it by realizing that it is at best a noetic expression of ontic reality: we can only, so to speak, make a model of ontic reality, and a model in wood is not necessarily better or worse than a model in clay. Our comprehensive view, then, will consist of a statement which is a synthesis of three types of constituent: postulates, which embody our convictions concerning ontic reality, but are themselves couched in noetic terms; areas of knowledge, which are ordered statements concerning definite areas of ontic reality, evident to us as phenomenal reality, and interpreted by us as noetic reality; speculations or hypotheses, which are necessary if the lacunæ among both postulates and areas of knowledge are to be tentatively filled, and are therefore necessary to make our scheme a unity.

Before beginning the statement, two remarks must be made: the form and order of the statement is to a great extent influenced by its objective, Christology; and the statement is given in coherent form as a unity, which is not necessarily the manner or order in which it would be presented if each part were being argued. It is to be read as a whole first and assessed afterwards.

We proceed first, then, to consider the creation of the Universe. This consideration soon brings confirmation of the importance of realizing that postulates are inevitably more fundamental to our thinking than is knowledge; for knowledge is merely a noetic interpretation of phenomena, and our noetic interpretation is futile unless we can postulate ontic reality behind the phenomena we interpret and the possibility of rationality in our interpretation. With tentative confidence in our framework of postulates we can now approach the problem of cosmogony and see how the data of observation and experience can be fitted into our framework.

The Universe of matter, energy, space and time, which constitutes the medium within which we experience, presents profounder mysteries to us than it did to our predecessors. Although its workings were evidently complex, and although scientists realized how numberless were the problems awaiting solution, there was nevertheless conviction that the categories of space and time were as they seemed, and that matter, built up of atoms, was ponderable and solid reality. Euclidian space, matter, Newton's laws of motion, vibrations and waves—on concepts such as these their view of the Universe was based. Even metaphysicians for the most part did not question such a view of the present Universe. They might seek to probe a little further into the reality behind the phenomenal, but few of them doubted that space, time and matter were real enough, and they considered that their task was to seek a fuller fundamental comprehension of them. Most scientists and philosophers, and all theologians, believed that the Universe must have had a beginning, just as they believed that it would have an end. But the reality of matter seemed the most obvious of the deductions from the data of experience, and though imagination boggled at the concept of the infinity of space and time, no other concept seemed feasible; and though it was realized, anyhow by theologians, that space and time as we know them belong only to this Universe, that 'time' has no meaning before or after the duration of this Universe, and that God is not to be thought of spatially, yet it was the objects and categories of this Universe that seemed compellingly real, while the categories of ultimate and eternal reality, whatever they might be, seemed remote and elusive.

During the last fifty years all that has changed. Scientific research into the nature of matter, space and time, research associated with the names of such men as Rutherford, J. J.

Thompson, Planck, Lorentz, Einstein, Weyl, Schrödinger, Jeans, and Eddington, has now reached a point where the interpretation of scientifically obtained data transcends the natural ability of the human mind. Matter, movement, vibration, waves, empty space, even space filled with some kind of immaterial wave-transmitting ether—these we could comprehend. But the physicists, astronomers and astrophysicists have pursued further researches and collected more data; the mathematicians have worked upon the data and have expressed them in the form of equations and formulas and have come to their conclusions: thus and thus the physical Universe works, and these equations are in correspondence with truth. When, however, we come to visualize the kind of Universe corresponding with these equations, we at once realize what has happened: man has probed sufficiently far into the structure of the Universe within which he lives to discover that "things are not as they seem"; but he is quite unable to form any clear mental picture of what things really are.[1]

Far from representing a bankruptcy of ideas, such a statement represents a very real advance in knowledge. We begin to approach true concepts as we sweep away erroneous ones, and it may be a definite advantage to realize that there are certain things which we can never know. We then endeavour to build up analogies or to institute parallels, saying of our analogies or parallels, "This is not an image of reality, but reality is something like this, or has similarities to this." It is to be understood that we dare not claim that our parallels are anything like so close as a statue to a man or a picture to a landscape. Our closest parallels with reality are probably much more remote than that— more like an attempt to explain music in terms of colour. Plato's hope that we might get as near an understanding of reality as a shadow is near to the substance is probably over optimistic (*The Republic*, vii. 514–515). The kind of analogy which is of most value is an analogy which can be shown to correspond in its variations due to time, place or condition in a parallel manner with the variations in the reality we are trying to understand. Thus if we were

[1] For footnote, see p. 259.

completely deaf and music had to be explained to us in terms of colour, and various pieces of music had been transposed for us into colour sequences and harmonies—which is quite easily done[1]—if, then, we were to receive the gift of hearing, once the key was given to us we should be able to understand exactly how our colour sequences corresponded with tunes. The glory of music would be a new and revealing experience, but our colour sequences and harmonies would have prepared the way. We cannot hope to get any nearer than that to reality; but, if we use all the resources God gives us here and now, we may hope to be able to get a view of things so parallel with reality that when hereafter we have all things revealed to us we may find that none of our main ideas was erroneous—only that reality is so much more full and glorious than we are now able to comprehend.

Now it so happens that recent trends in scientific thought have had the curious effect of increasing the difficulties of the mathematician, scientist, and metaphysician, but of decreasing those of the theologian. Things which the theologian had long felt must be so are now shown actually to be so, not by theology, but by science. As the objective simplicity of the Universe is discovered to be an illusion, the scientist is driven more and more towards metaphysics and theology, not indeed because he is a scientist, but because he is also conscious of being a man in a Universe. Thus Jeans says in his foreword,[2] "I am not a philosopher either by training or inclination," yet proceeds to write a book which implicitly displays a metaphysic and a theology. As a scientist he had no need to think on these things; as a man he was driven to do so. The safe solidity of the Victorian scientist's conception of the Universe has gone and, when the ground on which we stand sinks, we instinctively seek fresh standing ground. Time was when a cube of iron was not thought of otherwise than as a solid piece of metal, with straight rectilinear sides, and a definite position in space. But now we are bewildered strangers in a Universe our forebears thought they knew so well: solidity

[1] The colours red, orange, yellow, green, blue, and violet correspond in the scale of C with C, D, E, F, G, A.
[2] The Mysterious Universe, p. vii.

is an illusion, and the solid cube of iron is nothing but a system of vibrating wave circuits, vibrating we know not how in we know not what; definite shape is an illusion, and the supposed cube is continually changing its shape as other things move in relation to it, nor is there any such thing in the Universe as a straight line; as to its position in space, space and time may merely be aspects of some continuum quite different from either, whose real nature is far removed from our analogical interpretations of it. It may well be that our ideas of movement in space and of passage of time are no nearer reality than is the colour scale to the musical scale. There may merely be what mathematicians call a one-one correspondence. There may not even be that. But the increasing elusiveness of matter, space and time confirms the view of the theologian who has always felt that ultimacy is not in these things; and we shall find that modern physics fits in excellently with a view of the Universe which takes up without difficulty the ancient convictions and provides a framework into which we may fit all our knowledge and faith without distortion.

In setting out our view of things we shall be aware of two contrasting factors: first, that the great fixed convictions of Christian theists stand firm, and need no adjustment, though modern knowledge may enable us to interpret those convictions more precisely, and it may amaze us to realize on what slender data they came to such true conclusions— and this confirms our belief that God gives His servants inner conviction on the great fundamentals; and second, we shall keep in mind the limitations of our knowledge, avoiding precision where precision is not yet possible and perhaps never may be possible. We shall attempt a broad outline. Some parts of it we may be confident are absolutely as we portray them; other parts we sketch in hazily, confident that our view, though not necessarily an exact image of reality, is in close parallel correspondence with it; other parts are merely tentative, a solution being suggested but alternatives not being excluded.

We shall not make our description tedious by marshalling the evidence in support of every opinion we express. A metaphysic has to be judged as a whole, and may be considerably more convincing as a totality than any of its parts are when considered separately. Our judgment as to the amount of truth likely to be reflected in a metaphysical system depends on a great many factors, including our sense of total coherence. Thus we shall not endeavour to build up a logical scheme with what the mathematicians would call 'rigid proof' at each stage. But the mathematician is quite convinced of the truth of many propositions long before he has reached the stage when he can 'rigidly prove' them. We shall therefore present a scheme, admitting that parts of it are to an extent uncertain and even in some matters giving alternative possibilities, yet maintaining that the scheme as a whole carries conviction and brings into reasonable connection many hitherto isolated objects of belief. No metaphysic can hope to be final. It can only hope to give such a picture of reality as shall enable us to understand life more clearly and to approach it with better purpose.

Now let us see how Christian theism gives us a clear way through the perplexities of this present Universe:

We believe that before this present Universe was brought into existence God had His being: that God existed in and of Himself, without relation to or dependence on space or time or any such concept, an existence absolute, unconditioned, and self-sufficient, both as to every conceivable power and every conceivable satisfaction. As in so many matters, the instincts and enlightenments of the ancients are abundantly justified by every advance in the clarification of thought. We shall see that the ancient emphasis on the qualities of God is not only the tribute of piety, not only the due of reverence, but a necessary element in a coherent metaphysic. We must get this definitely in mind: God lacked nothing, and in Himself had every power and every satisfaction.

Then why and how came it about that God created the Universe, and such a Universe as we inhabit? It is presumption to think that we can answer either part of that question. The 'why' presumes understanding of infinite love and wisdom, and the 'how' presumes understanding of infinite power. But we may make certain tentative suggestions.

Why did God create the Universe? In order that sentient beings, free to choose, might have the opportunity of sharing in the knowledge and love inherent in God Himself; in order that sentient beings, who but for Him could never have been, might enter into relationship with God's own being and, to whatever extent might be possible, might share His blessedness and glory. However we care to express it, two things must be borne constantly in mind: first, that God did not create the Universe to satisfy any need of His own. He was complete and perfect without it.[1] Second, that possibility of profit and gain is entirely on the side of the sentient beings whom God creates, and that it is incumbent upon them ever to be mindful that there can never be anything in the nature of a pact or bargain between them and their Maker.[2] These two remarks, which historic theology has consistently emphasized in some form or another, are of fundamental importance in seeking to obtain a true view of the Universe: God is perfect and serene in Himself, and has nothing to gain; the creature is utterly dependent on and entirely indebted to God.

How did God create the Universe? To this question we can attempt a more complete answer than was possible even a few years ago, and yet at the same time a more guarded answer in that we are more aware of the limitations of our science and metaphysics. Recent research in science and recent speculation in metaphysics have two elements in common: they make us acutely aware of the mists which bound our range of clear vision, and they convince us there must as yet be great reservations in our speculations as to what lies within and beyond those mists. This is salutary, and in shaping a metaphysic makes two things necessary: first, to realize that though there are certain fixed points, ours by conviction and faith, many things must be conceded to be as yet doubtful, and alternative views may be permissible; and secondly, to realize that reality may be very different from our appreciation and interpretation of it, so that it is probably more reasonable to hope that our view of truth is parallel with ultimate

[1] This is very well expounded in Mascall, *He Who Is*, pp. 108–112.
[2] Luke xvii. 10.

reality rather than to dare to suppose that it is any sort of picture of ultimate reality itself. The bearing of these two remarks will perhaps emerge as this chapter unfolds.

The Creation of the Universe

Before the creation of the Universe of matter, energy, space and time, in which we have our being, God was. Even this statement is open to objection, for no concept of time is applicable to God. Time and space are mere elements in the schema[1] provided by God for the duration of the Universe, and have no reality or importance beyond that. In trying to think of God before the creation of the Universe, it is most important to realize how we must not think of Him. We must not think of Him as in any way limited, in any way needy, in any way unsatisfied, in any way dependent on a space factor, in any way dependent on a time factor. Space and time have no meaning except for the Universe. How then are we to think of God before the creation of the Universe? Perhaps a most important word is 'incomprehensible'. God had His being in a way utterly beyond our comprehension, unlimited and unconditioned by anything we can imagine or by anything beyond our imagination. If we use the convenient word 'continuum' to describe the space-temporal or other framework of this or any other existent or possible universe, we must recognize that God is in no continuum. He is of Himself. There is no continuum of any kind whatsoever that we can conceive as containing or conditioning God, or as constituting the framework of His being or activity. God is *extra omnia continua*. Let us refer to this most important fact by saying that God is *exoschematic*: not simply transcendent, that is, beyond the limits and definitions of this Universe, but beyond all limits and definitions whatsoever. Because God is exoschematic, there is no limit to His power, His perfection, and His glory. He is infinite in the most boundless interpretation of that word, infinite in the sense before which the mere infinity of space and time fades into insignificance and unimportance. For God there is no space

---

[1] 'Schema' (framework, general scheme of things) must not be confused with 'schêma' (mere appearance). Cf. pp. 108–109.

and time; He is outside all such restricting concepts: He is exoschematic. It may be desirable to introduce a term to symbolize the infinite realm and range of the being of God. Since God is exoschematic, we may use the term *exoschema* to convey the idea of ultimate infinite reality as it is to God. The exoschema is the infinite sphere of God's being and activity.

When God saw fit to create the Universe, He did so by causing it to come into being as a kind of bubble or *physema* within the exoschema, yet in such a way that the exoschema was in no way affected. To God, who is exoschematic, the existence or non-existence of any particular schema or continuum is irrelevant; for Him it is as though it were not, for all His qualities and powers transfuse it; nothing is hid from Him, nothing is away from Him, nothing affects Him. The method of causation of the Universe was the result of what in our ways of thought would be lengthy and precise calculation, but for God, for whom time is not, would have been no sooner willed than done. Just as a child laboriously works out on paper that 17 times 17 is 289, whereas the average mathematician no sooner sees 17×17 than he knows the answer, so with the calculations of God: God knows instantaneously what we would take minutes, hours or centuries to calculate. We prefer to use the expression 'God calculates instantaneously' for reasons which will appear later; and when we say 'God calculates' or 'calculated', we always imply 'instantaneously', and any who wish can say God 'knows' instantly instead of God 'calculates'.

God calculated, then, in the following terms: He intended, Himself exoschematic, to cause there to come into existence a continuum which was to be the scene for the life, development and opportunity of sentient beings. The first step was to create the continuum itself, the continuum which to us is space and time and contains matter and energy. This continuum He caused to come into existence as a kind of physema in the exoschema, a physema within which, and only within which, the realities whatever they may be corresponding with our concepts of space and time have meaning and relevance. The reality may be something totally unlike our concepts of space and time. All we can say with certainty is that we live in a continuum, in a physema, in which all experience is related to a schema explicable to ourselves in the two concepts of space and time. Mathematics, physics, astrophysics and metaphysics unite in warning us that the reality behind our concepts of space and time may be very different from anything we can conceive, and that space and time may indeed be merely aspects of some tertium quid: that we live in a four-dimensional continuum of which we interpret three dimensions as space and one as time.[1]

Incidentally, this view of our continuum brings a new check to our ideas of infinite space and infinite time. In the exoschema space is an irrelevance and is not to be thought of. The term 'space' is therefore only applicable to this Universe, and although this physema in the exoschema is undoubtedly very large (to our way of thinking) it is not infinite. On quite other grounds mathematicians, physicists and astrophysicists are coming to the same conclusion.[2]

As to time, this concept also only applies to this Universe, and for the same reason. Time began when God caused the physema, and will end when He ends the physema. Time is an irrelevance in the exoschema and to God: "One day is with the Lord as a thousand years, and a thousand years as

---

[1] It is not relevant to our present purpose to pursue this point, but one observation should be made: although mathematicians and physicists, applying the relativity theories of Einstein and others, find that the assumption of a four-dimensional continuum is of advantage for their calculations, it by no means follows that we actually do live in a four-dimensional continuum. A theory may over-elaborate or may over-simplify, and may nevertheless accurately fit all the known facts. All we can safely say is that there is a surprising correlation between space and time hitherto unsuspected; but it by no means follows that they are aspects of the same thing, even if for calculations we can so regard them, any more than years and rates per cent. are the same thing, even though for calculating simple interest we can multiply them together. As Lodge says (*Encyclopædia Britannica*, 14th Edition, xvii. 882): "Every differential equation is an expression in space with its three dimensions and the other abstraction called time; and some attempt has been made to unify these two great abstractions by aid of the velocity c. This however is rather verging on metaphysics, unless it is merely regarded as a legitimate convenience in calculation to deal with four similar variables instead of three and an odd one." It seems probable that space and time are distinct though related, and that both are in reality very different from our ideas of them.

[2] For footnote, see p. 262.

one day" (2 Peter iii. 8). This truth is felt after in the emphasis so continually placed on the contrast between 'time' and 'eternity', and the conviction or expectation that with the ending of this life we pass beyond the limitations of time as well as of space:

> "For tho' from out our bourne of Time and Place,
>   The flood may bear me far,
> I hope to see my Pilot face to face,
>   When I have crost the bar."
>   TENNYSON: *Crossing the Bar.*

But eternity rightly understood does not mean an infinite extension of time backwards before the creation of the Universe and forwards after its end. Eternity, in contrast with time, means a state of affairs in which time is irrelevant, in which time is merely a recollected element in a completed schema. The exoschematicity of God is absolutely independent of any such continuum elements as space and time. 'Infinite', therefore, is not an adjective to be applied to space or time. They are in fact not infinite. True infinity is something tremendously more comprehensive, and is relevant only to God. If we speak of infinite space or infinite time either we mean space or time so great that we cannot imagine it, or we are carrying the yard-sticks of the physema into the exoschema. If we do that, we of course find them completely irrelevant and completely swallowed up; in that sense the exoschematicity of God is infinite in space and time, because even the greatest measures of such concepts are irrelevant to Him. It is not so much that God is infinite in space or time, or above them or outside them; it is simply that they have no relevance to One whose being is not conditioned by any continuum, space-temporal or other. God is exoschematic.

Thus God first caused the continuum to come into being, which He did merely by willing that it should so come into being: for what God wills happens. It is to be postulated, for reasons which need not be detailed here, that whatever God wishes to be comes into being, and does so without in any way (1) reducing or impairing God, (2) taking from His substance or energy (whatever these words may mean as applied to God), or (3) becoming in any way necessarily related to God. That which God calls into being is itself and nothing else, and is in no way God, nor is to be thought of as being or having ever been in any way God.

Having caused the continuum to come into being, God caused to appear in it conglomerates of wave systems, each such conglomerate probably first appearing as what we call a nebula. Thus we picture the creation: first God caused a physema in the exoschema; in that physema He caused to appear conglomerates of wave systems.

What is our view of the physema, and what do we believe about the conglomerates?

Foremost, we know that in causing the physema and in originating the conglomerates God neither reduced nor impaired Himself, that these acts caused Him no effort or loss, and that neither the physema nor the conglomerates are to be thought of as derived from God's substance or being, or in any way related to Him, nor as being or ever having been in any way God. It is just as though God merely willed, wished or thought, and what He willed came to pass. We dare not try to picture the actual process, and so "God said, Let there be . . .: and there was . . ." is as good as any other way of putting it.

The physema, to our way of thinking, is characterized by extent and duration, space and time. It is like the inside of a bubble. But what is the inside? Is it 'full of nothing', a vacuum? It certainly may be a vacuum, but we have no idea what a vacuum really is. When science was purely mechanistic, and thought that the Universe could be explained in terms of hard round atoms, motion, and corpuscular radiation, the physema could well be thought of as 'full of nothing', a vacuum in the popular conception of the term. But when the idea of corpuscular radiation had to be abandoned, the physema had to be regarded as filled with something able to transmit waves, at least waves of heat and light. Thus arose the idea that the physema, 'space', was filled with a 'luminiferous ether', a hypothetical something with inconceivable qualities, far less dense than hydrogen, far more rigid than steel, with a higher co-efficient of elasticity than glass. Now, scientists are content not to know what, if anything, is in the physema. They realize that physics and mathematics, plumbing ever deeper and deeper into the nature of matter and space, and gaining ever more and more enlightening mathematical formulæ, are only approaching a parallel or parallels to reality. As Jeans says in regard to this question: "In brief, a mathematical formula can never tell us what a thing is, but only how it behaves."[1] We had better think of the contents of the physema as able to transmit waves or to permit the progress of waves, without pressing beyond that.

As to the conglomerates, caused by God to appear in the physema, here we stand abashed at the might and wisdom of the infinite and almighty God. A full description of them would be a recapitulation of all that science has discovered about them. But the following concise statements bear on our theme:

(1) Time (which is merely a measure of the sequence of events in this Universe) began when the first conglomerate or conglomerates of wave systems was caused by God to appear somewhere in the simultaneously or previously created physema. We like to think in sequences, but it seems more probable that the physema and the first conglomerate or conglomerates of waves appeared simultaneously. There seems no reason for supposing any interval, and in any case there would be no such thing as time in a physema which was a continuum only. If, on the other hand, the continuum and the waves are, as may very well be the case, states of the same thing, if the waves are distortions or contortions of the continuum, as Schrödinger and others think, then there is no reason why God should create the continuum and then cause the desired contortions to appear rather than that He should create it with a conglomerate or conglomerates of such contortions in such positions within it as He willed. We may, with this caveat, visualize the beginning of the Universe of matter and energy, space and time: God caused the physema to be, and thus there was a framework for space and time, the continuum of this Universe; then (or simultaneously) God caused great conglomerates of wave systems to appear in it, and there were the nebulæ, primal phenomena of the material

[1] *The Mysterious Universe*, p. 142.

Universe. Whether God created simultaneously all the nebulæ there ever have been or will be, or whether He created them in sequence or in groups with time intervals between each act of creation, or whether He creates them at regular or irregular intervals in units or groups all through time, is of little consequence. The fact that we can observe nebulæ in all stages from apparent pristinity to their ultimate contraction into cold dead stars might lead us to suppose that their creation has been in sequence. But there may be other reasons for their present differences in stage; it may be that dead stars, by collision or in some other way, can flare up again, become nebulæ, and thus renew their youth. Such speculations are not important for our present purpose, and it is enough for us to know that God directly made the first ones. How things have gone on since then is for the astrophysicists to determine.

(2) Why the physema contains so many conglomerates of wave systems, in all stages from apparent recent inception to apparent cold inertness—in other words, so many nebulæ, white stars, red stars, and dead stars—is not evident. It is impious to suggest that they are necessary for the proper functioning of the present Universe, though the present Universe may very well be so designed that all things in it comprise a grand and mutually compensating system; and it is futile to speculate as to any particular purpose for which God may have created any or all of the others. Our attention can only profitably be directed to the nebula which gave rise to the Solar system.

(3) Whatever happens to other nebulæ, we have a certain amount of knowledge of what has happened to that which gave rise to the Solar system. It was originated as a conglomerate of wave systems, and we do well to meditate on the calculations[1] made by God in originating that conglomerate. He had consideration for the number, direction and nature of the wave systems, so that they should eventually resolve themselves into a system consisting of a central luminary round which a number of planets should revolve, and that on one of those planets sentient life should be possible. This involved two interdepending problems:

[1] For the implications of this word, see p. 238.

the astrophysical problem, and the problem of the potentiation of matter. To solve the first, God had so to direct
the initial velocities, directions, number and properties of
the wave systems comprising the conglomerate, that they
should, starting as a whirling cloud of incandescent vapours,
condense and cool, and either by the condensation of rings
or whorls thrown off in its cooling, or by pieces rent off by
the near passage of other bodies, form eventually a system
with at its centre a source of radiant light and heat and
circling round that centre a company of planets. All this God
provided, and a hypothetical observer of our Solar system
would now have seen a glowing sun, emitting light and
heat, and round that sun at varying distances a number of
planets circling, round some of which yet smaller moons
revolved. One of these planets, he would have observed,
was set at such a distance from the sun that life was possible
upon it. He might well have reflected with wonder upon
the ingenuity which had devised the conditions making life
possible, and upon the fact that the particular planet on
which life existed was of such a nature and in such a position
relative to the Sun that great areas on its surface were
seldom colder than 0° C. or hotter than 40° C., a temperature
range within which life is possible, whereas the temperature range of the Solar system as a whole covers from
$-273°$ C. to at the very least 6,000° C., an estimate of the
temperature of the surface of the Sun. Life as we know it,
and we cannot conceive organic life of any very different
kind made with the elements as known to us, is only
possible within a range of about 40° C. We have reasons
for believing that life could not long endure in a realm
where temperatures remained continually at or below 0° C.
or at or above 40° C. 0°–40° C. may be taken as the life
range. 40 degrees out of a range covering well over 6,000!
If we considered the range in the Universe instead of just
in the Solar system, we should have a range of over 28,000
degrees, as it is estimated that the hottest stars are in the
region of 28,000° C. That particular range of 40 degrees is
therefore a 1 in 150 chance in the Solar system, and a
1 in 700 chance in the Universe. It may be argued that
a planet in cooling is bound to pass through this range at

some time or another. That is so, but to reason like that simply transfers our wonder to the mechanism of life itself: not that it is possible in a certain temperature range, but that it is possible at all. Thus God prepared the scene for life on this earth, and, after æons had passed, what was once a whirling white-hot flaming nebula had resolved itself into a solar system whose most important member, for us, was a little planet circling round a great sun, near enough to it never to get much colder than 0° C. and far enough away never to get much hotter than 60° C.

(4) It is now time to take a closer look at that planet. Like all nebulæ, stars, the Sun, and other planets, the earth consists of an agglomerate of wave systems. We use the expression 'agglomerate of wave systems' rather than 'concourse of atoms' because we wish to indicate both how much and how little we know concerning the ultimate nature of matter. There are two factors involved: knowledge, and the interpretation of knowledge. The physicists have been able to show that atoms consist essentially of electrons revolving round proton nuclei; but what exactly electrons and protons may be is a matter for speculation. The most generalized view would seem to be that they must be wave systems or wave circuits of some kind vibrating and moving in some way in the continuum. Whether the waves are something other than the continuum and move within it, or whether they are vibrations or distortions of the continuum itself, is open to discussion. The latter alternative is perhaps the more widely held. We had better regard these primal wave systems of which the electrons and protons would seem to be composed as to us the ultimate basis of the material Universe, and we may therefore conveniently refer to them as the *protocumata*.[1] We shall use the word protocumata to indicate the ultimate something underlying matter, waves of we know not what vibrating we know not how. Using the term protocumata, then, to indicate whatever lies behind matter, we may truly say that the protocumata by their first groupings or modes of interaction (so Schrödinger; cf. the note on p. 260) give rise to electrons and protons, and that these by their mutual

[1] τὰ πρῶτα κύματα, the primal waves.

association and relation in systems give rise to the atoms. The atoms seem to be composed on a common plan, a proton nucleus with electrons revolving round it. The nucleus always contains a whole-number of protons, some of which, then called neutrons, are neutralized by electrons directly associated in the nucleus. In a neutral atom the number of planetary electrons is always equal to the number of non-neutralized protons in the nucleus. In general, therefore, an atom is a system consisting of an equal number of protons and electrons, in which there must be at least one planetary electron, and in which there may or may not be electrons neutralizing protons in the nucleus. That is to say, an atom consists necessarily of protons with planetary electrons, and the proton nucleus may in addition also contain neutrons. The simplest atom is that of hydrogen (the lighter isotope), which consists of one proton and one electron. A more typical example would be aluminium, whose atom consists of 13 planetary electrons round a nucleus of 13 protons and 14 neutrons. There are about 240 known types of these electron-proton systems. Each separate example of any one of these types is called an atom.[1] Although a proton weighs as much as about 1,840 electrons, and the weight of an atom is therefore almost entirely in the proton nucleus, its physical and chemical properties seem to depend upon the number of planetary electrons, which vary from 1 to a maximum of 92. The 240 types of atom therefore fall into 92 groups according to the number of planetary electrons, some groups comprising only one type, while other groups comprise up to as many as six or seven types. The types within a group differ owing to a difference in the number of neutrons in the nucleus, and consequently differ in little but mass. Each group, no matter how many types it contains, is regarded as an 'element', and the various types within the group are called isotopes of that element. Several elements, for example helium, fluorine, sodium, aluminium, phosphorus, chromium, arsenic, iodine, and gold, constitute groups of one

[1] What a misleading name! The atom, far from being ἄτομος, uncuttable, i.e., an ultimate unit, is thus known to be a complex and wonderful system of electrons and protons, themselves complex wave circuits which we can only describe as derived from the protocumata.

type only, whereas most elements occur in several isotopic forms: carbon, nitrogen, and chlorine in two; oxygen, magnesium, and sulphur in three; and so on, up to xenon, which is near the head of the list with nine. The differences in mass between isotopes of the same element are not usually sufficiently great to have a noticeable effect upon its physical and chemical behaviour, apart from the slight differences that we should expect to follow from the slight differences in mass. The greatest difference occurs in the case of hydrogen, whose heavier isotope, composed of one proton, one neutron, and one electron, is thus twice as heavy as the lighter isotope. The heavier isotope is sufficiently distinctive to have received a name and symbol of its own—deuterium, D. Even so, its differences from the lighter isotope are not extraordinary; for example, its oxide, 'heavy water', is not very dissimilar from ordinary water, freezing at $3 \cdot 8°$ C. and boiling at $101 \cdot 6°$ C. Though we know a little more than our forefathers, it is still true to say that for most purposes we can regard the atoms—complex system though each is—as the 'bricks' of the Universe. These wave systems called atoms are so stable and inviolable, with a very few exceptions, that it is safe to say that the great majority of them endure unchanged for millions upon millions of years. So true is this that the law of the conservation of matter was until a mere fifty years ago generally held to be as certain as a 'law of nature' could be. Even now it is pragmatically sound in nearly every realm except atomic physics. It is probably safe to say that for one atom that is changed or disintegrated by natural process or by man's ingenuity, more than a million remain unchanged for more than a million years. The atoms are the bricks, and for all ordinary purposes we may say that there are 92 kinds of brick, the 92 elements. It was God who calculated[1] how to create a continuum in which He could cause systems of waves to subsist in these 92 stable forms, each form definite, each form inviolable, each form with its own characteristics. The complexity and wonder of these wave systems is only fully apparent to the mathematical physicist. It is little wonder that Jeans feels able to say:

[1] For the implications of this word, see p. 238.

"It is true, in a sense somewhat different from that intended by Galileo, that 'Nature's great book is written in mathematical language.' So true is it that no one except a mathematician need ever hope fully to understand those branches of science which try to unravel the fundamental nature of the universe—the theory of relativity, the theory of quanta and the wave-mechanics."[1] Well does he conclude "that the universe appears to have been designed by a pure mathematician."[2]

It is indeed right that we should stand in humble awe before the "Great Architect of the Universe",[3] who is such a "pure mathematician",[3] and that we should realize the infinite range and ingenuity of Him who is Eternal and Omnipotent. But it is even more important to realize that in the range of the purposes of God the working out of the mathematics of the Universe was a mere bagatelle, simply a means to an end; and although it is salutary to be reminded of the awe-inspiring mathematics of which God is master, before which even the acutest type of human mind reels, it it also salutary to remind ourselves that to God these stupendous calculations were merely a preliminary, and that God no more wants us to think of Him primarily or only as the Great Mathematician than a musician who can also play a good game of draughts wants to be thought of primarily or only as a draughts player. God's mathematics was a preliminary to a greater purpose, and, though He is both, He would rather that we came to know Him as 'Our Father' than as 'Great Mathematician'.

But we must not let our wonder rest in mathematics. We pass on to a consideration of the amazing properties which God has caused to be emergent in the derivatives of the protocumata. For the atoms, in their 92 main varieties, are not merely interesting as sets of varying wave systems. They are that, but God has given them other properties and potentialities which we must now briefly describe.

Let us pass back in imagination over several millions of years, to a time when this earth was becoming recognizable as it is to-day, but when neither vegetation nor animal life had yet appeared upon it. The temperature was rather

[1] *The Mysterious Universe*, pp. 127-128.   [2] Ibid., p. 132.   [3] Ibid., p. 134.

higher than it is now, for the Sun's radiation was a little stronger and the internal heat of the earth itself was somewhat greater. The scene was being prepared for the coming of life, and the landscape was beginning to take shape into a form not very dissimilar from some of the forms with which we are familiar. The atoms, the bricks of the Universe, of which this earth is composed, themselves wave systems, had been given properties, properties arising from the nature of those wave systems—how marvellous the devices of the Great Mathematician!—whereby they were able to form themselves into firm agglomerates which we call solids. Millions, then, of atoms, say of iron, being near to one another and the temperature being anything below 1,000° C., would form themselves into an agglomerate of such a kind that the relative position of each atom remained approximately fixed with respect to its neighbours, and the impression created upon our senses would be that of a firm solid. In similar ways other solids would arise, either of atoms all of one kind or of atoms of different kinds forming harmonious and orderly agglomerates. In a bar of pure iron all the atoms are iron atoms. In a piece of rock-crystal (quartz) the atoms are silicon and oxygen, two of the latter to each one of the former, and all of them arranged in symmetry and order. Some agglomerates, instead of being solid, are liquid, and the atoms instead of remaining always in the same relative position to one another move around, over and under one another, but remain in close proximity. In other cases, again, the atoms move freely about in space, either as units or in small groups, so that the agglomeration is neither solid nor liquid, but what we call gas or vapour.

Thus matter exists in solid, liquid, and gaseous forms, and the unit for any particular portion of matter is an atom or group of atoms. If quartz is made up of atoms of silicon and oxygen, two of the latter to each of the former, it is evident that we cannot imagine anything to be quartz unless there are at least three atoms in the group, one of silicon and two of oxygen. This smallest group of atoms making the existence of a given substance possible is called a molecule. The same fact is also expressible by saying that a molecule is the smallest possible amount of a given substance. The molecule might be divisible into its constituent atoms, but they would no longer be the same substance. In some substances, particularly gases, we know that the atoms move about in groups even when of the same kind, so that the molecule is a group of atoms of the same kind. Hydrogen, nitrogen and chlorine, for example, are gases in which the atoms always move about in pairs, so that the molecules of these gaseous substances consist of two atoms. In other cases, for example helium and argon, the atoms move about singly, so that the molecule is the atom. A substance, then, is an aggregate of molecules; and a molecule may consist of one atom or of groups of atoms of the same or of different kinds. Further, a substance may be solid, liquid or gaseous, and the same substance may change its form as the temperature and pressure rise and fall. Water, for example, is a substance whose molecules consist of a group composed of two atoms of hydrogen and one of oxygen; below $0°$ C. it is a hard solid (ice), between $0°$ C. and $100°$ C. it is a clear liquid (water), and above $100°$ C. it is a gas or vapour (steam).

God has thus devised that the atoms by their groupings and behaviour may compose a great variety of substances, some of which have molecules consisting of atoms of one kind (elementary substances, e.g., iron, copper, hydrogen, sulphur, 92 in all) and others of which have molecules consisting of groups of atoms of two or more kinds (compounds). There are certain laws and conditions governing the association of atoms into molecules, the study of which belongs to chemistry, and man has learned how to bring the various groupings about so that he may produce compounds of various kinds. A chemical formula is a concise statement of the kind and number of the atoms in the molecule of a given substance. Thus the formula of nitrobenzene, $C_6H_5NO_2$, tells us that each molecule of nitrobenzene consists of a group of six carbon atoms, five hydrogen atoms, one nitrogen atom and two oxygen atoms. Molecules, in fact, range from those consisting of only one atom to molecules containing hundreds or even thousands of atoms. The number of compounds, counting both those found in nature and those produced by human activity, is immense, and it is difficult to say where a limit could be fixed. In this respect the atoms are indeed like a box containing 92 varieties of brick: the ways of arranging them are almost incalculable. Sufficient to say that well over 200,000 different compounds containing the element carbon have been prepared and studied.

God has in this way made possible the existence or preparation of a great range of substances, all ultimately derived from the complex wave systems which constitute the atoms. Thus it appears that a material substance, a piece of marble for example, consists ultimately of an agglomerate of millions of identical complex wave systems, vibrating, reciprocating, revolving and intertwining in ways beyond our calculating. God has devised all that, and the devising is perfect. The wave systems are stable, their behaviour is invariable, and their formation into compounds obeys definite and inflexible laws. God has packed into each specific atomic wave system potentialities which stagger us, particularly when we remember that the atomic wave systems themselves derive from the potentialities put by God into the protocumata. Though ultimately they are nothing but wave systems, God has devised that various substances shall possess properties that seem entirely inexplicable in relation to their origin. We ought not to be unmindful of the wonder of our material environment, which derives from the wisdom and beneficence of God. There is stone and brick and concrete for every kind of building; there is wood of many kinds for varied uses; there are metals suitable for every variety of machine; there are materials from warmest fur to finest silk; there is paper on which to write and ink to use for writing; there is no need but the material is there for its fulfilling, no art but the material is there for its expression. Plastics, alloys, drugs, dyes—every new production is another triumph of man, because he has made a new pattern with the bricks; and is yet another proof of the wondrous wisdom and designing skill of God, because He made these things possible, He cached the potentiality which has been realized.

Before passing on we should emphasize three points:

(1) Matter is in no way God. It originated by His will, not as waves of power going forth from Him, but as waves caused by Him to arise spontaneously in appointed places within a physema which previously or simultaneously He had caused to come into existence within the exoschema, a physema which had no effect whatsoever on God in His exoschematicity. In the familiar words creation is ex nihilo by divine fiat.

(2) Matter has, apparently, been created exuberantly. God did not see fit to create a minimal Universe, with exactly calculated sufficiency of each constituent. The Universe is large beyond our power of imagining, product of One to whom space is an irrelevance; it contains stars as big as our Sun, and bigger, to the number of at least 300,000, and we have no means of knowing whether any other of these stars has, like our Sun, planets revolving round it. Even this earth, small as it is in the scale of the Universe, is a tremendous stage in comparison with the actors on it. So much water in the seas, so much sand in the deserts, such masses of rock—the creating God has made great reservoirs of matter, quantity is no concern to Him. There is a vast supply of atoms of every kind, a mighty reservoir of matter, so that nothing need be stinted.

(3) Although there is probably much matter which will never serve any more useful purpose than an odd rock on the moon, all matter has what may be called potentiation. God has given each of the 92 elements properties which endow that element with many potentialities. Thus atoms of carbon, in mutual arrangement according to one of their potentialities, may constitute a diamond; arranged on a different plan, the same group of atoms might constitute a stick of graphite; suitably co-operating with varying numbers of hydrogen atoms they could constitute petrol, acetylene or benzene; or they could form part of a piece of chalk, a lump of cheese or a leaf on a tree. God has given each atom its potentiation, which in some cases may be realized in any of various ways, or in some cases never seems to be realized at all: the reservoir is ample, the creation of matter was exuberant.

It is now possible to introduce some ideas which, applying in a simple manner to matter, will be found to lead on to a powerful method of analysis when dealing with life, man, and the Person of Jesus Christ. The ideas may be introduced by defining a number of terms:

(1) *Potentiation*

It is ever to be realized that all power and direction is of God, and that nothing has any possibilities except those given to it by God. God, for the fulfilment of His purposes, in the beginning caused the physema to come into being as a continuum with certain primal wave systems within it, the protocumata, and He potentiated the protocumata in such a manner that from them should derive electrons and protons, and that from these again should derive atoms. To the atoms was given the potentiation of aggregation into molecules and to the molecules of aggregation into substances. A substance is thus derived from the protocumata by the successive emergence of potentiations which God gave to the protocumata when He caused this Universe to come into being. It seems best to regard the original potentiation of the protocumata as a catenary quality, which revealed itself in successive and progressive stages. As each stage was reached so another became possible, and the potentialities emerged in due order. The primary potentiation of the protocumata was to give rise to, or themselves in some way to group themselves as, electrons and protons. These being produced, the second emergent potentiation of the protocumata became manifest, and the electrons and protons grouped themselves in the varying ways which gave rise to the 92 types of elementary atom. Atoms thus appearing, the third emergent potentiation of the protocumata became operative, and the atoms grouped themselves into molecules. The molecules, by the fourth emergent potentiation of the protocumata, were enabled to constitute the various substances which provide the material basis of this present Universe. The Universe of matter has thus arisen because of the potentiation given by God to the primal waves of the continuum: God caused the protocumata to appear in the physema, and potentiated them so that by successive emergence there should appear therefrom electrons and protons, atoms and molecules and substances. God's potentiation of the protocumata set the material Universe going, and we presume that it 'went like a clock' until at least the time for the appearance of life.

(2) *Integration*

The potentiation given by God to the protocumata led by a catenary process to the emergence of the substances which form the basis of the material Universe, and it will have been noticed that this process has one consistent feature: each successive step is the result of a number of smaller becoming one greater. However we like to think of the protocumata, whether, with Schrödinger, as 'ripples in a sub-æther' or otherwise, we cannot escape the conclusion that each electron and each proton is a new something that arises as the result of the protocumata becoming linked, combined or in some way mutually interacting, so that from few or many protocumata emerges one electron or one proton as the case may be. It is to be emphasized that this process is more than a mere grouping or congregating, as can be made clearer higher up the scale. Let us call this process "natural integration". Protocumata, then, naturally integrate into electrons and protons, electrons and protons naturally integrate into atoms, atoms into molecules, and molecules into substances. The wonder of natural integration is two-fold. First, that the product of a natural integration may possess properties quite unlike the properties of that from which it was derived. To think that the 92 types of element, so diverse in their properties, should all be derived by natural integration from electrons and protons, and that the immense variety of substances available in nature and by artificial means should be derived from these 92 elements! Successive natural integrations are accompanied by successive realizations of the potentiations given by God to the original protocumata. Second, that natural integration is a process of a powerful and uncontrollable kind, operating inevitably and certainly according to clearly definable laws. So definite is the potentiation given by God to the Universe of matter that we are impotent to affect it in the slightest degree. All we can do is to endeavour to discover the conditions under which certain things behave in certain ways, and, when we want these things to happen, to try to bring about the conditions.

By natural integration smaller systems or units become larger systems or units, and in this way God devised the coherence of the inanimate material world. But He carried the same principle several stages higher, one of which we must mention. Although animate creatures cannot affect the mode of natural integration, which takes place according to the operation of laws determined by God, God has nevertheless given animate creatures the ability to carry the progress of integration several stages further. Just as natural integration leads up from protocumata to substances, so God had given animate creatures the power to form larger systems or units from smaller systems or units, by assembling and interrelating the smaller units so that they constitute one large unit. For example, when a watch is made, matter in units of several kinds (pieces of steel, silver, copper, glass, themselves already naturally integrated from millions of atoms) is integrated into one system or unit. In contrast with natural integration, which is brought about by the definite laws of God, this process may be called *theletic*[1] *integration*, in that it is brought about by the will and operation of an animate creature to which God has given a real or apparent independence of action. Just as there are several types of natural integration so also are there several types of theletic integration. For the moment it is sufficient to recognize how far reaching a principle integration is: thereby God provides for the mechanism of the material Universe, by natural integration; and thereby He enables animate creatures to use that material, by theletic integration.

(3) *Unity*

It will be seen from the above section that the idea of unity is necessarily closely linked up with the idea of integration. The idea that many separate units can be integrated into one new unit implies that unity consists essentially in

[1] Θελητός, willed.

a special relationship of parts, the many parts being built up into one system. It is indeed well to use the word system side by side with unit, as it implies a necessarily correlative idea. To take a simple example: an atom is now supposed to be the integration of a number of wave systems, all of which are integrated into a system more complex than any of them regarded separately. The atom is therefore itself a complex system, which we nevertheless regard as a unit because it has properties and qualities which the wave systems from which it was derived do not possess. Similarly a number of atoms may combine to form a complex system which we call a molecule. We nevertheless regard the molecule as a unit, because it has properties and qualities which the atoms from which it was derived do not possess. Unity, therefore, does not necessarily imply homogeneity, indivisibility, indistinguishability of components, or even inseparability of parts. Rather does it imply definiteness of structure and definiteness of properties and qualities. Nor is the term exclusive. The various parts of a machine may separately be regarded as units; but the whole machine is also a unit. It may at this stage be said that an understanding of the nature of unity will follow from an understanding of the nature of integration. We may define the result of integration as a unit, and if we proceed to investigate and understand the different types of integration we shall also understand the different types of unity.

(4) Value

A system or unit of any kind may have value. It has functional value if it serves a useful purpose in some larger system or unit. Thus a bicycle wheel has functional value with respect to the complete bicycle. A system or unit has *pulchral*[1] value if it stimulates the sense of appreciation of beauty in an animate beholder. A system or unit has moral value if it is in some larger system which is subserving an end describable as "good". Value may be actual or potential. Functional value is actual if the unit is in fact functioning in a larger unit, like a wheel in a complete bicycle. Functional value is only potential if the unit is not so

[1] *Pulcher*, beautiful.

functioning, as would be the case of a bicycle wheel in a store. Such a wheel has potential functional value, but no actual functional value. We may say that a unit possessing potential functional value is functionally efficient, but not actually functionally valuable, only potentially functionally valuable. Pulchral value is actual or potential according as whether the system is in fact stimulating the sense of beauty in some beholder or not. Moral value is actual or potential according as whether the system is in fact in some larger system subserving an end describable as 'good' or not.

(5) Centricity

The idea of centricity arises from the idea of value. To consider the simplest case, functional value, we may say that nothing has actual functional value unless it is in a system greater than itself, though it may of course have potential functional value. But actual functional value depends on a less being integrated into a greater. That which is unintegrated has therefore no actual value. A cog-wheel, for instance, stored in a drawer, is not integrated into anything greater than itself, and therefore has no actual functional value. It has potential functional value, but that potential functional value will not become actual until the cog-wheel is fitted into a machine. While the cog-wheel is stored, and not integrated into anything greater than itself, it may be said to be *autocentric*: its existence is centred only in itself. But if the cog-wheel is integrated into a machine, it may be said to become *allocentric*: the centre of its existence has now been transferred to a greater unit, the machine. The cog-wheel has become allocentric, because it no longer centres on itself, and in becoming allocentric its potential functional value becomes actual functional value. In general, anything which is autocentric has no actual functional value —only potential functional value. When anything by integration into a greater unit becomes allocentric, its potential functional value becomes actual functional value. In the case of moral value the same reasoning applies. An object having potential moral value can only be made to have actual moral value if it is integrated into a system or unit greater than itself. Similarly pulchral value is potential or

R

actual according as whether there is a beholder or not. The desert flower may be beautiful, but its pulchral value is never more than potential unless someone passes by and sees it.

Autocentricity is the state of a unit which is not integrated into anything greater than itself, and in that case all its values remain merely potential. Allocentricity is the state of a unit which is integrated into something greater than itself, and in that case its values will be actual. It may at this point be suggested that the highest possible type of allocentricity would be the integration of a unit into the purpose of God: its complete dedication or surrender to His purpose. Theocentricity would thus describe the state of a unit which is integrated into that which is greater than all else, which is integrated as fully as its potentialities permit into the purpose and harmony of God Himself.

(6) *Perfection*

The idea of perfection gains definition when taken in conjunction with the ideas of value and centricity. Functional value, pulchral value and moral value are all scalar qualities, and we can readily admit the possibility of their being assessed on some scale, though it may be very difficult to devise a precise scale or an exact method of measurement. It is important to recognize that a system may have functional value and that its functional value may nevertheless not be the greatest possible. Consider, for example, a 'lead' refill for a propelling pencil. If the lead wrote smoothly, did not break easily, and did not wear away unduly quickly, we might agree that its functional value was high, say 90 per cent. of perfection. On the other hand, if the lead was gritty, liable to break too easily, or wore away unduly quickly, it would have a certain functional value in that it would be much better than no lead at all, but it would be far from perfection and we might agree that its functional value was not more than 20 per cent. of perfection. Proceeding still further, we might be offered a so-called lead which would not make any mark at all on paper. As a lead, its functional efficiency would be 0 per cent. of perfection. Obviously, anything less than 100 per cent. perfect is imperfect. But can imperfection rate lower than o per cent.? Yes, because we may find that a system or unit which we had integrated into a greater system not only fails to fulfil the hoped function, but does positive harm. A lead refill, for example, might scratch paper without writing on it and might in some way damage the inner mechanism of the propelling pencil. In such a case its perfection is not simply o per cent.; it is negative, and might be indicated by some negative percentage, say −30 per cent. A value may therefore scale down from perfection in its class (100 per cent.) not merely to complete uselessness (o per cent.) but to a corresponding degree of its active antithesis (−100 per cent. value). For example, a cogwheel that serves efficiently in a given machine has positive functional value; one that does not serve the purpose at all but does not do any injury to the machine has zero functional value; one that does damage if put into the machine has negative functional value. Similar arguments apply to pulchral and moral values. Debased "art" may have negative pulchral value. A corrupt form of religion may have negative moral value.

It is to be noted that functional value does not inhere in a system as such. An autocentric system may have functional efficiency, but it cannot have functional value, that is, actual functional value, though it may have potential functional value. A system only actualizes its functional value when it becomes part of a greater system, and it emerges that functional value depends upon the nature of that into which a unit integrates as well as upon the unit itself. A certain washer, integrated into a certain tap system, might have positive functional value; but the same washer, integrated into a different tap system, might be totally unsuitable and have negative functional value. In the same way pulchral and moral values depend not only upon the systems or units themselves but also upon those into which they are integrated.

In the next few chapters we shall see how the above ideas apply to matter, animal life, and man.

Footnote 1, *p.* 232: The general structure of the Universe as envisaged by modern scientists can be gathered from a great number of books of varying degrees of technicality and revealing a variety of metaphysical and even theological ideas. The following may be recommended as a short list in approximate order of non-technicality: Jeans, *The Mysterious Universe*; Eddington, *The Nature of the Physical World* and *The Mathematical Theory of Relativity*; Einstein, *Zur Einheitlichen Feldtheorie*; Weyl, *Raum, Zeit, Materie*.

It is difficult to express the findings of the 'new physics' clearly and at the same time concisely. For our present purpose the following points must suffice:

(1) The old ideas as to the substantiality of matter and of definite and permanent atoms have gone. It has been discovered that the atoms are miniature solar systems, electrons revolving round nuclei of protons. But the nature of electrons and protons eludes us. If an electron or proton is to be pictured at all, it should probably be as some sort of permanently closed wave circuit, the wave circuit itself giving rise to waves of some other kind. We may quote a few sentences from Eddington, *The Philosophy of Physical Science*: "Do not be misled by thinking of the nucleus as a sort of billiard ball. Think of it rather as a system of waves" (p. 111). "It is pertinent to remember that the concept of substance has disappeared from fundamental physics; what we ultimately come down to is *form*. Waves! Waves!! Waves!!!" (p. 110). "The statement often made, that in modern theory the electron is not a particle but a wave, is misleading. The 'wave' represents our knowledge of the electron. The statement is, however, an inexact way of emphasizing that the knowledge, not the entity itself, is the direct object of our study; and it may perhaps be excused by the fact that the terminology of quantum theory is now in such utter confusion that it is well-nigh impossible to make clear statements in it. The term '*electron*' has at least three different meanings in common use in quantum theory, in addition to its loose application to the probability wave itself" (p. 51). The last quotation is very illuminating. It is tantamount to saying that we can get no further than thinking of an electron as something that behaves as if it were a wave, though we have no way of discovering what in itself it is. It should be added that there are circumstances in which the electron behaves as if it were a particle. But it is not difficult to imagine that a closed wave circuit could so behave, for a closed wave circuit is very different from a progressing wave. As a very imperfect parallel we might instance a smoke ring, which is a very different phenomenon from smoke generally diffusing. Thus atoms are electrons and protons; electrons and protons are wave circuits, or behave as if they were; but waves of what vibrating how in what? There is no answer. "The real atom contains something which it has not entered into the mind of man to conceive, which has, however, been described symbolically by Schrödinger" (Eddington, *The Nature of the Physical World*, pp. 198–199). Eddington gives a useful summary of Schrödinger's theory (op. cit., pp. 211–220), from which the main trend of the opening paragraph may be quoted: "Imagine a sub-æther whose surface is covered with ripples. The oscillations of the ripples . . . by convergence and coalescence . . . conspire to create a disturbed area. . . . Such a disturbed area is recognized as a material particle; in particular it can be an electron."

(2) The elusiveness of matter would not unduly disturb us if we felt sure of our concepts of space and time. We could tolerably well imagine a Universe filled with some sort of tenuous elastic 'ether' of such a nature that wave circuits and vibrations within it gave rise to what we interpret as matter, electricity, light, and other natural phenomena. But the exponents of the new physics are very emphatic that our old ideas of space and time must be dismissed. "The space-time frame itself is known only in its abstract mathematical properties; there is no reason to suppose it similar in intrinsic character to the spatial and temporal relations of our perceptions as known in experience" (Bertrand Russell, *Encyclopædia Britannica*, 14th Edition,

xix. 100). "Space in itself and time in itself sink to mere shadows, and only a kind of union of the two retains an independent existence" (Minkowski, ibid., xix. 94). The physicists and mathematicians vainly endeavour to convince themselves and others that they have some idea of what space and time really are. Read, for example, Eddington's tenth chapter in *Space, Time and Gravitation*, from which these quotations are taken: "We thus get the idea that space-time may have an essential curvature on a great scale independent of the small hummocks due to recognized matter. . . . Spherical space is not very easy to imagine. . . . The difficulty is that we try to realize this spherical world by imagining how it would appear to us and to our measurements. There has been nothing in our experience to compare it with, and it seems fantastic. But if we could get rid of the personal point of view, and regard the sphericity of the world as a statement of the type of order of events outside us, we should think that it was a simple and natural order which is as likely as any other to occur in the world. . . . Spherical space-time, that is to say a four-dimensional continuum of space and imaginary time forming the surface of a sphere in five dimensions, has been investigated by Prof. de Sitter. If real time is used the world is spherical in its space dimensions, but open towards plus and minus infinity in its time dimension, like an hyperboloid. This happily relieves us of the necessity of supposing that as we progress in time we shall ultimately come back to the instant we started froml History never repeats itself. But in the space dimensions we should, if we went on, ultimately come back to the starting point. This would have interesting physical results, and we shall see presently that Einstein has a theory of the world in which the return can actually happen; but in de Sitter's theory it is rather an abstraction, because, as he says, 'all the paradoxical phenomena can only happen after the end or before the beginning of eternity.' The reason is this. Owing to curvature in the time dimension, as we examine the condition of things further and further from our starting point, our time begins to run faster and faster, or to put it another way natural phenomena and natural clocks slow down. . . . When we reach half-way to the antipodal point, time stands still. . . . There is no possibility of getting any further, because everything including light has come to rest here. All that lies beyond is for ever cut off from us by this barrier" (op. cit., pp. 158–160).

(3) Why, it may be asked, are the physicists and mathematicians, in spite even of their own difficulty in grasping their own concepts, nevertheless so sure that their views are right, or are at least moving in the right direction? They are so convinced because the mathematical formulæ which fit their observations and deductions can only be interpreted in some such way as writers like Jeans and Eddington endeavour to interpret them. The mathematical formulæ give a true picture of the way in which the natural Universe behaves, and formulæ assuming that the Universe is four-dimensional give results that fit the data more nearly than formulæ assuming that it is three-dimensional. It may be added that for certain purposes it is even better to assume a six-dimensional Universe (cf. Eddington, *The Philosophy of Physical Science*, pp. 140 and 164). Our mathematics has not run beyond our power to use it, but beyond our power to understand it. It is possible to work out the mathematics of space of four, five, six, and even more dimensions, and we have every reason to believe that our calculations are sound. But it is idle to pretend that we have any real idea of what our results mean, except in faint analogy. As Eddington says (op. cit., pp. 141–142), mathematics "dismisses the individual elements by assigning to them symbols, leaving it to non-mathematical thought to express the knowledge, if any, that we may have of what the symbols stand for." Perhaps a very simple illustration

should be given of the way in which mathematical methods so quickly transcend our conceptual ability. If we suppose x to represent a length, we readily concede that x^2 can represent an area, a square, and x^3 a solid, a cube. But x^4, x^5, x^6, completely baffle us. Our minds come to a stop at three dimensions of any one kind. Yet it is just as mathematically certain that $(a^2 + b^2) (a^2 - b^2) = a^4 - b^4$ as it is that $(a + b) (a - b) = a^2 - b^2$. But though the latter equation can easily be visualized in terms of lengths, the former cannot be visualized at all. To regard a and b merely as 'pure numbers' does not help us, as that at once drives us into the very difficult realm of the philosophy of pure number. Thus it is with the formulæ deduced by the mathematicians to correlate the data obtained by the physicists. The formulæ are doubtless true enough, but we cannot interpret them in the old familiar scheme of things: they presuppose a Universe consisting ultimately of vibrations and waves moving in, or themselves constituting, a medium we may call the space-time ether. If we can imagine something filling space, but not like matter of any kind with which we are familiar, either solid, liquid, or gas, and if we can imagine this something containing in itself curves and twists, rarefactions and compressions, closed systems of waves moving as systems and waves of various kinds travelling onward at varying speeds and in various directions, and all in some way linked up in one continuum at once spatial and temporal—if we can imagine all this it would be only a first faint approach to the real state of affairs, for nothing like this quite fits the formulæ. As Jeans remarks (*The Mysterious Universe*, pp. 142–143), "a mathematical formula can never tell us what a thing is, but only how it behaves; it can only specify an object through its properties. . . . We need not discuss whether the wave-system of a group of electrons exists in a three-dimensional space, or in a many-dimensional space, or not at all. It exists in a mathematical formula; this, and nothing else, expresses the ultimate reality, and we can picture it as representing waves in three, six or more dimensions whenever we so please . . . but none of these interpretations possesses any unique or absolute validity."

Footnote 2, *p.* 239: "Einstein's original theory of relativity supposed the presence of matter to be the only cause of the bending of space. An empty universe, totally devoid of matter, would have its space entirely uncurved, because there would be no matter to curve it, and so would be of infinite size. As the universe is not empty, its size is determined by the amount of matter it contains, the greater the amount of matter the smaller the universe" (Jeans, *The Mysterious Universe*, pp. 60–61). "A very different concept of the universe has been put forward by Professor de Sitter of Leiden. He supposed that even a universe totally devoid of matter would possess a certain amount of curvature, impressed upon it by the inherent properties of space and time" (ibid., pp. 62–63). But in either case the Universe is finite as regards space, for "the combined distortions of the four-dimensional continuum produced by all the matter in the universe causes the continuum to bend back on itself to form a closed surface, so that space becomes 'finite', with the results that have been already discussed" (ibid., p. 112). Eddington goes so far as to express the opinion that "to know the exact number of particles in the universe is a perfectly legitimate aspiration of the physicist". His tentative belief is that there are 136×2^{256} protons and the same number of electrons (*The Philosophy of Physical Science*, pp. 170–179).

It is for mathematicians and physicists to investigate further the nature of space and to determine how it is bounded in such a way as yet to give us the impression that it is infinite. But it is interesting to note that our metaphysic and modern physics alike arrive at the concept of a Universe which is spatially finite, whereas its infinity was regarded as almost axiomic less than a century ago.

The question may at once be asked: "If we suppose ourselves able to travel on and on in a straight line in some kind of trans-space airliner, what would happen? We have been accustomed to the idea that we should go on and on for ever and ever into infinite space, and if we said that that was unthinkable, we were asked whether we could imagine the end of space, and if so, what we thought could possibly be beyond that end if not more space. Now is it suggested that if we travelled far enough we should reach the boundary of the Universe, the 'skin' where the physema contacts the exoschema?" The answer is that God has so constructed the Universe that the physema seems infinite to those within it, and there is certainly no escape from it by travelling to its 'skin'. How God has contrived to do this is for the mathematicians to investigate, and they are working towards a solution from several directions. Their types of solution need not be considered here, but the non-mathematical reader may like a hint as to how these things can possibly be. Two suggestions may be made, neither of which is meant to be more than a hint:

(1) Just as it is possible in three-dimensional space to produce a two-dimensional surface on which it is possible to move indefinitely in any direction, so it should be possible in a four-dimensional continuum to produce a space in which it is possible to move indefinitely in any direction. An example of such a two-dimensional surface in three-dimensional space is the surface of a sphere. On such a surface one can go 'straight on' in any direction indefinitely, though to an outside observer the 'straight on' is seen to be the describing of a great circle. The illusion of going straight on indefinitely only arises because the surface is curved, not plane. Similarly, if it is possible for there to be a type of space in a four-dimensional continuum corresponding with the surface of a sphere in a three-dimensional continuum, it should be possible for the same illusion to be produced. If we call such space 'curved' (retaining an idea in parallel with the surface of a sphere), going 'straight ahead' would really be proceeding along an immense circle, and one would eventually return to the starting point. Some imagine that space may be curved in some such way as this. Two-dimensional creatures on the surface of an enormous sphere, ignorant that there were really three dimensions, might well be surprised that going straight ahead on what they considered (owing to its enormous radius of curvature) to be a plane surface brought them eventually back to their starting place. Further, if, like ants on the earth, they had no means of completing so long a journey, they would never have any reason to think otherwise than that the two-dimensional space in which they had their being was plane and infinite, when it was really neither. If we live in a 'curved' space with a radius of curvature so enormous that to us it seems a rectilinear space, very similar effects might be expected: every supposedly 'straight line' in the Universe leads into itself again. Einstein's earlier view was somewhat along these lines, and calculations based upon it give the length of the great circles as in the neighbourhood of 6×10^{21} miles.

(2) Those who prefer analogies not depending on more than three dimensions may be interested in considering another hint as to how the impression of infinity might arise in a finite continuum. The space-time continuum constituting the physema is of such a nature that it transmits light, or permits its passage, at a speed of approximately 186,000 miles per second. Let it be supposed, which is indeed highly probable, that all other speeds of motion and action in the continuum bear a direct relation to the speed of light; and let it further be supposed that as the 'skin' of the

physema is approached there is a progressive intensification, condensation or 'stiffening' of the continuum of such a kind that all movement in it becomes progressively impeded, so that light and every other kind of motion and action would be progressively slowed down. As the 'skin' of the physema was approached the impedance would become greater and greater, until finally the continuum would be so stiff that further progress would be virtually impossible. To express it mathematically, the continuum would have become so stiff that the limit of progress would approach zero distance per second, or the limit of time required for traversing unit distance would approach infinity. (A simple illustration is the covering of half the remaining distance to a given goal in each successive second. The goal is never reached, and the distance travelled in each successive second becomes smaller and smaller until it is conceivable but cannot be visualized.) It will readily be seen that an impedance building up in geometrical progression would fulfil the condition of this hypothesis. Indeed, a reduction by $\frac{2}{10^{16}}$ in the speed of light every second outwards from the centre of the physema would meet the case. Assuming that we are near the centre of the physema, such an impedance would make no appreciable difference within the limits of the solar system or indeed within the range of distances between us and the majority of the observed 'fixed' stars. For instance, assuming that the distances between ourselves and Sirius and Altair follow radii of the Universe, so that the differences in the velocity of light would be as great as possible, if we take the velocity here to be 186,000 miles per second, the corresponding velocities at Sirius and Altair would be in the neighbourhood of 185,999·9898 and 185,999·9825 miles per second respectively. These differences are too small for our present means of discrimination in such matters, and in any case to an observer on this earth the only effect would be that he would think that Sirius and Altair were slightly further away than they really are. As used to be said, there appears to be a 'conspiracy' to hide the real nature of space-time from us. But on the assumption of some such retardation in all velocities as the 'skin' of the physema is reached, a progressive stiffening of the continuum, the illusion of infinite space is perfectly accounted for. Light can travel 'for ever' in any direction and never reach the skin of the physema, as it progressively slows down as it encounters the progressive stiffening on approaching the boundary. Similarly, if a star approached the boundary, it too would be progressively slowed down until its motion had become infinitesimal. The skin itself, which neither light nor anything else from within the physema could ever quite reach would thus be virtually equivalent to an infinitely rigid and absolutely impenetrable barrier. The ancient idea of a 'firmament' may thus have had a greater element of truth in it than we formerly supposed. The view sketched above is in many ways parallel with de Sitter's view, as may be seen by reference to the note on p. 261. The chief difference is that we suppose the physema to reach its boundary at the skin of infinite stiffening, whereas de Sitter supposes that beyond that point a 'destiffening' takes place. But he admits that anything beyond the 'skin' (which on his view is 'half-way to the antipodal point') is quite outside our ken, as what happens there is "after the end or before the beginning of eternity." We of course agree, because beyond the 'skin' is the exoschema. He agrees that at the skin all time and action cease. De Sitter's theory leads to a Universe of much the same order of size as Einstein's, the radius being in the neighbourhood of 10^{21} miles. Light starting from the centre of such a Universe at 186,000 miles per second with a geometrically progressive retardation (due to progressive stiffening of the continuum towards the skin) of $\frac{2}{10^{16}}$ per second would take about 120,000 years to get half-way to the boundary.

CHAPTER III

WE have seen that God has potentiated matter in such a way that one of its fundamental properties is the power to form systems. In certain circumstances the many smaller become the one greater. This process we have called natural integration, and the result of the process is a new system or unit. In using the word unit we must not lose sight of the fact that the system is made of parts, and that its unity is more fundamentally a unity of function and purpose than of mere indivisibility or homogeneity. A system may be a real unity yet easily divisible or recognizable as composite. Integration is of two main kinds: natural integration, which is brought about by definite potentiations which God has placed in matter itself, and follows what are usually called 'natural laws'; and theletic integration, which is brought about by an animate creature, usually an animal or man. In this chapter we shall consider natural integration, which we shall find valuable in itself and also a useful introduction to theletic integration.

Natural integration may best be considered in an order which is both logical and chronological:

I. The integration of the protocumata into electrons and protons.

Concerning this we at present know nothing, and we must await further investigation by the physicists and the elaboration of corresponding theory by the mathematicians.

II. The integration of electrons and protons into atoms: atomic integration.

Here also we have little certain knowledge, though it may be hazarded with fair assurance that there must be certain conditions in which various definite numbers of electrons and protons become integrated into various definite atoms. Just as the protocumata integrated into electronic and protonic systems or units (electrons and protons), so also the electrons and protons integrated into atomic systems or units (atoms). Atomic integration, being a natural integration, takes place inevitably when certain conditions arise. Correspondingly, the process is reversed when certain other conditions arise, so that the possibility of integration is always balanced by the possibility of disintegration. There must be conditions, not yet fully understood, in which electrons and protons will integrate into atoms. There are other conditions, not yet fully understood but being sedulously investigated, in which atoms will disintegrate into electrons and protons. There are probably also conditions covering the whole range between the extremes of integration and disintegration:

(1) Further integration, whereby an atom resulting from atomic integration of electrons and protons may have additional electrons and protons integrated with it and thus become an atom of a different (larger or heavier) kind.

(2) Partial disintegration, whereby an atom, itself the result of the atomic integration of electrons and protons, may suffer the disintegration from itself of some of those electrons and protons and thus become an atom of a different (smaller or lighter) kind.

(3) Reintegration, whereby two or more atoms, by processes of complete or partial disintegration and complete or further integration from the results of the complete or partial disintegration, may become reintegrated as two or more atoms of a kind different from that which they were originally.[1]

In every case integration whether complete or partial, disintegration whether complete or partial, and reintegration of whatever kind are entirely dependent upon the fulfilment of conditions which God has imposed on the electrons and protons and prior to that on the protocumata. He has made them in a certain way, and the laws of their being are God-imposed and unalterable, except of course by Him.

An atom per se, that is, when not integrated into a further

[1] The present state of knowledge on these matters may be gathered from such books as Andrade, *The Structure of the Atom*.

system, has no actual functional value. It of course has potential functional value in view of the possibility of its integration into greater systems or units. When not so integrated it is autocentric, and anything which is autocentric has no actual value of any kind, functional, pulchral or moral, though it may have all these values potentially. Although it has no actual functional value it has a degree of functional efficiency, which is a scalar quality and corresponds with such ideas as durability and stability. Some atomic systems are very durable and stable and may therefore be said to be of high functional efficiency. Others are transient and unstable[1] and, as atomic systems, may be said to be of low functional efficiency. Thus electrons and protons, revealing the secondly emergent potentiation of the protocumata, have been so potentiated by God that in predetermined conditions they integrate by atomic integration into atomic systems (atomic units, atoms), which in themselves if not further integrated are autocentric systems or units with a degree of functional efficiency; in view of further possible integration, they are potentially allocentric and have potential functional value and, in some yet greater integration, even potential pulchral and moral value.

The first two processes in logical order in the development of the Universe were the integration of the protocumata into electrons and protons and of the latter into atoms, the two processes perhaps being simultaneous or immediately successive. At the very high temperatures which seem to have prevailed in the beginning, possibly because atomic integration is a highly exothermal reaction, the atoms were probably for some long period of time autocentric and isolated units, not integrated into any further

[1] The so-called radio-active elements, of which the best known is radium, are really elements whose atoms are atomic systems of low functional efficiency and consequently tend to break down with loss of electrons and protons. These they lose in units or groups, the most usual group lost consisting of four protons and two electrons, known as the α ray or particle, which later takes up two electrons and becomes a neutral helium atom. By these losses uranium, ionium, radium, thorium, actinium and various intermediate unstable atomic systems eventually partially disintegrate until they find stability as one of the isotopes of lead, which consists of a stable system of 82 planetary electrons and a nucleus of 82 protons and, according to the particular isotope, 121 to 126 neutrons. As an atom, lead may be described as very functionally efficient, as it is very stable.

systems and not associated by any ties other than those of
coexistence in the same continuum and the possession of
certain properties such as mass and position. But coexistence
in the same continuum and the possession of mass and
position are sufficient to establish certain inevitable relationships, and we must interrupt the sequence of progressive
integrations to interpolate a section on a type of integration
which may have a bearing on a complete philosophy.

Interpolation: Existential Integration

No atom which God has allowed to come into being (by
atomic integration from electrons and protons) is without
significance in the Universe. It may be, in the scale of
natural integration, autocentric and only of potential
functional pulchral and moral value; but it is nevertheless
an integral part of the Universe, and not only has potentiality but also has inevitable effect on every other atom in
the Universe. This fact of necessarily being an integral part
of the Universe enables us to appreciate an inevitable
"wholeness' in the scheme of things, even if many parts of
the whole never realize their full potentialities. This participation in the Universe by the fact of mere existence may
be called 'existential integration', by which we mean the
inevitable participation of every atom in the general scheme
of things by virtue of its mere existence and its fundamental
properties. Every atom has mass[1] and position, every atom
by its nature responds to gravitational and electrical forces
or, on the more modern view, itself helps to produce them.
In consequence the mass becomes weight[2] and the position
becomes subject to change, so that every single atom thus
takes its place in the balance and interaction of weight and
motion in the Universe. Every atom is thus existentially
integrated into the general scheme of things, and each
minute moving mass has its minute but real effect on every
other moving mass. Even the rock on the moon referred

[1] Mass: the amount of matter in a given body. This is independent of
where the body happens to be.
[2] Weight: the force exerted by a body by virtue of its being gravitationally
attracted by some other body or bodies. Force is needed to prevent a body
falling to the ground owing to the gravitational pull of the earth. Less force
would be required on the moon, but more on Jupiter.

to above (p. 252) has its small but real effect on the kinematics of the solar system: if God caused that rock to cease to exist there would be a minute but calculable change in the course of the outermost planet. Nothing, therefore, which God has caused to come into being is outside His purpose, even if, as part of the great reservoir of matter, it is only integrated existentially into the scheme of things and all its other potentialities remain unrealized.

III. The integration of atoms into molecules and substances: hylic[1] integration.

Once the atoms had been formed their existential integration into the general scheme of things was unconditioned and inevitable: by virtue of weight and motion they had their place in the general balance of weight and motion in the Universe. Many atoms probably never reach any higher integration than that. They just form part of the great reservoir of matter and their potentialities are never actualized. There are probably atoms which have never entered into any kind of greater integration, but have remained autocentric atomic systems moving about among their fellows and having no influence on or relation with them except that of existential integration by virtue of their weight and movement. At very high temperatures all the elements tend to exist as monatomic gases, which is the same as saying that all the atoms exist as autocentric atomic systems; and even at all temperatures likely to occur naturally on this earth for millenniums yet to come the atoms of helium, neon, argon and the other gases of that group do so exist and are likely so to continue to exist.

Although at very high temperatures all atoms tend to exist as separate autocentric units, as the temperature becomes lower a temperature range is eventually reached within which certain atoms tend to integrate in certain ways with atoms of the same or of other kinds. Such integration may be called 'hylic integration', and the result a hylic system or unit. Hylic integration is of two main types, which may occur separately or concurrently. The first type of hylic integration is molecular integration, by which we mean the integration of separate atoms into a

[1] ὑλικός, of or pertaining to matter.

system of atoms in which each of the originally separate atoms has a defined place. Such a system is a molecule and constitutes a hylic system or unit, in particular a hylic (molecular) system or unit. The chemist represents each atom by its initial or some other convenient letter or group of letters, and indicates a molecule by writing the symbols of the elements integrated into it with a subscript number to indicate the number of atoms of each element. Thus $C_6H_5NO_2$ represents a molecule of nitrobenzene, which is a hylic system or unit integrated from six atoms of carbon, five of hydrogen, one of nitrogen and two of oxygen.

The second type of hylic integration is aggregative integration, by which we mean the integration of separate atoms or molecules into liquid or solid aggregates, such aggregates being characterized and defined by their continuity: a quantity of liquid, from a lake to a drop; a lump of solid, from a great rock to a grain of powder. These are all hylic systems or units, integrated from atoms or molecules into liquid or solid aggregates. It should be noted that atoms may in certain cases undergo aggregative integration without having first undergone molecular integration. It is convenient to use the one term hylic integration although the two types have to be included: the integration of atoms into molecules, and of atoms or molecules into aggregated substances, liquid or solid. The one term is desirable because these two types of integration are often interrelated and interdependent. A hylic unit may be as small as one diatomic molecule or as large as an iron casting weighing many tons. In the former case two atoms have by hylic integration become one molecule. In the latter case millions of iron atoms have by hylic integration associated themselves into molecules and then into a solid substance. The term hylic integration includes all the ways in which atoms can form systems with one another in chemical or physical ways or in both combined. In general, a hylic system or unit consists of atoms mutually integrated together by a God-given potentiation which makes them cohere in groups known as molecules and alternatively or simultaneously in liquid or solid aggregates. The term 'hylic integration' thus includes all the phenomena known as chemical combination and physical liquefaction and solidification. It is the potentiality in atoms of hylic integration which enables them to combine chemically and to condense to the liquid and solid form.

It is not necessary for our present purpose to investigate the operation of hylic integration in any great detail, but the following observations are significant:

(1) As with atomic integration, which involves also atomic disintegration and reintegration, so hylic integration involves hylic disintegration and reintegration. Just as there are conditions under which atoms hylically integrate into hylic systems or units, so there are conditions under which hylic disintegration takes place and the hylic systems or units break down into other smaller hylic systems or units or into atoms. We should also distinguish other possibilities arising from the phenomena of integration and disintegration:

(i) Further hylic integration, whereby a hylic unit resulting from hylic integration of atoms may have additional atoms or other hylic units integrated with it, and thus become a hylic unit of a different (and larger or heavier) kind, or, if the other hylic units were similar to itself, of a larger and heavier kind.

(ii) Partial disintegration, whereby a hylic unit suffers disintegration from it of some of its atoms, as separate atoms or as smaller hylic units, and thus itself becomes a hylic unit of a different (and smaller or lighter) kind, or, if the smaller hylic units were similar to itself, of a smaller and lighter kind.

(iii) Reintegration, whereby two or more hylic systems by processes of complete or partial disintegration and complete or further integration from the results of the complete or partial disintegration, may be reintegrated as two or more hylic systems of a kind different from those which they were originally.

These three headings cover practically all types of chemical reaction and also physical processes such as change of state, the mixing and dividing of liquids and the composition and breaking up of solids. In fact, the idea of

hylic integration and its necessary consequents, hylic disintegration and reintegration, gives a comprehensive view
of the inevitable behaviour of atoms as their circumstances
and conditions change. All chemical reactions and physical
changes are simply due to the inevitable behaviour of the
atoms in accordance with the realization of the potentiations
God has given them, potentiations which are realized as
and when conditions so determine. It is in the conditions
governing hylic integration (and hylic disintegration and
reintegration) that we have the first indication of the higher
potentiations which God has given matter and of the conditions under which these higher potentiations may be
realized. Without unduly anticipating, it may be desirable
to make the following observations at this point:

(i) Hylic integration and reintegration take place under
conditions which God has determined, one of which is
temperature. As the temperature is raised higher and higher,
integrations and reintegrations are less likely to take place,
whereas disintegrations are more likely. This is familiarly
expressed by saying that most substances tend to decompose
or break down on heating. At very high temperatures almost
all forms of matter tend to exist in the form of gases whose
molecules are monatomic, that is, as autocentric atomic
units. But as the temperature is reduced, so the atoms tend
to integrate into groups, of the same or different kinds
according to contiguity, and to condense from the gaseous
to the liquid or solid state. In general, the most complex
integrations and reintegrations appear to take place in a
temperature range of from about 20° C. to 100° C., and it
is the lower part of this range, say 20° C. to 40° C., in which
are possible the integrations and reintegrations which make
possible the existence of those substances (organic compounds) on which life as we know it depends. But if the
temperature is progressively lowered further, the processes
of hylic integration and reintegration tend to slow down
and stop, and at temperatures much below the freezing
point of water (0° C.) a static condition is reached in which
the processes of integration and reintegration cease or are
in some cases even succeeded by disintegration. It thus
emerges that there is an optimal temperature range for

hylic integration, in which temperature range the potentiation of matter to form more complex aggregates is at its highest.

(ii) Hylic integration in no way depends upon the atoms themselves. Their potentiation has been given by God, and acts according to inevitable law. Given certain conditions hylic integration, disintegration or reintegration will take place; but the certain conditions may come about in at least two ways:

(*a*) They may arise in the course of the general progress of events in the onward trend of the duration of the Universe. For instance, as the earth cooled temperature and pressure conditions occurred which made certain hylic integrations possible. If the appropriate elements were contiguous, the integration accordingly took place. Such hylic integrations may be characterized as incidental: they are incidental to the general trend of events, and atoms incidentally hylically integrated into more complex groups may still have no more significance in the Universe than they had as individual atoms. Although incidentally hylically integrated, the group or complex into which they are incidentally hylically integrated may itself be no more than existentially integrated into the general scheme of things. A hylic integration is therefore not necessarily of more significance in the general scheme of things than an isolated atom. It may be, and often is, merely autocentric.

(*b*) Hylic integrations may also arise as a result of the exercise of man's will. God has given man free will, and he may exercise that free will to bring about the conditions in which certain atoms will integrate into certain groups or complexes or in which certain already existing groups will reintegrate into other groups or complexes. In that such integrations and reintegrations come about by the imposed will of man, they may be distinguished as theletic[1] hylic integrations. 'Theletic' indicates that it has been brought about by man's will, and 'hylic' indicates that it has only been possible for such an integration

[1] On the use of this word, see p. 255.

S

to take place because God has placed such possibilities in the atom, possibilities which are inevitably realized when and only when certain conditions arise or are brought about.

(2) The result of a hylic integration, whether incidental or theletic, is the emergence of a substance with properties different from those of the substances from which it was derived. If the integration has been brought about by man's will, it is often, though not always, possible to say that the new unit will be put to good or bad use. That is, the newly integrated hylic unit may itself be integrated into a bigger system or unit—not necessarily a hylic one—and that bigger system or unit may be efficient or inefficient, beautiful or ugly, good or bad. Not in itself, but in its possible uses, matter and its integrations thus have possibilities of opposite kinds from the point of view of values. It emerges that, as in the case of the atom, the hylic unit has no actual value in and of itself, though it may have considerable potential functional pulchral and moral value which may be realized if it is integrated into some suitable greater unit. So long as it is not integrated into a greater system a hylic unit is autocentric and has no actual functional value. It has a degree of functional efficiency, which is a scalar quality, and corresponds with such ideas as durability and stability. Some hylic units are very durable and stable (e.g., gold, granite), and may therefore be said to be functionally efficient as hylic units. Others are transient and unstable (e.g., dyes that fade, things that 'won't keep'), and may be said to be of low functional efficiency.

We may make this summary statement: The atoms have been potentiated by God, emergently from the protocumata through the electrons and protons, so that they should in predetermined conditions by hylic integrations integrate into hylic systems or units (substances), which are in themselves if not further integrated autocentric functional systems or units with a degree of functional efficiency, but in view of further possible integrations are potentially allocentric and have potential functional pulchral and moral value.

It may now be desirable to give a sketch of the operation of atomic and hylic integration prior to the appearance of life on the earth.

After the creation of this continuum we suppose that the first event was the integration of the primal wave circuits, the protocumata, into electrons and protons and of these latter into atoms. The methods of these integrations are not altogether outside our powers of investigation, but once the atoms had appeared they seem on the whole to be singularly stable, and although the processes of integration, disintegration and reintegration of atoms to some extent still continue,[1] both incidentally and theletically, we may for most purposes regard the atoms as the fundamentally abiding units of the material Universe.

We may well suppose that immediately after the formation of the atoms the temperatures in the first nebulæ were so high that the atoms could only exist as autocentric units. But as the temperature of a nebula became lower, so the temperature range was reached in which hylic integration, disintegration and reintegration became operative, and the formerly autocentric atomic systems began to integrate into various hylic systems according to the exactly predetermined potentiations placed by God emergently in the protocumata and consequently in the atoms. The conditions were mainly temperature pressure and contiguity, but other factors no doubt came into operation, such as catalysis and electrical conditions. Meanwhile, the nebula in which we are most interested, the one which gave rise to our solar system, was reaching the stage when it condensed out into a central sun and planets, and if we transfer our imagination to this earth we can picture the state of affairs as it cooled further. There must have been a turmoil of chemical and physical activity. The earth began to solidify, and violent chemical reactions took place between the various elements, vapours condensing, gases evolving and reacting with one another and, later, steam condensing to water and pouring down as the first rain to form the first rivers and seas. In all this welter of activity one great divine principle was at work:

[1] The cosmic significance of continuing atomic disintegration and reintegration is not overlooked.

hylic integration; and all that took place could be truly and completely represented by tracing for each atom a cosmic line and showing how that line intertwined (i.e. hylically integrated) with and disentangled itself (i.e. hylically disintegrated) from the cosmic lines of the other atoms. We can thus picture the then Universe as a flux of hylic units, atoms entering and leaving a succession of hylic systems according to the operation of definite God-determined laws. The Universe, prior to the entry of life, may be correctly and completely described as a flux of hylic systems or units, such systems or units consisting of atoms integrated into them by hylic integration, the atoms themselves being integrated into atomic systems or units by atomic integration from electrons and protons, and they from the protocumata, and the protocumata having been brought into being and potentiated by God in the simultaneously or previously created physema which appears to us as the space-time continuum.

IV. Biotic[1] Integration.

The next great stage in God's plan was reached when the earth had cooled to such an extent that the temperature on at least parts of its surface was within the approximate range 20° C. to 40° C. By that time the general features of the earth were not very different from those prevailing now. Continents and islands, rivers and oceans, mountains and valleys, all these had appeared. Indeed, could we be transported to the earth as it then was we should think we were in some tropical region where the scenery was singularly bold and rugged, wild and desolate, and it might be a little while before we noticed the significant characteristic: no life of any kind, neither tree nor bush, grass nor flower, neither insect, bird nor beast. But in the then prevailing temperature range, 20° C. to 40° C., hylic integration is at its highest peak from the point of view of the complexity of the hylic systems which in various circumstances can form. It is in this temperature range that a whole range of very important hylic systems known as organic compounds are able to be formed and to exist. These substances are the material basis of life, and plant and animal organisms

[1] βιωτικός, of or pertaining to life.

are built up of hylic units amongst which organic compounds play an indispensable part. No living organism exists into whose composition at least one hylic unit of the kind known as an organic compound does not enter.

Organic compounds are formed when certain atoms (or atoms already integrated by hylic integration into certain hylic units) are brought together under certain conditions of temperature and pressure, and with perhaps other accompanying circumstances, such as the presence of other substances or of light and electricity. In such circumstances a hylic integration takes place and a hylic unit of the type known as an organic substance is formed. It is a remarkable and interesting fact that all such substances contain at least one atom of the element carbon. In His marvellous planning God gave to this element (through the emergent potentiations of the protocumata atomically integrating to form it) the power of becoming the basis of a tremendous number of compounds of a very special kind, the organic compounds. It was formerly supposed that these compounds could only be produced by the activity of life, vegetable or animal, but, as in so many matters, God has made it possible for man to investigate the mechanism of the Universe, and we now know something of the way in which these marvellous compounds are constructed, and we are able to build up very many of them by bringing about the right conditions. The first success of this kind was achieved by F. Wöhler, a German chemist, who in 1828 succeeded in synthesizing urea. Such syntheses exemplify hylic integrations taking place not incidentally but theletically. Man does not cause the integration to take place. He merely arranges to bring about the conditions in which the integration will take place. Incidentally, let it be remembered that man's discoveries only reveal possibilities already latent in God's original potentiation of matter and that the ability to discover is itself ultimately a gift of God. We now know that the range of organic compounds, which are the raw material of all animal and vegetable life and are the material out of which leaf and stem, flower and tree, muscle, flesh, and sinew are made, depend on the ability of carbon atoms to form chains and rings in a way in which no other element can. It is very exceptional for an inorganic (non-carbon containing) molecule to contain more than seven or eight atoms of the same or different kinds. But it is very exceptional for an organic compound to contain so few as that. It may be of interest to mention the number of atoms in the molecules of a number of common organic substances: glucose, 24; trioleïn (a constituent of olive oil), 167; lecithine (a constituent of egg yolk), 145; taurocholic acid (which is found in bile), 80. Some organic compounds, such as the proteïns, are of such complex structure that it has not yet been possible to ascertain how many atoms their molecules actually do contain, nor how they are arranged. Naturally, such substances have not yet been made artificially in the laboratory. One of the most complicated organic compounds ever made in the laboratory was an octodecapeptide, synthesized by E. Fischer, having the formula $C_{48}H_{80}N_{18}O_{19}$, and thus containing 165 atoms in its molecule. In every case the possibility of these wonderfully complex substances depends upon the ability of carbon atoms to form chains or rings. This ability is an illustration of hylic integration, and just as carbon has a greater range and variety of hylic integrability than any other element, so have the carbon compounds a greater power of integration among themselves than have inorganic compounds, and this results in the possibility of the formation of what we call organisms.

Thus it came about that when the earth had cooled to a temperature within the limits within which we know life to be possible, the next great significant step towards the preparation of the scene of human life was taken. By the properties which He had made inherent in carbon and its compounds and the potentiality in those compounds of integrating into organisms, God had prepared the means whereby life could come into existence on this earth. How God caused life to appear, and in what stages, we are not certainly able to say, though during the past century an increasing amount of material has been collected and correlated which helps us to speculate more intelligently. The idea of organic evolution is only a theory, and must not be elevated into a 'law of nature', though the evidence supporting it is very strong. There is nevertheless no reason why those who wish to do so should not believe that God created the various forms of life in successive acts, beginning perhaps with the simplest marine organisms and culminating with man. Such a view could fit into our present scheme without undue difficulty, and we do not dismiss it. The idea of organic evolution, however, is in more harmonious conformity with our general scheme, and quite apart from the arguments of the biologists we are inclined to accept it for that reason.

Thus we can picture the wonderful divine scheme unfolding:

(1) God caused the Universe to be, creating the primal wave systems in the continuum and giving them their successively emergent potentiations. Thus protocumata became electrons and protons and these became atoms.

(2) As the nebulæ, and in particular the solar system, and still more particularly our earth, cooled, so further emergent potentiations became actualized: the ability of the atoms, given the right conditions, to form hylic systems or units—gaseous molecules, liquids, solids.

(3) When the temperature had dropped still further, the temperature range was reached on this earth when the atoms by hylic integration were able to form organic substances, and the next emergent potentiation of the protocumata became manifest: the ability of hylic systems, in particular those known as organic substances, to integrate by biotic integration into biotic systems or units, which are generally styled "living organisms". Thus in the warm swampy margins of the primeval seas, in conditions which God had foreseen and predetermined, a photosynthesis took place whereby the first organic compounds were produced and the first organisms emerged, the simplest forms of vegetable and animal life.

The significance of biotic integration must now be considered, and it will be desirable to indicate three differing views. It is to be strongly emphasized that any of these three views can be fitted harmoniously into the general philosophy which we are endeavouring to expound, and no one need be perturbed because he feels inclined to accept one of these views in preference to either of the others. It may perhaps be said that almost all modern biologists would support either the first or the second in some form or another.

(1) We may regard biotic integration as in exact line with the other natural integrations (atomic integration and hylic integration) and we may consider that God fully potentiated the original protocumata so that there should be an orderly emergence of that potentiation: the primary potentiation whereby the protocumata formed electrons and protons, the second emergent potentiation whereby these formed atoms, the third emergent potentiation whereby the atoms formed hylic systems, the fourth emergent potentiation whereby the hylic systems formed biotic systems, living organisms. Just as the protocumata formed electrons or protons according to divinely determined conditions of which we are so far ignorant, and as the electrons and protons formed the various atomic systems in accordance with varying circumstances and conditions, and as by further integration and reintegration atomic systems of varying complexity can be formed; and just as the atoms form different hylic systems according to circumstances and conditions, and as by further integration and reintegration hylic systems of varying complexity can be formed; so the hylic systems (in particular the organic substances) formed the first biotic systems (living organisms) when the appropriate circumstances and conditions arose.

Such a view is perfectly reasonable, and is one of the alternatives considered probable by most biologists.[1] It would simply mean that God, in His great wisdom, had so potentiated the protocumata that in due course atoms, substances, and finally living organisms emerged by successive and progressive integrations; and that just as atomic

---

[1] See, e.g., Grove and Newell, *Animal Biology*, p. 1: "What is life? This has been answered by saying that life is merely a property of certain kinds of matter (the mechanistic point of view). If, however, the question be answered by the statement that living organisms possess something additional to the material of which they are composed (the vitalistic point of view), then a second question arises, namely: What is the nature of this peculiar 'something'? Both these questions await a final answer."

integration gave rise to the 92 main types of atom, and as hylic integration of the atoms gave rise to hundreds of thousands of different hylic systems (substances), so biotic integration of certain substances gives rise to almost countless types of biotic systems (living organisms, vegetable and animal). Such a view supposes that God so planned the Universe that He did not have occasion to intervene in any way between the creation of the continuum and its wave systems and the emergence of the higher animals. Such a view, far from being irreverent or tending to agnosticism,[1] leaves us in awestruck wonder at the mighty ingenuity of God, who foreplanned and potentiated the physema and its contents in such a way that the mighty mechanism once set going would lead to the ultimate emergence of butterflies and bees, gazelles and antelopes.[2] It may be added that this view will become inescapable if man ever becomes able by laboratory processes to produce a living organism. So far this has not been done, but if it were done it would only prove that man had been able to discover yet another of the wondrous secrets of the methods of God's devising. Every discovery is but an enlargement of our comprehension of the marvels of the divine scheme.

(2) Or we may regard the biotic integration of hylic systems as a process involving something additional to matter, however integrated. We may consider that God definitely intervened at the appropriate moment and added something else to His Universe, or at least to that part of it on which we live, this earth. When the time had come that hylic integration was able to produce organic substances, God by divine fiat caused those first formed organic substances to come together into the form of an organism and gave that organism a new quality which we call "life", the quality which distinguishes living from dead matter, whether vegetable or animal, a quality which provides for organic existence, growth, development, and reproduction. Having given this new potentiation to the first organism, and having thus made it a living organism, God devised

[1] For footnote, see p. 296.
[2] Also cockroaches, lice, the hippopotamus and the tiger? Certainly, but see pp. 283–284.

that this quality, life, should always accompany biotic integration and be in some way handed on in successive biotic integrations. If we accept this view, biotic integration means the integration of hylic units into a biotic system, such integration being dependent not only on the availability of the appropriate hylic units and of the appropriate circumstances and conditions, but also on the presence of 'vital force', whatever that may be, but which is in some way not understood passed from one or more biotic systems to those which originate from it or them, such origination occurring in various ways. These various ways of origination are called 'reproduction'. If we accept the idea that biotic integration necessarily involves the presence of an additional something called 'vital force', we may further wish to subdivide that force into vegetable vital force and animal vital force, though the line is very difficult to draw between them and there are many who would regard vegetable and animal life as manifestations of the same force, the latter being merely more highly developed and working through a more complex and responsive biotic system.

We may mention two reasons given for holding this second view of the nature of biotic integration:

(i) No living organism has yet been proved to have originated except from antecedent living organisms. It seems as though some quite definite new force came into evidence with the appearance of life, a force which inheres only in and is transmitted only by living organisms. It would therefore seem reasonable to suppose that at the appropriate juncture God put 'vital force' into His creation and thus caused the first vegetable and animal life to appear.

(ii) Life, 'vital force', has properties which the mind finds it hard to suppose could inhere in the atoms, severally, jointly, or in any possible arrangement of them. It is hard to imagine that the brain and nervous system even of a frog consists of nothing but cunningly arranged atoms of carbon, hydrogen, oxygen, nitrogen, and traces of other elements. It is not impossible that God should have so devised, but many prefer to suppose that the 'vital force' in the vegetable and animal world owes its origin to a later and separate special act of God.

The first vegetable and animal life having been set on its way, the vital force appropriate to each form being transmitted from generation to generation, the next emergent potentiation became manifest. For just as matter was given potentiation so that it could be integrated and centred for better for worse, so life was given potentiation of an even more far reaching kind. The following observations may make the matter clear:

(i) Each individual living organism, whether vegetable or animal, has, in general,[1] its inception, its individual life, and its end. From inception to end is its 'life'. Its original integration was from matter and vital force supplied by its parent or parents. After that original integration it lives in relation to its environment, to which it is marvellously and ingeniously adapted, and finally, after a period peculiarly characteristic of each type, it disintegrates and its 'life' comes to an end.

(ii) Although in general types breed true, and like produces like, God appears to have provided for variation, and by natural selection, accidental variation, and in other ways, the first simple types of vegetable and animal life have in the course of the ages multiplied themselves in an astoundingly numerous and varied manner. It seems best to suppose that God put the potentiality of this variation into the original form or forms that He caused to be, so that the thousands upon thousands of varieties of vegetable and animal life were not designed one by one (though that is neither ridiculous nor impossible), but that God set a system into action which would produce a vast range of living organisms which He of course foresaw, but which He allowed to work itself out. Looking at some queer insect we may thus say, "How marvellously ingenious of God to make the evolution of this little creature possible!" This approach also fits in with our idea of inevitable antitheses: the potentiation of vital force can produce the beauty of the gazelle and the ugliness of the hippopotamus; the lithe grace of the tiger and the ponderous bulk of the rhinoceros; the song of the nightingale and the hoarse

[1] There are exceptions which need not concern us here, as they could be accounted for without dislocating our main contentions.

croak of the crow; the elegance of a red admiral and the repulsiveness of a louse. It is true to say that all these things are fearfully and wonderfully made. They indeed are, and they all 'work'. From one point of view the mechanism of a louse is as wonderful as that of a gazelle, and from that point of view it is in a sense a beautiful and wonderful work of God. But that is not quite the point. The point is this: just as matter is neutral, but can be used well or ill, so life is capable of being exemplified in higher or lower forms, and it seems that the possibility of great beauty and elegance is of necessity counterbalanced by the possibility of great ugliness and clumsiness, as though God said, "See, here is life, life abundant and varied. With this gift comes potentiation, and as the gift is a greater one than the gift of dead matter, so are the extreme realizations of its potentiation, upwards and downwards. Mark and learn." A mass of copper could be shaped into a spear or a lovely vase: its potentiation includes those extremes. But these extremes are not so great as the contrast between a dog faithful unto death to its master and a pack of wolves savaging its victim.[1] The vegetable and animal world is thus a great object lesson: wondrous beauty in the vegetable world and yet more to be educed by the cultivation of our gardens, for God has not arranged that the largest and most beautiful flowers should grow wild, but that they should be developable as a result of man's co-operation; and wondrous elegance and power in the animal world and yet more to be educed by man, for the various breeds of horse and dog are the result of man endeavouring to bring out the most useful or most beautiful potentiations.

(3) A third view of the coming of life on to the earth is the belief that the various types, or at least the main types, of vegetable and animal life were created separately, and that biotic integration consists of the biotic integration of hylic systems (substances) in conformity with the potentialities defined for each type, vital force appropriate to each type passing down from generation to generation within each type. We do not propose to deal with this view in

[1] Though a pack of dogs may savage a deer, and a wolf could presumably be tamed.—Jas. iii. 7.

detail. All we need say is that its adoption would entail some considerable modifications in the general view set out in this work, but no modifications of a disastrous character. We do not dismiss this view as unreasonable or discredited, although, as already stated, the first and second views given above are those now most generally accepted.

We shall proceed on the basis of the assumption of the first or second view as a working hypothesis, and whenever the term biotic integration is used it is to be taken to mean the integration of hylic units into living organisms, and we shall assume that vital force, whatever it is and however derived, is a necessary constituent of a living organism: no living organism can become such without vital force, and when vital force ceases or leaves, the living organism ceases to be such and becomes a mass of dead matter, a complex of hylic units which soon begin to break down into less complex hylic units. We leave it open as to whether vital force is a fourthly emergent potentiation of the protocumata or a special addition made by God to His creation at the appropriate time and transmitted only from precedent to consequent life. Even if vital force is only a fourthly emergent potentiation of the protocumata, it is of sufficiently outstanding distinction to justify reference by a special term. The reader must therefore interpret vital force as he wills: a special something added by God on the occasion of the first biotic integrations and transmitted only by and through subsequent biotic integrations; or a fourthly emergent potentiation of the protocumata which emerges concurrently with biotic integration.[1]

Let us now sketch the state of affairs on this earth after the appearance of vegetable and animal life but prior to the coming of man.

All three types of natural integration, with their corresponding types of disintegration, reintegration and intermediate stages, were in action: atomic integration, hylic integration, and biotic integration. The protocumata had been integrated (via electrons and protons) by atomic integration into atomic systems or units (atoms), and these

---

[1] A very good analysis of the various forms of these two views may be found in McDougall, *The Riddle of Life.*

are mostly fairly stable, though a certain amount of dis-integration and reintegration was taking place among the atomic systems as some atoms broke down and others were formed. Most atoms, however, remain as originally inte-grated. Their flux is comparatively slight, though by no means unimportant. The atoms, on the other hand, were actively and continuously integrating, disintegrating and reintegrating into and out of hylic systems or units (sub-stances). To trace the career of an individual atom would be to follow its entry into and departure from a succession of hylic systems, many of these hylic systems being them-selves integral parts of biotic systems. The flux of hylic systems is complex, continuous and very energetic. Biotic integration, the third and highest type of natural integration, was continually in operation in keeping the chain of 'life' unbroken. In the appropriate circumstances certain hylic systems would integrate into a biotic unit, living organism, plant or animal. That unit, the highest type of natural integration, was itself in a continual state of flux as the hylic units composing it themselves underwent continual integration, disintegration and reintegration.

With all three types of integration in operation a very complicated state of affairs arose, and the following points should be noticed:

(i) All three forms of integration are rightly called natural integration, by which we mean that the processes of integra-tion, disintegration and reintegration, whether atomic, hylic or biotic, are entirely and solely due to the operation of God-given laws and the realization of God-given potentia-tions, whether to the original protocumata or subsequently. Even vegetable and animal life is entirely dependent on natural integration in this sense: no animal 'causes' its own young. The processes of biotic integration, like those of hylic integration, follow inevitable and certain laws.

(ii) All three forms of natural integration result in natural systems or units, which are easy to identify and define at any given instant and in some cases remain practically unchanged over very long periods. But in other cases the system or unit undergoes successive and even rapid changes; so that although at a given instant we may say that the Universe consists of a complex of natural systems or units (some biotic, some hylic, some merely atomic), it is not so easy to define the beginning and end of a given unit. It may not be difficult to define the unit at any given moment, but it may be very difficult to say when the unit really began, the moment of its integration, and when the unit ended, the moment of its disintegration, because as has already been seen, integration and disintegration are scalar processes and take place partially as well as completely. To deal with this problem precisely and exactly would involve considering matters which are not relevant to our present purpose, so we had better accept a convenient working convention: that in the complex of natural integration, disintegration and reintegration whereby natural units are continually being formed, changed and broken up, there are points which we may call nodes at which it may be said that new and distinctive natural units have started their existences and other nodal points at which the units may be said to have ended their existences as such. We thus arrive at the conception of the continuity or duration of a natural unit, taking into account the fact that it may be in a state of flux, undergoing partial integrations and disintegrations, so that it is strictly a succession of slightly differing natural units. Yet we recognize the fact that there is some kind of continuity, and we may therefore speak of the continuity or duration of a natural unit, even though the unit is subject to some degree of integration and disintegration during what we consider the continuity of the same unit. The words inception and end are used in this special sense rather than major integration and major disintegration, because although some units arise from what may be called a major integration and end in a major disintegration, in other cases both processes may be so gradual that a nodal point may have to be arbitrarily or conveniently fixed.

Fortunately the cases which really concern us are not difficult, but our method must at least be patently potent enough to be applicable with perhaps necessary elaborations to cover all cases. We may therefore give two very different examples:

(i) Continuity or duration of a natural unit such as a snowball.

A snowball is a hylic unit, being a solidly aggregated compound molecular hylic system or unit (cf. p. 270). But when is its inception? A snowball is usually made by compressing snowflakes together. But if the snowball is no bigger than a marble we can hardly call it a a snowball; it is merely a snow pellet; and unless the snowflakes are compressed together so that they cohere we should only have a handful of snowflakes and we could not call that a snowball either. We must therefore define 'snowball', and say that unless there is a certain minimum amount of snow, and unless it is cohering to a definite degree, the material is not a snowball, but merely a snow pellet or a handful of snow. There is thus a point, difficult to define but conceptually real, when the handful of snow being compressed into a snowball becomes what may truly be called a snowball. That is the nodal point in the flux of natures when that particular snowball has its inception and begins its continuity or duration as a natural unit. Similarly, it may end with a major disintegration by being broken into pieces, when the natural (hylic) unit 'snowball' has disintegrated into a number of smaller natural (hylic) units which we may call 'irregular lumps of snow'. But it might end by gradually melting away, in which case there is no point of major disintegration, but a progressive disintegration into a pool of water or drops of water. Our definition of snowball must again be brought in, and when the snowball has melted away below a certain size or weight we must say that the natural unit 'snowball' has ended, by disintegration into a smaller but similar natural unit 'snow pellet' and some natural units known as drops of water.

(ii) Continuity or duration of a natural unit such as a plant or animal.

A plant or animal is a biotic unit, and during its continuity it undergoes continuous minor integrations and disintegrations as its tissues wear out and are renewed and as its various vital processes proceed. By the end of its duration there may be very little matter still integrated with it which was integrated with it at its inception, but we nevertheless recognize it as the same biotic unit: there have been continual integrations and disintegrations, but no nodal point at which we may say that the flux of natural units has given rise to a new unit or units. In such cases it is convenient to regard its inception as the moment of its derivation from its parent or parents, when it could be said to have begun its separately identifiable existence. In the case of biparental reproduction that moment may be conveniently defined as the moment of union of the gametes. Its end is not quite so easily defined, especially in the case of a plant. Perhaps we may define the end of a biotic unit as the nodal point beyond which it no longer has power to integrate further constituents into its system or unity: that is, when the biotic unit no longer possesses the characteristic power of biotic integration. It then begins to break down into its constituent hylic units. In an animal that point is reached soon after its breathing and heart beating cease.

To the whole flux of natural units (atomic, hylic and biotic) the following remarks apply:

(i) Any unit not integrated into a greater system or unit is autocentric, and though it may have a degree of functional efficiency and may possess potential functional, pulchral and moral values, those potential values cannot be realized while it remains autocentric.

(ii) Any unit integrated into a greater system or unit becomes allocentric, and may have functional value in that greater system. Its functional value may vary from 100 per cent. positive to 100 per cent. negative.[1] Pulchral and moral values do not arise at the level of natural integration, and therefore still remain potential.

In that it has an important bearing on our analysis of man it may be well to conclude this chapter with a brief description of the mode of inception of a typical higher biotic unit such as a vertebrate mammal.[2]

It must be emphasized that the production of a biotic

[1] An example of negative functional value might be the ingestion of a poison. A biotic unit might biotically integrate into itself a poison, which, biotically integrated with that biotic unit, would speedily lead to its end.

[2] Our description is naturally with a metaphysical emphasis. The scientific details may be found in any good text-book of biology, e.g., Grove and Newell, *Animal Biology*, p. 466 sqq.

T

system or unit, an organism, is entirely due to the realization of God-given potentiations, and is in no way dependent on the will of the parents except in so far that they bring about the conditions in which certain processes will take place. This utter dependence on God-given potentiation must never be lost sight of: we cannot make hydrogen and oxygen combine, but we can put them together in circumstances in which they will combine because God has so potentiated them; we cannot make a seed grow, but we can put it into an environment (soil, moisture, warmth) in which its God-given potentiation will be realized. So also no parents can 'produce' an offspring. All they can do is to make possible the operation of God-given (natural) laws. In bisexual reproduction, with which we are primarily concerned, there are two parents, biotic units. Each of these parents, in course of its biotic duration, produces at regular or irregular intervals by a process of minor partial biotic disintegration a small biotic unit called a gamete. In bisexual reproduction the male produces a gamete of one kind, called a spermatozoon, and the female produces a gamete of a different kind called an ovum. Each of these gametes is a biotic unit and its inception is at the moment of disintegration from the biotic unit which is its parent. These biotic units, the gametes, are not very durable, and left to themselves would soon come to an end by biotic disintegration, becoming resolved into a number of hylic units. That is, they would die and decompose. But God has devised that gametes of opposite kinds belonging to the same species shall, when brought together in suitable conditions, undergo biotic integration (or reintegration) into a new biotic unit known as a zygote: two biotic units (the two gametes, spermatozoon and ovum) by biotic integration integrate into a new biotic unit (the zygote). That represents the inception of a new 'life', a new 'individual', as a biotic unit of the animal organism type is usually called. The zygote develops in different ways and by different methods according to its species, in some cases within the body of one of its parents, in other cases outside, in yet other cases for a period within the body of one of its parents and then outside. But in any of these cases the zygote is to be regarded as a separate biotic unit, an 'individual', and its duration begins at the moment of biotic integration of the gametes. It is not here necessary to go into details as to the way in which the integration takes place, but emphasis must be laid on the fact of detailed contribution from each gamete. The zygote (embryo) is no mere mixing or addition of the gametes: it is a new unit produced by intimate and detailed integration, detail by detail. The mechanism of inheritance, genetics, has been investigated with such thoroughness that we now know that the specific character of the zygote is integrated from the specific characters of the gametes by the integration of unit-characters known as genes and usually associated in groups as chromosomes. Each unit-character in the new individual is the resultant of the interaction of the corresponding genes in the gametes. In general, each gene is duplex, and the new gene for the zygote is derived by the reintegration of the genes of the gametes in such a way that the new gene is integrated from two half portions of the genes of the gametes, one half portion from each gene.[1]

Now whether life, vital force, is a fourthly emergent potentiation of the protocumata, or whether it was added by God at the first biotic integrations and made by Him transmissible by the parent or parents at reproduction, just as are other characteristics of the offspring from the parent, we cannot escape this fact: in the reproduction of living organisms, life, whatever it is, is transmitted from parent to offspring; and in the case of biparental reproduction, where the possibility of the existence of the new individual depends on the integration of a contribution from each (spermatozoon + ovum = zygote), is evidently transmitted in some way analogous to the way in which unit-characters are transmitted, that is, by some kind of contribution from each parent, the new individual not being produced unless the contribution from each is present.[2] Let it be noted that

[1] For details see any text-book of biology, e.g., Grove and Newell, op. cit., p. 567 sqq.

[2] Parthenogenesis, whether natural or induced, becomes progressively rarer the higher we ascend the scale. We may suggest that God had special reasons for devising that reproduction in the higher animals and man should be biparental. Some of the reasons are quite evident, but attention may now be drawn to this: In parthenogensis the characteristics of the new

biparental reproduction is not the only possible method. Reproduction may be by fission and in other ways, in which cases vital force passes in some more simple and direct manner. But in the higher forms, in which life itself is manifested in a more developed and individuated form, the method of integration of contributions from each parent is evidently that which God has ordained.

We thus see that life is manifested in a range of complexity comparable to that of matter. Just as the most complex substances—certain organic compounds—are derived by successive integrations from the protocumata, successive potentiations being realized and manifested, so it would appear that once life, vital force, had been added to (or had emerged in) the natural flux, then successive integrations, revealing successive potentiations, would lead up to the highest animal forms. Whatever life is, whether merely a fourthly emergent potentiation of the protocumata, or a potentiation specially given by God to the first or even to successive biotic integrations, or a something akin to electricity, or a property possessed by matter in certain integrations, it is evidently something participating in the great principle of successive and progressive integration. We have the series protocumata, electrons and protons, atoms,

individual derive only from the genes of the one parent, whence it follows that all the new individuals deriving from that parent will be monotonously alike and lacking in distinctive individuality. But in biparental reproduction there may be as many as three possible types for each new gene; and as distinctive individuality depends to a very great extent on the different characteristics emerging through the genes, and as there may be many scores or hundreds of genes in the gamete of a high type animal, the same two parents may produce an almost indefinite number of offspring all of which may have distinct and definite individualities. On the purely biological side, it will be seen that two parents each possessing n heterozygous genes could in theory produce 3^n distinctly differing progeny. As n is a number running into scores or hundreds according to the type of animal, and as it only needs to be 20 for 3^n to exceed three thousand million, it at once emerges how, even on the purely physical side, it is so easily possible for each of us to be a really distinctive and unique individual. It could of course chance that two individuals might have exactly the same distribution of genes, as indeed happens in the case of uniovular (identical) twins. In such cases distinction in individuality can only arise from difference in reaction to environment, and those with identical physical equipment become distinct individuals as the result of a series of divergent personal choices. But life would be somewhat monotonous if we were all as alike as identical twins! To borrow Schrödinger's phrase (*vide* p. 296, *infra*), we do well to stand in awe before "the Lord's quantum mechanics".

molecules, substances, organic substances, organisms; and we have the series amœba, sponge, jelly-fish, sea urchin, lobster, frog, duckmole, rabbit, cat, monkey, gorilla. The second list is not parallel to the first in the sense that the later members are derived from the former by progressive integration, but the second list is parallel to the first in the sense that the later members exemplify 'life' in a more highly developed, more highly integrated, form than do the earlier members. We seem unable to escape the following general view:

Life is a discrete quality associated with and characteristic of biotic systems from the time of their integration to the time of their disintegration, and it may be manifested in degrees of varying intensity, quality and complexity. It is simple and diffused in plants and low forms of animal life, and gains both in complexity and centricity in higher forms of animal life. In a higher animal, say a cat or dog, life is both complex and centred. The brain is its primary instrument, and through the brain the life centre directs the biotic unit. As in all well designed machines much of the biotic unit functions automatically. By skilfully designed[1] tropisms, reflexes and instinctive reactions, God has made biotic units machines of the most amazing intricacy and precision. But in the higher animals at least there is more than automatic action and reaction. There is a continuity and a centre. It is futile to speculate as to what that continuity and centre is. If we must give it a name we can call it the centrum vitæ, and if we must in some way picture it, we may picture it as a kind of reticulum situated in or diffused within the brain, and composed of some organic substance integrated in some special way and with or without the addition of something electrical or non-electrical, specially adapted from existing matter and force or different from either and only describable as 'vital force'. Letting that suffice for a definition of the centrum vitæ, 'animal soul',[2] we must make the following remarks:

(i) The centrum vitæ of a higher animal is a higher

[1] It makes little difference if we replace 'skilfully designed' by 'evolved from skilfully calculated potentiations'.

[2] We avoid the term 'psyche' because we wish to keep a clear distinction between vital force as diffused and as centred.

integration with evidenced centricity of the same kind of vital force which, diffused, enables a tree to 'live'.

(ii) The centrum vitæ is of purely practical value, and relates the animal to its environment. An intelligent animal is one whose tropisms, reflexes and instinctive reactions keep the machinery of its body immediately safe and nourished, and whose centrum vitæ co-ordinates and directs the wider range of its conduct and behaviour. That conduct and behaviour is entirely bounded by the present material world: the only values taken into account by the centrum vitæ are functional values, the fulfilment of the biotic unit's purposes and satisfactions. It is to be recognized that God has so designed those purposes and satisfactions that many of them appear to us to have pulchral and moral as well as functional value. This, however, is an unjustifiable transference of human reasoning to animal behaviour. We regret that it is not relevant to discuss this point further, though it may be added that the natural world, inanimate and animate alike, has potential pulchral and moral value in view of its integrability into human theletic systems.

(iii) When an animal dies, its centrum vitæ has no longer any relevance. The animal when alive and conscious was in contact with its environment, and its centrum vitæ was the means for its maintenance of purposive and satisfying contact with that environment. Its outlook was purely empirical and pragmatic, and there was no relevance except to the environment. Dulling senses cease to bring in new impressions to work upon, failing circulation ceases to keep the brain functioning, lack of material and lack of power leaves the centrum vitæ with nothing to work on, with or for. The centrum vitæ therefore ceases to function. Its purpose as the continuity centre of that particular biotic unit has ended. What happens to the centrum vitæ? We cannot say. It probably disintegrates into whatever it is composed from, whether material, electrical or otherwise, and the components return to their appropriate reservoirs of matter, electricity, or otherwise. We do not dismiss the idea that an animal's centrum vitæ may possibly be a discrete unit which may pass into a kind of vital reservoir and be used again as a discrete unit. But it seems to us far more likely that the centrum vitæ is an integrated unit within the biotic unit and disintegrates with the disintegration of the biotic unit, so that its continuance is in the general flux of natural units (atomic, hylic and biotic) and not in itself specifically.

Before ending this chapter it may be profitable to recapitulate a few of the points we have endeavoured to make:

(1) The material Universe consists essentially of a flux of natural units (protocumatic, atomic, hylic, biotic), and this flux proceeds in accordance with the 'laws of nature', which are merely statements expressing and systematizing the consequences of the potentiations given by God to the protocumata and, emergently, to the higher integrations arising therefrom.

(2) The material Universe reveals progressively emergent potentiation, revealing itself principally by progressive integration, each successive integration revealing properties not before manifest, so that integration appears to be the means whereby God enables higher possibilities to be realized.

(3) Integration consists in the previously many becoming the new one, not one by mere conglomeration or homogeneity, but one in function and, where such a word is applicable, purpose. Thus a system and a unit are almost always interchangeable terms.

(4) There can be systems within systems and units within units, as smaller integrate into greater. Identity is not necessarily lost, and a greater system or unit may be readily recognizable as the integration of smaller systems or units.

(5) Value depends on integration, and to have actual value a unit must be integrated into something greater than itself. Value is functional, pulchral and moral, and all three types of value may scale down from 100 per cent. perfection through 0 per cent. perfection (uselessness) to — 100 per cent. perfection (maximum antithesis).

(6) The material Universe would thus be an admirable medium for the exercise of and testing of an independent

will. If we could imagine an independent will released into the Universe and able to control integrations, such a will would be able to use the material Universe to bring about integrations whose value could be assessed. The natural Universe is itself pulchrally and morally indeterminate, but can be made the medium for the expression of varying degrees of positive and negative pulchral and moral excellence. The bearing of this sixth point will emerge in the next chapter.

Footnote 1, *p.* 281: Although published forty years ago, Bastian's *The Nature and Origin of Living Matter* is still as forceful and cogent a statement of this view as we should wish to find, and its closing paragraph is to be noted (op. cit., p. 314): "As I have endeavoured to show, there are good reasons for the conviction that the same Forces which are now in action within and around us, have been and are constantly operative throughout the whole universe—everywhere producing the most uniform and complex results which combine in testifying to the existence of one supreme and all-pervading Power of which these results are the phenomenal manifestations." The significant capital P is of course Bastian's. A much more recent statement (1944) is to be found in Schrödinger, *What is Life?* This little book gives a concise and able sketch of the impact of the new physics on biology, and the following sentences are quoted from his seventh chapter: "We must therefore not be discouraged by the difficulty of interpreting life by the ordinary laws of physics. For that is just what is to be expected from the knowledge we have gained of the structure of living matter. We must be prepared to find a new type of physical law prevailing in it. Or are we to term it a non-physical, not to say a super-physical, law? No. I do not think that. For the new principle that is involved is a *genuinely* physical one: it is, in my opinion, nothing else than the principle of the quantum theory over again. . . . Thus it would appear that the 'new principle', the order-from-order principle, to which we have pointed with great solemnity as being the real clue to the understanding of life, is not at all new to physics. Planck's attitude even vindicates priority for it. We seem to arrive at the ridiculous conclusion that the clue to the understanding of life is that it is based on a pure mechanism, a 'clock work' in the sense of Planck's paper. The conclusion is not ridiculous and is, in my opinion, not entirely wrong. . . . Now, I think, few words more are needed to disclose the point of resemblance between a clockwork and an organism. It is simply and solely that the latter also hinges upon a solid—the aperiodic crystal forming the hereditary substance, largely withdrawn from the disorder of heat motion. But please do not accuse me of calling the chromosome fibres just the 'cogs of the organic machine'—at least not without a reference to the profound physical theories on which the simile is based. For, indeed, it needs still less rhetoric to recall the fundamental difference between the two and to justify the epithets novel and unprecedented in the biological case. The most striking features are: first, the curious distribution of the cogs in a many-celled organism, . . . and secondly, the fact that the single cog is not of coarse human make, but is the finest masterpiece ever achieved along the lines of the Lord's quantum mechanics." (Op. cit., pp. 80–86.) How splendidly significant the final turn of that last sentence!

CHAPTER IV

MAN

"The Lord God formed man of the dust of the ground, and breathed into his nostrils the breath of life; and man became a living soul."
GEN. II. 7.

THE Christian theist must never be unmindful of the nature of the framework of his approach to life, and he must realize that reasoning from postulates is just as valid as reasoning from 'knowledge', for, as we have already seen, the coherence of the entire framework in any case depends upon the validity of certain postulates. Postulates and knowledge alike can only be checked and verified by their coherence section by section and in the scheme of things as a whole. There may be a natural inclination to cast our views into a form which suggests that we have reasoned upwards from areas of knowledge, when as a matter of fact there were already certain postulates in our minds which, consciously or unconsciously, we had fixed upon as our goals. It is better to resist this inclination and, instead, frankly to state our postulates and to endeavour to show how consistent they are with all we know and sense. It serves no good purpose to try to persuade ourselves that we have reached *per gradus* what we have really reached *per saltum*; it is much better to show that there are steps leading down from the point we reached per saltum (which may of course include per fidem) meeting those leading up from the areas of knowledge. In considering man, therefore, we intend to begin on the higher levels and to work down. Ingenuity could readily invert the argument, and it would be equally true. But if we have really opened up a route from Khartoum to Calabar by working from each end and finding a meeting point, it is vain and foolish to make out that we have actually worked our way directly from Khartoum to Calabar or vice versa. After all, the important and valuable thing is the existence and discovery of the route.

We begin, then, with a question on the highest teleological level: Why did God create man? Our answer is:
God created man in order that there might come into
existence a company of sentient beings capable of appreciating and seeking truth and beauty and holiness (and
therefore inevitably equally capable of retroversion towards
their antitheses), a company of sentient beings who, being
given freedom of choice, should be able to choose to enter
into a blessed mutual relationship with God Himself, a
relationship which would enable them to be at one with
God in all His purposes, and which would enable them
to participate in all His qualities, so that there might
be for them in union with God a full realization and
appreciation of all truth and beauty and holiness, and a
complete accord between God and them in all will and
feeling.

We may amplify this statement to this extent:

(1) In creating man with this fulfilment as the highest
possibility, God was not doing anything which He needed
to do to complete or satisfy Himself. God was complete
and perfect without any such act.

(2) The union between man at his highest (a sentient
being voluntarily choosing union with God) and God is
to be conceived of as a harmony, a concord, an utter
sharing of all volition and love, and must not in any way
be thought of as an organic or merging union. God
remains God, and His being needs no addition and suffers
no subtraction. Perfected man does not become part of
God in the old essential sense; perfected man becomes
part of God in the sense of perfect harmony and concord
and the sharing of attributes in so far as the attributes of
the infinite can be shared with the finite. (We use the
words 'infinite' and 'finite' in a relative way. We prefer
to refer to God as exoschematic rather than infinite, as
exoschematic is a term of such wider meaning. In the
space-temporal sense man when perfected will be out of
this schema and to that extent 'infinite', for finitude is an
incidental of the space-time continuum. But perfected
man will still be dependent on and limited in relation to

God, in that man's perfection will always depend on God.)

(3) God is the only self-existent, and though perfected man live for countless æons in harmony and unity with God, man's being will always depend for its continuance on God's being.

(4) God in His inscrutable wisdom alone knows the conditions under which this mutual relationship and union between Himself and sentient beings can be possible, able to endure, and mutually satisfying, so that it should not depend entirely on God's will, though entirely on His grace, so that it should not depend entirely on man's will, though entirely on his surrender, so that it should be a bond precious because costing something on each side, so that it should be established in such a way that the bond should be dependent on a self-surrendering and self-sacrificing love, so that it should be based on a mutual knowledge of such a kind that man by adoption should know what it is to participate in God and God by condescension should know what it is to be man. The achievement of all this is the mystery of the Atonement, and the reason for God becoming man in Christ.

Such then, as far as we dare suggest an answer, is the reason for God's creation of man. Confident that we exist that we may seek and eventually find union with God, and trusting that by His grace that union may be brought about, we are able to look at the Universe with a new comprehension. Why does a Universe such as this exist? We do not presume to pretend to know all the divine purposes for which every part of this Universe exists; but we are confident that at least one of the reasons for the existence of that part of it in which we have our being is as follows: that there might be a prepared testing ground for sentient beings, a testing ground so prepared that they should be able in it to find and respond, if they would, to truth and beauty and holiness; a testing ground so exactly balanced that its opportunities should all be bivalent, so that error and ugliness and sin should always be possible alternatives;

and yet so adjusted that there should always be a greater urge towards the positive, and the negative would only be preferred by an act of rebellious self-will; and, in it all, if man would but respond, the gracious power of God Himself, ever ready to aid those seeking the right courses—indeed, so precisely balanced that no right course could be successfully followed without the aid of that power, so that God's grace and man's choice must ever be inseparable if the highest is to be achieved. The preceding chapters have included a very abbreviated survey of the principles of design of this Universe, our endeavour having been to sketch the main lines of its construction. For the testing of man the factor of overwhelming importance is the fact of integration: the fact that theletic integration, working with and beyond natural integration, can build up systems which have value, value which at the integrator's option may range from positive to negative maxima.

The next practical problem is a two-fold one: How could God place sentient beings for test in this environment, and at the same time make it possible for them to be able to live in harmony and union with Himself afterwards? It is evident that the sentient beings must be capable of living in the space-time continuum, as otherwise they would not be able to experience and function there; and they must also be capable of living outside the space-time continuum, in the unlimited realm of God. No being but God can ever be exoschematic in the sense of being outside the limitations of all schemata; but the redeemed sentient beings must be able to live limited only by God Himself, and therefore able to live outside the space-time continuum. All this simply brings inevitably and logically into our scheme what the religious instinct has always postulated: that man possesses a spirit,[1] which makes contact with this schema through a suitable body, and will make contact with its hereafter schema in some other manner or through another or a transformed body. However, the problem is not to be solved by the simple expedient of imagining that the spirit is a kind of tenant occupying a material body and then

---

[1] We use this word (πνεῦμα) in preference to 'soul' to avoid possible confusion with animal soul (ψυχή).

leaving it to live disembodied or re-embodied. Any such solution entirely fails to appreciate the fundamentals of the problem.

Before passing on, we ought to say that the Christian theist's preliminary idea concerning the nature of a human spirit is felt after by those ascending from knowledge. The steps descending from our postulation meet the steps ascending from the hypotheses striving up from knowledge. We need not dwell long on this point, as it is adequately dealt with in McDougall, *Body and Mind*,[1] and in Maher, *Psychology*,[2] from which works Relton deduces this concisely summarized conclusion: "If the soul is a simple, spiritual, substantial principle; if the most distinctive factor within man is an Ego, which, in the ultimate analysis, transcends completely the material organism of which it is the central principle, and knows itself as in some sense capable of leading an existence independent of the body; then we may say that an analysis of the human yields us at its very central and basic point, in the very central subject of human personality itself—the Ego—something which at the very least may be named immaterial, incorporeal, and in this sense spiritual. Whether from other considerations we may enrich this 'spirituality of the soul' with a much fuller content, and claim for it the possession of something infinitely more than the attribute of incorporeality, is a question for theology, and carries us beyond the realm of the science of psychology; but this conclusion at least seems legitimate as the result of our inquiry: that an analysis of human nature in the light of modern psychology yields us, in its most central and distinctive principle—the soul—an element which transcends the material and opens out into the spiritual" (*A Study in Christology*, pp. 135–136). In a sentence, the spirit is that which is able to maintain continuity of experience corporeally and incorporeally. From quite

[1] For footnote, see p. 336.

[2] This is the work of a Roman Catholic who has made a very complete study of all aspects of psychology. The concise statements in his Book II must therefore be read in the light of the detailed background provided by Book I and, though his discussion of this particular point is short, there is considerable weight behind his belief in the "substantiality, identity, simplicity, and spirituality of the human soul" (op. cit., pp. 459–473).

another angle, let us quote Schrödinger's conclusion as to spirit. After a most masterly explanation of the body as a mechanism, an explanation over which the materialist might well gloat right until the antepenultimate word of Chapter VII, to which we have referred on p. 296, *supra*, he nevertheless concludes his book thus: "Yet each of us has the undisputable impression that the sum total of his own experience and memory forms a unit, quite distinct from that of any other person. He refers to it as 'I'. What is this 'I'? If you analyse it closely you will, I think, find that it is just a little bit more than a collection of single data (experiences and memories), namely the canvas upon which they are collected. And you will, on close introspection, find that, what you really mean by 'I', is that ground-stuff upon which they are collected. You may come to a distant country, lose sight of all your friends, may all but forget them; you acquire new friends, you share life with them as intensely as you ever did with your old ones. Less and less important will become the fact that, while living your new life, you still recollect the old one. 'The youth that was I', you may come to speak of him in the third person, indeed the protagonist of the novel you are reading is probably nearer to your heart, certainly more intensely alive and better known to you. Yet there has been no intermediate break, no death. And even if a skilled hypnotist succeeded in blotting out entirely all your earlier reminiscences, you would not find that he had killed you. In no case is there a loss of personal existence to deplore. Nor will there ever be" (*What is Life?*, pp. 90–91).

We proceed, then, without feeling any need to argue any further that the spirit is "a substantial[1] principle having a persisting indivisible identity",[2] an identity able to endure not merely throughout life in this schema but also in life beyond this schema. But now we face the crux of the problem: how is the spirit related through the body to the material Universe? We have already hinted that it is quite inadequate to regard the spirit as a kind of tenant of the

---

[1] Substantial in the sense *id quod per se stat*, not in the sense of material substance.

[2] Relton, op. cit., p. 134.

body. If the spirit were only that, God's purpose would not be achieved, for He has created this Universe in such a way that it shall serve (perhaps among other purposes) as the precisely balanced sphere in which sentient beings should have the opportunity of choosing or rejecting union with Himself. That precise balance would be upset unless the sentient being felt that he was indeed inescapably committed to this Universe, so that his place of testing should seem utterly and compellingly real. God has succeeded in doing this with such precision that two alternatives are fully possible:

(i) A sentient being in a body can so persuade himself of his utter committal to this Universe that he may readily reject the idea that there is any reality beyond it.

(ii) A sentient being in a body can so accept God's offered grace that he may realize that this is but a temporary stage in his existence and that fuller self-development lies beyond it.

To re-read those two sentences should recreate wonder at the precision of God's devising: He has caused to exist the exact conditions necessary for the achievement of His purpose.

We may now suggest how He has brought that about. He has brought it about by integrating a spirit into a suitable body of the same general type as that possessed by a higher animal. A higher animal is a biotic unit maintaining relationship with its environment by virtue of its place in the flux of natural units and by virtue of its possession of a centrum vitæ whereby it reacts with an intelligence of an empirical and pragmatic kind. Man is a biotic unit maintaining relationship with his environment by virtue of his place in the flux of natural units and by virtue of his possession of a centrum vitæ whereby he reacts with an intelligence of an empirical and pragmatic kind. In addition, there is also naturally integrated into him, probably through the centrum vitæ, his spirit, whose essential quality is the appreciation of values. Great emphasis must be laid upon the words 'naturally integrated'. Man is a natural unit. It is to be strongly emphasized that from his birth to his death man is a natural unit. His spirit is not like the tenant of a

house or the driver of a vehicle. The tenant can leave and
return, the driver can get out and in. But the spirit cannot
act like that. The spirit is utterly committed to the body
and cannot leave it except in accordance with natural law,
and once having left cannot return. Further, the spirit is
integrated with the body in such an intimate manner that
all its experiences, to whatever they may be referred in
theory, are in practice all felt to pertain to the same 'I'. The
same 'I' is equally the subject of physical pain and of anxiety
in thought. Man is, and is meant to be, a natural unit of the
strictest kind. He is keyed inexorably into his environment,
the environment designed for the very purpose of giving
him the right sphere for making his fateful choice—acceptance or rejection of divine grace, and union with or eternal
disunion from God.

Perhaps we ought to say a word as to the way in which
this view links up with the ancient tripartite view. There is
a very real parallel, and a very real modification. The old
view, shortly, was that man was a sum or compound of
body, animal soul and spirit (σῶμα, ψυχή, πνεῦμα). Our
emphasis is that the sum or compound is of such a kind
that the constituents are so integrated that while the integration lasts we are to think of the integrated unit as itself,
man, and not as a sum or compound of these other things,
except for analytical thought. While integrated we do not
deal with a body, an animal soul and a spirit, but with one
integrated unit, man. A chemical illustration may help:
sugar is a hylic integration of carbon, hydrogen and oxygen. But, except for analytical thought, we do not and
should not think of sugar as a sum or compound of a black
solid and two gases. They are so integrated (not merely
mixed) that we shall only deceive ourselves if we think of
sugar as a kind of composite of a black solid and two gases.
We think of it as a white soluble sweet solid, and that is
what it is while it remains as it is. It is time to think of its
constituents as such when we break it down into them,
meanwhile not being unmindful of what its constituents are.
Just exactly similarly man is man until he is broken down
into his constituents, and not body plus animal soul plus
spirit. Integration is not mere addition.

We must now attempt a brief survey of the duration of the natural unit 'man':

(1) *Integration of the first man or men*

It is of the utmost importance that in this matter we should distinguish the relevant from the irrelevant. All that really matters is contained in the basic implications of the verse quoted at the head of this chapter: "The Lord God formed man of the dust of the ground, and breathed into his nostrils the breath of life; and man became a living soul." What does this verse mean? The first crude picture it presents to the mind is of an anthropomorphic god making a little reproduction of himself, breathing into it, and making it 'live'. No doubt it has meant no more than that to very many. It is, however, a noetic statement of an ontic reality of a profound kind, and perhaps we can get nearer the core of its meaning by paraphrasing and amplifying thus: When the appropriate time came in the course of the duration of the Universe, God chose a suitable biotic unit which had already evolved in accordance with His laws, or formed one *ad hoc*, and integrated into it a human spirit. In this way the first man appeared, differing from all else in the scheme of creation by the possession of a spirit, a spirit which was in some special way different both in nature and origin from all else in the material Universe.

As we must have working hypotheses, the following remarks may be made:

(i) What a human spirit in itself is it is useless to pretend to know. As Relton roundly remarks: "We can, of course, form no conception of what the soul is in itself, i.e. as an absolute substance."[1] All we can say is: (*a*) It is an entity which is able to be linked for conscious and continuous experience both with this material Universe and with the exoschema. (*b*) It is different from everything else in this Universe in that it is (α) not derived from the protocumata by any kind of successive integration, that is, it is immaterial, (β) able to appreciate pulchral and moral values, (γ) in some way nearer in nature to God Himself than is the matter of the Universe, in that it is able to enter into some special

[1] Op. cit., p. 144.

U

kind of union with Him. (c) It is derived from God in some way intentionally different from the way in which all else in the material Universe has been brought into being. The complete otherness of God from the material Universe is emphasized in the mode of creation. The material Universe was created by divine fiat ex nihilo. God caused it to be by an act of will: "God said, Let there be . . .: and there was . . ." As we said earlier, we are to picture the physema coming into existence and the protocumata within it not going forth from God but arising where He willed them to arise—on the surface a slight difference, but a tremendously significant difference. The creation of the material Universe in no way diminished, affected or exerted God. But the first man came into being because the Lord God "breathed into his nostrils the breath of life". This means that God caused the first man to come into being by integrating into a previously existing or specially formed biotic unit something which had itself come into being in a different way from that in which all else in the Universe had come into being, and which was integrated into the new unit, man, in a way in which no other integration had ever taken place. This is tremendously significant. It is of no use to push analogies too far, but we can at least say this: God has made the spirit of man of such a kind and in such a way that it bears both potentially and actually a relation to Himself of a unique kind. It is not of the same "stuff" as the rest of the material Universe, but is an entity of a kind which partakes in nature though of course not in degree of many of the divine attributes, and is capable of existing in some kind of special harmony and union with God. In some sense to be examined later, we may boldly assert: the spirit of man is in some way integrable with God, and can in some way become Theocentric.

(ii) It is to be hoped that it is recognized how totally unimportant is the precise method by which God integrated the first human spirit into the first human body. Any of the following methods might have been used:

(a) God, having by the process of emergent potentiation caused the Universe to run on until the higher animals had developed, may then have undertaken His first great 'interference', and created a creature on much the same lines as the higher mammals, integrating into it, probably via the centrum vitæ, the first human spirit. We may of course substitute 'them' for 'it'. God could have created a unit, a pair or a company.

(*b*) We may hold the same view as (*a*), except that we may hold that the first great interference was the giving of vital force, in which case the giving of the human spirit would be the second.

(*c*) God may have acted on the principle of minimum interference, and at the appropriate moment may have added a human spirit to the centrum vitæ of a highly developed animal of an ape-like type. There would have been a discontinuity, but not a discontinuity much remarkably greater than that evidenced when a 'sport' arises. We can, if we wish, picture a community of high ape-like animals. When God decided that the moment had arrived, He could have integrated (*in utero?*) into two or a group of them human spirits, so that thus the first men appeared.

(By contrast there is one type of solution which the Christian theist must definitely reject: that 'spirit' arose as an emergent potentiation from the protocumata. We surely need not elaborate this point.)

Thus the first man or men appeared, with spirit fatefully integrated into body.

(2) *Integration of subsequent men*

The first men having been created in some such way as indicated above, God ordained that the race should continue by processes quite similar to those which He had devised for the higher animals. Those processes have already been described (pp. 289–292), so need not be repeated. We need therefore only concern ourselves at this point with the mode of formation of the spirit of the newly conceived human child. Without discussing the various views which have from time to time been advanced, we may at once say that theological opinion recognizes two views between which choice or compromise must be made:

(i) Traducianism, the view that each new human spirit is generated from the parents at the same time as the body and in an analogous manner;

(ii) Creatianism,[1] the view that God creates a new spirit for each human body, and infuses that spirit into the body at some time between conception and birth, e.g. at the 'quickening'.

Grave difficulties are involved in the unqualified acceptance of either of these views, and it is presumably the recognition of that fact that has caused the question still to be left open.[2] Although Jerome strongly supported the creatianist view, and it certainly became the opinion of most medieval theologians, the traducianist view cannot perhaps be so summarily dismissed as, for example, by Maher.[3] A problem which so exercised Augustine[4] that he was never able to come to a definite decision cannot be regarded as one capable of easy solution. The direct and indirect implications of either solution present grave problems. It may well be that we ought not to adopt the creatianist view without endeavouring to see in what ways it needs to be qualified. To quote Nairne again, "Creatianism . . . became the general opinion of the medieval theologians, and Peter Lombard's 'creando infundit animas Deus et infundendo creat' was an accepted formula. . . . Peter Lombard's phrase perhaps shows that even in his time some union of the two opinions was needed, and Augustine's toleration pointed in the same direction, for the traducianism he thought possible was one in which God 'operatur institutas administrando non novas instituendo naturas' ".[5] We must obviously avoid a crude traducianism which supposes that a new spirit arises from the union of quasi-material 'spirit' gametes, as though there were something

---

[1] Often spelled 'creationism'. But the spelling 'creatianism' has the advantage of distinguishing the word from other meanings of 'creationism'.

[2] Although creatianism is the 'official view' of the Roman Catholic Church, it is not a Catholic dogma. "The question has never been authoritatively determined" (A. Nairne, *Encyclopædia Britannica*, 11th Edition, vii. 388). For references to the literature on the problem see Kidd, *History of the Church*, iii. 85.

[3] *Psychology* (9th Edition), pp. 572–576.

[4] See his letter to Jerome, *Epistol. Classis*, III. 166.

[5] *Encyclopædia Britannica* (11th Edition), vii. 388.

in the nature of a pneumato-spermatozoon and a pneumato-ovum corresponding to the spermatozoon and ovum which give rise to the body. On the other hand, Augustine's difficulties still remain very cogent if we suppose that God imparts a new spirit directly and unconditionally to every new human body.

Perhaps the difficulties in the creatianist position may be minimized if we approach the problem thus:

(i) We have recognized the principle of emergence, whereby an integration so frequently results in the formation of something altogether unlike those things from which it is integrated. God has so wondrously devised His Universe that natural integration has to be recognized as His means of bringing into existence things which are virtually 'new creations'. Nestorius was feeling after this when he said that "natural union is a second creation" (B. 236, and cf. pp. 86–88). It is as though the divine creative power makes its action concomitant with the fulfilment of certain conditions and dependent upon certain accompanying circumstances. God could create anything whatsoever whensoever He wished, ex nihilo by mere fiat. But in practice He does so rarely, and such an action would be regarded as a 'miracle'. (A miracle is not any more strange or surprising than a natural event. It is simply an *ad hoc* act of God out of the course of His usual mode of action through natural law. It is important to recognize that the day-to-day running of the Universe by natural law is just as wonderful and amazing as any series of miracles. The only difference is that of usual and unusual.)

(ii) In any natural integration, therefore, we see evidence of the creative and devising power of God. We do not know how or why natural integrations take place, nor can we control them. All we know is that given certain constituents and certain conditions the integration will take place, and the new unit will be formed, something which we recognize as quite distinct from its constituents.

(iii) It is also of paramount importance to remember that the mode of origin of a natural unit is of absolutely no consequence. Hydrogen, for example, can be prepared in dozens of different ways. But once the hydrogen has been prepared, its precise mode of preparation ceases to be of consequence.[1] All that matters is the nature of the unit, which is as God has devised.

(iv) We must therefore carefully avoid a merely materialistic and mechanistic view of the natural Universe, and we must never be unmindful of the activity and devising of God: that which comes into existence, whether by integration or ex nihilo, comes into existence only as He permits, and its mode of integration and its nature are alike dependent on Him.

(v) In the conception of a new human life we have already recognized the essentially passive part taken by the parents. This must be emphasized. The parents, obeying an urge which they can and should control, and which may have values functional, pulchral and moral from the highest to the lowest, make it possible by their act for a spermatozoon and ovum to come together. If they do so come together, the gametes combine to form a zygote, and the new life has begun. The parents do nothing more than we do in bringing about any natural integration: we can only provide the conditions in which by laws not of our ordering or controlling certain things happen. That is to say, the new life starts because God has ordained that in such circumstances a new life shall start.

(vi) As to the spirit, its immateriality excludes any idea of its formation by synthesis of contributions from each parent, whether inhering in or accompanying the gametes. But we have to recognize this fact, which distinguishes the creation of a new human spirit from other divine creations ex nihilo: God has made His creation of a new human spirit necessarily concomitant with and to that extent contingent upon the formation by coalescence of gametes of a new human body. So that if we maintain that the human spirit derives directly from God and not through the parents, we must nevertheless recognize that the procreative act of the parents is at once the occasion and the precondition of the infusion of the new spirit. That is to say, the gift of the spirit, the 'quickening', is a creative act which God has

[1] We do not overlook the possibility of difference in proportion of isotopes. If this point is considered important, instead of hydrogen an example could be taken from an element having no isotopes, such as fluorine, sodium or aluminium.

made contingent upon the parallel and simultaneous natural integration by bisexual reproduction of the body. Perhaps an analogy may be useful: it might be the practice on a railway system that the driver should start the train immediately after, and only after, some authorized person has blown a whistle and some other authorized person has waved a flag. The train will not be started unless the whistle is blown and the flag is waved, and the train will start if the whistle is blown and the flag is waved. But the train is not started by either the whistle or the flag or both together. Similarly there may be an ordained sequence, working through what divine method we cannot expect to probe, whereby God devises that there shall be infused into each human embryo a spirit, a spirit which is immaterial and immortalizable,[1] which shall come into existence integrated into the body being formed, and shall for its coming into existence be contingent upon the coalescence of the gametes of its parents. This latter fact is significant. The coming into existence of a new spirit depends upon the successful coalescence of the gametes. The coming into existence of the new spirit does not depend, apart from that, on any act of will on the part of the parents: there need not be a 'union of spirits' producing a spirit. In fact, the fact must be faced that genuinely loving kindred spirits may be unable to reproduce their kind, though their spirits are yearning together, because the gametes do not coalesce; and the coalescence of gametes in a brutish or unwanted union nevertheless results in a child possessing a spirit. This reflection rather suggests that the spirit comes by divinely ordained concomitance rather than causally or derivatively from the parents. Their part is no more than the agreed and accepted signal: God has decreed that a new spirit should arise whenever and however human gametes coalesce. Again we recognize our utter dependence on the divine planning. We should also recognize the tremendous responsibility of human parenthood, and the need for its highest safeguarding.

[1] 'Immortal' should only be applied to a human spirit if we clearly recognize that it is only immortal at God's grace and pleasure. Only God is immortal by His own nature and without qualification.

(vii) We are not at present concerned with working out all the implications of the preceding paragraph. But it has a very real bearing on some of Augustine's problems. It is as though the gift of an immortalizable spirit into a body were a covenanted act: the circumstances of the generation, and in those circumstances is necessarily included the nature of the parents, have their inevitable consequences on the nature of the newly integrated human being; for the hereditary factors affect the body and through the body the whole integration, and environmental factors likewise affect the whole being. It may thus be seen that the 'responsibility' is not so exclusively God's as Augustine may have supposed creatianism to involve. Mankind is responsible for propagating itself, and knows that God will give a spirit if 'the will of the flesh' leads to the provision of a body.

(viii) It is difficult to convey the exact nuance of significance distinguishing the creation of a new human spirit from an 'uncovenanted' act of creation. It is desired to express the fact that God indeed creates the spirit, but that He creates it contingently on human action, upon which to a great extent the nature of the integration into which the spirit enters would depend. By the successful accomplishment of the function which brings about the union of the gametes, human parents are, subject to the qualifications already explained, responsible for bringing into existence a new human being, body, centrum vitæ and spirit, though God gives the spirit and it is not integrated from previous constituents as is the body.

(ix) Human fatherhood involves the ability of a man to bring a human spirit into existence, not indeed by any power or right of his own, but because, certain functions being successfully fulfilled, God will add to the coalesced gametes a spirit. Similarly, motherhood involves the ability of a woman to bring a human spirit into existence, not indeed by any power or right of her own, but because, certain functions being successfully fulfilled, God will add to the coalesced gametes a spirit.

There are many complicated problems connected with this matter into which we cannot now enter. We only wish to qualify creatianism by emphasizing that God's act is contingent upon man's act, and that to that extent responsibility for bringing spirits into the world depends upon man; we emphasize that no human spirit is caused to come into existence by God unless man exercises or causes to operate his reproductive power. It must be pointed out that the power of parenthood as thus defined is equally effective whether exercised lawfully or unlawfully, lovingly or lustfully, willingly or unwillingly. The balance between divine gift and human responsibility for its evoking implied in this paragraph may enable us to retain a creationist view while at the same time recognizing and allowing for most of the facts for which traducianism seeks to account.

If our view must be given one designation or the other, we should unhesitatingly say it is a creationist view; but we would emphatically emphasize man's contingent responsibility, in that God does not create a spirit unless the powers of parenthood are exercised.

We may add:

(i) The newly created spirit has its inception contingently upon the union of the gametes, and although the question cannot be definitely settled, it seems best to suppose that the spirit is integrated with the zygote at the moment of conception. 'Quickening' is a purely physical phenomenon, and occurs in animals just as in human beings, so there is little reason to ascribe the infusion of the spirit to that particular stage.

(ii) The new spirit is inevitably linked with the organism, biotically integrated with it, most probably through the centrum vitæ, and in any case we can hardly fail to suppose that the spirit and centrum vitæ are most intimately related. It seems reasonable to suppose that the spirit and centrum vitæ are linked in the closest intermeshing,[1] and that a living man has the utmost difficulty in distinguishing what of 'I' pertains to the spirit and what to the centrum vitæ. Here is a sphere where comparative psychology (animal and human) may shed interesting light. The differences between the

[1] By 'intermeshing' is not meant intermeshing as of cog-wheels but intermeshing as of two materials woven in the making through and into one another in such a way that if all the threads of one were cut the other would remain intact, but so woven together that they could not be separated without such cutting.

highest type of animal mind, not so much the differences
of degree as the differences of kind, will indicate what are
the true and special characteristics of the spirit. It may well
be that all that pertains merely to adaptation to and manipu-
lation of the contents of the physema pertains to the centrum
vitæ, all, that is, that is empirical and pragmatic, and that
the essence of that which pertains to the spirit is in the
realm of pulchral and moral appreciation and volition:
appreciation and choice on the highest levels. The human
"mind" is therefore a complex of centrum vitæ and spirit,
and there may be a salutary sobering in meditating on that
fact: we do not carry forward excellencies of the centrum
vitæ, but excellencies of the spirit. Cleverness and skill
pertain to the centrum vitæ. Wisdom, character and love
pertain to the spirit.

(iii) It is inescapable that body, brain and mind (using
mind for centrum vitæ and spirit integrated together), being
naturally integrated, must all develop together. The body
and brain obviously develop in size and efficiency, and the
brain acts as the 'card-index' and automatic exchange of
experience and information which the mind uses. If we
abstract in thought the idea of 'the mind', we may well ask
whether it too develops. The answer would certainly appear
to be 'yes', though we must rigorously exclude any idea of
the centrum vitæ, and still more of the spirit, 'growing' in
a way comparable with the growth of the body and the
brain. The growth, anyhow of the spirit, is entirely non-
spatial and immaterial, and, if we must so think, had better
be thought of in terms of intensity, quality, appreciation
and feeling rather than in any way suggestive of space or
matter.

(iv) The natural immortality of the spirit is a Greek rather
than a Christian concept. The spirit as created by God is
a unit of exceptionally persistent and enduring kind, more
relatively indestructible than the stablest type of atom. We
know no means whereby a human spirit could be disintegrated. In any case, it is immaterial, and we have no
way at all of dealing with it on such levels. But that is not
to say that it is by nature indestructible or eternal. We must
remember two things: God can destroy (disintegrate) spirits;

and no spirit continues to exist except by the good-will of God. Against the idea of the natural immortality of the spirit we must set the fact that God is the only self-existent and that nothing exists or continues to exist except by His grace and will, within this schema or within any other. God only is exoschematic. When we use the word 'immortal', therefore, of anything but God, we must always realize that none but God is immortal by His own nature and without qualification. Anything or anyone else is only immortal at His grace and pleasure. 'Immortalizable' indicates ability to endure for ever if God so permits and wills, and necessarily involves the possibility of continuing to exist outside this continuum, for we have every reason to believe that this continuum as such will come to a definite and final end.

(3) *The life of man*

Man thus begins his life as the result of an integration which makes him a biotic unit of a special kind: a biotic unit with its place in the flux of natural units, and integral in that unit something (the spirit) which undergoes all the experiences, can assess them and react to them, can take its choice as to its line of conduct, can choose whether to endeavour to identify itself with the purposes of God by yielding to His grace. This complex biotic unit, man, is both a system and a unit, and we must be very clear as to the correlativity of the terms system and unit. Man is a system, because he is a complex integration of many parts. Man is a unit, because the many parts are integrated into one autocentricity.

Let us consider the relevance to the integration of man's body. His body is made up of organic and other substances naturally integrated together to form a wonderfully devised machine whereby he may be able to live in and react with his environment. A body is simply a means whereby a mind may be suitably related with a given environment. Given a different environment, the same mind might need a modified or quite different body. God has clearly demonstrated this fact by potentiating hylic units in such a way that biotic units can be formed capable of living in shallow water, deep water, or on the land; in cold, temperate or hot climates; and adaptable in various other ways to widely varying conditions of life. Similarly, if God wished us to live and experience in conditions very different from those prevailing on this earth, He could readily devise a body suitable for enabling us to be related to that environment. We must not digress on this point, though it illustrates a very important principle—that the function of the body is to enable a mind (and therefore, in man, a spirit) to relate itself to its environment. It may be suggested that "the resurrection of the body" is a noetic statement of an ontic reality which we may interpret thus: in the next life God will see to it that our spirits are suitably related to our new environment: we shall not be naked spirits, but "clothed upon" (2. Cor. v. 4). The whole passage, 2 Cor. v. 1–8, seems to endorse this view. There is nothing essential about our present senses. By sight, hearing and touch we appreciate our surroundings and, to an extent, other people. In surroundings of a different type God will devise suitable means of appreciation and communication.

But the body is more than a means of relation to environment. It is most carefully adapted to a specially devised environment, not merely in what may be called a mechanical manner, but, what is far more important, in a value-reaction manner. It is largely (but not entirely) through the body that a man realizes not only the fact but the pull of the ambivalent potentiation of the natural order. It is largely through the body that man can realize certain potentiations by theletically entering or declining to enter certain integrations, natural or otherwise, and, having entered or declined to enter such integrations, he realizes, clearly or dimly, the value of what he has done. Let it be emphasized that so precisely has the balance between the body and its environment been devised, and so exactly has the mind's sense of value been prearranged, that the choice of mode of integration is always a real one and the sense of value is always present (that is, of course, in normal cases. We are not at the moment considering abnormality, whether accidental, misfortunate, or self-induced). Thus the body is a sensitive instrument for healthy exertion, and responds to right use. One of the primitive satisfactions is a body functioning in accordance with its powers. Games and athletics minister to such satisfactions. On the other hand, the body is an instrument able to respond to perverted uses, and is adaptable to vices and follies of many kinds. It may be said that the body is morally neutral, but that with a little encouragement in either direction it readily becomes not merely the instrument but an intensifier of the decisions of the mind. The athlete desires that his body should serve as the instrument for his games and accomplishments. It readily does so, and there is a real pleasure in a well acting body. The vicious desires that his body should serve as the instrument for his depraved or uncontrolled appetites, and it readily collaborates, until it may seem that the body itself cries out for its drugs, abuses or indulgences. It is terribly true that a (normal) body is 100 per cent. functionally efficient,[1] but that its functional efficiency can be integrated into systems varying in functional and other value from 100 per cent. positive to 100 per cent. negative. As a specialized illustration, see St. James on the tongue: "Therewith bless we God, even the Father; and therewith curse we men, which are made after the similitude of God. Out of the same mouth proceedeth blessing and cursing" (Jas. iii. 9–10).

The perfect body is a machine without bias, and cannot overrule the controlling mind, nor can it crave a satisfaction the mind inhibits. The same body can equally subserve a love that waits years for its consummation or a lust that demands satiation every few days. The body may indeed be an amplifier and intensifier of whatever the mind sets in train, but the last word is always with the mind. We can let the body perish rather than yield to it.

Nevertheless, and this is very relevant to our view both of man and of Jesus Christ, the perfectly neutral and unbiassed body is probably an abstraction. Quite apart from any speculations as to the derivation of our bodies through progressive biotic integration from lower forms, our bodies have come to each one of us through a long line

[1] That is, in accordance with its purpose in the scheme of things, which is to serve as the instrument of an experiencing mind (and spirit) for about 70 years.

of ancestors, and in that long line there have been people of many types and of very varying character. Our bodies are therefore usually produced with predilections to certain responses, for tendencies to certain reactions undoubtedly inhere in the body. These predilections are not to be thought of as direct biasses, physical or mental, but rather as inclinations towards certain reactions which are recognized as potentially pleasing. Just as certain engines may run most easily at certain speeds or with certain fuels, so the body may be born with certain predilections as to treatment. Such a body may be easier or more difficult to control than the average; but control still resides in the mind, and no moralist or court of law accepts any such excuse unless the mind itself is also warped.

As to disease and infirmity, those are inevitable parts of the scheme of things. Their incidence is not even, and we have to accept our share of it with what equanimity we can. The body is designed to work for a number of years and then to wear out. The wearing out process is unpleasant, and may minister to petulance and complaint or to courage and patience. This is not an approach to the problem of pain, but merely a recognition of its existence. A discussion is irrelevant to our present purpose.

The brain is of course part of the body, but a few words must be said concerning it. Like the body, the brain may vary in efficiency and adaptability, but its functioning is controlled by the mind and its easiest tendencies need not be followed. The brain is an automatic exchange for the due working of certain reflexes and instinctive reactions, a means of storing impressions and experiences, and, in general, the machinery through which the mind operates in relation to its material environment. Like the body, accidental causes and inherited tendencies may make the brain efficient to a greater or less degree. We are not responsible for our type and quality of brain; but we are responsible for the way in which we use what we have.

In man, the mind is an intermeshed complex of centrum vitæ and spirit. In so far as it is a centrum vitæ it resembles the mind of other high type animals. In so far as it is a spirit it has a responsibility and power which no high type animal approaches. An intelligent animal may learn to be obedient and to respond to affection. These are functions of the centrum vitæ, and they are empirically and pragmatically sound. A man who believes that honesty is the best policy and acts accordingly is not acting on the spiritual level, nor is the man who is good natured and affable to those who respond: "If ye love them which love you, what thank have ye? for sinners also love those that love them. And if ye do good to them which do good to you, what thank have ye? for sinners also do even the same" (Luke vi. 32–33). It is in the spirit that the distinction of man resides, and it can elevate or depress the functioning of the mind of man so far above or so far below the level of the functioning of the mind of an animal. The centrum vitæ of an animal may be of a poor or high degree of development (cf. a rabbit and an elephant), but it essentially relates the creature to its environment in an empirical and pragmatic manner. That relating may depend very largely on the place of the creature in the scheme of things, which may display any of a number of divergent possibilities in biotic integration. The gazelle illustrates gentleness and fear, the tiger violence and courage. But each is as the potentiations have emerged, and their centrum vitæ acts accordingly. Either may be "good" of its type, and either may respond to kindness, but only because its centrum vitæ more or less automatically weighs up advantage and disadvantage.

The addition of spirit, however, introduces an element of an altogether different kind. God has caused the human spirit to partake in parvo of elements in His own nature, so that it appreciates ultimates regardless of empirics and pragmatics. We, as spiritual beings, can appreciate truth even if it is of no direct practical service to us; we can appreciate beauty apart from all functional association; and we can appreciate holiness irrespective of whether it 'pays'. Further, God has given spirit a natural yearning for these things, so that the spirit is not at peace unless it seeks and until it finds concord with all that is true and beautiful and holy. Here, then, is the meaning of human life: man is a complex placed in and related to an environment of many possibilities; he is given the ability to discern and seek that which is best, and he is given free choice of alternative satisfactions, higher and lower. Herein is the tragedy of human life: no man (except One), though given this discernment and this choice, has ever clearly enough discerned and definitely enough chosen to be described without qualification as completely wise and good. This is no accident or error on God's part. God knew what He wanted to make possible and He knew how it could be achieved. God knew that a self-perfectible man might enter into some kind of harmony and union with Himself, but not into the kind of harmony and union which God wanted to make possible —a harmony and union of love and dependence as well as of purpose and action. God therefore brought it about that the integration of man into Himself should take place not solely by man's choice and effort but should also depend on an approach from God Himself. This is the work of Christ, and the mystery and glory of the Atonement.

A brief digression must be made here on the relation of the study of psychology as ordinarily pursued to the view set out above. The study of psychology divides, implicitly even when not explicitly, into two divisions, which may be called the scientific and the metaphysical. The scientific approach to psychology regards mind as something intimately associated with the brain and nervous system, leaving aside the question as to whether mind is anything but a function of the brain and nervous system, and proceeds to study mind in relation to the machinery through which it works (or which it is). Such an approach leads to the discovery and systematization of a great amount of most useful information, enables us to form a clear idea of the way in which the mind 'works', and gives us an insight into what we may expect the reactions and behaviour of men and animals, normal and abnormal, to be. This aspect of psychology is often described, sometimes disparagingly, as "behaviourism". It should by no means be disparaged, as it has codified a great deal of most enlightening information, and enables us to assess spirit while making due allowance for the machinery, strong or weak, healthy or diseased, normal or abnormal, through which it has to work. But even those, like McDougall, who approach psychology in

this way, and it is a mode of approach which has largely
superseded the old "classical" approach, for the most part
recognize that, like all scientific approaches, it deals competently with phenomena but has little direct power in
interpreting ultimates. Science finds out 'how' in meticulous
detail, but science as such cannot tell us 'why'. To endeavour
to answer that latter question is the province of philosophy
and theology, and the psychologist who wishes to proceed
beyond the study of neural processes and behaviour must
nolens volens become at least some sort of philosopher.
As in all philosophical speculation, this means that postulation inevitably begins to assume increasing importance, and
whenever a psychologist begins to endeavour to explain
what mind really is we need to know or to deduce his
postulates before we can appreciate the value of his opinions.
Quite frequently we can readily transpose his views into
another framework, thus conserving what may be valuable
in them while not necessarily subscribing to his general
philosophy. We are not therefore greatly concerned with
the speculations of psychologists as such as to the ultimate
nature of mind. We can read their views, and without much
difficulty recognize whether the author is of the rational or
intuitive type,[1] and if of the latter the degree of his acceptance or rejection of the general Christian framework. By
way of illustration we may take Freud's general view, as
summarized by himself in the *Encyclopædia Britannica*.[2]
Freud reduces the ultimates of mind (and presumably of
spirit) to 'id', the reservoir of instinctive impulses, 'ego',
the plane of contact with the world, and the 'super-ego', the
complex of inhibitions. Such a view reflects an essentially
rational mind, and the analysis is quite sound so far as it
goes. We can readily equate it. Freud's 'id' is a term covering the workings of the brain and nervous system as a
'card-index' and automatic exchange under the general
vitalizing supervision of the centrum vitæ; his 'ego' is a
term covering the mind's assessment of and reaction to the
data of experience, thus corresponding with the reactions
and valuations of the intermeshed centrum vitæ and spirit
which we have related together as the experiencing and

[1] See Preface.   [2] xviii. 673 (14th Edition).

W

directing centre of living man; his 'super-ego' is a term covering what we should regard as the developing personality of the intermeshed centrum vitæ and spirit, the non-space-temporal values of which are retained and carried forward by the spirit. We are of course all endeavouring to interpret the same ontic reality, but our noetic interpretation inevitably greatly varies according to our framework of postulates. General shape is so much more important than detail. Detail takes a warp from a warped framework, and in assessing philosophical arguments this fact must always be borne in mind. The details of psychological speculation need not worry us; the essential point for the Christian theist is that spirit experiences in intimate and necessary association with body, with which it is integrated during life into a real unit, and that the spirit carries forward the appreciations and inclinations it has chosen to develop.

We may now consider how man may deploy his powers and endeavour to realize his potentialities. We therefore take up again the very important ideas of potentiation, integration, unity, value, centricity, and perfection, which were introduced on pp. 253–259. Applying them to man, we first observe that man is an integrated unit, a biotic unit of a special kind, in that there is integrated into him a spirit, which has powers of discernment and discrimination, of choice and action different not only in degree but in kind from the powers displayed by a higher animal. The essence of the difference is that man can appreciate and respond to pure issues related to truth and beauty and holiness without reference to empirical or pragmatic considerations. The characteristic of man is the possession of such a spirit.

The word 'unit' in the above paragraph must be emphasized. Man is not a spirit inhabiting a body. He is a spirit naturally integrated into a body, which is a very different matter. While a man lives he is not a spirit: he is a man, and 'man' includes body just as certainly as it includes spirit. He is a complex and he reacts as a complex, though that complex is a natural unit and therefore acts as a unit.

As man is a unit, he has a centricity. One unit implies

one primary centricity, the centricity into which all that is integrated into that unit is centred. Before integration each of those things which are to enter into the integration is autocentric. After integration, each of those things which have entered into the integration has become (if, as is legitimate, still regarded by analytical thought as discriminable though integrated) allocentric, the centricity being in that greater unit into which all have become integrated. Man as a unit is therefore autocentric, and the self-consciousness of his autocentricity is his individuality, which constitutes him a person. Each man realizes that he is an integration: he knows that he is made of 'bits and pieces'; yet each man realizes that he is a unit, and though parts of that unit are in a continuous state of flux of minor integration, disintegration and reintegration, there is a continuing autocentric unity which is 'himself'. Indeed, man is the apex of the series of natural integrations. He is the highest natural unit, and is the most complex natural autocentric system. It may be well at this point to recapitulate the ascending scale of natural integration:

(i) The protocumata, by the primary natural integration (the primary emergent potentiation of the protocumata), integrated into electronic and protonic systems or units (electrons and protons), which, if not further integrated, are autocentric systems or units possessing a degree of functional efficiency and potential functional value, which potential functional value becomes actual if the electrons and protons are further integrated into higher systems or units, in which case the electrons and protons become allocentric in a greater system and their value becomes actual in that system.

(ii) The electrons and protons, by atomic integration (the second emergent potentiation of the protocumata), integrate into atomic systems or units (atoms), which, if not further integrated, are autocentric systems or units possessing a degree of functional efficiency and potential functional value, which potential functional value becomes actual if the atoms are further integrated into higher systems or units, in which case the atoms become allocentric in a greater system and their value becomes actual in that system.

(iii) The atoms, by hylic integration (the third emergent potentiation of the protocumata), integrate into hylic systems or units (molecules and substances), which, if not further integrated, are autocentric systems or units possessing a degree of functional efficiency and potential functional value, which potential functional value becomes actual if the hylic units are further integrated into higher systems or units, in which case the hylic units become allocentric in a greater system and their value becomes actual in that system.

(iv) Hylic units, by biotic integration (the fourth emergent potentiation of the protocumata, whether sufficient in itself or in the first instances accompanied by the direct infusion by God of 'vital force'), integrate into biotic systems or units (organisms, vegetable or animal), which, if not further integrated, are autocentric systems or units possessing a degree of functional efficiency and potential functional value, which potential functional value becomes actual if the biotic units are further integrated into higher systems or units, in which case the biotic units become allocentric in a greater system and their value becomes actual in that system.

(v) Hylic units, by the special type of biotic integration appropriate to man (the fourth emergent potentiation of the protocumata, possibly in the first instance accompanied by the direct infusion by God of 'vital force', and certainly in the first instance accompanied by the direct infusion by God of 'spirit'), integrate into the biotic system or unit known as 'man', which, if not further integrated, is an autocentric system or unit possessing a degree of functional efficiency and potential functional, pulchral and moral value, which value may become actual if the man is further integrated into a higher system or unit, in which case he becomes allocentric in a greater system and his value becomes actual in that system.

Thus natural integration culminates in the biotic units and man, and at that stage one factor begins to assume diversity and at the same time clarification, and another emerges for the first time:

(i) Value, which in lower integrations is readily recognized in its functional aspect and is only very indirectly conceivable as potentially pulchral or moral, begins increasingly to display its threefold aspect, and in man, though functional and pulchral value is important, moral value is evidently the one of supreme significance. Functional value is linked up with the method of the Universe. Moral value is linked up with its purpose. Pulchral value is not easy to define or assess. It is probably a kind of efflorescence accompanying functional and moral perfection, earnest of something fundamental in the nature of God Himself. According to our appreciation of functional and moral excellence, so shall we see beauty in varying forms and degrees.

(ii) The biotic units and man, themselves the apex of the natural integration series, are themselves able to be both inceptors of and elements in integrations of a yet higher and far more significant type. We have already pointed out that natural integrations can arise incidentally or theletically. But biotic units and man are not only able theletically to bring about natural integrations, they are also able to form systems from natural units, interlocking, grouping or arranging natural units in such a way as to form a system or unit subserving some purpose or fulfilling some end. Such systems may be of many kinds, and it will be convenient to apply to all of them the adjective 'telic'.[1] It will be obvious that while a natural unit may arise incidentally or theletically, a telic system or unit necessarily arises theletically. A telic system is necessarily theletic.

We ought first to say something about telic integration as it may be observed among lower biotic units. Biotic units of the simplest types, such as plants, appear to live entirely naturally. From their inception to their end their course entirely depends upon the operation of God-ordained laws of natural integration and disintegration, and their life processes seem to depend on the conditions of temperature pressure humidity and so forth to which they are subjected, and the processes of biotic integration, partial integration, disintegration and reintegration and final disintegration, which constitute their life cycle, proceed with an apparent inevitability. In that sense their life can be described as entirely natural, as though it were the functioning of a complex but essentially calculable mechanism which God

[1]τελικός , of or pertaining to an end.

had devised. If the Universe showed no other kind of life or activity we could conceive of no higher actual value than actual functional value and of no higher centricity than the allocentricity of hylic units integrated into a biotic unit, itself inevitably autocentric except in so far as existentially integrated into the general scheme of things, and to that extent into whatever purpose God might have had in causing such a Universe to be.

But in the higher biotic units we see the increasing emergence of an ability to exercise an influence on the flux of natural units. They are themselves natural units, but not, like atomic units, hylic units and biotic units of a lower type, subject to the unmodifiable action of inevitable natural process. They can, on the other hand, themselves influence the course of events and in that way modify the course and character of the flux of natural units. This is done by what is usually called the exercise of volition or will, and is to be carefully distinguished from reflex action, which is purely natural. Without at this juncture making a precise distinction between volition and reflex action, which is by no means easy, we may define volition as the quality or power possessed by certain higher biotic units by the exercise of which they are able to bring about, or to endeavour to bring about, modifications in what would otherwise be the course of the flux of the natural units about them. That is to say, they are able by the exercise of volition to modify the course of events, usually, of course, in their own interests or in accordance with their own desires and inclinations. They are thus able to impose a pattern on the sequence of events or on to some section of that sequence, and there thus arises an area in the general flux of natures which has received its shape and character as the result of the volition of some biotic unit or units. Such areas constitute telic systems or units, and are, needless to repeat, necessarily theletic. Simple examples are the arrangement of twigs to form a nest (bird), burrowing into a bank to make a warren (rabbit), building a dam to provide a location for an under-water home (beaver). These types of telic integration may without doubt be referred to the centrum vitæ, and as with all functions of the centrum vitæ are based upon empirical and pragmatic considerations, to whatever extent, that is, that we are unable or unwilling to account for such actions as due to tropisms and reflexes. All we need say is that the higher biotic units seem to show a rudimentary ability to initiate telic integration. But this is a question we need not dwell upon, as the principle is so much more evidenced in man and we may therefore more advisedly set out a rising sequence going far beyond what we should expect to find in any other creature.

(1) Man can bring about the conditions (to a limited extent and only in some cases) in which atomic integrations, disintegrations and reintegrations take place. In such cases atomic integration has been brought about by the will of man, and is therefore to be characterized as theletic as opposed to incidental. It is nevertheless natural, in that man is only bringing about the conditions in which natural laws operate.

(2) Man can bring about the conditions in which hylic integrations, disintegrations and reintegrations take place. Here again such integrations are theletic but also natural. Every chemical substance produced by man is a theletic natural (hylic) integration; so is every piece of worked metal, every brick, every piece of shaped stone.

(3) Man can bring about the conditions in which biotic integrations, disintegrations and reintegrations take place. Theletic biotic integration means the formation of a biotic unit (a living organism, plant or animal) from hylic units or other biotic units by a process of biotic integration not arising incidentally in the general flux of natures, but by the exercise of will in some man or men. The integration is natural (biotic), and utterly depends on God's laws. But it is theletic, because it has not arisen merely incidentally. Examples are to be found in all cases in which a man plants a seed, indeed in all horticultural and agricultural processes, in which man is endeavouring to influence and control the course of biotic integration, and in all cases where man seeks to control or direct the production of animal life. Garden roses, racehorses and Wyandotte fowls are alike theletic biotic integrations. Let it be observed that the adjectives natural (which includes atomic, hylic and biotic) and theletic do not contradict one another. Integrations

described as theletic do not come about unless will has been exercised; but if they are also described as natural we are made aware that they do not take place except in accordance with the God-given potentiations governing such integrations. A theletic natural integration thus results from man making use of processes which God has made possible.

(4) But of far greater significance than his ability to bring about natural integrations theletically is his great power of bringing about telic integrations. This power, which, as we have seen, is possessed in a rudimentary form by the higher animals, is possessed by man in a highly developed degree and, like natural integration, is progressive. A few natural units (perhaps themselves theletically produced) may be integrated into a telic unit. That telic unit and others may be integrated into a yet more complex telic unit. That more complex telic unit may be integrated into a telic unit still higher in the scale. In every case, as with natural integration, the result is both a system and a unit: a system in that it is integrated from parts, and a unit in that it subserves a definite function and actual or potential purpose.

It is not necessary to work out an exact scheme of progressive telic integration. Rather would it be preferable to consider how man himself is able to use it and himself to enter into it. Herein lies the value of life as a testing ground, that God has given man the power to integrate himself and his environment into telic systems, and such systems have value. Telic integrations have value which can be assessed under the three headings we have already used: functional, pulchral, and moral. When we considered natural integration we found that functional value was prominently in our minds, whereas pulchral and moral value seemed less directly involved, and we saw that pulchral and moral value were largely to be regarded as potential and emergent "in some greater integration". But when we begin to consider telic integrations we shall see that functional, pulchral and moral value are more closely and directly correlated, particularly as the complexity of the telic integrations increases. It may be useful to sketch the way in which telic integrations increase in complexity and to see how man himself enters into them.

Let us start by considering the simplest type of telic system, an object such as a clock. A clock is made in two stages. First of all, the separate components are prepared by theletically induced natural integrations. That is to say, a number of little pieces of metal of various shapes and sizes, and various other little items, are prepared and shaped by the processes appropriate to the integration of hylic units. Each little piece is in fact a hylic unit which has been produced not incidentally but theletically. All these prepared pieces are then integrated by man into one new system or unit, the clock, which is a telic unit—that is, an integration, a system, a unit devised by man for the fulfilment of a certain end. All machines are telic units, produced by telic integration of a number of parts, the parts usually being themselves theletic natural units. A telic unit such as a clock in and of itself is autocentric and has a calculable degree of functional efficiency. It only acquires functional value if it is integrated into some bigger system, becoming for example, the time-piece in the living room of a family.

The idea of the integration of a simple telic unit into a larger unit leads us to the conception that, as we advance in the scale, telic systems pass beyond the idea of compactness which we have accustomed ourselves to associate with a natural unit. The ideas 'system' and 'unit' begin to acquire a deeper meaning as we realize that the significance of a system does not reside in the mechanical connection of its parts, nor does unity necessarily involve contiguity and continuity. In fact, a clock, which we have taken as an example of a simple telic unit, admirably illustrates the transition. Its parts are in contact, but they are not fused (naturally united) together. Their value in the unit depends upon their harmonious functional interrelation rather than upon any bonds of inevitability. In higher telic units we may therefore look for unity of purpose and function, unity of 'end', rather than mere substantial or organic unity, and if we use the correlative term system we think of it in terms of purposeful rather than merely membral association.

We thus pass on to telic systems in which the discrete parts are not merely separably discernible but may be actually separate in space. We can thus recognize a room as a telic unit, integrated from the lesser telic and natural units within it. The house itself is a still greater telic unit, so indeed is the town.

Human activity is thus seen to express itself in telic unities of great complexity and interdependence, and, passing over any detailed analysis of them, we may pass straight on to at least one of the legitimate ways in which we may analyse the whole complex of telic units. Each individual man goes through life continually integrating, disintegrating and reintegrating telic systems of many kinds. At any given moment we may picture that man as himself responsible for and himself the centre of a telic system which is the expression and realization of his impact upon his environment. As this telic system centred on himself is characteristic of and peculiar to the man himself, we may call it his idiotelic system. Life, looked at as a complex of human activities, is thus seen to be a complex of idiotelic systems, always in flux and often in conflict. The contents of an idiotelic system have potential value according to what they are and actual value according to their function in the system as a whole. If now we add the idea of duration to idiotelic unity, we get this comprehensive view of human life in relation to its environment: man's effective life is the duration of an idiotelic unit, which starts with his conception and continues to his death, which is indeed the man in relation to his environment, and is the expression of his impact upon it. If we like to form visual images, the duration of an idiotelic system or unit is a kind of labyrinth through the space-time continuum, having a nodal point of inception at the man's conception and a nodal point of termination at his death. Running all through like a thread, the continuing element of unification and continuity, is the natural biotic unit the man himself, round whom is gathered this idiotelic unit of his total activity and reaction. At a given moment there is the natural unit 'man' and the idiotelic unit centred on and telically integrated with him. He has his continuity, it has its continuity, both are in flux, both are inescapably related. Quite obviously, a man is assessed by the quality of the idiotelic system associated with him. There is no other way of judging him, for all his relations with other people and things are part of and evidences of his idiotelic system. Every man is evidently telically integrated into his own idiotelic system, and his actual value is his value in that system. Similarly, the value of the idiotelic system becomes actual according to its mode of integration into the scheme of things in general. It may not be difficult to arrive at general conclusions as to the value of ordinary human idiotelic systems. It has to be remembered that an idiotelic system can be considered instantaneously or duratively. Its value from instant to instant will vary greatly, but its value as a duration must obviously take into account the record of its total duration.

(1) *Functional value of an idiotelic system or unit*

This is very difficult to assess. It involves answering the questions, "What has been the value of this man and his activities to the general scheme of things? At what do we value all that he has done, all that he has been, his work, his influence, his effect on others? What percentage should this assessment be of the best he could have done?" It is fantastic to suppose that there has ever lived a man (save One) whose functional value in the general scheme of things has, taking his life right through, been anything but a very small percentage of what it should ideally have been. Every slightest error takes from it. We have to take account of all work imperfectly done, of all failures, of all omissions, indeed of everything open to any kind of criticism on the grounds of functional imperfection. Scales are exceedingly difficult to devise, but we may most certainly assert that the functional value considered over its whole duration of any ordinary human idiotelic unit has never approached anything like 100 per cent.

(2) *Pulchral value of an idiotelic system or unit*

We are not going deeply into the problems of æsthetics, and pulchral value is only included because there is almost certainly a deep and fundamental connection between beauty on the one hand and truth and holiness on the other which we must not overlook. Let it suffice to regard the pulchral value of an idiotelic unit as the contribution made by it to the sum total of all in the world that is beautiful in the widest sense of that word: not only contributions towards the ideal of beauty as sought after in music, art and literature, but beauty in life and conduct, beauty in the sense of whatever is done in the fittest possible manner. Here again there would be none to dispute that the life of no ordinary man has ever been an idiotelic unit of anything approaching 100 per cent. pulchral value.

(3) *Moral value of an idiotelic system or unit*

Here again "there is none good but one". The finest ordinary man who ever lived could not be assessed as having been an idiotelic unit of anything like 100 per cent. moral value. That would be equivalent to sinlessness, but "all have sinned, and come short of the glory of God".

Consideration of the three types of value leads to one inescapable conclusion: no ordinary idiotelic unit has ever had perfection of functional, pulchral or moral value. There has never been a perfect ordinary man.

We may now ask a question of far reaching import: What is the centricity of an ordinary idiotelic unit? This question is in general very difficult to answer, though its two extremes are plain. One extreme is this: the worst type of idiotelic unit is that which is centred exclusively and continuously on the man who is the integrator as well as part of the unit. Such a man retains himself as the centre of the idiotelic system to which he gives rise. The system is autocentric, and further its autocentricity is centred on its integrator, a human biotic unit. The man whose idiotelic system is centred on himself is necessarily autocentric. Autocentricity means self-centredness, self-interestedness, selfishness of an utter kind; autocentricity is the fundamental sin. Such complete autocentricity is, fortunately, rare. The other extreme is Theocentricity. Can we suppose a man deciding that he would like his entire life and all its concerns and ramifications—his entire idiotelic system—to be completely subordinated to the will and purpose of God, to transfer its centricity to God Himself, in fact, to integrate his idiotelic system into God's purposes voluntarily and entirely, so that his idiotelic system should become incorporated into the

Theotelic system, the Theotelic unit? There are two obvious comments. Could a man actually so will, and, if he so willed, could he so surrender? And, if a man could so will and so surrender, would God accept into His perfection an imperfect idiotelic system? We need not pursue these questions, because no ordinary living man has ever been able to transfer his centricity in that complete sense.

What, then, is the centricity of an ordinary idiotelic unit? Herein lies man's struggle and unhappiness, for his centricity is subject to continual flux and stress. One strong pull, the pull of selfish egoism, is towards autocentricity. Another strong pull, the pull of divine love and grace, is towards Theocentricity. This is exactly felt and expressed by St. Augustine: "Thou hast made us for Thyself, and our heart is restless until it rests in Thee." Intermediately, there are pulls which we might, if we wished, analyse as varying compromises between autocentricity and Theocentricity, but which we may more easily describe simply as allo-centric. Genuine regard, love and concern for other people or groups, for causes, for organizations, all such love and concern is a factor which may wholly or in part transfer the centre of an idiotelic system from its human integrator to some other centre, some cause, movement or ideal. With all these pulls operating with intensities and effects which are continually varying it is a matter of considerable difficulty to say exactly what is at any moment the centricity of an idiotelic unit, and far more difficult to ascribe to it a continuing centricity. In fact, the actual centricity is what mathematicians would call the 'resolution' of varying degrees of autocentricity, Theocentricity and various allo-centricities. The resolved centricity is thus a complex, and furthermore a complex in a continual state of flux. It is nevertheless a real continuity, and the human unit who is the integrator of the idiotelic unit is aware that his and its centricity is subject to these continual variations. Our selfishness (autocentricity) ebbs and flows; our faith and loyalty to God and the degree of our willingness to depend on His grace (Theocentricity) waxes and wanes; our concern for family, group, other causes (allocentricity) varies from time to time. No wonder we are unhappy. Our centricity is in continual flux, and even if at any given moment we can regard it as definite, it is even so an averaged compromise point resolved from several others. If we could only achieve it, committal to Theocentricity would solve our problems and give us peace. The perfect man, who has never existed (save once), would be perfect in functional, pulchral and moral value, would integrate himself into an idiotelic unit which he would surrender to and integrate into the Theotelic unit, and he would surrender his autocentricity in order that he and everything pertaining to him might become Theocentric. God, in His gracious mercy, has made it possible for man ultimately to acquire a place in the Theotelic system and to become Theocentric. The Atonement wrought by Jesus Christ is the means, a means which involved God in Christ Himself becoming the only Perfect Man. It is not necessary to discuss the life of man further, as our analysis has proceeded far enough for our present purpose.

(4) The death of man

A time comes when the human biotic unit disintegrates. It disintegrates because the machinery of the body for one or several reasons has arrived at such a condition that it is no longer a functionally efficient unit, and is consequently no longer able to fulfil its rôle of maintaining a sentient being in contact and relation with its environment. The body, as a machine, has worn out or broken down, has developed a fatal fault or has received some grave injury making its continued functioning impossible. When that event occurs, 'death' occurs. Death is the end of the biotic unit man, and he disintegrates into his constituents. Those constituents are in the main three: body, centrum vitæ and spirit. As we have seen, these three constituents are in most intimate mutual relationship, interpenetrating and intermeshing with one another in ways which we cannot exactly determine. We may, however, be sure of two things: the body, which is itself an integration of hylic units, will, bereft of centrum vitæ and spirit, slowly or speedily break down into hylic units of various kinds, which will thenceforward continue in the flux of natural units, "earth to earth, ashes to ashes, dust to dust"; and the spirit, having been given its opportunity of experiencing and making its choice in this continuum, will pass on to the next stage of its existence in accordance with its deserts and God's mercy and grace. We may be a little uncertain as to the centrum vitæ. To what extent is it merely an adjunct of the body, the conscious centre of vital force, which is presumably its rôle in the case of the higher animals? We are convinced that the spirit carries forward the result of its earth-life experiences, and that its quality and worth depend on the reactions and decisions of its earth-life. But can we be certain to what extent it carries forward actual memory of its earth-life? Some may say that it does not do so, and that such actual memory is unimportant, that what matters is the quality of spirit that the earth-life experiences have produced, and that at death "mind and memory flee". Others may prefer to think that memory is carried forward, as they cannot imagine the continuance of personality without it. We had better not pretend that we can answer such questions. If we hazard a view, it would be that although memory appears to be primarily a function of the brain and centrum vitæ, as in higher animals, that is no reason for supposing that it is impossible for there to be a corresponding capacity in the spirit for retaining definite memory as well as carrying forward definite character. There may be a parallel retention. But the point may not be so important as we may imagine. The significance of our earthly life will surely tend to fade in any case as we pass on to higher stages and richer fulfilments. We may, however, feel justified in supposing that continuity of personality and of mutual recognition will be unbroken.

The disintegration of man is a natural disintegration, that is, it takes place in accordance with inevitable laws. It is therefore beyond man's control, except in so far that he can place himself or others in circumstances in which the natural laws will operate which will cause the disintegration to occur. Its irreversibility is the reason for our dread of it. It is a river we can only cross in one direction: "death is so final". Its painfulness is usually exaggerated. Death is quite often painless, and the average person probably suffers far more in non-fatal illnesses than at his end.

It is not within our present purpose to discuss in detail

what happens to the spirit after death, but we may make two brief observations:

(i) Death is the end of man. The human biotic unit begins at conception and ends at death. When the spirit has disengaged from the dying body it is no longer a man. A spirit might say, "I was a man"; it could not say, "I am a man". To have been man will be one experience through which we shall have passed.

(ii) It must be remembered that the body serves two linked purposes. It is our means of contact and communication with an environment; and, like the environment itself, it has been carefully designed to serve as a means of test and presentation of opportunity. When, therefore, its purpose has ended and we pass into a different environment, perhaps (indeed almost certainly) outside this physema, we shall need a different means of contact and communication with our new environment. God will provide us with bodies suitable for that environment.

Footnote 1, *p.* 301: See particularly his last chapter, from which the following sentences are taken: "We must maintain that the soul is in some sense a unitary being or entity distinct from all others; for we found that prominent among the facts which compel us to accept the animistic hypothesis are the facts of psychical individuality, the fact that consciousness, as known to us, occurs only as individual coherent streams of personal consciousness, and all the facts summed up in the phrase 'the unity of consciousness.' We found that these facts remain absolutely unintelligible, unless we postulate some ground of this unity and coherence and separateness of individual streams of consciousness, some ground other than the bodily organisation" (op. cit., p. 366). "It is open to us to believe that the soul, if it survives the dissolution of the body, carries with it some large part of that which has been gained by intellectual and moral effort; and though the acceptance of the view we have suggested as to the essential part played by the body in conditioning the sensory content of consciousness, would make it impossible to suppose that the surviving soul could enjoy the exercise of thought of the kind with which alone we are familiar, yet it is not inconceivable that it might find conditions that would stimulate it to imageless thought (possibly conditions of direct or telepathic communication with other minds) or might find under other conditions (possibly in association with some other bodily organism) a sphere for the application and actualization of the capacities developed in it during its life in the body" (ibid., p. 372). *Body and Mind* was published in 1911, and it is interesting to observe that the author's main contentions have not been shaken by his continued attention to the problem, as in *The Riddle of Life*, published in 1938, he says that the view he has formulated "gives us a glimpse of an intelligible possibility of the continuance of the activity of each one of us beyond death of the body, and hence of the continuing influence of whatever of positive value in our personalities may have accrued from our individual efforts" (op. cit., p. 273).

CHAPTER V

GODHEAD AND TRINITY

AT no time is it more necessary to bear in mind our
Seventh Postulate, that ontic reality is beyond human
comprehension (p. 229), than when we endeavour to comprehend the nature of God. Our first realization should be
that we are endeavouring to comprehend the incomprehensible, and we must therefore be fully aware that any
ideas we may hold concerning God will be at best but a
dim approach to something in some way parallel with
the reality.

Hitherto we have used the term 'God' in a general sense
to indicate the divine nature or activity as immanent in
some process to do with or within this continuum. We can
indeed have no other direct evidence of Him, but a comprehensive view of things soon obliges us to postulate far
more than is deducible from this continuum, and as these
postulates are of very fundamental importance to the
Christian theist they must be indicated at least in broad
outline. Although our present purpose is not the elaboration of a metaphysic of Godhead and Trinity, much that
has emerged incidentally in the preceding chapters must be
systematized and certain positions upon which the following
chapter will depend must be stated.

Our first concern is to avoid one of Nestorius' con-
spicuous faults—over exactness in realms where exactness
is not humanly achievable. It is futile to be more precise
than the data warrant or the nature of the problem permits.
It is therefore best to avoid ascribing a list of attributes to
God until we have envisaged as clearly as may be possible
a general concept of Him.

General concept of God

As Christian theists we unhesitatingly agree with St.
Anselm in postulating that our God is *id quo maius cogitari*

x

non potest.[1] God is beyond and above our most ideal concept of every kind. He is beyond limitation of any kind and is more completely perfect than we can imagine in all qualities which we regard as desirable, and, if there are any good qualities beyond our imagining, those also are attributable to God. He is inconceivably perfect in wisdom, love, power, and all other such qualities. To avoid a fulsome because inadequate compilation of epithets, we may say that God is the Supremely Perfect, both these words being interpreted in the grandest and greatest manner.

It would be sufficient if our minds could dwell in that: God is the Supremely Perfect. It may well be that this is the cardinal postulate of Christian theism. The non-Christian may be a little irked at what he regards as an almost irrational elevation by the Christian of the idea of God, that God must be above every limitation and above every criticism. But this postulation of God as the Supremely Perfect is of a depth of significance which it is difficult to put into words. What does the acceptance of this postulate imply and what does it involve? It implies that we are confident that the general scheme of things has an Originator and Controller whose plans and purposes are in every way above reproach and question, and that we believe that in the end the whole panorama of history will be justified; and it involves our willing personal surrender to that God and to His purpose. There is, further, this very real and cogent intellectual difficulty: that God is really the Supremely Perfect will only be conclusively demonstrated when this Universe has come to an end and the venture can be assessed in its entirety. How then can one accept that God is the Supremely Perfect, and how can one be expected to act on that assumption? An attempt to answer that question must begin with the recognition that the difficulty is itself fundamental to God's purpose, and that it is not God's intention that we should be able to overcome it intellectually. If it could be conclusively proved that God is the Supremely Perfect, subservience to Him would merely be wisdom and

[1] Vide Anselm, *Proslogion*, cap. II. We might not state the argument in his form, but we certainly concur in his faith: "Et quidem credimus te esse aliquid quo nihil maius cogitari possit." (Accessible in Migne, *Patrologia Latina*, clviii. 227C–228A.)

to accept Theocentricity would merely be the selfish achievement of our own highest satisfaction. But, as it cannot be proved, the acceptance of this postulate is a venture of faith, and the Christian life consists in living as though our faith were proven fact. It is more splendid in God's sight that we should act because we believe than because we know. Here we approach one of the final mysteries: God wants us to seek Him because we have faith that He is the Supremely Perfect, not because, knowing Him to be so, we wish to identify ourselves with Him. Faith, moreover, is inalienably linked with love, and it is here that we find one approach to the doctrine of the Atonement. The acceptance of and action upon the postulate that God is the Supremely Perfect depends on faith, not on proof. Faith involves the surrender of autocentricity and the acceptance of Theocentricity. This implies the abnegation of selfhood, which is virtual self-extinction, or at least a willingness to take the risk of it. Such a willingness could only arise from utter pessimism or utter devotion. But how can we utterly devote ourselves to One whom we believe, but cannot prove, to be Supremely Perfect? Only by a venture of faith and love, a venture only possible because God has made it possible for us to make it, and because He comes out to meet us: Jesus Christ is God coming to meet us, and enabling us to step blindly but fearlessly across the abyss, our faith and love answering to His prevenience and love, and our finding in Him the peace and fulfilment we could never have found apart from Him: "Cor nostrum inquietum est donec requiescat in Te."

The cardinal postulate of faith, then, confirmed in us by the evenient love of God, is that He is the Supremely Perfect. This postulate, in some form or another, has been emphasized by Christian thinkers all up the centuries; for Christian philosophers have unerringly realized that unless God is recognized to be the Supremely Perfect all philosophy tends to pessimism, and Christian theologians have equally unerringly realized that unless God is recognized to be the Supremely Perfect the Christian faith has no right to claim a man's complete surrender and his faithfulness unto death. For it has to be recognized that the Christian faith does in fact require that a man's natural autocentricity shall be surrendered, and that he shall voluntarily give his being over to a Theocentric unity, forsaking his auto-centricity in a willing surrender to God who thenceforward shall be the centre of all purpose and the fulfilment of all desires.

How could such a surrender be demanded unless there were an overwhelming and compelling confidence that God is indeed the Supremely Perfect? If God were less than that, man might be justified in preferring defiance and perdition, and there would be no more admirable type of character than Horace's 'justus et tenax propositi vir', whom nothing in heaven or earth could intimidate, not even 'fulminantis magna manus Iovis'.[1]

But the Christian theist accepts with confident assurance that God is indeed without limit or imperfection, that He is indeed the Supremely Perfect, and that full surrender to Him will be gloriously justified. This confidence is the distinguishing mark of the true Christian, and is evidenced by the life absolutely committed to God in Christ. From New Testament times onwards Christian consecration has been characterized by this complete abandonment to the will of God, this complete confidence in Him and in Him revealed in Jesus Christ: "And he saith unto them, Follow me, and I will make you fishers of men. And they straightway left their nets, and followed him" (Matt. iv. 19–20). "Then answered Peter and said unto him, Behold, we have for-saken all, and followed thee" (Matt. xix. 27). As William James puts it: "Self-surrender always must be regarded as the vital turning point of the religious life." It characterized the first disciples. It must characterize all who would be His disciples: "There is but one salvation for all mankind, and the way to it is one; and that is, the desire of the soul turned to God. This desire brings the soul to God, and God into

1 "Iustum et tenacem propositi virum
   non civium ardor prava iubentium,
   non voltus instantis tyranni
       mente quatit solida neque Auster,
   dux inquieti turbidus Hadriae,
   nec fulminantis magna manus Iovis;
       si fractus illabatur orbis,
       impavidum ferient ruinae."
   HORACE, Carmina, Lib. III, Car. 3.

the soul; it unites with God, it co-operates with God, and is one life with God" (William Law). This surrender, made with the confidence of responding love, passes over into an assurance which its possessor regards as knowledge. Thus St. Paul feels able to assert: "I know whom I have believed, and am persuaded that he is able to keep that which I have committed unto him against that day" (2 Tim. i. 12). Indeed, it may be questioned whether there is any knowledge so real and final as that based upon the proven assurance of faith, a postulate confirmed by experience and by that which comes forth from God to us, the divine evenient grace confirming the inner conviction—this is illumination.

Before considering the attributes of God in the light of the postulate of His Supreme Perfection, we ought perhaps to digress a little in order to consider a criticism which the Christian theist is frequently called upon to meet: that the Universe in which we live itself challenges the idea of God as the Supremely Perfect. This criticism usually has two aspects: that the Universe, being part of whatever God's general scheme of things may be, is an imperfection and limitation in which He Himself must be involved; and that the Universe, as God apparently allows it to run, leads us to doubt His power, His love, or both. In endeavouring to formulate some kind of answer it is well first of all to state that our confidence in our postulates is sufficient to leave us unshaken by arguments based on difficulties arising only from within this continuum, and that we have confidence in our postulates to carry us through realms in which reason is unable to tread with confidence, if only because we are by nature unable to deal adequately with questions with linkings outside our continuum. The following remarks must therefore not be taken as an attempt to solve all the difficulties arising from this criticism, but merely an attempt to indicate the lines giving the direction in which solution may lie:

(i) As to the existence of this Universe adversely affecting God, we emphasize that in comparison with the exoschematicity of God this Universe is completely negligible, a mere physema in the exoschema, having no effect whatsoever on the completeness and perfection of God, for whom, in comparison with all else that pertains to Him, it is as though this Universe does not exist. He both transcends it and is yet immanent in it. But He does not transcend it merely in the sense that He is greater than the Universe and that there is more of God outside the Universe than is manifested within it. That is a quite inadequate idea of transcendence. God transcends the Universe to such a degree that its existence makes absolutely no difference to Him. If, as a feeble analogy, we transferred the idea of a space-time continuum to the exoschema, we should have to say that this Universe had less than the relative significance of a point. This is only another way of saying that God is in no way limited by the Universe He has created. It takes up no more 'space' (to use an entirely misleading term) in His exoschematicity than music takes up in a room: "All time is but a fleeting wave upon Thy calm, deep sea" (Robert Dawson). Similarly, God's immanence in the Universe does not in any way obligate or implicate Him of necessity. He can pervade it and be aware of it with entire disjunction. Grasp the complementary thoughts whether we can or not, these are postulates: God is so great that the Universe is as nothing; God is so aware that its smallest detail is known to Him.

(ii) It has to be remembered that God having called the Universe into existence is the sole arbiter of its destiny and the sole ground of its continued existence. He who creates can destroy, and that which He creates only continues while He wills that it shall. There is perhaps something unreasonable as well as impious in a creature presuming to judge its creator. Whence can it derive its standards of judgment except directly or indirectly from its creator? Perhaps an adverse judgment, even if sincerely held, cannot be in any case based on anything but ignorance or misunderstanding.

(iii) Some would extend the idea in the above paragraph to the extent of saying that the continued existence of the Universe from moment to moment depends upon God's continued concern for it: if God ceased to care about it it would ipso facto cease to be. To that extent they are feeling after a truth who talk of things as "thoughts of God". If we know exactly what we mean, there is truth in saying that the Universe only exists because God "thinks" about it.

(iv) We must retain enough sense of proportion to realize that when this Universe comes to an end, as it will and must, its ending as such will not make the slightest appreciable difference to the exoschema. It will merely be equivalent to the bursting of a non-existent bubble. As Prospero said after his magic pageant,

> "Our revels now are ended. These our actors,
> As I foretold you, were all spirits and
> Are melted into air, into thin air:
> And, like the baseless fabric of this vision,
> The cloud-capp'd towers, the gorgeous palaces,
> The solemn temples, the great globe itself,
> Yea, all which it inherit, shall dissolve
> And, like this insubstantial pageant faded,
> Leave not a rack behind."

The Tempest, Act IV, Sc. 1.

How can a continuum, which is a framework for limitation, have any relevance or effect in the limitless and illimitable? The extinction of the physema would affect the exoschema less than the blowing out of a candle would affect the brightness of high noon.

(v) Not until there is humble realization of the incomprehensible greatness of God in comparison with the Universe is there likely to be a dawning realization that His creatures, owing everything and with no title for claiming or expecting anything, should contemplate with grateful wonder that He, who needs nothing, is nevertheless willing of His great condescension to enable those whom He has permitted to exist to feel the need of Him, and, Himself unneeding, to permit Himself to satisfy that need and to be to them as though He too needed them. Here again we cannot state our postulate so precisely as we might wish. The paradox of the Needless Being willing to need is only a way of saying that the condescension and the graciousness is all of God, who has nothing to gain, and the profit and indebtedness is all on the side of man, who without God would not be and without God can have no abiding purpose or hope.

(vi) No sequence can be rightly assessed until it is complete, and this must be remembered in criticizing the present Universe. We have to remember that God has purposes for us far transcending the space-time continuum. Having permitted man to be, and having designed this transient Universe as his testing stage, God has made it possible for man's spirit, having here acquired character and made choice, to enter into a relationship with Himself which shall transcend and outlast this Universe. This relationship of human spirits with God is described as union, and consists in a relationship higher than and different from the relationship of creator to created. It consists in the human spirit so identifying itself in humble and thankful dedication with God that it has no wish to will aught but what He wills and no desire to fulfil any purposes but His purposes. There is thus established a state of affairs in which the human spirit offers no impedance to God's purpose, that is, has ceased to be autocentric. Such a spirit is ready to be freed from the designification which existence in a continuum involves and can be welcomed into the exoschema. There it will joyfully accord with all that God will and will to that extent share the life of God. We must set ourselves against mechanical images of spiritual realities. But if we really cannot do without one, let it be put this way: Let God be likened to a mighty stream, the onward purpose of which demands perfect fluidity and freedom from all solid content; and let human spirits be likened to separate molecules of some solid substance, corrupted, if you will, with some insoluble impurity. If these separate molecules are to become part of the mighty stream they must (*a*) be freed from the insoluble impurity, which can never have part in the stream which must ever have perfect fluidity, (*b*) must be willing to lose their solid independence and commit themselves to the stream, (*c*) must be willing to dissolve in the stream so that they lose their isolating solidity and partake of the stream's fluidity. Nevertheless, the molecules remain as discriminable units in the greater unit of the stream. The stream indeed is not affected, for its volume and fluidity are too great to be affected by the solution in it of a few molecules more or less. Yet the molecules are one with the stream, flow with it, act with it, rejoice with it. Material and inadequate though such an analogy necessarily is, it may yet serve to indicate dimly and faintly something of the nature of the relationship of the redeemed human spirit with God: God, like a mighty stream, continues in His purpose, a purpose unaffected by the presence or absence of aught else; yet He is willing to accept into Himself spirits who shall thus become one with His purpose and movement yet still discrete units: units within a unit, spirits within God: God so great that His oneness is unaffected, for of Him they had their being; they so one with God that the only consciousness of separateness is the joy of knowing that they have become one with Him. But how can we put mysteries into words, however confident we may be of the truth underlying them? Suffice to say we shall become one with God, yet still know we are ourselves; we shall have no purpose but His, yet still know we are making that glad surrender.

(vii) However inscrutable to him the means, the Christian theist is confident that God's ways will be fully justified when it is realized whither those ways lead. Before the human spirit is set the goal of perfection, a perfection to be reached in union with God Himself, when autocentricity has surrendered itself to Theocentricity and the human spirit has integrated its idiotelicity into the Theotelic unit which is God and all His. This end is only possible of achievement because God Himself in Jesus Christ became Perfect Man in order that imperfect men might be raised to His perfection.

Still confident, then, in the Supreme Perfection of God as a cardinal postulate of our faith, we can consider the attributes which have historically been ascribed to Him without fear of becoming involved in any real difficulties. Such difficulties as arise, arise from the limitations of our forms of expression, not from the nature of God Himself. It is well to remember that no attribute ascribed to God must be interpreted otherwise than as an exemplification of His Supreme Perfection, and before we proceed it may be desirable to make three observations:

(i) We need to remember that all attributes rightly ascribed to God are ascribed by those who implicitly or explicitly recognize Him as the Supremely Perfect, and all the attributes they ascribe to Him are ascribed with the intention of adding explicitness and definition to the concept of Supreme Perfection. It should thus be clear that no attribute ascribed to God can be intended to raise difficulties or to lead by any process of reasoning to restrictions, limitations or absurdities. God's Supreme Perfection is always to be taken as antecedent to the implications of any attribute. The latter must be considered in the light of the former and not vice versa.

(ii) Attributes can only be described in terms conceptually possible to us who dwell in a space-time continuum. If they are positive terms, they can only be some faint parallel to the reality. If they are negative terms, they can only describe that which seems inappropriate to God to those whose experience is limited to this continuum. A positive term may therefore assert too little and a negative term may deny too much.

(iii) We must not think that God can be delimited by a framework of attributes. It is futile to ascribe an attribute to God because we think God is like that, and then to suppose that God must be like that because we have ascribed the attribute.

Nevertheless, we shall find that the historic attributes crystallize much valuable conviction which has been verified by experience across the centuries. That is why the rejection of a dogma is always so grave and often so foolish an act, as the reasons for it are often very subtle to disentangle, and the greater our historic sense the more cautious we become. Wisdom consists rather in endeavouring to get a little closer to the reality underlying the noetic statement.

We shall probably find that the ancient attributes may, for the purposes of our present approach, be conveniently grouped under two broad and significant headings. There are two qualities of Godhead which may include all the others: that God is exoschematic, and that God is endoharmonic. These two terms cover two complementary aspects of the Supreme Perfection: perfection in ability of being and perfection in quality of being, perfection, that is, in what are sometimes classified as the physical and the ethical attributes. All perfections of ability of being are included in the term exoschematic; all perfections of quality of being are included in the term endoharmonic. The Supreme Perfection is comprehended by the balance of these two qualities, which have always to be considered in mutual relation.

I. *God is exoschematic*

The idea to which the word 'exoschematic' endeavours to give expression has already been put forward (pp. 237–240): God cannot be subordinated to anything whatsoever; there is no schema or continuum able to contain, bind or limit Him; He has absolute power of every kind and in every realm; neither time nor space has significance for Him. We readily see that many of the traditional attributes are simply ways of expressing this one fact, that God is beyond all limitation and restriction. Hence the traditional attributes are only particular statements of some of the ways in which God is exoschematic, for it is evident that this term at least includes that God is eternal, uncreated, immortal, timeless, unchangeable (immutable), incorruptible, without needs, impassible, omnipotent, omniscient, omnipresent, invisible, incomprehensible, infinite, perfect. It is far better to endeavour (so far as is possible) to grasp these attributes as a unity, and to envisage them as partial statements intended to emphasize the Supreme Perfection of Him who is exoschematic and endoharmonic rather than to press each attribute to its logical (or illogical) conclusion. If we examine these attributes carefully we shall perceive that they all have one intention: to emphasize that God is not subject to control or restriction of any kind. This can be expressed in one sentence: God is exoschematic.

II. *God is endoharmonic*

Just as exoschematicity endeavours to convey the idea of the limitless range of God's abilities, so endoharmony endeavours to convey the idea of God's absolute perfection of quality. God within Himself possesses perfect inner harmony, because His Supreme Perfection includes the perfect interworking of every true satisfaction and the complete expression of every moral quality. Within the Godhead there is the full realization beyond anything we can conceive of the utmost ideals of love, compassion, benevolence, wisdom, mercy, and all else that we associate with perfect holiness and beauty, and all these coexist in such perfect mutual relationship that the Godhead is in perfect peace and abides in perfect satisfaction. This inner harmony of the Godhead is epitomized by saying that God is endoharmonic. Nothing that disturbs harmony can disturb God, because no such thing is in or can find entrance into Him: no sin, no ugliness, no discord, no conflict.

By taking exoschematicity and endoharmony together, as we must, we recognize their interdependence. We also recognize the line of approach to the solution of some of the difficulties which were supposed to arise from a contemplation of the attributes of God. There is no need to deal with them in detail, but a few remarks ought perhaps to be made about two of them:

(i) *Omnipotence.* The ascription of this attribute has sometimes given rise to anxiety as to its exact meaning. Without entering into pointless discussion, let it suffice to say that by interpreting it as an exemplification of exoschematicity and endoharmony we at once perceive that 'omnipotence' implies that God's power of action is not controlled or restricted by anything whatsoever other than Himself, and that He can do anything He desires to do. At the same time, the ascription of omnipotence is only an attempt to render more explicit what we already cover with the terms exoschematic and endoharmonic, and we must not let the implications of a term carry us beyond what the term is intended to convey. In particular, if it is ever argued that the idea of omnipotence can be made to lead to absurdities, the short answer is: "The fact that God can do anything does not involve that He does or would do everything." There is nothing God could not do, but there are many things we can certainly assert that He would not do, simply because He is Supremely Perfect and because He would not disturb His own endoharmony. We are definitely entitled to assert that God would not do anything which on ultimate views could be termed unjust, unloving, or capricious.

Omnipotence means that nothing in any way controls or limits God, and that His actions are able to give full expression to His endoharmony. (Nestorius is very sound on this point: see pp. 123–124.)

(*ii*) *Omniscience*. The ascription of this attribute raises similar problems to those arising from omnipotence, though they have a more practical bearing on the question of the Person of Jesus Christ and on the question of free-will. We might cut the Gordian Knot by suggesting that just as omnipotence does not necessarily mean actually doing everything, but rather the ability to do everything He wishes and deems it desirable to do, so omniscience does not necessarily mean actually knowing everything, but rather the ability to know everything He wishes and deems it desirable to know. Though we may feel that this is a parallel worth investigating, there is nevertheless felt to be a real difference between choosing not to exercise a power and choosing not to know a fact. We have to remember, moreover, that all our processes of awareness, memory and calculation are processes devised by God as suitable to our existence in a special continuum, and we have no idea what corresponds in God to our awareness, memory and calculation. But we can certainly assert that God's awareness is not limited and conditioned, as is ours, by a restricted set of senses and a material medium; nor is whatever corresponds with memory in God to be thought of as a repository of stored impressions and ideas; nor, and this is most important, does God need to 'calculate' in our sense: God knows instantly (see p. 238) what we should calculate laboriously, and knows instantly what we should not be able to calculate at all. However, we must always remember that the fundamental quality of Godhead is Supreme Perfection, expressing itself through exoschematicity and endoharmony, and we do well to remind ourselves that we must not limit God by our interpretation of the attributes which were originally ascribed to Him with the intention of expressing His illimitability. Can God choose not to know? Or can He know or not know at His own choice? Or can He ignore His own knowledge and act as though He did not know? These questions are not so much the raising of difficulties as reminders that our categories are quite inadequate for real knowledge of the inner functioning of Godhead. We can, however, without hesitation say this: there is nothing, past, present or future, which God cannot know, just as there is nothing He cannot do. The root of the problem is not so much in the paradox of omniscience, which of course includes prescience, in balance against man's supposed freedom of will, but in our total ignorance of the meaning of awareness in the Godhead. The relation of divine omniscience to human free-will does not here concern us. Its relation to knowledge in Jesus Christ will have to be considered in our next chapter.

We must now outline a more precise use of terms. 'The totality of Godhead' implies everything that is God. It is a term of a significance entirely beyond our comprehension. It may be preferable to keep the word 'Godhead' for this meaning, so that by 'Godhead' we mean the totality of that which is God. 'God' simpliciter, on the other hand, is used in a number of ways, between which it is not easy to distinguish. Perhaps most of the usages would be included if we said that 'God' was a word used to indicate our concept of the essence, nature and activity of the Godhead, especially when emphasis was upon nature and activity rather than upon totality. Any direct or indirect manifestation of the nature, purpose, will, love or grace of the Godhead is 'God', equally 'God', for the Godhead is indiscriminable in quality, though not in function. It is very important that this distinction in idea should be borne carefully in mind, whether the exact allocation of the terms is acceptable or not. Every theophany is truly God, every direct manifestation of the Godhead is God. But a theophany is not Godhead in the sense of 'the totality of all that is God'. To anticipate, we shall maintain that Jesus Christ is God, and that Jesus Christ is of the Godhead. To say that Jesus Christ is God means that in Jesus Christ the essence nature and activity of the Godhead is directly manifested. To say that Jesus Christ is of the Godhead means that Jesus Christ is a manifestation of the totality of all that is God, though that totality exceeds the manifestation, not indeed in essence or in nature, but in totality of harmonic function, both immanent and transcendent. The terms should seldom be capable of misapprehension if used in this way. 'Godhead' will always mean 'the totality of that which is God', and 'God' will always mean the divine essence and nature, whether thought of generally or as particularly manifested. Any manifestation of the Godhead is equally God, and anything we can properly name 'God' is a manifestation of the nature and purpose of the Godhead.

We must now consider the terms to be used with regard to the Trinity, and their bearing upon the question of three Persons being nevertheless a real One. We have already discussed with some care (pp. 127–141) an interpretation of the Trinity in the ancient terms, and it may be doubted whether we can get much further, except perhaps by endeavouring to relate the ancient terms to more modern categories; for this is a matter in which we are wise to recognize our inability, and all we can hope to do is to formulate some dim idea as to how the things we assuredly believe can actually be as we believe them to be. Hodgson, in *The Doctrine of the Trinity*, gives a timely warning as to the limits of philosophical speculation in this matter: "The doctrine of the Trinity is thus an inference to the nature of God drawn from what we believe to be the empirical evidence given by God in His revelation of Himself in the history of this world. I have argued that this evidence, as viewed from within the fellowship of the Christian Church, requires us to believe in a God whose unity unifies three activities each of which is made known to us as a distinct Person in the full sense of that word. . . . Where we cannot reconcile the deliverances of empirical evidence with the demands of logical consistency, it is better to maintain an attitude of suspended judgment as to the mode of reconciliation than to distort or explain away the evidence in order to procure an immediate result. I therefore make no apology for the fact that in this would-be philosophical lecture I can say no more about the nature of the divine unity beyond what I have already said. I have attempted to show that the idea of what I have called an internally constitutive unity is not repugnant to reason; I have called attention to certain idealist arguments which encourage us to believe that in God both the Unity and its Constituents may be personal; and I have pointed out that it is generally characteristic of our earthly experience to know the ultimate unities not in their unity but in their multiplicity. There I must let the matter rest" (op. cit., pp. 140–141).

We may, however, make a few additional observations:

(i) The totality of Godhead contains within Itself[1] every perfection, is independent of all restriction or control (is exoschematic), and is in a state of perfect inner harmony and bliss (is endoharmonic).

(ii) The totality of Godhead is a unity, which means that there is no divergence of purpose within Itself, and that It possesses complete and unbroken self-awareness. Any revelation or manifestation of Godhead is equally 'God', for there are no qualitative distinctions within the Godhead.

(iii) The Godhead nevertheless, perhaps in realization of Its endoharmony, maintains, both within Itself and in relation to all else, a threefold simultaneous functionalization, so that there is always being expressed, both within Itself and in Its outer relations, those attitudes and functionings which make Godhead Itself endoharmonic and maintain It in perfectly just, merciful, loving and gracious relationship with all else. We can only quote again from p. 130: "Thus there is always in the Godhead creative and sustaining impulse; there is always the urge to bring into willing harmony with Himself[2] that to which He has given volition; there is always a surging forth of Himself in aiding power to those who will respond thereto. These phases of the divine nature are not successive: they co-exist." Within

---

[1] For footnote, see p. 355.

[2] It is significant that in interpreting Nestorius we did not feel the need to make such a careful distinction between the suprapersonal unity of the totality of Godhead and the individuation of the Persons. In the Nestorian terms, it was sufficient to recognize one ousia and nature of Godhead and three simultaneously existent phases of that ousia, each phase being a prosôpon or hypostasis, using both those words in the special Trinitarian sense. There was thus little difficulty in using 'He' in reference to the ousia or to a prosôpon. But with our endeavour to obtain more exact ideas as to personality and individuality it is necessary to recognize a distinction between the focus of personality manifested in Jesus Christ and the suprapersonal totality and unity of which that focus was a manifestation and revelation.

the Godhead, we can only suppose that these three simultaneous phases exist eternally and by their perfect harmony and balance account for the needlessness and endoharmony of the Godhead. In outer relations, we may usually correctly identify the phase of Godhead which is relevant to the circumstance or the need. It is not that God manifests Himself capriciously or fortuitously now as Father, now as Word, now as Holy Spirit; rather is it thus: God, in external relation, being One and perfect, reacts in all circumstances with complete appropriateness (which includes supreme wisdom and love), and it will therefore inevitably come about that certain external relations will fall naturally into accord with one phase of the divine being and others will fall into accord with some other phase of the divine being. There is thus both irrelevance and relevance in ascribing 'Person' to God in His dealings with other things or with ourselves. It is in any case God simpliciter, God and none else, and God will deal with every circumstance and person as His perfect nature deems right. We cannot, that is, 'choose' to deal with God the Father, God the Word, or God the Holy Spirit. We deal with God, and He deals with us as the circumstances indicate. He may appropriately react creatively, enharmonizingly, or energizingly. It is one and the same God, though we may characterize those respective appropriate responses as those of God the Father, God the Word, or God the Holy Spirit. The phases are distinct in complementary function, but they are phases of a One. There is no appeal from one to the other: God the Word is in perfect accord with God the Father, for God the Word and God the Father are One simultaneously expressing Itself according to the perfection of Its nature (John x. 30). However we attempt to clarify and crystallize our ideas, we shall probably not get anything more parallel with the reality than to recognize that Godhead is one ousia with one nature, revealing Itself in three simultaneously existent and mutually self-infolding phases which we may call hypostases or 'Persons'. We may refer again to Fulton's excellent summary quoted in the note on p. 147.

Our consideration of the Trinity brings us to the two aspects of the divine nature which are of most direct

Y

significance to us: the divine endoharmony, and the divine love. We have seen that God alone is endoharmonic. In Him is perfect self-accord, perfect peace, perfect satisfaction, perfect love. In God alone, therefore, is there possible a final centricity. God alone is satisfied centred in Himself, for in Himself is all perfection and all satisfaction. Integration and centricity find climax and finality in Him. Whatever is, according to its possibilities, integrated into God, and consequently has transferred its centricity to God, has thereby attained its highest condition. There is no higher state than integration into God (union with God) and centricity in God (Theocentricity); and herein lies the wonder of the divine nature: God, Himself endoharmonic, is yet willing of His love and grace to receive into union with Himself those who in that way and in that way only can find their complete fulfilment. We thus see human life as a sending forth by God into inanimate creation of that which, given the power of choice, by choosing to accept that grace which alone will enable it to return again in willing union to God can establish by that willing return a loving bond of union which could not have been brought into existence in any other way. The grand consummation of human life is integration into the divine unity, a sacrifice of autocentricity into the highest of all allocentricities and that which alone is finally satisfying—Theocentricity—and finally satisfying because God alone has that which gives final satisfaction—endoharmony. None but God is endoharmonic.

The abiding and central marvel is God's perfect love. It is this which accounts for His endoharmony, and it is this which expresses itself in His willingness to seek and to save. As Otto so fittingly phrases it, "The real Christian God, whom neither theism nor any other religion whatsoever conceives in the same way, is the seeking God, i.e. the God who seeks the lost. He is the God who does not wait upon righteousness but, with seeking and pardoning love, takes the initiative; who does not thrust the lost one deeper into his lost state, but seeks him out in his lost state in order to save him; who does not wait for love in order to pardon for its sake, but pardons in order through love to produce love" (*The Kingdom of God and the Son of Man*, English translation, pp. 393–394). How God came forth to seek and to save is the theme of our next chapter.

Footnote 1, p. 352: It is difficult to decide what pronoun to use in referring to the totality of Godhead, to the Trinity. How can we use 'He', when 'He' is used of each Person? It is correct to refer to any particular manifestation, any particularized focus of self-manifestation of the Godhead, as 'He', because any such manifestation, being functional, is necessarily expressive of Godhead as manifesting through a Person. 'God' simpliciter is 'He', because when we use the term 'God' we almost inevitably think of God as manifesting or expressing Himself, and that must always be in Person. But the concept of the totality of Godhead, of the Trinity as a comprehensive totality, is very different. To think of the totality of Godhead, the Trinity, as 'He' suggests Sabellianism, and to think of the same concepts as 'Them' is tritheism. With hesitation and diffidence I therefore suggest 'It', emphasizing that the use of the initial capital is intended entirely to discriminate such usage from the usage of 'it'. 'It' refers to the incomprehensible suprapersonal totality of Godhead, the Trinity in toto, which is a unity of a kind which precludes the use of 'Them' and is yet, containing three Persons each of whom is correctly 'He', seen to require, for distinction, some pronoun other than 'He'. The initial capital in our use of 'It' must be continually recognized as the symbol of a very special usage. However, if anyone scruples at this usage, let him by all means substitute 'He', though in that case he must remember that 'He' as applied to the totality of Godhead must be of very different significance from 'He' as applied to each of the Persons.

This may be the appropriate point for the following remarks: If the ancients are to be criticized for their inadequate concepts of personality and individuality, it may well be that we are in danger of applying our more exact ideas of personality in an undue manner to the problems of Godhead and Trinity. We are inclined to consider that personality consists essentially in a continuing unified centre of awareness, judgment, and appreciation of value. So indeed it may, and a perfect continuing centre of that kind might be a perfect personality according to our ideas. Jesus Christ, whom we believe to have been such a perfect continuing centre during His earthly life, would therefore be the perfect personality in that sense. But when we consider the extension of the continuity of Jesus Christ, as God the Word, backwards and forwards from His earthly life, we should at once see the inadequacy of our idea of personality when applied to His Person. There are 'stops' in our mind on account of our nature and our existence in this continuum, and it may be suggested that our idea of personality is inevitably too tinged with autocentricity, idiotelicity, and unification of focus. But all these things are imperfections and limitations, for the ideal personality will be Theocentric, in the Theotelic unity, and a focus of awareness within that greater unity. Jesus Christ alone fulfilled these conditions, and was therefore the only perfect personality the world has known. The Persons within the Trinity, therefore, must be thought of as differing from our idea of 'persons' in that they are one in their centricity, each not being autocentric; they are one in telicity, each not being idiotelic; and the omniawareness of the Godhead involves many foci of awareness, not merely one or three. Yet the many foci constitute one omniawareness. Thus our ideas of personality tend to make us individualize the Persons of the Trinity unduly, just as our unification of focus makes it difficult for us to comprehend a multifocal unity. We thus need to be very circumspect in using the word 'Persons' of the three members of the Trinity, just as we need to be very aware of what we mean when we describe the totality of Godhead as suprapersonal. It is therefore important to keep these distinctions in mind when using 'He' of a Person of the Trinity, and still more important to realize that the omni-awareness of the totality of Godhead, a multiplicity of foci of awareness in one unity, is something entirely outside our experience or our ability to conceive. To use 'He' in such a case seems illogical and misleading, and I feel that a reverently applied 'It' has to meet the case, an 'It' not of less content than 'He', but of vastly more.

CHAPTER VI

THE INCARNATION

"God was in Christ, reconciling the world unto himself."
2 COR. v. 19.

JUST as the first consideration in attempting to answer the question "What is man?" is teleological, so also is it in seeking to understand the meaning and method of the Incarnation and the nature of the Person of Jesus Christ. Why was the Incarnation necessary, and why did God will to become man? A brief answer will surely be in terms such as these: God, of His gracious condescension willing to offer every assistance to the sentient beings whom He had caused to be and to whom He had given the opportunity of eventually achieving oneness with Himself, for reasons not entirely within our comprehension but accepted by us as undoubtedly needful, resolved Himself to become man, to dwell and experience as a man among men, and Himself as man to die for man's redemption and salvation.

On this statement several preliminary observations may be made:

(1) The Incarnation consisted in God becoming man, not in man becoming God, nor in God and man in some way combining. The glory and wonder of the Incarnation does not consist in a man being elevated and accepted into Godhead nor in a man becoming in some unique way united with Godhead; the glory and wonder of the Incarnation consists in God condescending to become man, in that thus it pleased Him to reconcile mankind unto Himself. Having stated this, we may nevertheless recognize the proportion of truth in the antitheses which some have always found attractive: that in Jesus Christ there was a movement of man Godwards as well as of God manwards; that He was perfect man as well as true God; that in Him Godhead and manhood met in perfect union. These statements are true, but we must appreciate what makes them true: that in Jesus Christ God, having assumed humanity and made possible

the perfect man, was leading Godwards the manhood He Himself had assumed; that He was perfect man because He Himself perfected man; that the perfect union of Godhead and manhood depended only on the gracious acceptance into Himself of manhood which He Himself was perfecting. We must definitely state that these antitheses must not be understood as though they envisaged an equal partnership and reciprocation between Godhead and manhood, between God going forth as Christ and man coming forth as Jesus, and the two somehow becoming the God-man Jesus Christ. The Incarnation consisted in God becoming man, not in man becoming God, nor in God and man in some way combining.

(2) God Incarnate—Jesus Christ—is thus in the continuity of Godhead, and in particular is the continuity of Godhead in the Person distinguished as God the Word. From eternity to eternity is God the Word, and during the space-temporal existence of Jesus Christ God the Word manifested Himself in no other way than as Jesus Christ, and Jesus Christ was none other than God the Word manifested as man.

(3) The ancient postulates, that Jesus Christ must be God, man, and one, may be preliminarily[1] explicated thus:

(a) Jesus Christ is certainly God, by which we mean that God thus revealed Himself in the way most fully possible to beings in the present space-time continuum, and that from Jesus Christ we believe that we receive the fullest revelation of God's nature and purpose, that His words are words of fully divine authority. In all matters the words of Jesus Christ are a revelation of the love and wisdom of God, and in all matters His words are infallible. In no way was He isolated from the continuity and unity of Godhead, and if in any particular matter, for the sake of consistency in His humanity, there were facts of which He appeared to choose not to be aware, the willingness to submit Himself to the consequences of the Incarnation was of His own volition entirely, and He could instantly have negatived

[1] The complex of ideas to be expounded in this chapter is of such a nature that it is requested that the complex be grasped as a whole before criticism is made of any part. Some of the parts cannot rightly be judged unless they are understood and interpreted in the light of the complex as a whole.

the apparent unawareness by a mere lifting of the self-imposed inhibitions. The obvious difficulties arising from this statement will be considered later. Further, no such apparent unawareness in any way affected His essential judgments or pronouncements: His outlook and judgment in all matters were those of omnipotent and omniscient Godhead, even though for the fulfilment of His purposes He had voluntarily and temporarily circumscribed the effective operation of His omnipotence and omniscience: just as omnipotence, rightly and intelligently understood, is seen to mean not necessarily actually doing everything but the power to do or not do anything, so omniscience, rightly and intelligently understood, may equally mean not actually at every moment being effectively aware of everything past, present and future, but the ability so to know and the power to utilize or to ignore what is known at His own but at no other will. The very real difficulties arising from this statement will also be considered later. It is thus abundantly true for us, as for the first disciples, that Jesus Christ has, in Bishop Gore's apt phrase, "the values of God".[1] Of anything which Jesus Christ said we may truly say: "God has spoken." In every relevant sense Jesus Christ is God: "For in him dwelleth all the fulness of the Godhead bodily" (Col. ii. 9). It may be necessary to supply an answer to an anticipated question: Was Jesus Christ totally God and nothing but God? The following two points are relevant:

(i) The totality of Godhead is incomprehensible to those living in a restricted continuum, and in Jesus Christ God was revealing Himself as fully as the circumstances permitted. Jesus Christ was the fullest possible revelation of the nature and purpose of the Godhead that could be made to beings living in this continuum. Jesus Christ was not the totality of Godhead—how indeed could it be conceived that the totality of Godhead should restrict Itself to bodily form?—but was a perfect and complete revelation of the nature and purpose of God. Anyone seeing Jesus Christ could truly say: "This

[1] *Belief in Christ*, p. 68.

is God in bodily form. Godhead in Its totality transcends my comprehension, but this is Godhead revealing Itself to me as fully as I can comprehend."

(ii) Since God is invisible, illimitable and impassible, it should be evident that Jesus Christ cannot be "God and nothing else". "No man hath seen God at any time", and the fact that Jesus Christ appeared in form as a man is sufficient evidence that He was not God in His essence without intermediation. God, who is exoschematic, condescended to reveal Himself in a particular schema, the space-time continuum in which we exist. To do so He necessarily used an instrument which could establish contact on the appropriate terms with that continuum and those living in it, and the instrument He chose was the body of Jesus Christ.[1] It is true to say that the body of Jesus Christ was God's body, and, in the sense of total revelation, to look at Jesus Christ and say: "This is God." But it must ever be remembered that the actual body per se is an element in the continuum, and therefore of the continuum and not of the eternity, illimitability and impassibility of Godhead. There were nevertheless linkages of a very special kind between God and the body, which will be considered later.

(*b*) A similarly reasonable interpretation must be applied to the statement "Jesus Christ is man". Jesus Christ is indeed truly man, in that He experienced this world through a body in touch with it in exactly the same way as are the bodies of ordinary men, and in that He submitted Himself to the restrictions of our continuum. If it be said, "But Jesus Christ cannot be an ordinary man, for is He not also God?", the answer is: "Jesus Christ is certainly not an ordinary man. It is maintained that He was truly man, indeed perfect man, the only perfect man who ever existed." The implications of these remarks will emerge later.

(*c*) The unity of Jesus Christ will not present difficulties so long as it is remembered that the continuity is that of

[1] Without further qualification or explanation this sentence may seem to suggest Apollinarianism. Qualifications and explanations will follow later, but the present point is to emphasize the functional significance of the human body of Jesus Christ.

God the Word. God the Word became man—in a way to be considered later—and there was never any 'man Jesus' apart from God the Word's sojourn in this continuum as the man Jesus Christ.

With these preliminary remarks we now pass on to examine, parallel with our examination in the case of man (*vide* pp. 305–336), the birth, life and death of Jesus Christ.

I. The integration of Jesus Christ

When God the Word willed to become man, He willed to become man in such a way that He should know what it was to be in the 'nature' of man, so that the body He assumed might be no mere vehicle for His self-revelation to those in this continuum, but a body to which He would voluntarily restrict Himself and whose limitations He would endure, just as ordinary men are restricted to their bodies and endure their limitations. He therefore became Incarnate in a manner the general principles of which must have been somewhat as follows:

(1) God chose from amongst the women of the Hebrews one of the line of David whom He knew to be suitable to be the mother of His humanity, though we shall see that that phrase is itself inadequate. The Blessed Virgin Mary was His mother just as truly and just as fully as any woman is the mother of her child. As we have seen, there is a very real sense in which no parent is more than a steward of the mysteries of God, and parenthood is one of the ways in which the successive generations are linked "in bonds of sweet necessity", for the body is formed by a natural (biotic) integration for which we merely provide the conditions, and the spirit is the gift of God. We are but the agents of God in making the adventure and opportunity of life possible to another spirit experiencing as man. Nevertheless, great must ever be our respect and veneration for the Blessed Virgin Mary, whom God chose for this preeminent part in the divine scheme: "Blessed art thou among women, . . . the mother of my Lord" (Luke i. 42–43).

(2) Having chosen the Blessed Virgin Mary, at the appointed time there took place the third act of divine

generation of humanity. The first act of divine generation of humanity was the generation by God of our first ancestors, however and whenever that took place. The second act of divine generation of humanity was the provision for biparental reproduction with the concomitant gift of each new spirit which has been the regular method for all men and women since our first parents. But let it here be noted that method of generation is no criterion of being man. If God caused a full-grown man to appear—as He easily could[1]—full-grown and mature, such a person would be really and truly a man, even though he had not originated in the usual manner (cf. pp. 71–72, 84–86); and on any view it seems inescapable that our first parents became truly man (and woman) by a means other than biparental reproduction from parents of the same type. The third act of divine generation of humanity must be described with all reverence but with necessary detail:

The Blessed Virgin Mary contributed to Him who was to be born all that any mother can contribute to her child: that is to say, the human ovum and her participation, in this case exercised by humble submission,[2] in enabling a new spirit to come into existence. From the father, ordinarily, comes the spermatozoon and his participation by the act of fatherhood in enabling a new spirit to come into existence.

It may be well to consider body and spirit separately:

(i) As to the body, the normal mode of formation in bisexual reproduction has been outlined in pp. 289–292 above, and it has been seen that the zygote arises from a union of gametes, the genes of which contribute the unit-characters of the zygote, each new duplex gene arising from the integration of two halves, one half from each corresponding duplex gene in the chromosomes of the integrating gametes. We have seen some of the reasons for this. But even in cases where bisexual reproduction is the usual method, cases of parthenogenesis are not unknown, a

---

[1] "And think not to say within yourselves, We have Abraham to our father: for I say unto you, that God is able of these stones to raise up children unto Abraham" (Matt. iii. 9).

[2] "And Mary said, Behold the handmaid of the Lord; be it unto me according to thy word" (Luke i. 38).

suitable stimulus serving to set the ovum on a course of development which normally would only follow its integration with a spermatozoon. In such cases the zygote may be perfectly normal, though obviously its unit-characters have to derive from the genes of the one gamete, the ovum. This fact is of real theological and religious significance. Reverence somehow prefers to contemplate the sufficiency of a divine stimulus to start the development of our Saviour's physical frame, rather than the provision of the equivalent of a spermatozoon. Moreover, it follows that the body of Jesus Christ was formed entirely from human material, all of it deriving through the Blessed Virgin Mary. His body was as human as are our bodies, though it may have borne a striking resemblance in physical character to that of His mother, though not more so than is frequently the case when a son is born to a mother whose genes are markedly dominant to those of the father. ('Dominance' in genes, of course, has nothing whatever to do with dominance in general character or personality.) The Blessed Virgin Mary was thus in a very distinctive sense the mother of His humanity so far as the body was concerned.[1]

(ii) As to the spirit, we have expounded our belief that in the ordinary way God creates and infuses a new human spirit into each newly integrated human zygote, that concomitantly with the union of the gametes God adds the spirit. We have also seen that this act of God is made contingent on the function of parenthood, human parents by their act setting in train the biotic integration of a new body into which God infuses a new spirit. After this infusion the zygote or embryo is an integrated unit, body, centrum vitæ and spirit being naturally integrated, and so remaining until its disintegration at death. Now in the integration of Jesus Christ we have constantly to remember the teleological aspect: the integration of Jesus Christ took place in order that the Word might become flesh and dwell among us. If the Word was to become truly man, His integration in Jesus Christ must include a truly human spirit as well as a truly human body. We have already seen that there is no

[1] Those interested may find further information bearing on this point in Barnes, *Scientific Theory and Religion*, pp. 451–452, 457–458.

doubt as to the true humanity of His body; but can we understand how Jesus Christ could have been God the Word and yet truly be said to possess a human spirit?

Let us consider the following points:

(a) When God caused the first human spirits to be, He created them in a different way from the way in which He created all else in this continuum. He did not just cause them to come into existence at a predetermined place in the physema; He created them by means of a directly emittent action from Himself (Gen. ii. 7), yet so as not to lose from Himself nor yet to cause the spirits to be in any way Himself. It came, however, as near to those prohibited categories as we can conceive. We can truly say that the spirit derives from God in a very different way from that in which we can say that matter derives from God. Matter arose by *fiat*: spirit by *empneusis*.

(b) The difference between creation by fiat and creation by empneusis distinguishes matter from human spirit, and suggests a distinction prior to the act of creation: in causing the physema and the protocumata within it, God was exercising whatever corresponds within the divine nature to power and thought; but in creating the first human spirit God was sending forth into the space-time continuum a focus of sentience which would, on a smaller and more restricted scale, appreciate and find satisfaction in that which constitutes the endoharmony of God Himself, would appreciate and find satisfaction in all that we include in the concepts of truth and beauty and holiness.

(c) That which God causes to be must first[1] come into ideal existence in whatever corresponds in Him with mind, and subsequently[1] comes into existence apart from Himself as where and how He plans[2] and intends. Prior,[1] therefore, to the creation of a human spirit there must have been within God a precise concept of the powers, appreciations and capacities deemed by Him suitable to a spirit intended to gain experience in this continuum.

[1] It is difficult to avoid the use of space-temporal terms when referring to God and the exoschema; but we must always remember that it is an improper use only justified by our complete inability to think in other terms.
[2] This word is used with implied qualifications similar to those applicable to 'calculate' when used of God. See p. 238.

(*d*) Having formed this precise concept, God in effect dismitted it from Himself into the first man, though we must not use quite that phraseology. To be more exact, we must say that God caused the concept to actualize itself and integrate into the first man in such a way that it integrated into that first man not as if it had come into existence at that point by fiat, but as if it had come from God by empneusis. It indeed had, if we can realize that empneusis represented no loss from God and did not make the spirit in any way 'God' or part of God. The concept was dismitted as an idea simultaneously with the realization of the concept in actuality in the physema.

(*e*) It is therefore clear that God could very readily set apart within Himself, could particularize within Himself, what we can only call an 'area'[1] of function and appreciation exactly corresponding with the nature and extent of function and appreciation pertaining to a human spirit: God could set aside such an area which, being dismitted in the sense explained in paragraph (*d*) above, would constitute a spirit suitable for a human body.

(*f*) It is extraordinarily difficult to convey spiritual ideas except in material images, but it is earnestly desired that the images be resolutely interpreted in a non-mechanical manner. With that reservation we may picture the inception of the spirit of Jesus Christ thus: God the Word, having set apart within Himself an area of function and appreciation which, had it been dismitted from Him (in the sense explained above) would have given rise to a human spirit, instead of so dismitting this area, resolved that while still within Himself it should be infused as the spirit into the zygote formed parthenogenetically in the Blessed Virgin Mary; and that this area still within Himself should nevertheless be integrated into that zygote in exactly the same way (subject to the qualifications given in the next section) that the spirit would be integrated in an ordinary case.

It is to be noted:

(α) The difficulties in which we become involved in endeavouring to envisage how an 'area' can remain 'in'

[1] See note 1 on the preceding page.

God the Word and yet still be integrable with a body
arise from the limitations of our space-time minds. 'In'
of this 'area' is not a spatial concept, and we must dismiss
from our minds any idea that the internal or external
relationships of the Godhead are in any way affected by
the incidental conditions of this or of any other schema.
God is exoschematic, and His relationships are not limited
or controlled by anything other than Himself. Thus the
discrete area set apart within God the Word as an area
exactly corresponding to the range of function and appreciation of a perfect human spirit remained truly part of,
truly 'in', Himself, and at the same time was capable of
integrating into a human body.

(β) This area which God the Word thus established
within Himself was in effect an area equivalent to perfect
human spirit within Himself. This area comprised exactly
what the hypostasis (in the literal sense) of a human spirit
would comprise, and as it nevertheless remained entirely
within the hypostasis (in the Trinitarian sense) of God
the Word, we may usefully call it a potential hypostasis.

There are two possibilities:

(א) The potential hypostasis might (as it in fact did)
remain for ever within God the Word. It would thus
never have come into existence as the hypostasis of a
distinct and separate being; it was a potential hypostasis
within and never separate from the hypostasis of God the
Word. We may call it the human endohypostasis within
God the Word.

(ב) God the Word might have performed an action
equivalent to the dismission of this area equivalent to a
perfect human spirit from Himself; not that there could
be an actual dismission, for it is not possible to subtract
from the essence of the Godhead; but that simultaneously
with the departicularization of the area within God the
Word, so that there was no longer within Him the
potential hypostasis as a discrete area (though all its potentialities would of course still be within Him), there should
have been caused by Him to arise a human spirit with
precisely corresponding characteristics. It is indeed thus

that we picture the creation of the first human spirit: the actualization apart from Himself of that which within Himself He had contemplated as an adequacy of appreciations and abilities for the formation of a sentient being able to respond to and seek harmony with Himself. But once God the Word had particularized such an area with the intention of thereby making possible His Incarnation, any such dismission (i.e. simultaneous departicularization and external creation) would have been equivalent to a failure in His chosen purpose, would have been equivalent to what in the first part of this work we called schizo-hypostasia (cf. pp. 160–161). We cannot imagine such a thing happening; it is counter to all our ideas and impressions of God's nature. But, as said earlier, it is sometimes necessary and illuminating to consider theoretical possibilities which we are absolutely confident could never eventuate. God the Word retained, and we dare think still retains, His human endohypostasis within His own hypostasis; and though eradication and dismission would have been possible to Him, we are confident that in no circumstances would He have exercised those powers.

The human endohypostasis having been established within God the Word in some such way as set out above, God the Word had thus particularized within Himself an area of function and appreciation corresponding exactly to the totality of function and appreciation pertaining to a perfect human spirit. If and while God the Word particularized His awareness to that area He would be availing Himself of a means whereby He could appreciate and if He so desired exercise exactly the powers and no more than the powers exercisable by a human spirit. It is as though a king had set apart within his palace a suite of rooms furnished and equipped exactly like the living quarters of one of his peasants. If the king chose to go into that suite and remain there for a short or long period, while there he would appreciate exactly how a peasant lived and, if he so wished, could restrict himself to the peasant's chairs, cooking utensils, books and other properties, not making use of anything other than that of which a peasant could make use.

(g) It must be pointed out that the word 'integration' used in the above section in reference to the integration of the human endohypostasis of God the Word with the developing human zygote has to be understood with due reference to the nature of Godhead as compared with the nature of all things else. God is omnipotent, and can do what He wishes, and He is not to be debarred from undergoing any experience He wishes; God can therefore enter into what would be for anything else a natural union. But, if He does so, there is one most significant qualification: although the union may be one which would be natural (and therefore inescapable) for anything but God, for God this is not so, and He could depart from it at His own wish; for natural unions are in accordance with God's devising and intention, and God cannot be of necessity restricted by that which He Himself has chosen to impose. In the case of God, and of God only, a natural union is therefore also and inevitably a voluntary union. Subject to this, we assert that God the Word integrated 'naturally' the area within Himself equivalent to a human spirit, the human endohypostasis within Himself, with the embryo which He had caused to begin to develop parthenogenetically within the Blessed Virgin Mary. Thus God the Word, through a particularized area within Himself which He had made equivalent to the function and appreciation of a perfect human spirit, had voluntarily linked to Himself and adopted to Himself by those ties which would have held it to an ordinary human spirit, a gamete which by a special stimulus He had started on the course of its development into a human body. Thus voluntarily He committed Himself to the equivalent of natural union with that developing body. Further, he decided that so long as the union between that developing body and an ordinary human spirit would have lasted, so long would He remain voluntarily united with it: He would accept voluntarily that which in any other case would have been inevitably accepted naturally (i.e. inescapably); and further, He decided that so long as that union persisted, He would use no other focus of awareness but that going forth from His own being into and through the area set apart within Himself as equivalent to a perfect human spirit and through that area into and through the body which He had accepted. To put it in inadequate imagery, He would only "look out" through that human body; or He would only use that part of His "palace"; or He would only use that equipment and resource. We may not so much like to call this a kenosis as a voluntary self-restriction. This we shall discuss on pp. 379–393. We thus conclude that from the conception *in utero Virginis* God the Word chose not to express or reveal Himself except through the body which He had adopted, with which He had united Himself; and that in expressing or revealing Himself through that body He would observe and restrict Himself not simply to the limitations of that body as such, but also to the powers of function and appreciation which He had particularized within Himself as equivalent to that of perfect human spirit.

(*h*) It may now be desirable to be reminded of the two significant linkings:

(α) God the Word is ever of the Godhead, indistinguishable in ousia and nature from all else that is God, yet ever the hypostasis of seeking love ever existing within the Godhead for Its endoharmony and ever functioning from the Godhead as Its evenient love. This essential oneness could not be broken by anything whatsoever, and never has been or can be broken. From eternity to eternity God the Word is God, is of the Godhead, is of the divine essence and nature.

(β) God the Word, united indeed voluntarily but in a way which for any other would have been naturally with a human body, had chosen to remain so linked for the natural duration of that body, and to use it alone as the means of His self-revelation and self-expression, in such wise that during the duration of that body through it and it alone would God the Word be known *ab extra*, though still *ab intra* retaining the unbroken endoharmony of the Trinity. While the body formed from the Blessed Virgin Mary existed, God the Word would not be known otherwise *ab extra* than as Jesus Christ, and Jesus Christ was God the Word in the flesh: nay more, as already expounded, God the Word become man.

z

(*i*) Here we may interpolate a paragraph on *Theotokos*. The ancient questionings concerning this word can surely here find an answer. The Blessed Virgin Mary most decidedly contributed to Jesus Christ all—no more and no less—than any mother contributes to the new life that comes into being in and through her. She was therefore mother of Jesus Christ as truly as Sarah was mother of Isaac. Further, as Jesus Christ was God the Word and none other, the Blessed Virgin Mary was certainly mother of God the Word, and as God the Word is God, the Blessed Virgin Mary was Mother of God. The Blessed Virgin Mary was *Theotokos*, *Deipara*, Bearer of God, nor need we scruple at the phrase *Mater Dei*, Mother of God. As in all these matters, it is only important that we should know exactly what and how much is meant,[1] and that we should use the terms with knowledge and reverence. The possible abuses of the term 'Mother of God' are too obvious to need mention. Sufficient to remark that motherhood implies neither creation nor equality. To recapitulate, then, the Blessed Virgin Mary contributed to Him who was to be born all that a woman can contribute to any child of hers. She was Jesus Christ's mother as truly as any mother is mother of any child.

(*j*) We must now examine the nature of that which had thus been formed: In what sense had the newly integrated embryonic babe a human spirit?

Not in any easy but misleading mechanical interpretation of what has been said above, but by endeavouring to grasp the meaning of the underlying symbols, we may begin dimly to perceive the tremendous truth felt after in the enhypostasia concept. God, from whom the potentiality of the human spirit derived, quite evidently contains within Himself the fulness and perfection of anything which He causes to be manifest—the Creator transcends His creation in total, in general, and in particular. There is therefore nothing in a human spirit at its most ideal and perfect other than what was designed by God to be its highest possible state: God knows exactly what the perfect human spirit should be, and could quite readily realize within Himself the appropriate circuits of appreciations and responses. God

[1] Cf. pp. 450–451.

the Word, that is, could very easily condition Himself to appreciate the reactions which would come to Him through a body in this continuum and, having Himself devised the appreciations and responses suitable to an ideal human spirit, would be able to know what human life was like. Thus we readily conceive that a human body could be made the medium of experience of God the Word, who, having caused the human spirit to be, is not less than His creation, but could if He so wished experience in the way it has to experience. This, of course, is Apollinarianism, which is neither unreasonable nor impossible, though it was not actually the mode of the Incarnation, because it would not have been adequate to the purposes which God had in view. For God the Word in fact did much more than this. He did not simply become, with part or a function of Himself, the competent indweller of a body. He chose instead to integrate Himself, in the sense carefully explained above, into a complex precisely similar to that into which each of us is integrated, the complex of body, centrum vitæ and spirit which is one system, one unit, unified by the bonds of natural unification, bonds from which we cannot escape and from which He would not. Further, the human spirit of Jesus Christ was a real functional entity, in that God the Word had set apart a focal centre within Himself which should constitute exactly and no more the appreciations and responses characteristic of a human spirit, and a mere act of will and disjunction on the part of God the Word would have enabled the human spirit so generated to become a separate existence. But God the Word did not so wish or disjoin. He kept what could have been a separate spirit still part of Himself, yet aware that He had set apart a focus within Himself which could fulfil the functions of perfect human spirit: God, from whom human spirit arose, Himself as God the Word prepared to experience as that which He had caused to be experienced, and linked Himself thus with a human body.

We may note incidentally how precisely the Gospel ascribes the appropriate functions of Godhead to each Person of the Trinity: "The Holy Ghost shall come upon thee, and the power of the Highest shall overshadow thee"

(Luke i. 35). Although Godhead in evenient love functions as and is the Person God the Word, Godhead as operating power in and through humanity functions as and is the Person God the Holy Ghost. We therefore correctly understand that both from the point of view of His endoharmony and of His appropriateness of function God initiated as Holy Ghost His integration into humanity as Word.

We thus have four elements, God the Word, the human spirit, the centrum vitæ, and the body. It is most important that we should recognize the nature of their integration, so that we may see whether they really constitute one Jesus Christ, a true unity, one Person.

The elements in Jesus Christ and their unity:

(1) *Was Jesus Christ truly God?*

Most certainly. The Godhead, whose self-manifestation and self-revelation at any time and in any manner is truly 'God', though the self-manifestation and self-revelation vary according to the circumstances and His intention, was revealing Himself in Jesus Christ in a full and true manner, not, as in a prophet, by a general direction and inspiration (the special function of the Person of the Godhead distinguished as the Holy Spirit), but completely and directly, so that Jesus Christ of all in human form was alone able to say "I and my Father are one" (John x. 30). Although a prophet could say "Thus saith the Lord", thereby making it clear to his hearers that a message from God was being transmitted through him, he and they were alike aware that the message was God's and not his, and that he was but the instrument of God. Jesus Christ, on the other hand, was Himself aware, and His perceptive hearers soon became aware, that His message was the immediate utterance of God, that He Himself needed no mediation from God, that He was in fact one with God. Jesus Christ was God, in the sense that His utterances were the direct expression of God Himself, directly using the mechanism of the human body to communicate with those in this continuum.

(2) *Was Jesus Christ truly man?*

The answer to this question requires that another question be answered first: What is man at his highest and best? An ordinary man is a creature in a continual state of stress, due to the conflicting possibilities of his integrability and centricity. As we have seen, a man is integrated into his idiotelic unit, his 'world labyrinth', which is a unit of varying value and of varying centricity, the centricity varying between autocentricity on the man himself at one extreme and Theocentricity at the other, varying degrees of allocentricity being intermediate. That is the picture of an ordinary man. But we readily see that man at his best would be a man whose idiotelic unit represented a perfect world labyrinth, that is, an idiotelic unit of the highest possible value in all its relations, an idiotelic unit which the man had centred, and with it of course himself, on God, so that the unit would be completely Theocentric. It follows that the idiotelic unit would therefore itself, and necessarily the man with it, be integrated into the great divine unity of purpose, the supreme Theotelic unity. The perfect man, therefore, is one who has integrated himself as far as possible into God, and, as we saw, that will presumably mean complete identification with the will and purpose of God, complete surrender to Him, and awareness of separateness only in so far as the senses of self-identity and glad dependence will be preserved. In Jesus Christ God the Word realized these conditions: He Himself showed what perfect manhood could be by Himself dwelling, as we do, naturally integrated into a human body, and in that body remaining in perfect accord with the totality of Godhead, Himself thus realizing what dwelling in a body meant for His creatures, and Himself none the less retaining perfect harmony[1] with His own eternal purposes.

(3) *Was Jesus Christ a unity?*

We have advanced from the old ideas of unity which were based on a mechanical metaphysic, and we recognize that the real concept of unity is to be sought in terms of

[1] Cf. Berguer: "He suffers from no division of mind" (*Some Aspects of the Life of Jesus* (English trans.), p. 146).

function and purpose, and that unity is not of one kind but of many kinds. We have seen that the ideas of integration, system and unit have to be considered together, and that just as there are many types of integration so there are many types of system and unit. In the case of a person, we have seen that the unit is an integration commencing at conception and ending at death, and that a human being, a man, is a complex integration of body, centrum vitæ and spirit, each of these constituents themselves being complex integrations. The thread of continuity and of unity, however, is the spirit, and though this may develop and undergo changes, it is aware, and others are aware, of its essential continuity and unity. The spirit, on our view, comes into existence as such at conception, and at death, when the man as such disintegrates, the spirit passes onward to whatever God in His mercy has prepared for it. A man is a natural unit, though of course discriminable into integrated parts.

In the case of Jesus Christ, these special considerations are to be noted:

(i) Jesus Christ's body and centrum vitæ call for little comment, as they were exactly similar to our own, except that His body arose parthenogenetically. But that is of little consequence physically, the only marked result being that His physical idiosyncrasies (eye colour, hair colour and texture, etc.) would be more than usually likely to resemble His mother's, though no more so than in the case of an ordinary child whose mother's unit-characters (borne by the genes) were dominant to those of the father.

(ii) The 'mind', as we have seen, is an intermeshing of centrum vitæ and spirit, working through the brain as its instrument. In the case of Jesus Christ, we need to consider the following observations:

(*a*) God the Word particularized within Himself a focal centre having exactly the potentialities of a human spirit, that is, a complex of reactive abilities possessing the abilities of appreciation and response characteristic of a human spirit, and integrated that focal centre with the gamete of the Blessed Virgin Mary which had been started on its course of development (parthenogenetically) by divine impulse. It is this consideration which adds reality and cogency to God the Word's great condescension: to become man He condescended to receive from humanity that which should complete that which He had caused to arise within Himself into humanity. In considering this mystery we must get our minds away from the more rigid implications of some of the ancient terms. God's abilities are not restricted by our metaphysical concepts, and we believe that God the Word was able to take into His own being, or to react with, that which arose in the Blessed Virgin Mary, and, integrating the physical frame deriving from her with His own prepared focal centre, to provide for Himself within this continuum a focal centre of real and perfect manhood. It may be asked, "Can God the Word suffer addition?" He can certainly take to Himself what He wills, though what He takes to Himself does not "add" to Him, for the Supreme Perfection of Godhead cannot be enriched or extended, nor, being endoharmonic, does It require any satisfaction coming from without. Nothing taken into Godhead "adds" to Godhead. The right approach is entirely otherwise: God the Word completed His focal centre into true humanity by adopting the physical frame which as God[1] He had caused to start its development within the Blessed Virgin Mary, not because He could not have completed that focal centre by a mere act of His own will, but because He wished to take up into Himself, of His gracious condescension, as much as was possible from the humanity He was ready to become and to redeem. The wonder is God's willingness to take into Himself from humanity. True, the result is exactly as though He alone had caused it to be; but the fact remained, and remains, that to bring His humanity into being God the Word chose to receive into Himself all that humanity could give.

(b) The focal centre representing ideal humanity within God the Word has this further significance: it of course partook of the endoharmony of Godhead, being wholly of and within God the Word, and, if, for purposes of thought only, we regard the focal centre as an entity, we must keep it clearly in mind that it was nevertheless perfectly integrated into and completely centred in God the Word: its integration

[1] Cf. the comment on Luke i. 35 on p. 372.

was in God, and its centricity was Theocentricity. This is the ideal for perfect man, and we thus see that in, and only in, the focal centre of human reactability set apart within God the Word does the ideal of perfect humanity stand revealed.[1]

(c) The focal centre representing ideal humanity within God the Word, made functional in this continuum by His gracious acceptance to Himself of that which came from the Blessed Virgin Mary, obtained through that acceptance and integration a natural intermeshing through the centrum vitæ with the body. Thus had God the Word naturally integrated Himself into humanity.

(d) Thus the integration is complete and unbroken: body, centrum vitæ, and focal centre of perfect and ideal human spirit intermeshed therewith, yet still in and of God the Word, so that the focal centre within God the Word, and therefore God the Word Himself, was a natural unity with His body just as we are, and realized within and of Himself the perfect manhood which is a human being telically integrated with Godhead and whose centricity is Theocentricity. Jesus Christ was, by the completion of human nature by the focal centre within God the Word, a perfect human being perfectly telically integrated with Godhead and with His centricity Theocentricity, for there can be no closer harmony than that of a focal centre within Godhead with the Godhead in which it already is. The further conditions—

---

[1] It is interesting to notice that Relton, approaching the problem in quite a different way, reaches a comparable conclusion: "The Divine Logos, prior to the Incarnation, already possessed everything needful to enable Him to live a truly human life. It is the same conception which we have seen was so strong a point in the Apollinarian Christology, namely, that there is in God a human element. His advent, therefore, in the flesh brought to the human nature He assumed, not an alien element such as would render a truly human life for the God-Man an impossibility, but just that which alone could make the life of Christ in every stage of its growth and development a truly and perfectly human life. The Divine Logos was capable of being the Ego, not only of His Divine but also of His human Nature; because His Personality in virtue of its Divinity already embraced all that is most distinctive of a truly human personality. The human and the Divine are not two contradictory, but two complementary terms, and the less is contained in the greater. His Divine consciousness was, in virtue of its Divinity, a truly human self-consciousness. His Ego was Divine—it was also human; therefore it could be the subject of both natures" (A Study in Christology, pp. 226–227).

consciousness of self-existence and of self-surrender—are also fulfilled, for God the Word was of course aware that He had set apart the focal centre and was of course aware that He had done so in self-surrender to the urge humanitywards of His own seeking love.

(e) How can we speak of natural integration when God the Word is involved? Does not our concept break down on this very point, that God cannot be supposed in any way to enter a natural unity? The answer is this: God indeed cannot be constrained by natural law, for natural law is His will as regularly operating. But God can most certainly do as He wishes, and if He wishes to allow natural law to apply to Himself He can do so, though He could at any moment release Himself from it. That is to say, with God, and with God only, submission to natural law is voluntary, and God, and God only, can at any moment cease to be subject to it. Just as God can, by mere fiat, abrogate any natural law, so God, and God alone, can enter into relations which in the case of any but God would be natural and inescapable (except by the operation of natural law), but which with God are entirely voluntary. When, therefore, we speak of the natural integration of God the Word through the focal centre of humanity into His body, we mean 'an integration which for any other would have been natural, which in fact has all the characteristics of a natural integration, but which from God's point of view is of course voluntary, in that He can make, break or vary it just as and when He wills. For God, and for God only, natural bonds are also voluntary bonds.' This merely adds to our wonder and awe at the Incarnation: that God the Word should voluntarily have endured for a human life-time bonds which He could at any moment have broken. If, therefore, we ever speak without qualification of God in natural integration or with natural bonds, it must always be understood that the prime characteristic of natural integration as it affects all but God is absent, namely, inescapability.

(f) We have got so far as to envisage Jesus Christ thus: God the Word, having set apart a focal centre of ideal humanity within Himself and having integrated Himself through that focal centre into a human body, voluntarily remained in what (in the case of any other) would have been a natural unity.

(g) God the Word, having thus adopted humanity, decided that during the duration of the unity Jesus Christ He would use no focus of awareness in this continuum other than the focus of awareness functioning through the focal centre of ideal humanity within Himself and that in turn operating through a human centrum vitæ, brain, and body.

(h) God the Word, having so decided, could at any moment have reversed His decision. He did not choose to do so, because He gladly yielded Himself to His own impulse of evenient redemptive love.

(i) God the Word chose to centre Himself in Himself as Jesus Christ, so that the amplitude of the Godhead's hypostasis of evenient seeking love should be concentrated in the focus Jesus Christ. God the Word was still indiscriminably Godhead. The Trinity was still complete. Its inner harmony and Its outer functioning were unimpaired. Its infinite and indiscriminable substance suffered no imposed restrictions. But during the lifetime of Jesus Christ God the Word nowhere evidenced Himself except as Jesus Christ, and during the lifetime of Jesus Christ, Jesus Christ was never other than God the Word Incarnate: yet also perfect man; for we have seen that perfect manhood consists in all that constitutes man (body, centrum vitae, and focal centre of appreciation and response) being telically integrated with Godhead and with its centricity become Theocentricity. In Jesus Christ God the Word both completed the manhood by Himself supplying the focal centre of appreciation and response (accepting voluntarily the necessarily concomitant self-restrictions) and also (being still Himself in the unbroken continuity and unity of the Godhead) fulfilled the requirement of telic integration with and centricity in Godhead. This is the doctrine of enhypostasia; for Jesus Christ was not God and man dwelling together ("Nestorianism"), nor God replacing the spirit in man (Apollinarianism), but God supplying from Himself in union with humanity (as derived through the Blessed Virgin Mary) the perfect man: the manhood was not anhypostatic, its hypostasis was from and in God the Word.

We conclude that Jesus Christ was truly a unity, truly one, and that One was God the Word Incarnate, God the Word become, during that lifetime, God-man. Before the Incarnation eternally was God the Word. During the Incarnation God the Word was Jesus Christ and no other and Jesus Christ was God the Word and no other. After the Ascension eternally is God the Word, God the Word carrying forward to all eternity what it was to have been man as Jesus Christ.

Lest our mode of approach may have appeared to avoid certain familiar difficulties, we had better remark on our attitude to them:

(1) *Kenosis*

In becoming the perfect man did God the Word empty Himself or depotentiate Himself, and if so in what manner and in what degree?

In considering this question we have carefully to distinguish between choice and compulsion, between conditions accepted and conditions imposed. In becoming Incarnate, God the Word was fulfilling His own purpose and carrying through a plan upon which He Himself had decided. It is surely inappropriate to use such words as "emptying" or "depotentiating" in reference to processes self-determined, particularly when we are unaware of the exact nature of the processes involved. It may be nearer the truth to think of God the Word as Jesus Christ adapting Himself to earthly conditions and suspending certain of His powers rather than emptying Himself of them or depotentiating Himself. Kenosis and depotentiation may be words carrying with them the danger of implying more than is needful and more than is right. We need therefore first of all to free our minds from many of the ideas which have gathered round the word "kenosis". The text from which the word derives, Phil. ii. 7, ἑαυτὸν ἐκένωσε, μορφὴν δούλου λαβών, has probably been interpreted far more rigidly than St. Paul ever intended that it should be. Just as do

we, St. Paul often found it difficult to find the word exactly
to cover his meaning neither more nor less, and he would
most certainly have been horrified if he had thought that
the word ἐκένωσε would have been seized upon by some
later writers as the starting point for the expounding of
views contrary to the whole tenor of his Christology. It
seems inconceivable that St. Paul meant more than this:
"God the Word as Jesus Christ voluntarily and temporarily
suspended the exercise of certain of His powers, willingly
adapting Himself to the conditions of earthly life." For the
moment, let us set aside both the words kenosis and
depotentiation, and let us consider what actually happened.

God the Word, in order to fulfil His purposes—the
loving seeking of mankind and its redemption—decided to
become man, that is, to integrate Himself with a human
body in the same way in which a human spirit is associated
with a human body and to live life in the same conditions
as does a human being. Further, He not only condescended
so to integrate Himself, but also condescended to become
man in the sense of self-focalizing into the sphere of appreciation and reaction characteristic of a human spirit. To
fulfil this purpose properly involved deciding to accept
certain restrictions inherent in what He wished to accom-
plish. We must now consider these restrictions in a little
more detail.

God the Word had decided to associate Himself with a
human body in such a way that He should be integrated
with that body in the same way as a human spirit is
integrated with a human body. He had, in fact, taken to
Himself (from the Blessed Virgin Mary) that which provided, in union with that which He Himself supplied within
Himself, all that is required to make possible the perfect
functioning of a human spirit; and through that which He
had accepted from the Blessed Virgin Mary He established
a linkage, through the centrum vitæ, with the body, a
linkage exactly analogous to that of an ordinary human
spirit. God the Word, therefore, was linked integrally with
a human body, and there is only one difference between
His linkage and ours: we are integrated with our bodies
naturally; that is to say, we have no control over the

linkage. We cannot make it and break it at will. We are bound into it by natural law, and we can only break it in accordance with natural law. But natural law does not bind God. God the Word, therefore, was integrated with the body in a way which was in every respect natural, except that He, being God, was not bound thereby, though any but He would have been bound. This point is of the utmost importance in realizing the true humanity of Jesus Christ. The perfect human spirit which God the Word actualized within and of Himself was integrated into the body in exactly the same way as every human spirit is integrated into its body; but God the Word could not be bound by natural integration, so that for Him the integration must further be described as voluntary: voluntary, but nevertheless natural. We may regard, if we wish, natural bonds as bonds of which God alone has the key. God the Word, therefore, could at any moment have left the body with which He was naturally, and for Him also voluntarily, integrated. But He had chosen, for the fulfilment of His purpose, so to integrate Himself, and He had decided that the mode and medium of the manifestation of His Person (God the Word) should for the period of an earthly life be nothing other than the body into which He had integrated Himself. So He decided: none constrained Him, none could constrain Him. From the conception to the death on Calvary, God the Word chose to manifest His Person in no other way, at least in this continuum. Passing for the moment over the problems of childhood and development, let us consider what this meant in the time of His bodily maturity.

God the Word voluntarily restricted Himself to manifestation through a human body. He therefore made use of that body in exactly the same way as we should. If He wanted to get to another place, He walked or rode there, using the body He had adopted. If He wanted to communicate with anyone, He used the voice of His body. He looked after the body as we do, washing it, feeding it, clothing it. He could at any moment have transported His body wherever He willed. He could have sustained it without food. He could have done anything whatsoever by the mere willing, for

He was God. But He did not so will. He had decided to be truly man, and He fulfilled all the conditions without flinching or failing. He could have done anything, but He would not. He would only do what man, perfect man, could do. If He wanted to go from Nazareth to Capernaum, He went as we should have to go. To use a simile, He had made His own rules, and He was determined to keep them, cost what it might. If bodies were limited in mobility, endurance, and in other ways, His body was to be limited in exactly the same way as others. With respect to the body, is it right to call such an attitude a kenosis or a depotentiation? He had not emptied Himself. He was still God, and contained the fulness of His power, though He was not choosing to exercise it all. He had not depotentiated Himself. He was still God and Lord of all. May we not rather speak of a voluntary self-restriction, a temporary cessation, an *anapausis*?[1] There was no emptying (kenosis) of any power or attribute of Godhead from God the Word. But there was indeed a temporary cessation (anapausis) of the exercise of some of His powers and attributes. Omnipotence is meaningless unless it can choose not to use its powers as well as to choose to use them. We think, then, with reverent wonder, of God the Word as Jesus Christ, walking, hungering, being tired, aching, feeling everything that can be felt through a body, not of necessity—that would have been limitation and passibility—but because He chose to endure in the course He had chosen: not a kenosis, but an anapausis of His powers. We may therefore expect divine intervention in Jesus Christ's earthly bodily affairs in exactly the same circumstances, and in no others, which would have justified divine intervention in the earthly bodily affairs of a prophet or messenger of God. God the Word did not favour Himself. We believe that God has from time to time intervened, as He so easily can but in wisdom rarely does, in human affairs on the bodily plane. According to our historical sense, our critical faculties, and, most crucial, our general view of things, we may narrow or extend the list of cases in which we believe it to have happened, but it is not to be doubted that when His purpose so requires God can sustain,

[1] ἀνάπαυσις, cessation, desistance.

levitate, transport, super-empower a human body, or indeed do anything He wishes with it or give it power to do anything He wills. Why indeed not? We thus see that on those occasions when Jesus Christ's body appeared to transcend the powers of an ordinary human body—and such occasions were very few—it was not that He was arbitrarily exceeding His self-accepted limitations, but that for the fulfilment of divine purpose Godhead so imposed; it was not that God the Word as Jesus Christ, to ease the strain of bodily existence or limitation, did certain things; but that God the Word, ever in perfect harmony with all that is God, being Himself indiscriminably of the Godhead, acted in such a way for the fulfilment of His all-embracing purposes. Let one example make this distinction clear. If we believe, as some do, that Christ's escape from the angry crowd referred to in Luke iv. 30 was miraculous, the reason for the miraculous escape was not that God the Word as Jesus Christ wished to save Himself from bodily pain or death, which He would have scorned to do, but that God the Word as of the Godhead knew that His purpose on earth was not yet fulfilled, and that the body must be saved from premature destruction. The distinction is very real and very important. God the Word as Jesus Christ did not do for Himself what He would not have done for another in similar circumstances. To hold otherwise leads inevitably to some kind of modified docetism. God the Word as Jesus Christ, shall we say, obeyed His own rules, not because He had had to but because He wished to. Unless the circumstances were such that in them God would have transported a prophet or apostle from one place to another miraculously (cf. Acts viii. 39–40), neither would He so transport Himself. Voluntary anapausis and condescending self-restriction is neither kenosis nor depotentiation, unless those words are interpreted in a very much more carefully circumscribed manner than is frequently the case.

We now pass to a more difficult problem. Was there a kenosis or depotentiation as to knowledge? Was God the Word as Jesus Christ omniscient? We may perhaps have no great difficulty in conceding the suspension of omnipotence, on the grounds that He could have acted but did not choose so to do. Can we deal with the problem of omniscience in a similar way? To do so may be to suggest some degree of hypocrisy on Christ's part, which we dare not for a moment contemplate. There is a very real difference between not using power and not using knowledge. To refrain from using power does not involve pretending to be powerless; but to refrain from using knowledge seems inevitably to involve pretending to be ignorant. There is, however, an approach to this problem which does not lead to this quandary.

The totality of Godhead, ever harmoniously simultaneously existent as Father, Word, and Holy Spirit, is in Its totality omniaware: aware of all that has been, is, and will be. Godhead is omniscient, and all the Persons are therefore omniscient, all being one in Godhead. But each Person of the Trinity can and does make contact with that which is within this continuum. Such contacts when revealing the phase of Godhead characterized as the Person of God the Father are usually called Theophanies. From the side of man they are revelations of God as Father. From the side of God they are foci of particularized awareness, particularized, and yet part of the omniawareness of Godhead. In the case of God the Holy Spirit, by which phase the Person of the Trinity who goes forth in aiding power manifests Himself, such contacts are evidenced by men in greater or less degree thinking or acting under His direction and with His power. Each such object of aid, each such act, is for the human being an awareness of the power of the Holy Spirit, and for the Holy Spirit is a focus of particularized awareness. There may be, and indeed are, countless such foci of particularized awareness simultaneously existent for the Holy Spirit, and they all constitute accentuations, in a sense duplications, of the omniawareness of the totality of Godhead. God can be aware of the same event from two or more aspects of awareness.

In the case of God the Word, during the earthly existence of Jesus Christ we believe that He chose to limit His particularized awareness in this continuum to one focus, Jesus Christ, so that all His awareness as God the Word came through that one channel. As of Godhead, God the Word as Jesus Christ was omniaware, omniscient. But He was aware of all events which came to Him as Jesus Christ in a double way: aware of them as mediated through the focus of particularized awarnesss, His earthly body, and aware of them because He was of Godhead. Now we are ourselves aware that we can struggle in a real and genuine way to find out something we already know. This can readily be illustrated from mathematics. We may strive to solve by algebra a problem we have already solved by the aid of the differential calculus, and we may strive to solve by projective geometry a problem we have already solved by analytical geometry. In both cases we wish to reach our destination by a certain route, and we are able to ignore other means of reaching it, even though we know perfectly well what the result is. We can do more than that. We can so fix our intention on solving the problem by a given mode of approach that to solve it by any other method would be unthinkable. We can ignore what we know, because we ardently desire to arrive at it this other way. This is a weak and inadequate analogy, but it serves as a preface to this: God the Word, determining that, as Jesus Christ, Jesus Christ should be the only focus of His particularized awareness, determined not to act on any knowledge except that which came to Him through that focus. His attention, so to speak, was turned away from the omniawareness He possessed as of Godhead and was directed only to the awareness particularized in that focus. That is to say, the omniawareness was actual in Him in that He was Godhead, but was ignored. He actually knew everything, but He restricted Himself to the use of such knowledge as came to Him through the particularized focus.

Let us consider how this would work out in some of the stages of His life:

II. *The human life of Jesus Christ*

(i) *Babyhood and childhood*

God the Word, as of Godhead, was omnipercipient and omniaware. Nothing within or without the Universe was

AI

outside His knowledge. But God the Word, as the Person of the Trinity willing to go forth in seeking love, had chosen as the only focus of His particularized awareness the body whose development had begun in utero Virginis. His awareness was thus turned in that direction of His own will, and He was determined to attend only to the impressions that came to Him through that focus and to restrict Himself to expression through that focus. It was as though a teacher of the blind closed his eyes so that he might put himself on the same level as his pupils. At any moment the teacher could open his eyes. But he might choose to keep them shut, so that he might realize what blindness meant, determining that in no circumstances would he open them until a definite period had been fulfilled. So God the Word refused to admit or to use anything other than that which came to Him through the medium of His human body. He would not talk until He had learned to talk as we do, nor would He use words until He had learned them as we do, nor would He use knowledge until He had acquired it as we do. The reader must clearly distinguish "would not" from "could not". God the Word as the infant Jesus could have spoken words of omniscient wisdom. But to have done so would have been to transcend the very conditions He had chosen to fulfil. He would have had to withdraw His focus of awareness from His body (to others the infant Jesus), and given expression through the mouth of that infant to that of which He was aware as Godhead. The infant Jesus would have become a mere instrument. God the Word would not do that. From the moment of conception He had directed His awareness entirely in one direction—through the body of His adoption. We may suggest another analogy. A man with inherited riches might decide not to use those riches, but to restrict himself to the use only of such money as he was able to earn. He might set to work and gradually accumulate reasonable means. He would then be able to buy anything within those means, but, although possessing fabulous wealth by inheritance, he might keep to his resolve not to go beyond his earned means. As his earned wealth increased, so would his power to buy. While still poor (on his earnings), he might say, "I cannot buy that, I cannot afford it." He could not afford it; that is, if he remained true to his decision not to use his inherited wealth. Thus it was with God the Word as Jesus Christ. He would not use anything other than that which came to Him as it comes to us. It is impious and unnecessary to think of a kind of "black-out" of the knowledge and awareness of God the Word, and His feeling His way back to knowledge and awareness as Jesus Christ grew up. It is equally distasteful and unnecessary to think of a deception: that He was aware of all power and knowledge all the time, but pretended to be unaware. There is an intermediate explanation. He had decided on a certain course, and with magnificent consistency He went forward on it: unwilling to use the wealth of power and knowledge He knew He had, yet aware that they were there. Suspension of known power and knowledge is easily possible with us, and we can readily act, think and feel within accepted limitations, and can make our effort and struggle genuine and unfeigned within limitations we have accepted and could easily break, but will not. We can strive to capture a piece in chess in accordance with the rules of that game, when we could easily snatch it off the board in a moment; but to do that would give us no satisfaction, for we wish to capture that piece in accordance with certain rules which we have accepted. So also God the Word as Jesus Christ knew that He had all power and knowledge, but He made Himself as one of us by refraining from power He could not command as man and from knowledge He had not acquired as man. Thus He passed through infancy and childhood, speaking no word till He had learned it as we do, using no knowledge He had not acquired as we acquire it.

(ii) Maturity

We have envisaged in Jesus Christ a double awareness: an awareness of the existence of sources of knowledge and power within Himself, but which He had chosen not to use, because to do so would have been to belie His purpose; and an awareness which came to Him as awareness comes to us. His experiences were indeed real, and so was the struggle and effort to acquire physical and mental competence. To return to the analogy used above, if we are playing chess, our efforts to capture a piece by the proper means are not reduced because we know that we could snatch it off the board with our hand. God the Word had become man, and He would equally have scorned to use power or knowledge impossible to man. Did He wish to go to Capernaum? Then He would walk, He would not miraculously transport Himself thither. Did He wish to talk of Old Testament times? Then He would gain His knowledge from the Old Testament scriptures, not by drawing on His divine omniscience. He discussed matters on the basis of that which was true to His hearers, realizing the futility of questioning postulates which they regarded as fundamental and realizing that what matters is not so much the factual as the value correspondence between noetic impression and ontic reality. Consider, for example, His treatment of the story of Jonah (Matt. xii. 39–40, xvi. 4), neither affirming nor denying its historicity, which is, after all, relatively unimportant, but emphasizing its importance as a type and sign. There was thus a kind of circum-progression as the humanly acquired keyed in with the divinely known. It is naturally impossible for us to know how this process appeared from within, to hazard how Jesus Christ ignored or recessed His divine omniscience. It is particularly puzzling in relation to the years of growth. We might wish to picture it as a kind of unwillingness to turn, as if all were recorded in 'the back of His mind', but that He would not turn and use 'the back of His mind'; He would only use what came to Him through His humanity. It was not that He did not know, but that He only chose to use what He knew as man.

The above paragraph may at once raise the problem of inerrancy. How, then, could Jesus Christ have been free from error? If He so restricted Himself, to what extent are His statements and judgments to be relied upon? To this question we may make a two-fold answer:

(i) Never let it be forgotten that Jesus Christ was God the Word, and however God the Word chose to restrict Himself, it is absolutely unthinkable that He should err in judgment. Even if He restricted Himself to partial data,

His judgments and pronouncements would be true not merely in reference to those data but in reference to the actualities behind those data. Every less was by Him assessed in the light of appreciation of its greater. Jesus Christ transcended His self-accepted context.

(ii) If by any chance mistaken information had been passed on to Him through ordinary human channels, we cannot but suppose that He would have at once registered a 'stop' in His mind. He would have known, even without 'turning round', that what He had been told was not so, whether a matter of history or of contemporary event. We are therefore absolutely confident not only that all His judgments on partial data were in conformity with the total data, but that no erroneous opinions or distorted facts could possibly affect His inerrant judgment. He would perceive exactly how and to what extent a noetic expression distorted or misrepresented an ontic reality, and it is illuminating, as has been hinted above, to consider how Jesus Christ dealt with problems arising from the conflict between what He knew to be true and what was firmly established in current thought. He did not needlessly confuse His hearers by shattering views they could not readily alter without a profound disturbance of their whole scheme of thought, yet He never said anything which was out of accord with ultimate values.[1] We may instance His treatment of Old Testament history, nature, reincarnation, angelology, and demonology.

The next problem that arises under this head is the problem of the miraculous. If, it may be asked, God the Word as Jesus Christ restricted Himself to human powers, with an anapausis of certain of His divine powers, where is the place for miracles of healing, of power over nature, and such personal feats as walking on the sea?

We may first of all remark that we are not really in a position to define the powers of perfect man. God the Word as Jesus Christ was ideal perfect man, and perfect

[1] Cf. Mascall, who points out how Christ "fully and naturally adjusted himself to the mentality of the questioner"; nevertheless, "The conformity of the mind to the situation being perfect, positive error is altogether excluded from the utterances that Christ makes" (*Christ, the Christian and the Church*, p. 60).

man is in perfect accord and harmony with the will and purpose of God, submitting His will to God's will and identifying His purposes with God's purposes. It is therefore difficult to say what we could do if we had achieved perfection and had integrated ourselves into God's purposes and had centred ourselves in Him. Much that Jesus Christ did may simply be evidence of the normal power of perfect man.[1]

Further, we have to remember that not Jesus Christ only has wrought miracles. Miracles wrought by others are to be explained thus: God, for the fulfilment of His purpose, may put it into the mind of one of His servants to do certain things, and, parallel with his so doing, He effects what He wills. Thus we must not think that God answered Elijah's prayer because God wished to fulfil Elijah's purposes; we must suppose rather that God guided Elijah in his procedure and at the appropriate moment sent fire[2] (1 Kings xviii. 36–39). Similarly it was not Elisha's inbreathing that revived the Shunammite woman's child, but God's revivification of the lad was concomitant with Elisha's actions: God could have revived the child without the co-operation of Elisha, but Elisha could not have revived the child unless God had so willed (2 Kings iv. 32–35).

In the case of Jesus Christ, then, we see that His working of miracles in no way brings into question His true humanity. On the other hand, in the case of Jesus Christ we have a most illuminating illustration of divine-human working, and an informative insight into the nature of the Trinity both as to inner harmony and outer functioning. It may be useful to consider the miracles of Jesus Christ as they are related to His real deity, His completely accepted manhood, and His Oneness:

---

[1] Libbey has written two short works in which he emphasizes that an outstanding characteristic of Jesus is His normality: "His complete normality . . . is itself the assurance, the guarantee, that He was the Son of God" (*The Boy Jesus*, p. 83). "He is not abnormal. That is the arresting feature. He is so extraordinary in being so peculiarly ordinary, so perfectly balanced" (*Science looks at Jesus*, p. 56).

[2] The actual historicity of this and other illustrations has no bearing on the principles involved.

(i) Miracles of healing

Many of Christ's miracles of healing may well have been merely due to the exercise of the powers of perfect man. It is not unreasonable to suppose that a pure and powerful personality might be able to bring about the cure of morbid conditions due to mental, nervous, or functional disharmonies. But the cure of organic disease and of diseases involving actual loss of parts (e.g. leprosy), cannot be explained in any such way. We may suggest the following:

Jesus Christ, drawn by loving compassion to desire to heal some particular case or being willing to accede to a request to heal, stretches forth His hand to touch—symbol of loving identification with His suppliant—and at the same time wills the disease or infirmity to depart. In the case of a grave organic disease we have already dismissed the idea that suggestion, hypnosis, or anything of that sort, would be of avail. Moreover, as self-limited to manhood, and as acting through His body, God the Word as Jesus Christ could not consistently effect the profound changes necessary to effect a cure. But God the Word, though Jesus Christ, was none the less God and none the less of Godhead, and through that oneness His will found immediate expression: what God the Word as Jesus Christ willed, God the Word as God fulfilled. For intellectual coherence we may thus picture a circuit: Jesus Christ did not heal gross infirmity as man; He healed it as God. The same God who was God the Word in Jesus Christ was God the Almighty Father and God the Holy Spirit—God, one in substance, one in will, purpose, concern, expressing Himself in three Persons for His endoharmony and for His outer functioning—God at once in Jesus Christ and working a beneficent cure through that natural order which He had created and of which He never ceased to be master: God yearning, feeling, laying on His hands as Jesus Christ; God mightily operating through the hidden forces of nature. Jesus Christ was able to heal the sick because Jesus Christ was God the Word and God the Word was God. This concept surely underlies Jesus Christ's own explanation of the mode of His interworking with God the Father: "The Father that dwelleth in me, he doeth the works" (John xiv. 10). Compare also

John v. 17–21. It may be supposed that some such ideas as these may have given rise to the "subordination" concept of Jesus Christ in relation to God the Father. It is not so much a case of subordination as of co-ordination and parallel exercise of complementary function. The word subordination is best avoided unless used in a carefully defined technical sense.

(ii) Nature Miracles

In these cases (e.g. stilling the storm, feeding the multitudes) a very similar explanation holds: what God the Word as Jesus Christ willed, God the Word as integral in Godhead through the appropriate functional Person of Godhead fulfilled.

(iii) Personal transcendence of nature

Under this heading we must consider any occurrences between conception and the death on Calvary in which Jesus Christ personally appeared to be superior to the limitations of bodily human nature. We think of such events as His walking on the sea (Matt. xiv. 22–27) and His escape from the crowd at Nazareth (Luke iv. 28–30). Actually such occurrences appear to have been very few, which is significant. Here again our solution depends upon a proper realization of the significance of the endoharmony of the Trinity and Its distribution of function. God the Word as Jesus Christ restricted Himself to the powers possible to perfect humanity, and we have already noted that we are not competent to describe or delimit even those powers; but it is to be remembered that the power of God to fulfil His purpose through Jesus Christ was not limited by the fact that God as God the Word was Himself Jesus Christ. If Jesus Christ had been man and nothing else, if it suited divine purpose God could have miraculously transported or empowered Him. We may think of numerous examples in Old Testament history; in the New Testament there is the case of Philip (Acts viii. 39–40). We may, I think, take this view: though Jesus Christ was God the Word, God the Word as man would not have exercised for His humanity powers He would not have exercised in similar circumstances for any other man if it were necessary for the fulfilment of divine purpose. That is to say, God the Word as Jesus Christ would not, being God, exercise functions of other Persons of His being in order to save Himself trouble, pain or difficulty. He would only do so if, some other servant of His being similarly placed, He would have done so for him. If the passing through the Nazarene crowd was miraculous, it was effected by God as Almighty controller of all things, with whom as of Godhead God the Word was perfectly one, in order that the human life and work He had undertaken as Jesus Christ might not come to a premature end. God would equally have saved any other special agent of His whose appointed task had not yet been done. Similarly, the walking on the sea was not the exercise of a capricious power. It was a necessary sign. It was not done for Jesus Christ's sake but for His work's sake. Herein is wonder, that God the Word as Jesus Christ, though able as of Godhead to exercise any function on His own behalf, none the less, except in these few exceptional cases, chose to accept all the limitations and restrictions appropriate to the manhood with which He had integrated Himself. God the Word, as Godhead, had all power of every kind. God the Word, as Jesus Christ, chose not to use any power He would not have used on another's behalf in similar circumstances.

(2) *Omnipotence and omniscience*

Our attitude to these attributes in reference to Jesus Christ has emerged in the course of the preceding section.

(3) *Impassibility*

Our approach to the problems arising from the ascription of the attribute of impassibility to the Godhead, and therefore to God the Word, is similar to our approach to the problem of omnipotence. We have to remember that the ancient attributes were ascribed to Godhead in a very proper endeavour to emphasize the Supreme Perfection of God in every conceivable way; and we have seen that we must not allow an end to be obscured by the means taken to reach it. God is Supremely Perfect. He is exoschematic, and He is endoharmonic. Nothing can limit or control Him, nothing can deflect Him from His purposes, one of which is manifested to usward in seeking redeeming love. All this being so, can God suffer? Let us vary the question slightly: Can God be made to suffer? To that we have not the slightest hesitation in answering with an emphatic negative. Nothing conceivable could make God suffer. But if God, for the fulfilment of His purposes, wished, of His great love, to identify Himself with humanity's suffering, to suffer with and for us, who could deny Him the right and power so to do? We may perhaps rightly postulate that, in the old terms, the actual essence of Godhead cannot suffer; but that does not prevent God knowing what suffering is like, and appreciating it through the human body and centrum vitæ which He had integrated into His assumed humanity and thereby into Himself. He thus of His own volition accepted suffering, suffering which we believe was integral in the plan of redemption. We must, however, emphasize this distinction: human passibility implies an inescapable liability; but in the case of God the Word He could at any moment have released Himself from the experiences He underwent. Therein is added wonder in Christ's life and work for us: He bore unflinchingly and of His own volition that from which the mere wish would have released Him. His passibility was voluntary, every moment of it and every aspect of it. If we scruple in any way to dethrone the old term, we may retain it simply by defining it in parallel terms to those in which we define omnipotence: God is impassible in the sense that nothing can make Him suffer. Nevertheless, for our sakes God in God the Word as Jesus Christ did suffer that He might bring about our redemption. This matter need not be laboured further.[1] We surely get the matter into right perspective when we balance up the glorious and central fact of divine love with the over-forcing of a metaphysical attribute: "If the Heart of God thus revealed is a heart of mercy and compassion, redemptive love and consequent suffering are not alien to Him, and the doctrine of His impassibility, as we have seen, will have to be modified.

[1] It is dealt with exhaustively in Mozley, *The Impassibility of God.*

The lesson revealed by the Incarnation and the Cross is the
lesson of a Suffering God, and nothing less than this can
constitute the foundation-stone of the atoning work of
Christ."[1]

III. The death of Jesus Christ

Great significance is, perhaps rightly, attached to the
answer a Christology provides to the question as to whether
the death of Jesus Christ meant to God the Word what
death means to us. Human death was described on pp.
334-336, and we must ask what were the parallels and what
were the differences between the death of Jesus Christ and
our death.

Jesus Christ was perfect man, a biotic unit integrated
from a body (itself a complex hylic integration), a centrum
vitæ, and a human spirit which had never been other than
perfectly integrated into God the Word, God the Word
having set apart within Himself a focal centre of perfect
humanity. Jesus Christ was thus a perfect man in perfect
integration with God and perfectly Theocentric, and the
mode of His integration was what in any case but His
would have been natural. In His case, uniquely, the natural
bonds were also voluntary, because, being God as truly as
man, He could at any moment have broken those bonds
and released Himself, as God, from all implication in the
body and humanity which He had adopted and become.
The supreme test of the love of God for humanity consisted
in His willingness to endure as Jesus Christ until that unity
should be disintegrated as it would have disintegrated had
any but He been its continuity. We recognize that there
would have been at least[2] two ways in which Jesus Christ
might have come to an end as such:

(i) God the Word could have chosen to withdraw Himself from the unity by an act of will, disintermeshing
Himself from the centrum vitæ and thereby from the body.
This He could have done painlessly and instantly. We just
dare not contemplate what would have resulted from such
an action, nor whether what was left would have been

---

[1] Relton, *A Study in Christology*, pp. 160–161.
[2] A third possibility is considered on p. 406.

alive or dead. It would certainly not have been a human being. But God did not do any such dreadful thing.

(ii) God the Word could have determined to endure in the unity until it came to an end in the same way as the ordinary human biotic unit comes to an end, that is, He could await the time when old age, disease or accident would make it impossible for the unit any longer to function as a unit, so that its disintegration would inevitably take place. God the Word did in fact remain as Jesus Christ until this end came, in His case brought about by the grave injuries, shock and exhaustion accompanying His Cruci-fixion. The pain and agony inflicted on the body is trans-mitted through the nervous system and the brain to the intermeshed centre of appreciation and consciousness which we believe is composite of centrum vitæ and spirit (ψυχή approximately and πνεῦμα). Until the nervous system and brain cease to transmit, the centrum vitæ and spirit do not cease to appreciate. Finally, consciousness fades, the link-ages break, the body becomes nothing but a complex of hylic units which will soon disintegrate further, the centrum vitæ, so dependent on the brain, will break down into what-ever its constituents may be (material, electrical, 'vital force'?), and the spirit will be released as the last inter-meshings fade, fail, or break. All this is involved in death, after which we presume and believe that the spirit, freed from its outworn instrument, with which it had been so intimately integrated, passes whither God's mercy will receive it and eventually clothe upon it the glorious body of the resurrection.

God the Word as Jesus Christ did not flinch from any-thing involved in dying. His death, moreover, was not of the easy and merciful kind human death so often is, uncon-sciousness supervening before the final disintegration, so that the final breaks are made without our awareness, and the spirit emerges into new consciousness free from its burden. But it was not so with Jesus Christ. He endured consciously to the bitter end, agonizingly aware of every pain in the racked and failing body. Can our reverent wonder and thankful devotion ever be sufficient to appre-ciate the love that was willing, though able instantly to release itself, to endure thus for us? God the Word allowed the natural bonds to tear painfully apart naturally, when He could have released them voluntarily and instantly. God the Word, not bound by nature, chose to die naturally, though none could make Him do so. He accepted, as man, man's lot:

> "O generous love! that He Who smote
> In man for man the foe,
> The double agony in man
> For man should undergo."

Jesus Christ, God the Word, died as all men die. God the Word, as Jesus Christ, died. True then, if we understand them aright, are those words we almost scruple to utter: God died. Those two words mean that God Himself, God the Word as Jesus Christ, knows what death means, and died because His loving purpose for us required it of Him.

It might now be expected that we should endeavour to show how our Christology fits the data of the New Testament. To do that would involve going yet again over much familiar ground, and the reader is probably sufficiently versed in the New Testament to have decided already whether, for him, the Christology here proffered is acceptable or not. We shall therefore make only these observations:

(i) In using the New Testament as a source for data on the one hand and as a standard for checking theories on the other, we have to remember that the use we make of the New Testament is itself conditioned by our attitude to the whole complex of things. However dispassionately we endeavour to assess the results of textual and higher criticism, we ultimately base our judgments on our total view, which indeed includes the New Testament as a datum, but also reacts on the New Testament in such a way as to incline us to interpret it in conformity with our view of totality. The latter is a most important consideration, and militates against a completely objective view of the New Testament, as indeed it does of most other things. Critical and historical judgments are far more intimately bound up with our general philosophy of life than is sometimes realized.

(ii) We accordingly submit the outline of a view which

conforms with the general trend of our postulates and fits into our framework without distortion:

(a) The details of the gospel narrative are not important; and though it may be interesting to endeavour to arrive as near to the facts of history as possible, it does not really matter whether there were two blind men at Jericho or one, or whether there were one, two or several occasions on which Christ fed the multitudes.

(b) To recover the ipsissima verba of Christ would be interesting, but not vital. Whether Christ actually said, in those words, what is recorded in St. John's Gospel is not important. What is important is that the words express something eternally true. What matters is not whether Christ ever actually said "I am the way, the truth, and the life", but whether He is in fact that. If He said it, and was not that, we are indeed lost. If He is that, whether or not He expressed it in just those words is of no consequence.

(c) Although we may by no means subscribe to the views expressed by Berguer in *Some Aspects of the Life of Jesus*, we must at least commend the penetration which enabled him to drive home the great truth that the meaning and work of Jesus Christ is quite independent of the details of the historical narratives. The narratives might be distorted out of all verisimilitude (though I certainly do not believe they are), and yet Jesus Christ might still be the centre of our being, our Saviour and our God. As Berguer remarks, "Above the historical truth, the truth of facts, there is a moral and psychological truth, a truth of states of mind, which can only be expressed under the cover of more or less adequate symbols and which must be respected quite as much as the other."[1] Berguer is willing to abandon much more than most of us see any reason for abandoning, as may be seen by reference to pp. 95–129 of the work quoted; but he nevertheless holds as firmly as any of us to the centrality of Jesus Christ in our understanding of the purpose of life.

(d) It might well be that the nearer we approached integration with God and Theocentricity the less dependent we should become on records and researches. It might well

[1] Op. cit. (English trans.), p. 100.

be that the illumination of faith would check and test history rather than vice versa, so that there would be in ourselves a faint parallel to that which existed perfectly in Jesus Christ, whose judgment could not be distorted by any inadequacy or distortion in data.

With the attitude indicated, it is possible to read the New Testament with an understanding and freedom from anxious care which enable us to sense its profound meanings without becoming unduly perturbed by text-critical and other problems. Essential truth will evidence itself; irrelevant detail will sink to its own level. Further, the Christology we have been endeavouring to expound is not something new and strange, which might send us anxiously to our New Testament to see whether it indeed fits the data. What we have been endeavouring to do is to show that the ancient faith in Jesus Christ as at once God, man, and one Person, is a faith which can be held without difficulty or anxiety by one who takes into account all that modern science, psychology and philosophy have to say. There is therefore no need to deal in general or in detail with the way in which that faith partly derives from the New Testament and how, in the light of it, various New Testament passages are to be understood. There is already a voluminous literature on that subject, and our present purpose will not be forwarded by any brief and therefore inadequate comments.

Our object has been at once simpler and wider. We have not endeavoured to solve the problem of Christology. It would be presumptuous and foolish to imagine that we can ever hope to reduce to some concise formula the mystery of God the Word in Jesus Christ. That is why this work is called only "an approach" to Christology. Our intention has been to show that modern knowledge and the ancient faith are not incompatible; that a general view of things can be constructed which leads up to and includes the most important fact in history, the fact of Jesus Christ, and which makes it possible for us to realize in some dim way how He could indeed have been truly God, truly man, and One. Moreover, we have found that our view provides indications of a way of approach to an understanding of the mystery cognate with that of the Incarnation, the mystery of the Atonement. If our ideas of integration and centricity are in parallel with the truth, we begin to see how Jesus Christ, at once true God and perfect man, is the means, the only means, whereby mankind can be integrated into the divine telicity and whereby that which God sent forth may turn again to Him and find the centre and purpose of its being in Him, so that "that which drew from out the boundless deep turns again home". We thus set side by side "No man cometh unto the Father, but by me" (John xiv. 6) and "I, if I be lifteth up from the earth, will draw all men unto me" (John xii. 32). To be drawn to Christ, our Brother, is to find in Him our Lord and our God, and to find in and through Him our oneness with the fulness of the Godhead, the fulfilment of our Saviour's prayer "That they all may be one; as thou, Father, art in me, and I in thee, that they also may be one in us" (John xvii. 21).

We have endeavoured to outline an approach, and we have tried to indicate a view of life and the Universe which both includes and depends on the central fact of God in Christ condescending to come amongst us and seeking to reconcile us unto Himself. In an endeavour to keep the outline clear, and owing to the many problems inevitably touched upon, the writer is sadly aware of the inadequacy and brevity of treatment. But the temptation to deal as fully as might be desired with various aspects of the main and subsidiary problems has had to be resisted in the interests of the continuity and coherence of the work as a whole. For similar reasons supporting and parallel quotations have been reduced to a minimum, not because indebtedness is not fully realized, but because there is inevitable modification if only in nuance when we fuse our gatherings and siftings into a coherent scheme, and we do not wish either to appear to be misinterpreting others or to break the continuity of the exposition of our own view of things.

We find it difficult to state our results in a just summary. We have been endeavouring to convey a point of view, to sketch a background, to indicate an approach. Unless these aims have in some measure been reached as the book has been read, they are not likely to be accomplished in a few terse and inadequate sentences now. It may, however, be desirable to bring this work to a close by seeing whether our study will have enabled us to read the Definition of Chalcedon with increased understanding. That Definition is not intended to set forth a metaphysical Christology. It is a statement of fact, and it is for us to endeavour to comprehend it as fully and as deeply as our resources and insight permit. It is a legitimate aspiration to hope that as the departments of human knowledge are extended so shall we be able to appreciate more fully the profound truths the Definition embodies.[1]

Let us therefore read the Definition phrase by phrase and discover whether it has gained yet more meaning for us, and whether we can the more readily fit it into the general scheme of our thought:[2]

"Following therefore the holy Fathers, we all with one voice teach to confess one and the same Son, our Lord Jesus Christ, the same perfect in Godhead and the same perfect in manhood, the same truly God and truly man of a reasonable soul and body, consubstantial with the Father as to the Godhead and the same consubstantial with us as to the manhood, like unto us in all things except sin; before the ages begotten of the Father as to the Godhead, and the same in the last days, for us and for our salvation, of Mary the Virgin the God-bearer as to the manhood, one and the same Christ, Son, Lord, Only-begotten, acknowledged in[3] two natures, unconfusedly, immutably, indivisibly, inseparably; the distinction of the natures by no means being taken away by the union, but rather the peculiarity of each nature being preserved and concurring in one prosôpon and one hypostasis, not parted or divided into two prosôpa, but one and the same Son and Only-begotten, God the Word, the Lord Jesus Christ; according as the prophets taught concerning Him from the beginning, and as the Lord Jesus Christ Himself taught us, and as the Creed of the Fathers has delivered to us."

[1] Cf. *Doctrine in the Church of England* (*The Report of the Commission on Christian Doctrine appointed by the Archbishops of Canterbury and York in* 1922), p. 81.
[2] The Greek is quoted on p. 203.
[3] Or 'of'. Reference to this disputed point is made on p. 202.

The detailed exposition of the Definition would involve a recapitulation of all the arguments of our book. But the writer is confident that nothing we have written is incompatible with the Definition. If anything seem to be so, let blame be put on lack of clarity in expression, not on any intention of innovating.[1] It may, however, be desirable to make brief comments on one or two points, not by way of full exposition but in an endeavour to indicate how our approach helps to comprehend the Definition yet more fully. Relevant phrases are grouped, and are not necessarily taken in the order of the Definition.

"Son."

As was implied on p. 15, we are entitled to seek as deep an understanding of this word as we can; and it is hoped that our study has helped us to realize at least a few more of its tremendous implications. We appreciate that 'sonship' and 'fatherhood' in reference to the Persons of the Trinity are terms of far greater significance than any human analogy can suggest. They have a significance as indicative of a continuing relationship which is of much more importance than the metaphysical problem concerned with 'eternal generation'. The endoharmony of the Godhead includes the fulfilment and satisfaction of all that is implied in the reciprocal relationships of idealized fatherhood and idealized sonship. To speak of 'God the Father' and 'God the Son' expresses the fact that the endoharmony of the Godhead realizes this satisfaction in the highest sense. There is, so to speak, a directional yearning within the Godhead which is satisfied within Itself in the direction Father to Son and Son to Father, and which is expressed ad extra by the yearning of the Godhead through the Son towards humanity. Sonship is therefore correctly predicable of God the Word before the Incarnation, and an added significance attaches to it after the Incarnation in that God the Word in becoming incarnate consented to identify Himself with that which was

[1] May it again be stressed how very difficult it is, unless our style is to be made intolerably wearisome by the constant repetition of qualifications, to avoid the occurrence here and there of sentences which out of their contexts might misrepresent our intention. Our ideas must be grasped as a complex, and cannot be tested by the consideration of isolated sentences.

derived in the closest analogy to parenthood. God the Word
therefore possesses something we can only describe as "sonship" both prior to the Incarnation as well as in the Incarnation. He was 'Son' before the Incarnation in the sense both
of mode of existence within the Godhead and of mode of
harmony within the Godhead. God the Word possesses
'sonship' after the Incarnation in the additional sense that
He had allowed Himself to undergo a process of integration
in utero Virginis as nearly as possible the kind that is undergone by ordinary human beings. He thus made Himself
"son" of the Blessed Virgin Mary just as truly as any human
being is son of his mother. (It is important to bear constantly in mind the precise significance of human parenthood: see pp. 310–313.) He also thus became "Son" of
God in the sense of self-restricting emergence into this
continuum from the totality of Godhead, as though He
were being derived from that totality by emission or
egression, though, as we have seen, there was no emission
or egression in a separative sense—God the Word as Jesus
Christ was still in the unbroken continuity and unity of the
Godhead, was truly God and truly indiscriminably of Godhead. Thus 'Son' is a title of a content far beyond our
describing, and is a symbol of much more than could ever
be conveyed by any human analogy. (What is said above
refers more particularly to Son of God and Son of Mary.
The parallel and supplementary implications of 'Son of
man' are not here so relevant.)

"Begotten of the Father."

From the considerations set out in the preceding paragraph it will readily be perceived that all human analogies
must be firmly excluded from our minds in contemplating
the meaning of 'begotten of the Father'. The endoharmony
of the Trinity is entirely independent of a space-time or any
other continuum, and did not arise in 'time' or in anything
analogous to time. It is as timeless and eternal as the Trinity
Itself, and, as the endoharmony never was not, so therefore
the Three Persons never were not. There is something
much more deeply significant in endeavouring to realize
that the generation of the Son from the Father is a

continuing and abiding relationship, rather than something happening once in or outside time. We dislike analogies; but as the idea cannot be conveyed in any other way, we suggest that the circumincessio (περιχώρησις) of the Persons of the Trinity is of a kind having a distinction for each Person, so that the Son returns into and proceeds from the Father, whereas the Father receives and sends forth the Son, while the Holy Spirit circumgresses. This is very inadequate; but it may faintly suggest the fact that Sonship and Fatherhood are both eternal and continuous within the Godhead. The Son is indeed begotten of the Father. But there never was when He was not, and there never is when He is not being begotten. Continuing relationships are of far greater significance than isolated events in or outside time. In fact, it might be argued that events are only significant as they establish or affect continuing relationships.

"Perfect in Godhead, truly God, consubstantial with the Father as to the Godhead."

Jesus Christ was perfect in Godhead, truly God, because He was God the Word and no other, and at any moment God the Word could have released Himself from all implication with humanity, could have escaped from the integration into which He had entered. That integration, which involved particularizing an 'area' within Himself and integrating that area through a centrum vitæ, brain and nervous system into a body, was the only focus of particularized awareness which God the Word used during the duration of the biotic unit Jesus Christ, and during that duration God the Word voluntarily restricted Himself thereto in the way which we have considered. But God the Word as of the Godhead was at once initiator and subject of that integration, and it was none other than He. Jesus Christ was none other than God the Word, and while Jesus Christ continued God the Word revealed Himself in no other way. No self-imposed restriction or limitation impairs the absoluteness of God the Word, nor did what He had accepted affect His own essence. God the Word remained indiscriminably of the Godhead, and therefore consubstantial (co-essential, homoousian) with all else that is God, including of course the Person God the Father. (Cf. also pp. 358–360, 372.)

"Perfect in manhood, truly man, consubstantial with us as to the manhood."

Jesus Christ was perfect in manhood because He had revealed, for the only time in the history of the world, what perfect manhood should be. Perfect manhood is to live in this world, in a human body, sensing through a human nervous system and brain, functioning for animal life through a centrum vitæ, appreciating and reacting on the higher levels through an enduring focus of consciousness, a human spirit, the whole naturally integrated in a unit dissoluble only by death, and so to live that the highest integrability of that unit is realized, namely integration into the purpose of God, and its highest centricity is achieved, namely Theocentricity. Only in Jesus Christ was all this realized, for in Him perfect manhood emerged by the gracious condescension of God the Word in self-restricting Himself to a focus of particularized awareness exactly equivalent to a perfect human spirit. (This section should be taken in close connection with the next; and cf. p. 373.)

"Of a reasonable soul."

A reasonable soul (ψυχὴ λογική) may be taken to be almost exactly equivalent to what we have endeavoured to describe under the figure of the intermeshing of centrum vitæ and spirit. We posit that intermeshing as it seems to be the only way of accounting for the difference between animal and human mental life and the only way of providing for at once the interrelation and distinction of space-temporal and exoschematizable qualities (cf. pp. 313–314). Does our Christology really allow that Jesus Christ had a 'reasonable soul'? This is a most vital question, because if we fail to give a satisfactory answer our system reduces to a form of Apollinarianism.

We therefore state:

(i) In our view, Jesus Christ possessed a truly human spirit, though His unity necessarily involved that that human spirit was never a separate and distinct hypostasis, never had a distinct and separate existence, either as such or integrated with a body. But it was a truly human spirit because God the Word had set apart within Himself exactly that which dismitted (see pp. 364–365) would have constituted a human spirit. Further, while still integral with Himself, this 'area' had been integrated into a human centrum vitæ, brain, nervous system and body, so that not only in range and quality of function and appreciation but also in means and mode of operation and expression Jesus Christ possessed a truly human spirit, God the Word particularizing Himself voluntarily thereto: "The Word became flesh."

(ii) The crucial test arises from the contemplation of the awful possibility of failure of the purpose of God the Word. We shrink from this contemplation, but it is of such significance that it must be considered. We dealt with this matter in the old terms on pp. 160–161, using the concept of 'potential schizohypostasia'. We would retain the essentials of that argument, merely transcribing it into more modern and less rigid terms, perhaps thus: If God the Word did not end His duration as Jesus Christ in one or other of the ways mentioned on pp. 395–397, there would have been yet a third awful possibility. He could have decided to let Jesus Christ continue to live, but without Himself being implicated in him. This He could have done by dismitting (cf. pp. 364–365) from Himself the focus of particularized awareness, and letting that become the now separate and independent spirit of Jesus Christ, or rather of Jesus, for such a terrible act would have been a schism in God the Word and a dereliction of His chosen means of manifestation. It is terrible and unthinkable: but it is an event within our powers of imagining. The unity of Jesus Christ depended on His human spirit never being other than the human endohypostasis within God the Word; but the dismitting of that human endohypostasis would have given rise to a spirit, separate, distinct and complete. It is exactly this consideration which makes us able confidently to assert that our view holds Jesus Christ as at once truly God and truly man, and distinguishes our view definitely and decisively from any form of Apollinarianism. Our view admits cognateness with the idea of enhypostasia, but not with Apollinarianism. The true humanity of Jesus Christ arose from the ideally perfect human endohypostasis within God the Word.

"Body."

We do not doubt in any way the complete similarity of Jesus Christ's body to an ordinary human body. The fact that it was parthenogenetically produced is irrelevant in this respect, as has already been mentioned. (Cf. pp. 361–363 and 374.)

"In (of) two natures."

There is no need to enter into a discussion on the matter of the prepositions, because rightly interpreted either preposition gives a right meaning. In fact, 'of two natures' should be taken as describing the mode of the Incarnation and 'in two natures' should be taken as describing the state of the Incarnation. Jesus Christ was by origin of two natures, the divine and the human, and He was during the period of the biotic integration in two natures, the divine and the human. As of the Godhead, God the Word was certainly in the divine nature, and nothing but His own will retained Him in the humanity of Jesus Christ. He could at any moment have disintermeshed Himself. There was no abrogation of His divine nature, no 'kenosis' (in the modern understanding of that word); there was indeed an anapausis of certain divine attributes, but they would have been instantly reactive at His will. As Jesus Christ, God the Word was certainly in human nature. He had so decided to continue during the duration of the biotic unit Jesus Christ, and He had set apart that within Himself which would enable Him to experience exactly as man experiences. He was truly in human nature. God the Word was truly in the divine nature and truly in human nature: in both, not in a nature fused from both. Monophysitism is definitely excluded.

"Unconfusedly" (ἀσυγχύτως) (inconfuse).

Although God the Word was in the two natures, and as
Jesus Christ was of the two natures, the two natures were
nevertheless not fused into one new or composite nature.
They were not 'poured together' (συγχεῖν, to pour together,
whence ἀσυγχύτως, not as if poured together, uncom-
mingledly). We are to think of the unity of God the Word
in Jesus Christ thus: a unity so firm that its bonds would
have been natural had any but God the Word been
involved; but because He was in fact involved, and the
unity was therefore voluntary so far as He was concerned
(though He observed it as though it were natural), the two
natures, which in any other case would have been fused
into one nature, were not so merged, and God the Word
was perfectly aware of the delimitations of His experiences
as man and of His existence as of the Godhead; He was
perfectly aware of the intermeshing of that which He had
set apart within Himself with the centrum vitæ and through
the centrum vitæ with the brain, nervous system and body
which He had adopted and whereby He had become man;
He appreciated all that came through that channel, so
that being God He yet knew what it was to be man, and
being man He knew what it was to be centred in God.
The experiencing subject of the communicatio idiomatum
(ἀντίδοσις ἰδιωμάτων) was God the Word, who was
experiencing at once what it was to be man and remaining
in the telicity and centricity of Godhead with which He
was never other than indiscriminably integral. ἀσυγχύτως,
rightly understood, excludes Arianism, Eutychianism, and
any other form of monophysitism.

"Immutably" (ἀτρέπτως) (immutabiliter).

Neither nature is to be regarded as in any way changed,
either by combination or transformation (τρέπειν, to
change, whence ἀτρέπτως, not as if liable to change,
unchangeably). The divine nature remained essentially
unaffected by its linkage with human nature, and the human
nature became by the linkage simply that which it was its
highest destiny to become, that which alone could make it
perfect human nature—entry into the telicity of God and

centricity in Him. ἀτρέπτως excludes all ideas of combination or transformation of natures as understood in the ancient metaphysic, and like ἀσυγχύτως definitely excludes Arianism, Eutychianism, and all forms of monophysitism.

"Indivisibly, inseparably" (ἀδιαιρέτως, ἀχωρίστως) (indivise, inseparabiliter).

Although the two natures are not confused, commingled, combined or transformed, and remain distinct, it is nevertheless to be recognized and emphasized that their union in Jesus Christ was a real union and not a mere juxtaposition. We can neither divide them nor separate them. If we wish to see a distinction in the two words, ἀδιαιρέτως (from διαιρεῖν, to divide, whence ἀδιαιρέτως, not as if able to be divided) may be taken to imply that we cannot say "Here functions humanity, and here divinity." Jesus Christ was One, and behaved as a single Person experiencing simultaneously in two natures of whose distinct properties He was well aware, but which in Him were equally within His unity. We approach comprehension of this when we appreciate that His humanity was telically integrated in the Theotelic system and its centricity was Theocentricity. The unity of Jesus Christ's Person was only possible because in His Person humanity is integrated into and centred in God, which is the ideal for all that is human and is made possible for us through Christ. Here is one aspect of the mystery of the Atonement, that thus He, though His Sonship is unique in that He alone is the Eternally Begotten, is nevertheless "the firstborn among many brethren" (Romans viii. 29). ἀχωρίστως, on the other hand, from χωρίζειν, to separate, whence ἀχωρίστως, not as if able to be separated, emphasizes not so much the fact of the natures being unified as a basis of experience, but that they could not be separated in the sense of duplex personality. Jesus Christ was not Jesus (humanity) on the one hand and God the Word (divinity) on the other somehow united in one bodily person (crude "Nestorianism"). There was no separation of any such kind, nor could there have been without the unthinkable disaster of schizohypostasia or dismission of the human endohypostasis; the natures were united in bonds which for any but God the Word would have been natural and inescapable; and though God the Word could have escaped from them, He had determined to observe them as though they were as binding on Him as they would have been on any other. None but He could have separated them; He would not.

"One prosôpon."

Jesus Christ was certainly one person (πρόσωπον) in the objective sense—one presence, one appearance, one person objectively from the point of view of an observer; for Jesus Christ was none other than God the Word, and during the duration of Jesus Christ God the Word manifested Himself in this continuum in no other way than as Jesus Christ. God the Word and Jesus Christ are not one and another, for while Jesus Christ was, God the Word revealed Himself in no other way in this continuum.

"One hypostasis."

Jesus Christ was certainly one person (ὑπόστασις) in the sense of discrete individuality, one personality in our sense of the term. The one hypostasis was that of God the Word in whom the human endohypostasis (see pp. 364–369) provided by enhypostasia that which completed the perfect manhood of Jesus Christ, so that the one hypostasis of God the Word was at once the individual subject, the hypostasis, of both the Godhead and manhood which found one another in Jesus Christ.

We find ourselves confirmed in our acceptance of the Definition, and able to read it with more assurance and understanding. The above comments serve to link up the phrases mentioned with the general arguments we have been advancing, and the phrases not commented upon are deemed to need no such linking.

Our task is ended, and it is our hope that these pages may have helped to confirm the faith of those to whom God in Christ is the supreme and central fact in the Universe, and may add to the certainty and assurance of those whose privilege it is to expound to others "the faith which was once delivered unto the saints".

APPENDIX

NOTES ON THE BAZAAR

NOTES ON THE BAZAAR

THESE notes are not intended to provide a general commentary on the Bazaar, but merely to enable the metaphysical and Christological ideas to be followed, so that the consistency of Nestorius' views may be tested. It is assumed that the reader will have accepted as a working hypothesis the metaphysic and Christology set out in Part I of this book, and that he will now check through the Bazaar itself to see how far the hypothesis fits the actual words of Nestorius.

References will be given by means of the page numbering of Bedjan's edition of the Syriac text,[1] as explained on p. 50 above. In Book I of the Bazaar it may sometimes be useful to quote the Book, Part and section numbers. Thus I. i. 12–20 means Book I, Part I, sections 12–20. But Bedjan's numbers will also be given in such cases. There are a few places where the numbering in Driver and Hodgson's translation[2] may not be quite clear. These should be noted, so that references may always be definite. Driver and Hodgson's page 1 is B. 1; their p. 3 is B. 2–3; the Syriac reference on their p. 4 should be 3, not 2; on their p. 6, 4–10, not 6–8; their p. 7 is B. 10–11, and the stroke before 'Preface' should be omitted, as B. 10 begins just before the end of the Translator's preface; the Syriac reference on their p. 8 should be 11, not 12; the stroke on their p. 51, dividing B. 74 from B. 75, has been omitted, and should be inserted between 'upon' and 'the' in line 12; the stroke on their p. 70, dividing B. 102 from B. 103, has been omitted, and should be inserted between 'nature.' and 'Thus' in line 12; the Syriac reference on their pp. 81 and

[1] *Nestorius: Le Livre d'Héraclide de Damas*, édité par Paul Bedjan, avec plusieurs appendices. Reference to 'Bedjan' will always imply this work, and as his page numbering is used as our basis, it will not usually be necessary to repeat his page number to enable a reference to be found.

[2] *Nestorius: The Bazaar of Heracleides*, newly translated from the Syriac. Reference to 'Driver and Hodgson' will always imply this work.

82 should be 119, not 120. The transposition of B. 137–146 to between B. 270 and B. 271 has already been noted (p. 50). The Bazaar is divided into five parts:[1]

Book I, Part I (B. 10–125).

This contains a refutation of the principal types of erroneous solution of the Christological problem, followed by the exposition of Nestorius' own views, and ends with some additional arguments against erroneous solutions.

Book I, Part II (B. 126–137).

This is in effect a summary of Book I, Part I. The erroneous solutions are summarized in six sections, then follows a concise statement of his own views, and the part ends with an attack on the idea of hypostatic union.

Book I, Part III (B. 146–193).

This is mainly concerned with criticisms of Cyril's motives and methods in bringing about the Council of Ephesus and in causing it to be constituted with undue haste. Nestorius explains how Cyril had interfered with Nestorius' handling of the 'Theotokos' problem at Constantinople, and how he had dominated both the preliminaries and the Council. It relates mostly to events between Nestorius' consecration as bishop of Constantinople, April 428, and the first session of the Council of Ephesus, June 431.

[1] The divisions here given are those in the Syriac text of Bedjan and followed by Driver and Hodgson. But Nau, drawing his own conclusions from the Syriac translator's preface (B. 4), prefers to make the divisions thus:

Book I,   Part I.   B. 10–125.
          Part II. B. 126–209 (omitting B. 137–146).
          Part III. B. 209–270.
Book II, Part I.   B. 137–146, 271–459.
          Part II. B. 459–521.

This explains why Driver and Hodgson in the note on their p. 95 say that, with Nau, they transfer B. 137–146 to the beginning of Book II, Section I. Using Nau's divisions, that is its new position; but with Bedjan's divisions the transferred section comes about one-fifth of the way through Book II, Part I. We must take Driver and Hodgson's "Book II, Part I" on their p. 131 to be in accordance with Bedjan, and "Book II, Part I" on their p. 186 to be in accordance with Nau.

Book II, Part I (B. 193–459).

This contains Nestorius' detailed comments on the charges made and the documents presented at the first session of the Council (June 22nd, 431), and an account of the trend of events after the Council, including the enforced peace between the Easterns and Cyril (433) and Cyril's correspondence with Acacius of Melitene (435).

Book II, Part II (B. 459–521).

This part gives a commentary on the events from the time of Flavian's consecration as bishop of Constantinople (446) until just before the Council of Chalcedon (October 451). Nestorius sees in Flavian's unequal contest with Eutyches and Dioscorus a repetition of his own struggle with Cyril, and believes that very shortly, with the triumph of Leo, will come the vindication of all for which he has contended.

Book I, Part I, contains practically all Nestorius' ideas, and if this part is mastered the rest of the Bazaar presents little difficulty. Apart from the historical setting, the remainder of the Bazaar amounts to little more than variations on the same few themes, Nestorius dealing with the same familiar points time after time as they arise in different settings. The two occurring most constantly are: that hypostatic union is not a solution of the Christological problem, for it involves ousic and natural union and the suppression of human nature (B. 133–137, 225–240, 257–270, 405); and that from the Incarnation to the death on the Cross reference should be made to 'Christ', 'Lord', 'Son', or some such term, as 'God the Word' properly bears reference only to the divinity in Christ, though apart from Christ there was no God the Word during the period of the earthly life (B. 201–204, 211–225, 245–270, 141–146, 271–363, 404–459). As has been pointed out (pp. 184–186) Nestorius regarded these two matters as of fundamental significance, and laboured them ceaselessly. The arguments on these and other matters which arise in the course of the parts subsequent to the first are not difficult to follow if Book I, Part I, has been mastered. For this reason the notes on

Book I, Part I, are fuller than on the remainder, it being needless to deal with the same points every time they arise in slightly different settings. Once the general principles of the Nestorian metaphysic have been grasped, it is not difficult to make sense even of his most involved passages. The tedious repetition of similar explanations is therefore omitted; otherwise the whole of the first part of this book would need repeating in the course of the notes. Passages will only receive comment if there is any real difficulty. If it is desired to refer to comments on particular passages which may have been made in Part I of this book, reference should be made to the 'Index to Passages in the Bazaar' (pp. 490–491).

Book I, Part I

Erroneous views discussed and refuted (I. i. 1–53) (B. 10–69). Nestorius' views expounded (I. i. 54–88) (B. 69–117). Additional arguments against erroneous views (I. i. 89–93) (B. 117–125).

Erroneous views discussed and refuted (I. i. 1–53) (B. 10–69)

Nestorius has his own method of classifying heresies and prefers to classify them according to his own metaphysic rather than under descriptive names. The only heresies he mentions by name are those which are simple in metaphysical concept, such as Manichæism, Paulianism, Arianism and Apollinarianism. Their more complicated derivatives he prefers to deal with in accordance with his own metaphysical approach, disposing of them according to classes and types rather than by specific names: "We wish to decline to [give] the names of their chiefs, so as not to prolong our discussion nor to be found to have omitted any point in the inquiry by first becoming entangled in [questions of] names" (B. 14). Except when engaged in the immediate controversy with Cyril his analysis of views is therefore little encumbered with names.

He starts by distinguishing three groups: (i) those who deny that Jesus Christ was God, (ii) those who deny that Jesus Christ was man, (iii) those who endeavour to solve the problem by positing the natural union of something of

Godhead with something of manhood. To these three groups names can be given: (i) is Paulianism, (ii) is Manichæism, (iii) is Arianism. He reckons as derivatives and modifications of Paulianism those theories which accept the true manhood of Jesus Christ but fail to find place for more than an impaired or partial Godhead in Him; he reckons as derivatives and modifications of Manichæism those theories which accept the true Godhead of Jesus Christ but fail to find place for more than an illusory, impaired or partial manhood in Him; he reckons as derivatives and modifications of Arianism those theories which explicitly or implicitly depend on ousic and natural union, particularly Apollinarianism and the views of Cyril. He does not work out his scheme with any degree of precision, owing to the digressiveness of his style; but the various arguments will be followed more readily if this classification is borne in mind.

Nestorius deals with the erroneous views in the following order:

(1) I. i. 1–4 (B. 11–12). Those who do not attempt to interpret Jesus Christ as God-man at all: the heathen, the Jews, and the Paulinians, who deny Him to be God, and the Manichæans, who deny Him to be man.

(2) I. i. 5 (B. 12–13). The Arians, who impair both Godhead and manhood and suppose a natural union.

From the opposite errors of excluding manhood by considering Christ as nothing but God (Manichæism) and of excluding Godhead by considering Christ nothing but man (Paulianism) there arise two contrasted types of heresy (I. i. 6) (B. 13). The one, though accepting the true Godhead of Christ, errs through inability to account for His true manhood; this type is the main subject of I. i. 10–37 (first paragraph) (B. 14–41). The other, though accepting the true manhood of Christ, errs by conceiving an impaired, partial or separated Godhead; this type is the main subject of I. i. 51–53 (B. 63–69). From Arianism there arise Apollinarianism and other erroneous views depending on ousic and natural union. These developments are the main subject of I. i. 42–50 (B. 49–63).

CI

(3) I. i. 10–30 (down to "Further, we have already said the same thing.") (B. 14–34). There are those who say that Christ was truly God, and suppose that God became man by the exercise of the power of His own nature, which, being omnipotent, includes the power to be man.

(4) I. i. 30 (from "Let us turn . . .")–35 (B. 35–38). There are those who say that Christ was truly God, and suppose that the manhood was taken up into the divine ousia, and made one with it.

I. i. 36 (B. 38–40) adds comments bearing on both the above headings (3) and (4).

(5) I. i. 37 (first paragraph) (B. 40–41). There are those who say that Christ was truly God, and suppose that God changed a part of His nature into the nature of man.

I. i. 37 (second paragraph)–41 (B. 41–49) is a digression on the problem of transubstantiation.

(6) I. i. 42–50 (B. 49–63). There are those who say that Christ was a natural union of God the Word and a human body and animal soul (Apollinarianism), or a natural union of God the Word and a human body, soul and intelligence.

(7) I. i. 51–53 (B. 63–69). There are those who say that Christ was only a man, but so obedient to and aided by God the Word that he gained the honour and name of Son by God's grace. There are thus two Sons, God the Word and Jesus Christ.

The various heresies are dealt with in the anciently popular dialogue form, Nestorius arguing with a certain fictitious Sophronius. Sophronius represents in turn the various heretical ideas, asks questions, and suggests difficulties. No consistency is to be looked for in Sophronius, as his business is to marshal objections of all kinds, whether self-consistent or not. This is made clear in I. i. 37 (B. 42), where Nestorius says to Sophronius: "Speak confidently, undaunted, using manfully and adequately every one of their arguments even as they themselves [do]."

Throughout this division the arguments almost entirely depend on a right understanding of the metaphysic of ousia and nature, and on a proper realization of the implications of the attributes of God. The reasoning will be easily followed, and often readily anticipated, if we bear constantly in mind the fundamental propositions on ousia and nature, which are set out on pp. 83–88. It may be convenient to repeat them:

(1) The real and true existence of any object depends upon the real and true existence of the appropriate ousia with its corresponding nature.

(2) There is an absolute correspondence between an ousia and its nature. ('One ousia, one nature.')

(3) A transformed ousia is that into which it has been transformed, and is nothing else.

(4) An ousia cannot change or add to its nature.

(5) The result of a combination of ousias and their corresponding natures into a new ousia with its corresponding nature is the formation of one ousia with its corresponding nature, which is to be regarded as a distinct unity just as though it had been newly created, and is not to be regarded as in any way still containing the original combining ousias or natures as such.

Of the attributes of God and their implications it is particularly necessary to recall that:

(1) The ousia and nature of God, being eternal and unchangeable, cannot be created, transformed or annihilated (p. 124).

(2) The ousia and nature of God cannot take part in integrations or disintegrations; that is to say, God can never enter into ousic or natural union (p. 125).

(1) *I. i.* 1–4 (*B.* 11–12). Those who do not attempt to interpret Jesus Christ as God-man at all: the heathen, the Jews, and the Paulinians, who deny Him to be God, and the Manichæans, who deny Him to be man.

These sections allude to those who regard the problem of Christology as insoluble. They cannot conceive of a Christ who is a unity, and both truly God and truly man.

I. i. 1 (*B.* 11). The objection of the heathen is, on the surface, a reasonable one. How can a passible Christ be thought to be God, who is agreed to be impassible? One of the major difficulties in formulating a Christology which can claim to be orthodox is to show how possibility can be predicated of Christ without predicating it also of God. It is assumed that the heathen accept the axiom that God is impassible (p. 122).

I. i. 2 (B. 11). The objection of the Jews is based on the same difficulty. They also regard passibility in Christ as incompatible with His being God. The Messiah will presumably partake of the impassibility and omnipotence of God, "in all great glory and dominion."

I. i. 3 (B. 11–12). The Manichæans also recognize this difficulty, but resolve it by denying the reality of the manhood of Christ. Whatever in Christ appears to be inconsistent with the nature of God is to be reckoned as illusory. This view leads to a consistent interpretation of the person of Christ, which in the terms of the Nestorian metaphysic could be summarized thus: God the Word, wishing to reveal Himself as a man among men, created by fiat (p. 70) an instrument having the schêma of a man, and used it as His allogenous prosôpon; Jesus Christ was God the Word revealing Himself by means of this schêma. But this is not an orthodox Christology, for the conditions of the problem are not observed: that Christ must be not only a unity, but truly man, as well as truly God. In fact, the Manichæan Christ is simply a theophany (p. 126).

I. i. 4 (B. 12). The Paulinians and Photinians do not accept Christ as God for the same reason as the heathen and the Jews: they feel that passibility in Christ makes it impossible to regard Him as God.

(2) I. i. 5 (B. 12–13). The Arians, who impair both Godhead and manhood and suppose a natural union.

In the terms of the Nestorian metaphysic the Arian Christology would represent Christ as a union of two ousias, one of which is incompletely human and the other divine but without certain of the attributes of God. Such a Christology is defective for three reasons: first, such a Christ is admittedly not fully man; second, such a Christ is admittedly not fully God; and third, a union of ousias is postulated, which necessitates the disappearance as such of the individual ousias and the emergence of a new and different one. The latter part of the section emphasizes some of the implications of a union of natures, showing how it involves the passibility of God: for if we suppose that God could in any way be supposed to remain in the united nature, this nature, being necessarily passible, involves God in its passibility. Thus a Christology involving a union of natures is both a failure to solve the problem and a contravention of the axioms as to the nature of God.

(3) *I. i.* 10–30 (down to "Further, we have already said the same thing.") (*B.* 14–34). There are those who say that Christ was truly God, and suppose that God became man by the exercise of the power of His own nature, which, being omnipotent, includes the power to be man.

I. i. 10 (*B.* 14–15). Nestorius vaguely indicates a heresy which he regards as approaching Manichæism, but which differs from it in that those who hold it suppose themselves to be avoiding the Manichæan error that the human qualities of Christ were illusory.

Sophronius undertakes to expound this view. He first advances the idea that, if God is omnipotent, His powers include the ability not to be God. The implication is that God could become man by virtue of His omnipotence, and thus become incarnate as man within His own nature. But metaphysically this should mean that the nature of God includes the property of becoming man, that is, presumably, of becoming the ousia of man with the corresponding nature. Sophronius recognizes a difficulty in this proposition, and says that it is not held that "the flesh truly came into being". This implies either (i) that that which seemed to be flesh was not actually the ousia of flesh; in that case the flesh is a mere schêma, and the position is simply Manichæism; or (ii) that that which seemed to be flesh actually was flesh, but was not to be regarded as coming "into being", in that it had already existed as God; a continuity of existence is to be supposed, but a change of ousia. Any such idea is counter to the fundamentals of the Nestorian metaphysic: a transformed ousia is that into which it has been transformed, and is nothing else (p. 84).

If, therefore, God were to be supposed to transform Himself or any part of Himself into flesh, that which thus came into being would be flesh in ousia and nature, and nothing else.

I. i. 11 (*B.* 15–16). Sophronius, however, continues to advance this idea, adducing a clever analogy from the behaviour of water. Water, whose nature is to be liquid and infrangible, can become ice, which is solid and frangible. Water thus becomes another nature, while, presumably, being the same ousia. Thus also God, whose nature it is to be impassible and omnipotent, can become man, who is passible and limited. God thus becomes another nature, while, presumably, being the same ousia. But this ingenious reasoning is inconsistent with the fundamental positions of the Nestorian metaphysic: an ousia which appears to possess two alternative natures simply possesses a nature parts of which are described by the supposed two alternatives: the nature is one, not two. So that if God seemed to become man in this way, He would still really be in His own ousia and nature, and if He were supposed to be a man, it would only be because He was presenting a prosôpon with the schêma of a man.

The last sentence of this section should surely be punctuated thus: "For as water, which cannot be broken, because it is frozen can in truth be broken, . . ."[1]

I. i. 12 (*B.* 16). Sophronius applies the analogy of water exercising two natures to the Incarnation and to Old Testament theophanies. When God appeared to Abraham, Isaac and Jacob, He was simply making use of His power to become human nature. The theophanies in mind are probably of the types recorded in Gen. iii. 8–9 (God walking and talking), Gen. xvii. 1 (God talking), Gen. xviii. 1–16 (God, as one of the three men, walking, talking, eating and drinking), Gen. xxvi. 24 (God talking), Gen. xxxii. 24–30 (God walking and talking).

According to the Nestorian metaphysic such theophanies are simply allogenous prosôpa of God with the schêmata

[1] Cf. Nau: "C'est ainsi que l'eau qui ne peut être brisée, l'est cependant en vérité lorsqu'elle est congelée . . ."; also Connolly, who translates thus: "For as water which is not-subject-to-breaking, when it is frozen may truly be broken" (*Journal of Theological Studies*, vol. xxvii, p. 195, January, 1926).

of men. Obviously they in no way fulfil the conditions of the Incarnation—Christ a unity, truly man, truly God.

In the latter part of this section Sophronius makes an assumption convenient for the view which he is defending: "The creator does nothing in *schêma* and in illusion". This, as we shall see, is an assumption which Nestorius does not accept. When it serves His purpose, God certainly uses schêma and illusion, if by illusion we mean the use of an allogenous prosôpon intentionally presenting the schêma of some other ousia. As Nestorius says, "There are many changes through which he appeared in *schêma*" (B. 29), and again, "And wherein he took the *schêma* of a man or of fire, it is said that God appeared or that one saw God" (B. 77).

I. i. 13 (*B.* 16–17). Nestorius asks whether those holding this view maintain that God truly became flesh. Sophronius repeats the argument in a slightly different way. He attempts to draw a distinction between being a nature and being in a nature. Being 'in a nature' would seem to correspond with the Nestorian definition, and includes definition and circumscription, properties and defects; being 'a nature', on the other hand, would appear to imply temporary possession of the qualities and properties appropriate to some particular nature without permanent subjection to its circumscriptions. Just as water, which in its nature is fluid and infrangible, can temporarily by freezing become a nature (ice) which is solid and frangible, but is not permanently limited to that nature because it can be melted again; so, Sophronius suggests, God could become the nature of flesh without being circumscribed by that nature, without being 'in' that nature. (The argument in this section makes it evident that the word 'in' is being used strictly to mean 'in naturally' (see pp. 145–146).) Any such idea is of course totally incompatible with the fundamental propositions on natures (pp. 83–88): to be a certain nature involves being in (naturally) that nature.

As *bsar* (flesh) is masculine, it is not always clear in this section whether the pronouns refer to God or to the flesh. In two places where Driver and Hodgson give 'his', 'its' may make easier sense: "We confess that he became flesh truly but not by its nature, . . ." and "Thus also has God truly become flesh, and he is the nature of the flesh and not in its nature, in that he is not it always but he became [so] afterwards."

I. i. 16 (*B.* 20–21). In this finely conclusive passage Nestorius condemns any method of explaining the Incarnation by the idea of transformation of divine ousia. Ousia and nature being inseparable correlatives, if God became any other ousia and its corresponding nature He would make Himself cease to be God. In the Nestorian metaphysic this conclusion is inescapable. Nestorius makes another sound point: our idea of omnipotence must not include absurdities: "In remaining God he wills not everything nor again does he wish not to become God so as to make himself not to be God."

But Sophronius repeats his point. He agrees that God cannot wish not to be what He is: He remains in His own nature. Nevertheless, being omnipotent, He can become any nature He wishes, though He is not circumscribed by the nature, that is, in (naturally) the nature.

I. i. 17 (*B.* 21). Nestorius asks whether 'truly flesh' means 'truly in ousia' or 'truly in illusion and fiction', since 'truly in nature' has been ruled out. Sophronius' answer must mean that he would consider it 'truly flesh' if God, remaining in His own nature, transformed His ousia into ousia of flesh. The flesh would be truly flesh in ousia, but illusory and fictitious so far as being flesh in nature was concerned. This is obviously a quite impossible idea, being contrary to the fundamental relationship of ousia and nature.

I. i. 18 (*B.* 21–22). Nestorius, assuming that existence depends on the real existence of an underlying ousia, points out that, if God remains in His own nature, His own ousia also continues; and if He is existing also according to the flesh, there must be ousia of flesh. That is to say, there are two ousias in the one nature of God, which is absurd.

Sophronius now suggests that there is only one ousia, ousia of God, but that it possesses the ability also to become ousia of flesh. He endeavours to make this apparent contradiction reasonable by referring again to the water analogy, as if the ousia of water constantly remained, but could also become ousia of ice.

I. i. 19 (*B.* 22–23). It may be well to ignore the Syriac translator's heading to this section, for the first sentence of the text seems to indicate that for 'schêma' he should have written 'prosôpon'.

Although it somewhat complicates matters, it seems advisable to apply the first three lines of this section both to the case of water and ice, and to the case of God in Himself and God in the flesh. Hodgson would refer it only to the former, and Nau to the latter. But analogy and argument are so interdependent that the lines must be understandable in application to either.

In reference to water the application is simple: running water and ice are the same in ousia and nature, but their instantaneous prosôpa differ owing to differences in their circumstances of pressure and temperature.

On the other hand, if the reference is to God in Himself and God in the flesh, an exactly similar explanation would apply. If it were conceivable that God, without making use of an allogenous prosôpon could remain as He is or at will appear as man, it would simply mean that for differing purposes His autogenous prosôpon presented itself in differing ways. Any such idea is contrary to the nature of God, which includes invisibility; but even if we were to suppose that God could present an autogenous prosôpon with the schêma of a man this would not be an incarnation.

The water analogy is thus completely disposed of; the true interpretation of the two states of water and ice has been given, but to use the analogy for solving the problem of God in Himself and in the flesh is of no value.

"But [to be distinguished] by the *prosôpon* without nature is a *schêma* without *hypostasis* in another *schêma*." This sentence completely disposes of the idea of God becoming man in His own ousia and nature. For if God, who is invisible (p. 123), were to be supposed to possess a visible prosôpon without making use of anything but His own ousia and nature, such a visible prosôpon would by hypothesis be without nature, for visibility cannot be predicated of a nature one of whose attributes is invisibility;

that is, such a prosôpon without a nature would be a mere appearance with nothing underlying it, a schêma without hypostasis, which is inconceivable. Further, this prosôpon without a nature, this schêma without hypostasis, would be presenting the schêma of a man: a mere appearance based on another mere appearance with nothing underlying it, "a *schêma* without *hypostasis* in another *schêma*".

I. i. 20 (*B.* 24). Finally, any such idea, even if it could be logically stated, would not be an incarnation. For Christ must be God and man, and if the manhood is attained by changing the ousia of God to that of manhood, where is the divine ousia in Christ? If you say it still remains ousia of God, where is the human nature of Christ?

I. i. 21 (*B.* 24–26). If we imagine a man made from the ousia and nature of God, it is the same kind of thing as if a man were made from wood or stone; the appearance might be that of a man, but the material in ousia and nature is wood, stone or God, as the case may be. Such a man would be a deceiving prosôpon of wood, stone or God, presenting the schêma (mere appearance) of a man.

Sophronius counters this by citing cases in which God effected transformations. Why cannot He transform Himself? It may be remarked that all these transformations are easily explained in terms of the Nestorian metaphysic (see p. 71). The most interesting of these cases is that of the transformation of Lot's wife into a pillar of salt. Lot's wife was a natural unity integrated from body, animal soul and spirit. The disintegration of that unity into its three constituents was accompanied by the simultaneous transformation of the first, or first and second, into a pillar of salt. The spirit, presumably, returned "unto God who gave it".

Nestorius admits that such changes can take place, but once they have taken place they are absolute, and the former condition is as though it had never been. In particular, if God changed the material basis, the hylê (see pp. 88–91), of His own ousia into the material basis of the ousia and nature of flesh, that material basis would, by definition, be the ousia of flesh and nothing else. The word hylê is probably used here in preference to ousia to suggest a possible common basis for all ousias, even ousias so different as those of God and flesh. But even if it is conceivable that God could detach some of His own ousia from Himself, reduce it to characterless hylê and form that hylê into ousia of man, even then Nestorius' conclusive argument still stands: "Things which are changed from their first *ousia* possess only that nature into which they have been changed." An intermediate hylê stage makes no difference. "He possesses that *ousia* which he has become without having been [it]." This may mean either "He possesses that ousia which he has become and which he was not (formerly)" or "He possesses that ousia which he has become and is as though he had not existed (formerly)." By the supplied 'it' it appears that Driver and Hodgson prefer the former alternative, as does Nau, who translates: "Il possède cette essence qu'il est devenu et qu'il n'était pas." But the latter alternative seems to accord better with the general trend of Nestorius' argument.

Sophronius next endeavours to support his argument by referring to the transformations of the staff of Moses and of the waters of the Nile.

I. i. 22 (*B.* 26–27). Nestorius has a complete answer to this, which is explained on pp. 84–86.

Sophronius endeavours to rebut this by quoting a case of conscious identity as two natures: Abraham, a man, yet aware that he was also 'dust and ashes'. This is supposed to support the idea that one ousia can have two natures. If the ousia of Abraham can be man by nature and dust and ashes by nature, surely the ousia of God can be God by nature and man by nature.

I. i. 23 (*B.* 27–28). If this is so, there must be one ousia underlying alike the natures of dust and ashes, man, and God, which we may consider indifferently as the ousia of dust and ashes, man, or God. We should, likewise, have to posit that its nature, necessarily one, included all the qualities of dust and ashes, man, and God—a reductio ad absurdum. Alternatively, if we agree that it is unthinkable to identify the divine ousia with the ousia of dust and ashes, we presumably must suppose that the nature of man can be based on either of two ousias, that of God or that of dust and ashes. But this is contrary to the fundamental concept of 'one ousia, one nature'. So that if man has the ousia of dust and ashes, and the ousia of God is something different, the ousia of God could not be the basis of the nature of man except possibly in mere schêma, and we are back to Manichæism. In other words, if one ousia were supposed to be recognized in two different ousias, it could only, in reality, actually be one of those ousias, and the manifestation as the other supposed ousia would simply be a schêma.

This paragraph illustrates Nestorius' skilful handling of scriptural difficulties. He implies that scripture is to be interpreted intelligently, and that isolated sentences must not be used as the bases of unsound arguments.

Sophronius then asserts that Nestorius is suggesting that God should be both God by nature and man by nature. (Nestorius would not suggest that God should be God by nature and man by nature, but that Christ should be God by nature and man by nature.) The paragraph ends with a crude misrepresentation of Nestorius' views. What Sophronius here suggests would be a syntactic unity consisting of God the Word, from whose point of view the unity would be a voluntary syntactic unity, and the man Jesus, for whom it would be an imposed syntactic unity. The quasi-prosôpon of this syntactic unity would have the schêma of a man and would be an allogenous prosôpon of God the Word. Such a syntactic unity is by no means an impossibility. It would constitute a theophany. But it would not provide a Christ with the kind of unity which the agreed conditions of the Christological problem imply. This misrepresentation is sufficiently like the first stage in the Nestorian Christology (pp. 152–153) to show how easily the idea of Nestorianism as a duality could gain currency.

I. i. 24 (B. 28–29). Without yet dealing with the difficulties involved in the use by God the Word of an intermediary, which are, of course, very real, Nestorius suggests that there are equally grave difficulties in the supposition that God the Word did not use an intermediary. If God remained in His own ousia and nature, and as man, or supposed man, was still only ousia and nature of God, how then can He be the mediator? As God only He cannot mediate between man and God. (This obviously powerful argument still leaves Nestorius the obligation of proving that Christ is not only God, but also something other than God, that He may have status as a mediator. The maintenance of this duality in a unity is the crux of Nestorius' problem.) "Consequently he cannot be God but the mediator of God." This means: He (Christ) cannot be God (and nothing else), but the mediator of God (that is, if not other than God, some kind of unity of God and something other than God).

I. i. 25 (*B.* 29). If the Incarnation took place as Sophronius suggests, how did it differ from God's appearances to Abraham, Jacob and others? Nestorius would consider that these appearances were merely in schêma, that is, they were theophanies of the allogenous prosôpon type presenting various schêmata appropriate to the circumstances (see pp. 126–127). "There are many changes through which he appeared in *schêma*." This sentence provides a belated answer to Sophronius' assumption in I. i. 12 (B. 16): "The creator does nothing in *schêma* and in illusion." When it suits His purpose, God certainly can and does use schêmata. Every theophany is an appearance in schêma.

Sophronius next attempts to distinguish between appearances to particular individuals and a general appearance to all mankind. The latter is the Incarnation.

I. i. 26 (*B.* 29–30). If the Incarnation is defined as a general appearance to all mankind, there never was an Incarnation, for Christ was not seen by men of all times and places.

I. i. 27 (*B.* 30–32). If the Incarnation had been a general appearance to all mankind, it would not have been an Incarnation as man, for it is the nature of man to be limited by time and space. The next sentence is an example of Nestorius' most characteristic fault. Although he exposes with minute care the flaws in the arguments of his opponents, he often states his own fundamental positions in vague and ill-defined terms. His meaning is so obvious to himself that he thinks it will be equally so to his readers. To understand these few lines, it is necessary to have grasped the whole tenor of his argument, which is hardly to be expected of a reader who has only reached his thirtieth page: "But in the *ousia* of man [he is] truly man, of the

true nature of the true man in which he became incarnate
altogether for all and which he made his *prosôpon*, and he
was revealed in the things of men in comporting himself
in the nature of man, being God in human nature." The
lax use of the expressions 'in ousia' and 'in nature' must
be observed. 'Ousically in ousia' and 'naturally in nature',
the strict and proper meanings of these expressions, are
obviously excluded. Only the manhood of Christ, the potentially separate man Jesus, was ousically in his ousia and
naturally in his nature; and the expression "God in human
nature" must mean in human nature in some way other
than naturally. (See the uses of 'in' on pp. 141–146.) The
uses of 'in' in this passage are remarked upon on p.
146, but there is also lack of definition in the use of
'he'. It may suffice at this point to indicate how much
Nestorius expects his reader to comprehend, by merely
inserting what must be understood by each use of 'in' and
'he': "But in" (naturally in reference to the potentially
separate man Jesus, syntactically, voluntarily and prosôpically in reference to God the Word) "the *ousia* of man [he]"
(God the Word in that part of His durative prosôpon in
which He voluntarily, syntactically and prosôpically united
Himself with the potentially separate but never separately
existing man Jesus) "[is] truly man," (in that He is voluntarily self-limited to the nature of man, from which if He
escaped, as He could, He would cause a separate man Jesus,
truly and only man, to come into being) "of the true nature
of the true man" (the potentially separate man Jesus) "in"
(syntactically, voluntarily and prosôpically) "which he"
(God the Word) "became incarnate altogether for all and
which he made his *prosôpon*," (allogenous) "and he was
revealed in" (circumstantially) "the things of men in comporting himself in" (syntactically, voluntarily and prosôpically in so far as He was God the Word, naturally in
so far as His allogenous prosôpon, the potentially separate
but never separately existing man Jesus, was continuously
His prosôpon in the duration of God the Word incarnate)
"the nature of man, being God in" (syntactically, voluntarily and prosôpically) "human nature." It can readily be
imagined that if anyone else had written such a sentence,

Nestorius would have been among the first to point out its incongruities. It must of course be admitted that the sentence is only capable of one right interpretation if the Nestorian metaphysic is securely in mind. But here, as so often, Nestorius expects too much of his reader.

In the remainder of this section, a very important distinction is drawn between the two ways in which a king can assume the schêma of soldierhood. A king can assume the clothing and equipment of a soldier, laying aside, for the time being, the purple of royalty but still retaining his royal dignity and authority. A king so doing would not, in any true sense, have become a real soldier. On the other hand, a king could assume the clothing and equipment of a soldier and voluntarily restrict himself to the powers and circumscriptions of soldierhood, not going beyond those things which a soldier as such could do. A king could so limit himself as long as he wished, and during the continuance of this self-limitation his power and dignity as a king would be completely laid aside—though naturally, if he wished, he could at any time lay aside the schêma of soldierhood and resume his full kingship. It is, however, interesting and relevant to observe that if a king had assumed the schêma of soldierhood with a view to the fulfilment of any specific purpose, it would be a confession of weakness on his part so to lay aside the schêma of soldierhood before his purpose had been fulfilled. Another very important point to observe is that in order to become a soldier permanently or temporarily a king needs only the clothing and equipment of soldierhood. Given these, there is within himself, merely by self-limitation, all that is required for his being a soldier. His bodily presence and physical powers are of the same kind as those of a soldier, and his mental powers will include all that a soldier needs for the execution of his duties. All the king needs to do is to forfeit or suspend his power and dignity. The implications of this have been considered on p. 154.

There are a few particular points in this section which call for brief mention:

In the first paragraph we have a reference to the typicality of the Incarnation: "He has become the *schêma* of one soldier, even that which clothes all the soldiers. So he became incarnate in one man for all men who are of the [same] nature."

In the same paragraph there is another example of the unqualified use of 'he' and 'in': "So he became incarnate in one man for all men who are of the same nature, since he was in their nature, and in it he spoke to all men, as if he spoke in his own nature." The meaning is clear and correct if we know when 'he' refers to God the Word in His eternal duration, when to God the Word in His duration as Jesus Christ, when to Jesus Christ as a prosôpon, and whether 'in' is used naturally, syntactically, voluntarily, prosôpically, circumstantially, or otherwise.

Not unnaturally, Sophronius takes this last sentence as sufficient opportunity for returning to his argument that God the Word became incarnate in His own nature, which could become the nature of man. Nestorius' reply (the last paragraph of the section) leads to the completion of the very useful distinction between the two ways in which a king can use the schêma of soldierhood. The first way, which would correspond with the position put forward by Sophronius, would amount to Manichæism, being an appearance of God in His own nature, using a mere body with the schêma of manhood as His allogenous prosôpon. Like all analogies, these analogies of the king using merely the schêma of soldierhood, or using that schêma and also self-limiting himself, must not be pressed unduly far; but the distinction suggested is of sufficient importance to bear very strong weight in freeing Nestorius of the charge of Nestorianism.

I. i. 28 (*B.* 32–33). The first paragraph is another example of lack of precision, though the meaning is quite clear. The underlying idea is simply the absolute correspondence of each ousia and nature, and the impossibility of any nature including the ability to be another nature. There would be no continuity if God the Word were supposed to pass from one nature to another. This would involve a change of ousia, which involves loss of continuity. "He is by nature in both of them, but the man is only man and God is only God." Rightly understood, this sentence is very significant. 'He' is Jesus Christ. Jesus Christ is the continuity of the prosôpon of God the Word during that period of His eternal duration in which He voluntarily accepted syntactic union during the whole of its natural duration with the durative ousia and nature of the potentially separate man Jesus, from which voluntary syntactic union He could have escaped, but would not. During that union, God the Word was in His own nature. In His syntax He was also in the nature of man, but as man the manhood had no powers but those of man, and had schizohypostasia taken place, the potentially separate man Jesus would have come into existence as a true man and nothing else. Similarly, God the Word suffered no restriction except such as He accepted voluntarily; and had He withdrawn from the syntax by miracle or schizohypostasia, He would have remained God and only God.

In the second paragraph of this section Sophronius raises a cogent objection, which is carefully met in the next section. "Or how is this God of the nature of men and not of the *ousia* of God?" This means: Or how is Christ to be truly called God if He is in the nature of men and not entirely of divine ousia?

I. i. 29 (*B.* 33–34). This chapter, continuing the analogy of the king in the schêma of a soldier, is very helpful in making clear how Nestorius conceived the unity of Christ. It also reveals one of the causes of his being misunderstood. In the first six lines, Nestorius emphasizes that the king is one, "has not become a double king"; and yet he talks of the potentially separate soldier, which the king could become if his self-limitation to soldierhood became fixed and final, as though he were already conceivable as a separate entity. Consider these sentences: "The king exists not apart from him", "He is in him", "He is not revered apart from him in whom he is known". In each case "him" is simply the king himself regarded as a potentially complete and separate soldier. These lines give a very clear indication of the way in which we are to take similar references to Christ being in man. In all such cases Nestorius means the potentially complete and separate man who would have arisen if God the Word had suffered schizohypostasia, and thus brought such a separate man into existence. In fact, there never was such a separate man, though Nestorius' phraseology so often reads as though the man is conceived as a separate entity.

The immediate transition to a consideration of the pro-sôpon of the Incarnation suggests an important parallel. The soldier has no existence apart from the king, and so the prosôpon, the self-manifestation, is that of the king only. It is the same prosôpon, whether we regard it as that section of the durative prosôpon of the king during which he was in syntactic union with the ousia and nature of that which provided him with the ability to present the schêma of soldierhood, or whether we regard it as the quasi-prosôpon of that syntax. It must be remembered that the quasi-prosôpon of a syntax, which includes a directing animate nature, is the same thing as the prosôpon of that directing animate nature (see pp. 105–107).

Similarly, there is only one prosôpon in the Incarnation, the durative prosôpon of God the Word, which includes in its duration the total duration of the ousia and nature of the potentially separate man Jesus, whose potentially separate prosôpon is never actually other than an element in the syntax, and forms part of the allogenous prosôpon of God the Word. There were never two prosôpa brought into union, for "he has received his *prosôpon* as something created, in such wise as not originally to be man but at the same time Man-God" (B. 87). When we refer to the one prosôpon as a prosôpic union, we mean two things:

(1) The prosôpon is the basis of unification of the syntax, belonging to and including within itself the two natures to each of which it equally belongs: it is the allogenous pro-sôpon of God the Word and the autogenous prosôpon of the potentially separate man Jesus.

(2) Though the integration of the syntax took place in such wise that the constituent prosôpa were never separate, it has been seen (pp. 160–161) that an essential characteristic of the syntax is its potential disintegration by schizohypo-stasia. If this potentiality had ever eventuated, two prosôpa would have resulted, that of God the Word self-freed from the syntax and that of the now separate man Jesus.

The following points in this section also require notice:
"Nor did he receive any addition of the *ousia*, because the *ousias* remain without change." This emphasizes the fact that the ousias are never combined ousically, although they are in prosôpic union. Although this in a way answers Sophronius' question, it also emphasizes that integrity of the ousias in the person of Christ which makes the establishment of a real unification so difficult.

"For then there is an addition in the *ousia* when it accepts another *ousia*, an equal *ousia*." There would have been an addition to the ousia of the Godhead if it had accepted union with any other ousia. If any such union were conceivable, there would be a new ousia. But no such union is conceivable, because union of any other ousia with the infinite ousia of God would necessarily result in the absorption and cessation as such of that other ousia. This is the significance of the expression "equal ousia". The ousia of God has no equal ousia.

I. i. 30 (*B.* 34–35). The part of this section which falls on B. 34 is in direct continuation of section 29, whereas the part falling on B. 35 begins a new main division in the argument. As Driver remarks, the Syriac translator's heading might well be transposed to the top of B. 35.

The portion of I. i. 30 falling on B. 34 brings this division to an end with a final argument against the possibility of the Incarnation being due to any change in the ousia of God. The only way in which this could conceivably occur would be for a detachment of divine ousia to take place, which would necessarily thus acquire its own prosôpon. This ousia could then become flesh by a transformation, and then recombine in some way with the ousia of God the Word. Any such view involves objections which have already been fully considered: "We have already said the same thing." In addition, this paragraph throws very valuable indirect light on the sense in which we are to understand 'homoousian' (ὁμοούσιος) in a Nestorian Christology. As has been pointed out on pp. 138–140, in the case of the Trinity homoousian implies unbroken continuity of ousia and not merely precise similarity. The three hypostases are homoousian to one another not because they are identically similar in ousia and nature, but because they form an unbroken continuity. Even if such a thing could be conceived, 'ousia of God the Word in detachment' is not 'ousia of God'. It has become another ousia, and is no longer homoousian with the ousia of Godhead.

(4) *I. i.* 30 (from "Let us turn . . .")–35 (*B.* 35–38). There are those who say that Christ was truly God, and suppose that the manhood was taken up into the divine ousia, and made one with it.

These suggest that in the Incarnation real human ousia was taken, but that it was received into the ousia of God in ousic and natural union. This involves either the disappearance of the human ousia altogether, as addition to infinity leaves infinity unchanged, in which case it is as though the manhood had never been; or we should have to suppose the formation of some new ousia, neither God nor man. Neither alternative is an incarnation, and both run counter to the fundamental ideas of the Nestorian metaphysic. This division presents little difficulty and calls for no comment, with the exception of the second half of section 32. This would appear to advance the following view: Although the ousia of the flesh has been changed into ousia of God, the hylê underlying this ousia is still discriminable; and this hylê, ousia of God from the former ousia of flesh, was used as the basis for the visible flesh of the Incarnation. God incarnate would thus be of one ousia, the divine, but for the purposes of the Incarnation makes use of fleshly hylê, which, formerly underlying the ousia and nature of flesh, is now nevertheless part of the divine ousia and nature. Any such view is quite incompatible with the Nestorian metaphysic, doing violence to all ideas and definitions regarding ousia and nature, as well as to all ideas of the unity and incorporeality of the divine ousia. If the ousia of flesh has become ousia of God, it is as though it was never otherwise, and if hylê of flesh is still discriminable in the ousia of God, it is evidently not part of the divine ousia and nature.

I. i. 36 (*B.* 38–40). This section briefly summarizes the conclusions arising from the views considered in the above divisions (3) and (4), and adds some further comments.

The Incarnation cannot consist either in changes in the ousia or nature of God, or in changes in the ousia or nature of man. The section enunciates some of the fundamental distinctions between the ousia of God and the ousias of all things else, and states some of the inevitable consequences. There is a fundamental distinction between the unmade eternal ousia and nature of God and all other ousias and natures which He has made "of nothing". The idea of creation ex nihilo is difficult but necessary. Without it we lose the absolute distinction between the ousia of God and all other ousias. For if God created by breaking down some of His own ousia into hylê, and from that made other ousias, and could then break down these ousias to hylê and make yet other ousias, it would be evident that His own ousia could differ only in degree, not in kind, from other ousias. God is to be thought of as causing hylê, the raw material of all ousias other than His own, to come into existence, and from that hylê making such ousias as He wishes. Presumably He could make an ousia directly without first making hylê, and could transform one ousia into another without an intervening hylê stage. But hylê is to be thought of as the unifying common basis of all ousias. Quite apart then from the fundamental concepts summarized on pp. 83–88, it is thus evident that transformations between divine and human ousias and natures are unthinkable: if divine ousia becomes human, that which is unmade and eternal in its nature has become something whose nature is made; if human ousia becomes divine, that which is made has become that which is unmade. All this illustrates the logical coherence of the Nestorian metaphysic. The phrasing of this section may seem a little involved, but it will read quite clearly if it is remembered that the expressions 'eternal', 'uncreated', 'unmade', 'which was', 'which has not come into being' are to be referred to the divine ousia and nature, and the expressions 'temporary', 'created', 'made', 'which was not', 'come into being' all refer to any ousia and nature other than the divine. "But it is impossible that [he should make] that which is unmade and that which was not from that which was, as thou sayest." The reading of V gives a much better balance and seems in every way preferable: "But it is impossible that [he should make] that which is made from that which is unmade and that which was not from that which was, as thou sayest." Nau evidently prefers V: "Mais qu'il fasse du créé l'incréé et ce qui n'est pas de ce qui est, comme tu le preténds, c'est impossible."

(5) *I. i.* 37 (first paragraph) (*B.* 40–41). There are those who say that Christ was truly God, and suppose that God changed a part of His nature into the nature of man.

This section disposes of the idea that the Incarnation could consist in a part of the divine nature being separated from the rest and transformed into human nature. Even if such a separation could be contemplated, the separated part would still be of divine ousia and nature, and could not be conceived of as being transformed into anything made and temporary.

I. i. 37 (second paragraph)–41 (*B.* 41–49). This is a digression on the problem of transubstantiation. The problem is dealt with by a close application of the Nestorian metaphysic, and the section illustrates Nestorius' skill in the handling of scriptural difficulties.

I. i. 37 (fourth paragraph) (*B.* 42–43). Sophronius suggests that, when the bread becomes body, it has become body of Christ in ousia and nature, and is only bread in schêma. Besides that, there remains the awareness of what it formerly was: "It is no more conceived in its former nature but as itself in that which it has become." This is why the Apostle decries those who consider it common, that is, presumably, of human ousia and nature. Further, as the Son of God, that is, God the Word incarnate, is of the same ousia and nature as God the Father, it would follow that the bread is really of the divine ousia and nature, though retaining the schêma of bread and having been derived therefrom. (It should be noted that a superfluous 'and' has found its way into the last few lines of Driver and Hodgson's version of this section: ". . . the Son of God is consubstantial with God and the Father." This should of course be ". . . the Son of God is consubstantial with God the Father". There is no conjunction in the Syriac.)

I. i. 39 (*B.* 44–46). Nestorius indicates the various meanings of the Greek word κοινόν ('common'), and asks

Sophronius which applies in the expression "has considered common the blood of his testament". Sophronius thinks that 'common' here means of human ousia and nature. Nestorius points out that if the body and blood is not that of man but of God, it must either belong to the ousia of the Son of God or, originally of human ousia, have been taken into the nature of divinity; for, on the view which Sophronius has been putting forward, the flesh has in any case ceased to be flesh, having by change or mixture or union entered into the ousia of God the Word. In that case the Apostle's reference is in reality to the ousia of God the Word, and is a condemnation against the impiety of those who consider that to be impure.

Sophronius shifts his ground and suggests that the Apostle is directing his scorn against those who consider the flesh and blood real, but still consider them common. Nestorius replies that Sophronius' position would just as easily be supported by interpreting the ousia of the flesh and blood as ousia so changed from that of God the Word. Sophronius has no more to say and leaves Nestorius to explain the matter.

I. i. 40 (*B.* 46–48). Our oneness with Christ depends on likeness of ousia. But there is no likeness of ousia between us and God the Word. Since, therefore, the blood of sanctification had to be from one of our ousia, God the Word by voluntary and prosôpic union with humanity ('a man')[1] established in Christ a unity with all humanity. Correspondingly, Christ by an identification of His body with the bread establishes a unity with those who accept that bread.

I. i. 41 (*B.* 48–49). This unity brought about through the mystery of the bread explains 1 Cor. xii. 27: "You indeed are the body of Christ and members in your parts." But Nestorius hastens to make clear that all these unities are of another type than ousic or natural. Nestorius at last gives his explanation of the passage under discussion. It refers to those who, understanding the true faith, none the less reject it. As to κοινόν in this verse, it means polluted or unclean, not human or shared. He ends the section by

[1] See p. 163.

re-emphasizing that our unity with Christ is through the possession of the same ousia as His humanity.

The implications of sections 40 and 41 are:

(1) Our oneness with Christ is a real oneness due to possession of the same ousia, the ousia of humanity.

(2) In Christ there is a unity of God the Word and man, this unity not being ousic and natural but voluntary and prosôpic.

(3) Hence, through Christ man acquires a type of unity with God.

These implications have an important bearing on Nestorius' view of the Atonement (see pp. 180–184).

(6) *I. i.* 42–50 (*B.* 49–63). There are those who say that Christ was a natural union of God the Word and a human body and animal soul (Apollinarianism), or a natural union of God the Word and a human body, soul and intelligence.

This division deals with Apollinarianism and similar views. The refutation is based on an application of the principles of the Nestorian metaphysic, and is not difficult to follow. Indeed, sections 44–49 (B. 53–60) are amongst the most valuable sources from which to deduce some of Nestorius' main principles, as may be seen by reference to the 'Index to Passages in the Bazaar' (p. 490). It is, however, sometimes necessary to observe carefully whether Nestorius is stating his own views or stating a case in order to show its absurdity or subsequently to refute it. Thus the greater part of I. i. 47–49 (B. 55–60) is taken up with showing the absurdity of accounting for the Incarnation by the natural union of divinity and humanity. This must be borne in mind, or we may fail to distinguish clearly between what Nestorius is supporting and what he is attacking.

One minor point calls for notice:

I. i. 42 (*B.* 50–51): "From no nature he became and he is the nature of a man." This may mean, as Driver and Hodgson suggest, that the manhood did not become a nature until God the Word added Himself to the body and vegetative soul. Or it may mean that no other nature was involved in God the Word becoming the nature of man, in that what He took to Himself was not a nature but only two constituents of a nature: there was never more than

one nature, whether God the Word in His own nature or
God the Word as the nature of man. Nau seems to favour
the latter interpretation: "C'est donc sans partir d'une
nature (complète) qu'il est devenu et qu'il est la nature de
l'homme." Neither interpretation is in accordance with the
Nestorian metaphysic, nor is it meant to be, as the passage
is part of the presentation of Apollinarian views.

(7) I. i. 51–53 (B. 63–69). There are those who say that
Christ was only a man, but so obedient to and aided by
God the Word that He gained the honour and name of
Son by God's grace. There are thus two Sons, God the
Word and Jesus Christ.

The Paulinian view, already mentioned in I. i. 4 (B. 12),
is taken up again. Section 51 reintroduces it, and a brief
reference to Sabellianism (section 52) leads on to an
exposition of Paulianism in greater detail. Unlike the
Sabellians, the Paulinians believe in God the Word as a
hypostasis, but regard Christ as only a man obedient to
and aided by God the Word. By His obedience, He received
the honour and name of Son by God's grace, and it thus
comes about that there are two to whom the title 'Son'
may be applied.

In the second paragraph of section 53 Nestorius riddles
the Paulinian position with rhetorical questions. Before
continuing with the implications of Paulianism, there is a
short and somewhat irrelevant passage (the first half of the
third paragraph of section 53) dealing with those who say
that Christ was eternally existent as such, Himself God, and
including His life and death on earth within the power of
His own nature. Nestorius then continues with the question
of the two Sons. He shows, by quotations mostly from
John i., that the Paulinian way out of the Christological
difficulties is simply a fleeing from the facts of the problem.
Having indicated the facts as they are stated in scripture,
that God the Word, the Son, the Only Begotten, is one, he
poses the problems: how could He, who is by nature
immortal and impassible, voluntarily become incarnate, and
how can the Son, by nature immortal, be said to die in
nature? It is again to be noted how skilfully Nestorius
handles scriptural difficulties. With genuine reverence, he

never even faintly suggests any fallibility in the scriptures; but he implies that the surface meaning is not to be seized upon and used to support fallacious arguments. The scriptures must be interpreted logically and self-consistently, and the proper elucidation of an apparently very simple statement (e.g. "the Word became flesh") may require a highly complex metaphysic.

In the last paragraph of this section Sophronius, somewhat irrelevantly, accuses Nestorius of predicating two sons by nature. This provides transition to the next main division, in which Nestorius sets forth his own views.

Nestorius' views expounded (I. i. 54–88) (B. 69–117)

In these sections Nestorius sets out many of his main ideas and emphasizes his salient points: the continuity of God the Word, Jesus Christ a unity, the union in prosôpon, God the Word in Jesus Christ gaining the victory first for Himself and then for us all, Satan defeated, God triumphant. As always with Nestorius, there is much repetition, and the ideas overlap and run into one another. An exact analysis is therefore difficult, but the main trend of the sections is broadly as follows (the references are to section numbers): God the Word is one, and in Jesus Christ united humanity to Himself by bonds of love, adoption and acknowledgment in a prosôpic union, thus making possible similar bonds between God and mankind (54–55); God the Word in Jesus Christ is in both natures, but by perfect accord and mutual use of the prosôpa of the two natures there is but one prosôpon, that of the union, which links Godhead and manhood in Christ, and, through Him, God and humanity (56–61); atonement required that the mediator should be Man-God, which came about in the prosôpic union (62–65); God the Word in Jesus Christ humbled Himself in obedience and death, and thus conquered, first for Himself, and then for us all (66–77); Satan was thus foiled, but God allowed him still to assail humanity, though victory could be obtained by all who availed themselves of the victory won by Christ (78–87); hence, by a consideration of the means of atonement, the Nestorian Christology is confirmed (88).

I. i. 54 (*B.* 69–71). God the Word is one, not two, and in that He was with God in the creation of the world, so in the Incarnation He came unto His own, and while some receive Him not, others do, and to these He gives authority to become sons of God, not indeed in nature, but by adoption and acknowledgment, even as He, taking our flesh by adoption and acknowledgment, has become our kin-by-adoption.

Nestorius expects that the answers to the questions on B. 71 will be obvious. This is one of his faults, though in this case the answers are not difficult to supply. To the first question the answer is "He spoke of God the Word"; the second question is answered in the last seven lines of the section; the third and fourth questions each need "No" for an answer; the answer to the fifth question is "Yes", and this implied answer is then amplified.

The Syriac of the fifth question begins in the singular, "Or has he remained . . .". Both Driver and Hodgson and Nau correct this to the plural, which certainly makes smoother sense and provides a logical sequence in the questions. The singular, however, makes quite good sense, and brings out an antithesis: God the Word by entering our nature, not indeed naturally, but by love, adoption and acknowledgment, enabled us to enter His and become His kin, not indeed naturally, but by love, adoption and acknowledgment. This antithesis is continued in the next sentence, so perhaps the Syriac needs no emendation.

I. i. 55 (*B.* 71–76). The first part of this section merely reiterates the argument with which section 54 closed. Nestorius then returns to the question of the continuity of God the Word and His identity as Jesus Christ: Jesus Christ was God the Word in His fulness, revealing God as far as was possible in our nature. The section ends with an objection from Sophronius, who says that God the Word, consubstantial with the Father, is invisible, and therefore Jesus Christ cannot be the same as He: was not Jesus Christ merely similar to Moses and the prophets, God working through Him as through them?

A few points need remark:

Near the bottom of B. 72: "As those who have received

him have become voluntarily by reception the natural
[sons] of God, so also he, in that he received the flesh and
sojourned in it, became their flesh by adoption and not by
change of *ousia*." How can we become "natural [sons] of
God", seeing that our nature is quite other than His? The
argument would seem to be as follows: God the Word,
having linked the flesh with Himself by every possible tie
except the impossible one of natural union, "became flesh"
to the fullest extent open to Him; those, then, who accept
Him, being already of the same nature as the flesh which
He has adopted, and having to that extent a common
nature with Him, on being adopted and acknowledged by
God as His sons through God the Word in Christ,
"become" His natural sons by the same links and in the
same way as God the Word "became" flesh. This is one of
those many cases in which what Nestorius says is quite
true and valid "if we know what we mean". But he would
probably have scorned anyone else who had suggested that
we could have become "natural sons of God". How indeed,
seeing that "In God the Word is fact there is not anything
whereby he and we should be of one" (B. 46).

In B. 73 Nestorius again emphasizes the complete correspondence of God the Word with Christ, pointing out that
the epithet 'full of grace' indicates identity and not mere
participation. Note also the indication of continuity in "is
that which the beloved son was".

Halfway down the same page there is a contrast drawn
between the fullness of God dwelling in Christ and the
naturally limited ability of humanity to receive that fullness.
His is the fullness; we can receive, not the fullness, but of
the fullness: "For the fullness consists in being deficient in
nothing, as God."

I. i. 56–61 (B. 76–85). God the Word in Jesus Christ is
in both natures, but by perfect accord and mutual use of
the prosôpa of the two natures there is but one prosôpon,
that of the union, which links Godhead and manhood in
Christ, and, through Him, God and humanity.

I. i. 56 (B. 76–77). Nestorius points out that there is a
fundamental difference between Christ and all theophanies.
Christ identified Himself with God, but no prophet or

angel ever dared to do that. They were aware that they were the mere agents or mouthpieces of God, and, though they might say "The Lord said", none but Christ ever dared to say "I and God are one". Such phrases as "God appeared" or "God gave the law" are not misunderstandable if the general principles of theophany are understood, nor is any exception to be taken to God using schêmata (cf. on I. i. 12, p. 420, and on I. i. 25, p. 427).

I. i. 57 (*B.* 77–78). This section describes the interrelation of the two natures in Christ, and is readily understood in the light of the arguments set out on pp. 171–174. We have to recognize at each occurrence whether 'prosôpon' is autogenous or allogenous and whether 'in' is being used naturally or syntactically (see pp. 143–146).

The latter part of the section shows how the names 'Son of God' and 'Son of man' are equally applicable to Christ. It is a matter of approach: as Son of God, Christ is the durative prosôpon of God the Word, made visible in an allogenous prosôpon based on the autogenous prosôpon of the potentially separate man Jesus; as Son of man, Christ is the autogenous prosôpon of the potentially separate man Jesus in syntactic union with God the Word, thus producing the syntax Christ, whose quasi-prosôpon is at once the autogenous prosôpon of the potentially separate man Jesus, the allogenous prosôpon of God the Word, and the total expression during the continuance of the syntax of the durative prosôpon of God the Word.

The last six lines are an example of the fondness of Nestorius for setting out his ideas in reciprocal balance. The meaning is, however, quite clear: God the Word as Christ is aware of His divine nature, and all His utterances and actions are in accordance with it; but He is also aware of the urges and limitations of humanity, and His utterances and actions also take those into account, especially when bodily sensations are concerned (e.g. "I thirst."[1]); in general, He was aware of both natures, and comported Himself as "God in human nature". There is the obvious reciprocity that as God the Word He was in divine ousia and human prosôpon, and that as potential man He was in human

[1] John xix. 28.

ousia and divine prosôpon. But antitheses and reciprocities are dangerous modes of thought to force, and it is better to hold firmly to the statement of facts in the simplest forms to which we can reduce them.

I. i. 58 (B. 79–81). This whole section is quite intelligible if we have clearly in mind the connotation of all the terms, especially 'became flesh', 'prosôpon' and 'in'.

There is a significant sentence towards the end of the section: "The distinction of nature, one *hypostasis* and one *prosôpon*, is theirs, the one being known by the other and the other by the one, so that the one is by adoption what the other is by nature and the other is with the one in the body." Each nature is necessarily based on its own hypostasis. This follows from the fundamental concepts concerning ousia and nature, for hypostasis is here absolutely identical with particular ousia so far as the humanity is concerned, and with ousia of Godhead hypostatic to God the Word so far as the divinity is concerned (see pp. 112–120 and 130–137). These hypostases are never united, for divine and human ousia and nature cannot possibly be united ousically and naturally, or, in the Nestorian connotation of the term, hypostatically. Each nature also has its own prosôpon, but owing to the special bonds between the divinity and humanity, the prosôpon of the human nature has completely surrendered itself to be the allogenous prosôpon of God the Word, and the prosôpon of God the Word has entirely self-restricted itself to expression through the prosôpon of the humanity. Thus each is identically the other, and there is only actually one prosôpon during the duration of God the Word as Jesus Christ.

The king and servant analogy with which the section ends is not very helpful. We are probably not to think of the king and servant as two separate persons, as a first reading would suggest, but to link this passage with the similar idea (king and soldier) worked out more fully in I. i. 27–29 (B. 30–34). The king decides to express himself through servanthood, to take the "means of self-manifestation of a servant as his own means of self-manifestation" ("the prosôpon of a servant as his own prosôpon"). Letting this be known, he accepts the abasement necessitated by restricting himself to servant status, but is revered by those who know that he is nevertheless still king: "(He) is content to be abased in the *prosôpon* of the servant while the servant is revered in the *prosôpon* of the lord and king." Nestorius himself does not seem to regard the analogy as a very exact one. It is still less helpful if we suppose the king is actually changing place and status with a real servant.

I. i. 59 (B. 81–83). This section disposes of the difficulties involved in the divine omnipresence. God pervades His entire Universe, and therefore "is in all creatures". But this indwelling can vary from mere conspatiality upward through varying stages to that complete mutual accord between Godhead and humanity found only in Jesus Christ. The varying uses of 'in' are to be observed; indeed, this passage is a valuable source for determining the possible shades of meaning of 'in' (see pp. 143–146).

The latter part of this section enunciates one aspect of Nestorius' view of the Atonement: as in Christ is established the closest union with Godhead, so we, linked with Christ through His humanity, through Him are linked with God, who adopts and acknowledges us as sons.

I. i. 60 (B. 83–84). The Incarnation consists neither in a mere allogenous prosôpon with the schêma of manhood nor in a theophany, but in a complete reciprocal adoption of ousias and prosôpa, so that the ousia of divinity (in the hypostasis God the Word) is voluntarily restricting itself to expression through an allogenous prosôpon (Jesus Christ), a prosôpon whose allogenous element is that which the vivifying power of God the Word is completing into manhood; and the ousia of humanity (the potentially separate man Jesus) is voluntarily submitting itself to being the perfectly according expression of the purpose of divinity, whose prosôpon it thus is.

The second half of this section illustrates the confusing effect of the undefined use of 'he'. The meaning of the first three lines appears to be: "God the Word as Jesus Christ has made use of His very own nature (in that the divine nature found full expression, so far as the self-imposed limitations allowed, in the prosôpon 'Jesus Christ') and of

His own prosôpon (for the quasi-prosôpon of the syntax Jesus Christ was at once the autogenous prosôpon of the potentially separate man Jesus and the allogenous prosôpon of God the Word), and was thus able to say truly, 'I and the Father are one'."

"He is whatever he is in *prosôpon* and whatever he is in *prosôpon* he is." Here again it is a little difficult to see to whom each 'he' refers. The meaning would have been clearer if Nestorius had replaced the pronouns by names or descriptions. The antithesis would appear to be between 'I' and 'the Father', that is, between God the Word as Jesus Christ, and God the Father or God undiscriminated: "God the Word as Jesus Christ is a true revelation of whatever God is in the self-manifestation of Himself; and the self-manifestation and self-expression of God the Word as Jesus Christ is a true revelation of God." That is to say, "Jesus Christ is a complete expression of the self-manifestation of God, and in whatever way Jesus Christ manifests Himself He is revealing the nature of God." Nau translates "Lui, il est ce que celui-ci est dans son prosopon, et ce que celui-ci est dans son prosopon, lui il l'est", thus taking the antithesis a little differently, though the general sense is the same.

I. i. 61 (*B.* 84–85). The reciprocity of the prosôpa is again emphasized, though the meaning is still needlessly obscured by lack of definition in the use of 'he'. But the leading idea is simply that there is but one prosôpon of Jesus Christ— at once the (allogenous) prosôpon of God the Word expressing Himself and the (autogenous) prosôpon of the potentially separate man Jesus submitting Himself.

I. i. 62–65 (*B.* 85–88). Atonement required that the mediator should be Man-God, which came about in the prosôpic union. I. i. 64 is of particular importance in endeavouring to establish a coherent Nestorian Christology. Its implications are fundamental to the arguments on pp. 155–157, 166, and 171–174.

I. i. 66–77 (*B.* 89–103). God the Word in Jesus Christ humbled Himself in obedience and death, and thus conquered, first for Himself, and then for us all. These sections only present difficulty in so far as they require a clear understanding of the shades of meaning to be attached to 'prosôpon' and 'he'. Reference may be made to pp. 154–184. On 'he', see particularly pp. 169 and 187. For a useful note on I. i. 72 see an article by Burkitt in the *Journal of Theological Studies*, vol. xxvii, pp. 177–179, January, 1926.

I. i. 78–88 (B. 104–117). Although Satan was foiled, God allowed him still to assail humanity; but victory could be obtained by all who availed themselves of the victory won by Christ. Thus, by a consideration of the means of atonement, the Nestorian Christology is confirmed. These sections provide much material for deducing Nestorius' views on the Atonement. Cf. pp. 182–184.

Additional arguments against erroneous views (I. i. 89–93) (B. 117–125)

These sections are mainly a recapitulation of positions already established in I. i. 1–53 (B. 10–69), as confirmed by the views on soteriology set out in I. i. 54–88 (B. 69–117). (It is necessary to recognize when Nestorius is stating views to show their untenability or subsequently to dismiss them —a favourite but sometimes confusing device. Examples occur in I. i. 90 and 91 (B. 117–120).)

I. i. 89 (B. 117) is parallel with I. i. 3 (B. 11–12), and repudiates Manichæism.

I. i. 90 (B. 117–119) begins with what is in effect a summary of the matters dealt with in I. i. 10–34 (B. 14–38), and ends with a reassertion of the views expounded in I. i. 54–77 (B. 69–103).

I. i. 91 (B. 119–121) deals rather more fully with some aspects of I. i. 30–34 (B. 35–38).

I. i. 92–93 (B. 121–125) deals largely with Arianism and Apollinarianism, covering again the matters dealt with in I. i. 5 and 42–50 (B. 12–13 and 49–63).

Characteristically, Nestorius ends Book I with a sentence meaningless to anyone who has not grasped the intricacies of his metaphysic: "Therefore the words of the Divine Scriptures befit not Christ in any other manner than this; but as we have examined and found, all refer not to the union of the nature but to the natural and hypostatic prosôpon." That is to say, Jesus Christ is not a natural unity (which to Nestorius would imply also a hypostatic unity), but is one prosôpon, a prosôpon at once expressive of the nature and hypostasis of God the Word (allogenously), and of the by Him completed nature and hypostasis of manhood. As is usual when trying to express himself concisely and neatly, Nestorius is in great danger of falling into unintelligibility. The idea is set out in detail on pp. 171–174.

Book I, Part II

The second part of Book I is little more than a summary of the first part. Following Sophronius' formal request, Nestorius gives in six brief sections a summary of the principal erroneous views. Then he provides a concise statement of his own teaching, which passes over into an attack on the idea of hypostatic union.

I. ii. 1 (*B.* 126). This is Manichæism, already dealt with in I. i. 3 and 89 (B. 11–12 and 117).

I. ii. 2 (*B.* 126). This section refers to a view which Nestorius regards as a derivative of Manichæism. It has already been dealt with in detail in I. i. 10–30 and 90 (*B.* 14–34 and 117–118).

I. ii. 3 (*B.* 127). This is Arianism. Cf. I. i. 5 and 92 (B. 12–13 and 122).

I. ii. 4 (*B.* 127). This is Apollinarianism. Cf. I. i. 42–50 and 92–93 (B. 49–63 and 121–125).

I. ii. 5 (*B.* 127–128). Though not very clearly expressed, this view seems to amount to a theophany, God the Word using as His allogenous prosôpon a specially created instrument with the schêma of a man.

I. ii. 6 (*B.* 128). This section is very illuminating in that it gives Nestorius' summary of what he thought Cyril's teaching involved. Note that he says 'united in ousia', being quite sure that Cyril's 'hypostatic union' could be nothing else. The last three lines are intended to present Cyril's view as metaphysically fantastic: as if an ousia could keep changing backwards and forwards from one nature into another and still remain the same ousia! This point has been dealt with exhaustively in I. i. 15–23 (B. 19–28).

I. ii. 7 (*B.* 128–133). This is Nestorius' own view. Note, incidentally, how much Nestorius expects of his readers. He introduces his own view in just the same anonymous way as the others, leaving the reader to infer that the first six are wrong and the seventh right. He also expects his readers to sense the proper shade of meaning to attach to the various terms. The word 'in' occurs constantly on B. 128 and 129, and a proper understanding of the passage is impossible unless we are able to recognize how 'in' is being used in each instance: is it being used to mean 'in (naturally)', 'in (syntactically)', 'in (prosôpically)', 'in (voluntarily)', 'in (conspatially)', 'in (circumstantially)', or 'in' in some other way? Reference to pp. 143–146 should enable the reader to solve the difficulties, and one particularly important passage is dealt with in detail on pp. 146–147. Maclean is justified in calling the passage "hopelessly confused",[1] though the confusion is in Nestorius' way of expressing himself rather than in the ideas themselves. We can read the passages with perfect understanding if we know how Nestorius thought.

The transition to the attack on the idea of hypostatic union is preceded by a paragraph which, taken by itself, looks very like "Nestorianism" (B. 131–133). But it must be read in conjunction with I. i. 64 (B. 87) and I. i. 27–29 (B. 30–34). See pp. 154–157. The opening sentence, "Consequently this man has attributed nothing in the Incarnation to the conduct of the man but all to God the Word", is singularly unfortunate. Nestorius provided—and provides—plenty of weapons for his enemies.

The rest of this part is quite easy to follow, the key simply being Nestorius' fixed idea that hypostatic union was necessarily natural and ousic. So it was by his own definitions, but not by Cyril's.

Book I, Part III

This part is mainly concerned with criticisms of Cyril's motives and methods in bringing about the Council of

[1] Article 'Nestorianism', *Encyclopædia of Religion and Ethics*, ix. 331.

Ephesus and in causing it to be constituted with undue haste.[1]

Nestorius opens with a rhetorical outburst against Cyril (B. 146–148), accusing him of intrigue and high-handedness: "Wickedly thou hast separated off a party . . . Thou hast all the support of the Empire . . . Because indeed I made not use of the support of the church nor of the support of the chief men nor of the support of the Empire, I am come to this extremity. . . . Thou wast bishop of Alexandria and thou didst get hold of the church of Constantinople—a thing which the bishop of no other city whatsoever would have suffered." He also complains (B. 148) that Cyril had an ally in Pulcheria, eldest and most influential sister of the Emperor Theodosius II, whom Nestorius' bluntness had alienated from himself.

Nestorius then gives a brief disquisition on Apollinarianism (B. 148–151). This adds nothing to what has already been fully dealt with in B. 49–63 and 121–125, q.v.

Arising from this, Nestorius explains how the "Theotokos" controversy began (B. 151–152). It is to be feared that his record of this matter does more credit to his later judgment than to his memory. As Kidd quite clearly shows,[2] Nestorius' recognition of the real meaning of the term, and therefore of its permissibility, was the result of a painful transition taking from November 428 to Easter 429; and although he had had perforce to recognize the permissibility of the term, even at the time of writing the Bazaar objection to it still rankled in his mind, and he admits that he "would have persuaded every one by words not to call the holy virgin the mother of God" (B. 218). If only all concerned had recognized that, rightly understanding the terms, the Virgin Mary was at once θεοτόκος, ἀνθρωποτόκος, and χριστοτόκος! The Virgin Mary was θεοτόκος, for He whom she bore was indeed truly God; she was ἀνθρωποτόκος, for He whom she bore was indeed truly man; she was χριστοτόκος, for He whom she bore was indeed the Christ, God the Word Incarnate, God-Man. θεοτόκος, or even

---

[1] As Nestorius' account is not unbiassed, his version of the events should be compared with others. Reference may be made to p. 59, footnote 3.

[2] A History of the Church, iii. 201–207.

Μήτηρ Θεοῦ or Mater Dei, was quite an unexceptionable term so long as it was realized that it meant "Mother of Him who is God" and not "Mother of all that is God". Jesus Christ, whom she bore, was indeed God, in that Jesus Christ was the self-manifestation and self-expression of God the Word; but the totality of all that is God, the totality of Godhead, was not born of the Virgin Mary, nor did anything to which we may apply the term 'God' originate in her. Who, however, but the most ignorant and unthoughtful could misunderstand the term? It had been used by Origen, Gregory Thaumaturgus, Archelaus of Kashkar, Alexander of Alexandria, Eusebius of Cæsarea, Athanasius, Basil of Cæsarea, Gregory of Nazianzus, and Gregory of Nyssa.[1] Further, its connotation was well understood. As Maclean so well remarks,[2] "It enshrined the vitally important doctrine that the same He who was born of Mary was from all eternity God the Son, and not only one who was inseparably connected with Him. It ought to be added that θεοτόκος is not designed to honour Mary, but rather to explain the position of her Child." As so often, Nestorius failed to express himself clearly, possibly failed even to clarify his own thought. But we may probably ascribe his objection to the term to two fears: fear that the use of the title would encourage Mariolatry,[3] and fear lest the idea 'Mother of Him who is God' should not be distinguished from the idea 'Mother of the totality of that which is God'.[4]

[1] It is surprising that Nestorius was apparently so ignorant of the previous usage of the term. Cf. his question and statement on B. 219–220: "How then sayest thou, O calumniator," (i.e., Cyril) "that 'we have found that the holy fathers thought thus and that they thus were confident in calling the holy virgin the mother of God. Thus we say that he both suffered and rose'? First prove unto us that the fathers called her the mother of God". On this passage see also pp. 458–459.

[2] Article 'Nestorianism', *Encyclopædia of Religion and Ethics*, ix. 328.

[3] Cf. Seeberg, *Lehrbuch der Dogmengeschichte*, ii. 212: "Nestorius hat freilich gewarnt: μόνον μὴ ποιείτω τὴν παρθένον θεάν."

[4] Without any intention or desire of condoning Nestorius, it may be interesting to notice that Bethune-Baker sees the effect of a similar fear in the omission of the term from public use in the Services of the Church of England: "For members of the Church of England it is interesting to remember that the great divines of the Reformation period, of whose loyalty to the orthodox doctrine of the Incarnation there can be no question, shared the apprehension of Nestorius as to the term 'Mother of God'. They withdrew it from public use in the Services of the Church. . . . The invocation 'Saint Mary, mother of God, our Saviour Jesus Christ, pray for us',

The term 'Christotokos' is of course perfectly true and innocuous, except in so far that its use might suggest that 'Theotokos' is impermissible.

Nestorius then continues with the history of the controversy, and the rest of this part throws no fresh light on his Christology. It deals with the events leading up to the Council of Ephesus, and with some aspects of the constitution and conduct of the first session. It is thus mainly concerned with the sequence of events from about Easter 429 to June 431, though detailed comment on many matters is reserved till later. Nestorius recounts how partisans of Cyril in Constantinople fomented trouble, and, flouting Nestorius' authority, communicated with Cyril (B. 152–154). He then quotes parts of Cyril's letter to his supporters in Constantinople, and gives his comments (B. 154–157). He quotes Cyril's letter to himself, and comments on that (B. 157–160). The next page of the Syriac is missing. This, as Driver and Hodgson suggest, must have dealt with the injustice of Cyril's insistence on the Council of Ephesus being constituted before all had assembled. Nestorius sweeps aside the trivial reasons given for the need of haste (B. 161–162), and quotes the request of the sixty-eight bishops that Cyril "should await the coming of the excellent bishops our colleagues" (B. 162–164), and tells how Count Candidianus "commanded them that the Council should not be held incomplete" (B. 164–165). But, erring in judgment, Candidianus read to the assembled bishops the Emperor's letter (B. 165), whereupon they regarded the Council as constituted, drove Candidianus out, and proceeded with the business. Nestorius discusses this error in procedure at some length (B. 165–170), and quotes in full Candidianus' own protest to Cyril (B. 170–174), a copy of

which had been retained in Cranmer's Litany, was omitted altogether in the First Prayer Book of Edward VI, and of course not reinstated in subsequent revisions. 'Mother of our Saviour' or 'of our Saviour Jesus Christ', or 'Mother of the Lord' or 'of our Lord Jesus Christ' are the titles which, since the Reformation, members of the Church of England have commonly been content to use, while at the same time firmly holding the belief that He who was born of her was God as well as man. These titles are enough to secure to her all the affectionate devotion and reverence that such Motherhood inspires. The faith in the Godhead of her Son is guarded in other ways" (*Nestorius and His Teaching*, pp. 66–68).

which Candidianus sent to the Emperor Theodosius II. The Emperor's reply (B. 176–177) supporting Candidianus is quoted; but Cyril himself wrote to the Emperor, maintaining the validity of the Council—"the holy Gospel having been placed in the midst, and we declare that Christ Himself, the Lord of all, was present"—and inviting the Emperor "to send for the most noble Candidianus and five of the holy Council, that they may vouch for what has been done before your Piety." Nestorius quotes sections from Cyril's letter and comments hotly on them (B. 178–186), passing from that to strictures on the Records of the Council (B. 186–193), which he proposes to examine in detail in the next part of his work.

Book II, Part I

This part deals in detail with the charges made and the documents presented at the first session of the Council of Ephesus, and with the events immediately following.[1] It falls into seven main divisions:

(1) Criticism of the proceedings at the first session of the Council (B. 193–208).

(2) Justification of Nestorius' position by two deductions from the Creed of Nicæa (B. 208–209).

(3) Comments on Nestorius' second letter to Cyril and Cyril's second letter to Nestorius (B. 209–270).

(4) Consideration of the extracts from the 'Book of Nestorius' which were put before the first session of the Council (B. 137–146, 271–366).

(5) An account of the events from Nestorius' deposition and excommunication at the first session of the Council (June 22nd, 431) till the accord of John of Antioch and the Easterns with Cyril (433) (B. 366–403).

(6) Nestorius quotes from the correspondence of Cyril with Acacius of Melitene, who was anxious lest Cyril had compromised orthodoxy by coming to terms with the Easterns (B. 404–452).

(7) After the enforced peace, Cyril continued to impose his will on all and to set himself up as the standard

[1] See p. 450, footnote 1.

of orthodoxy, even against Fathers anciently accepted (B. 452–459).

(1) Criticism of the proceedings at the first session of the Council (B. 193–208).

Nestorius criticizes the method by which he was charged and the substance and manner of the charges put forward by Theodotus and Acacius.

(i) The method of charge (B. 193–199)

Quoting from the Records of the Council, Nestorius cites the words with which Peter, priest of Alexandria and chief of the secretaries, introduced the case against him. Commenting on this, Nestorius complains that Cyril was behind everything: "And I was summoned by Cyril who had assembled the Council, even by Cyril who was the chief thereof. Who was the judge? Cyril. And who was the accuser? Cyril. Who was bishop of Rome? Cyril. Cyril was everything" (B. 195). Not only was Cyril prime mover and self-appointed director of the proceedings, but he would not even wait until all entitled to be present had had reasonable opportunity of assembling: "You were not ashamed to have written this as an excellent reason whereby you were constrained not to wait for the bishops who were far off who were constrained to come, and who had been delayed in coming by an important reason and besought you to wait for them" (B. 197).

(ii) The reason for his absence (B. 199–200)

Nestorius refused to attend the Council on the ground that it had assembled prematurely. But Juvenalius, bishop of Jerusalem, suggested that his absence was due to a guilty conscience, and that for the same reason he had guarded his house with soldiers. Nestorius pointed out that a guard was necessary for his personal safety: "Thou accusest me of posting soldiers around my house: [it was] not that they might do any wrong unto you but that they might hinder you from doing wrong unto me" (B. 199).

(iii) The accusation of Theodotus (B. 201–205)

Theodotus, bishop of Ancyra, charges Nestorius with having asserted that it was "not right to say of God that he has been suckled nor that he was born of a virgin"; also, said Theodotus, Nestorius had many times said, "I say not that God was two or three months old."

The crux of this matter is the use of the word 'God'. Theodotus would reason thus: Christ is God, and therefore all Christ experiences can correctly be described as experience of God. Contemplating Christ's infancy, it could be said "God is two or three months old", meaning that God in Christ is experiencing what it is to be two or three months old. Who could misunderstand what was meant? But Nestorius, with his rigid metaphysic, could not say such a thing without a far greater consciousness of the qualifications. To Nestorius, 'God' without qualification implies the ousia of God in its nature, whether that ousia is hypostatic to God the Father, God the Word, or God the Holy Spirit. 'God' refers to the divine ousia. 'God the Father', 'God the Word', 'God the Holy Spirit' refer to the divine hypostases specifically. But we ought not to refer to a prosôpon as if it were identically that of which it is the prosôpon, nor ought we to refer to a complex as though it were identically one of its constituents, nor to a phase as if it were a whole. Jesus Christ, to Nestorius, was indeed the prosôpon of God the Word, but an allogenous prosôpon, and as God the Word had existed eternally it would, to Nestorius, seem absurd to say that God the Word was born or was a certain age. It would, however, be correct to refer such expressions to the prosôpon which was the manifestation of God the Word during the period of His self-manifestation as Jesus Christ. Nestorius would therefore prefer to say that Christ was born, was suckled, was two or three months old, and would agree that these things were true of the hypostasis of God in that prosôpon; but to refer them to God without qualification seemed absurd. "Christ is God but was not as God born nor [as God] became two or three months old" (B. 203).

The answers to the rhetorical questions (B. 203–204) are not particularly difficult to supply, though some of the later

ones could be answered "Yes" or "No" according to the
interpretation we put upon them. But probably it is only
the last question which Nestorius would answer in the
affirmative: "Or was he born by adoption of the *ousia*
in the birth of the flesh?" Then follows an antithetically
phrased statement which brings out the Nestorian emphasis
on the oneness of Christ yet the integrity of the two ousias.
No adverse criticism can be passed on it, except to point
out that all the experiences belong to the one Christ, and as
Christ was God the Word in the flesh, all the experiences
belong to God the Word. Thus "God was born" has a real
meaning, though obviously not in the sense that ousia of
Godhead originated in utero Virginis. It is this inability to
concede to others the right to know what they mean which
contributes so largely to Nestorius' aversion to the title
Theotokos (see pp. 450–451).

(*iv*) The accusation of Acacius (B. 205–208)

Next came Acacius, bishop of Melitene, who charged
Nestorius with having put a certain question in such a way
that any answer would involve the answerer in error. As
Acacius gives no details and does not even record the
question—"For what reason dost thou not utter this absurd
question whereby you wish to condemn me?" (B. 207)—
the matter is not worth pursuing.

(2) Justification of Nestorius' position by two deductions
from the Creed of Nicæa (B. 208–209).

We cannot tell what arguments Nestorius intended to
base on the Creed of Nicæa at this juncture because, unfortunately, after his introductory remarks and the quotation
of the first few sentences of the Creed a number of pages
are missing. The next page of the Syriac is evidently not
very far after the commencement of a section dealing with:

(3) Comments on Nestorius' second letter to Cyril and
Cyril's second letter to Nestorius (B. 209–270).

Nestorius quotes a number of extracts from these letters
and makes his comments on them. Very little that is new
emerges, as Nestorius' arguments follow from his rigid
metaphysic, his careful discrimination in the use of the

terms God the Word and Christ, and his uncompromising opposition to the idea of hypostatic union.

He considers seven extracts:

(i) An extract from Nestorius' second letter to Cyril. (Only the latter part of the quotation is available in the Syriac, owing to the missing pages referred to above.) (B. 209–211.)

Nestorius' comments on this extract illustrate the difficulties arising from his lack of precision in the use of the word 'in'. Reference is made to this on p. 145, q.v. It is to be noted that Nestorius' very consciousness of his own meaning led him to use expressions apparently mutually contradictory. Thus at the end of B. 210 we have "God the Word was at the same time in the humanity", whereas halfway down B. 211 we have "God the Word is not in two natures." Although these sentences verbally contradict one another, there is no confusion in Nestorius' thought. In the first case 'in' means 'in syntactically, voluntarily, prosôpically, adoptively'; in the second case 'in' is used strictly and means 'in naturally'.

(ii) Extract from Cyril's second letter to Nestorius (B. 211–220).

Nestorius uses this quotation as the starting point for a disquisition on the distinction which should be observed in the use of the words 'Christ' and 'God the Word'. The ground is quite familiar, though one or two points call for comment:

B. 215–216: "Now God the Word is not of them both in *ousia*, nor again is God the Word in flesh, nor is God the Word of two nor is God the Word two natures. For herein only, in his being co-essential with the Father, is God the Word conceived. For he was made flesh and was revealed in flesh; but if he was made flesh in the flesh, it is evident that [it was] in that flesh which had been made, and he who was made flesh in that which was made made not his own *ousia* the flesh." Here we have another bad example of the undefined use of 'in'. "Nor again is God the Word in flesh"—that is, naturally. "For he was made flesh and revealed in flesh"—that is, prosôpically.

B. 216: "For he made use of the likeness and of the

prosôpon of a servant, not the *ousia* nor the nature, in such wise that he was by nature in them both, as being Christ." The first 'he' is simply God the Word, but the second 'he' must be taken to mean God the Word during that period when His durative prosôpon was expressing itself allogenously in the unique syntax Jesus Christ.

B. 219: On the first half of this page Nestorius deals with the implication that Cyril was attacking him not for failing to confess that Christ was God, but for confessing that He was also man. The answer is confusingly involved, because Nestorius adopts the unhelpful expedient of saying what he supposes he would have said if he had held the wrong view, i.e. Cyril's view. A paraphrase, with asides to show the trend of Nestorius' thought, might read thus: "I am accused, then, for confessing that Christ is man as well as God. If Christ is man as well as God (and indeed He is), and if I had not confessed Him to be so (though I of course do), I should have taught thus: Christ is God (only) and consubstantial with the Father and yet (somehow) at the same time also man consubstantial with us. (How absurd!) I should have emphasized the one prosôpon as arising from the ousia of the divinity, itself sufficing to provide a pro-sôpon both divine and human,[1] so that both divinity and humanity would be ousia of God! And I should have ascribed everything, including whatever pertains to the flesh, to the one ousia and nature of Christ, Himself God and nothing other!"

B. 220: "First prove unto us that the fathers called her the mother of God." Nestorius does not help himself much by taking up this point. As has been indicated (p. 451), the titles 'Theotokos' and 'Mother of God' had already been used by theologians of acknowledged standing. Only two explanations seem possible:

(*a*) Either Nestorius was aware that the title had been used by those quoted, but did not consider them to rank as 'fathers'. Such an attitude would be very difficult to justify. Even now it is uncertain what exactly is meant by

[1] Cf. Nau: "Je n'aurais pas passé rapidement sur le prosôpon de l'union et j'aurais commencé par l'essence de la divinité comme prosôpon commun de la divinité et de la humanité; comme d'une seule essence de Dieu le Verbe qu'elles étaient toutes deux."

'the Fathers', as Swete points out.[1] The Apostolic Fathers are admitted by all to include Clement of Rome, Ignatius, and Polycarp, most also including Barnabas, Hermas, and Papias; the Catholic Fathers are generally agreed to be Irenæus, Clement of Alexandria, and Tertullian. But those who assembled at Nicæa are often referred to as 'the three hundred and eighteen fathers', and many would consider that orthodox theologians till the time of Gregory in the West and John of Damascus in the East are entitled to be reckoned as 'fathers'. The question was just as open in Nestorius' time, and it would probably have been considered that all Catholic orthodox bishops of former days were 'fathers'. Any explanation depending on the connotation of the word 'fathers' therefore seems unsatisfactory.

(b) Or Nestorius was not aware that the title had been used by those quoted. This, though somewhat surprising, seems to be the only likely explanation. It has already been remarked (pp. 61–62) that Nestorius was an original thinker rather than a well-versed student, and once again Socrates may have been right: having remarked on Origen using 'Θεοτόκος', Socrates says: "Nestorius therefore appears ignorant of the works of the ancients: on which account, as I said, he shunned the special term."[2]

(iii) Extract from Cyril's second letter to Nestorius (B. 220–222).

Here again everything hinges on a proper understanding of the terms 'Christ' and 'God the Word'.

(iv) Extract from Cyril's second letter (B. 222–225).

By criticism of Cyril's somewhat unfortunate wording, Nestorius endeavours to show that Cyril himself is guilty of teaching a duality in Christ's person: "For the [word] 'with' is not said of one but [of one] with another, and the one, who is with the other, is seated with the Father; how will he not introduce a semblance of separation?" (B. 222). The argument is not of much interest or value, as it is hardly fair to base an argument on an obviously ill-worded

---

[1] *Encyclopædia Britannica* (11th Edition), x. 200–201. (Slightly abridged and uninitialled in the 14th Edition, ix. 110–111.)

[2] Socrates, *Historia Ecclesiastica*, Bk. vii, Ch. 32: Φαίνεται τοίνυν ὁ Νεστόριος ἀγνοήσας τὰς πραγματείας τῶν παλαιῶν. Διὸ, καθὼς ἔφην, τὴν λέξιν μόνην περιίσταται. (Accessible in Migne, *Patrologia Græco-Latina*, lxvii. 812B.)

sentence. Such a method would find no easier victim than Nestorius himself.

(v) Extract from Cyril's second letter (B. 225–233).

Cyril roundly states that we cannot avoid predicating 'two sons' unless we accept the idea of hypostatic union. The burden of Nestorius' comment is that he cannot conceive hypostatic union without at the same time oneness of ousia and nature. He asks a number of questions in a feigned endeavour to discover how any sort of hypostatic union could preserve the integrity of the ousias and natures; but the questions are merely rhetorical. In one passage (B. 229) he wonders whether what Cyril means by 'hypostasis' is really the same as what he himself means by 'prosôpon'. This might indeed have been a starting point for the reconciliation of the two points of view; but Nestorius concludes, perhaps a little too hastily, that there is no hope of this identity being established.

(vi) Extract from Cyril's second letter (B. 233–245).

Here again Nestorius charges Cyril with inconsistency. He endeavours to show that his own ideas are coherent and logical, whereas Cyril's views lead to confusion and contradiction.

(vii) Extract from Nestorius' second letter to Cyril (B. 245–270).

He uses a quotation from his own letter for a further exposition on the right understanding of 'God the Word' and 'Christ'.

(4) Consideration of the extracts from the 'Book of Nestorius' which were put before the first session of the Council (B. 137–146 and 271–366).

Part of the evidence against Nestorius presented to the Council had consisted of a number of extracts from his own writings or records of his own utterances. These extracts are quoted as if from the 'Book of Nestorius', and reference is made by 'chapters' or 'rolls'. There may have been some inexactitude in the citing of the work or works from which the extracts were taken, in the mode of reference, and in the exact wording of the quotations: " 'From the Book of Nestorius, from the sixteenth[1] chapter, con-

[1] See p. 461, footnote 1.

cerning the Faith.' From which book of mine? From which sixteenth[1] chapter?" (B. 141); "I pass by the things which they have omitted, and they have clearly not preserved the coherence [of the argument]" (B. 142). Having made these remarks, however, he proceeds to discuss the quotations with little further question as to their authenticity or accuracy, so we may take it that apart from trivial errors in citing and reference[2] the quotations are nearly enough in Nestorius' own words.[3]

Nineteen of these extracts were presented to the Council, and Nestorius devotes his next hundred pages to justifying the opinions he had expressed. The arguments are not difficult to follow, and for the most part cover ground already familiar. He deals with the extracts in the order in which they were presented to the Council:

(i) From the sixteenth[1] roll (B. 141–146).

From the birth to the death 'Christ', 'Son', 'Lord', are the appropriate terms because they are indicative of the two natures, whereas 'God the Word' indicates only the divine nature. He gives a quotation from Ambrose (B. 146) which he claims expresses the same view. We have not Nestorius' full comments on this extract, because a number of pages are missing after the quotation from Ambrose, and the next extant Syriac page is dealing with an extract from the twenty-first roll. The Syriac copyist says that twelve pages are missing, but Nau does not think the gap is so considerable as that. In these extracts Nestorius follows

---

[1] 'Sixteenth' should be corrected to 'seventeenth'. The Syriac of Bedjan gives 'seventeenth' without an alternative, and Nau translates 'dix-septième'. Loofs (*Nestoriana*, p. 273), Mansi (*Sacrorum conciliorum collectio*, iv. 1197A), and Labbe (*Sacrosancta concilia*, iii. 519B) all give 'seventeenth' (13'). Professor Driver concurs in this correction.

[2] The citing of numbers in ancient records is notoriously liable to error, and it may well be that Nestorius' query is to some extent an endeavour to make capital of unimportant mistakes in the reference to the roll numbers. Compare also the uncertainty as to the numbers for rolls 17, 7 and 24 (see below, pp. 464, 466 and 467), but in these cases the numbers may be due to the Syriac editor rather than to Nestorius.

[3] Loofs (*Nestoriana*, pp. 225–292) has endeavoured to reconstruct this 'Book of Nestorius', which is evidently simply a collection of sermons. He places them in order and recovers the original text as far as possible from the available ancient sources. The differences and omissions in the citations as made at the Council may be observed by comparing Loofs with Mansi, op. cit., iv. 1197A–1208B.

the same order as was followed at the Council, and we know that the twenty-first roll was considered immediately after the seventeenth.

(ii) From the twenty-first[1] roll (B. 271–276).

Owing to the lost pages, the citation and the earlier part of Nestorius' comment is lost. But the extract can be recovered from the Greek record of the proceedings of the Council, and is quoted in Nau (pp. 170–171).

The extract is a defence of his understanding of the term 'Mother of God', and his comments elaborate his views in the familiar manner: God the Word exists eternally, Christ is God the Word from the birth to the death; God the Word signifies the divinity, Christ the divinity and the humanity as united in the one prosôpon.

The relevance of the quotation from Athanasius is perhaps not clear owing to the absence of the immediately preceding pages, and the word 'artificially' (B. 271) presents some difficulty. The Syriac (*bash'îlû*) might mean by entreaty, by seeking, by desire, by pretext, by assumption (cf. R. Payne Smith, *Thesaurus Syriacus*, ii. 4008, and *Supplement*, p. 325). Hence Driver and Hodgson are able to say it means literally 'metaphorically', while Nau says it means literally 'par emprunt' (by borrowing). But, as always, we must remember that it is the original Greek which signifies, and in this case we know that it is θέσει. This, unfortunately, is almost as indefinite as the Syriac, and might mean by placing, by setting, by ordinance, by deposit, by adoption, by position, by affirmation (cf. Liddell and Scott, *A Greek-English Lexicon* (new revised edition 1940), i. 794–795). Taken in conjunction with the words φαντασία and δόκησις used in the same passage from Athanasius, it would seem sufficiently clear that all three words (θέσις, φαντασία, δόκησις) are used in opposition to that which exists in reality and truth (ὄντως and ἀληθείᾳ). The precise connotation of each term is not for our present purpose important, for a detailed investigation of the matter would involve an analysis of Athanasius rather than of Nestorius. The important point is this: nothing satisfies the conditions of the problem

---

[1] This number is inserted in accordance with the numbering in Loofs, op. cit., p. 277, Mansi, op. cit., iv. 1197C, and Labbe, op. cit., iii. 519.

which is otherwise than in reality and truth (ὄντως, ἀληθείᾳ), and any view of the Incarnation which depends in any way on θέσις, φαντασία or δόκησις—and however we translate these words they are meant to be antithetic to that which is ὄντως and ἀληθείᾳ—cannot be valid. To use Nestorius' wide and useful term, any such view of the Incarnation would be a mere schêma. The lack of precision arises from the fact that Nestorius is taking over into his own argument words used by Athanasius in a somewhat different setting and with a not identical metaphysic. Driver and Hodgson translate the three words (θέσει, φαντασίᾳ, δοκήσει) 'artificially', 'fantasy', 'fictitious', while Nau translates them 'par apparence', 'imagination', 'en imagination'. It is not relevant to pursue the matter further. Nestorius' implication is simply this: God the Word was not in Christ θέσει, φαντασίᾳ, δοκήσει (by imposition, by mere appearance, in mere seeming, or whatever else these datives may mean, and all of them are probably nearly enough equivalent to κατὰ σχῆμα), nor, at the other extreme, hypostatically; but voluntarily, adoptively, by love, by acknowledgment, prosôpically.

Near the end of B. 272 there is a translator's slip: the sentence beginning "For thou sayest that God the Father is body and man, . . ." should read "For thou sayest that God the Word is body and man, . . .". (Noted to the author by Professor Driver.)

(iii) From the twenty-fourth[1] roll (B. 276–281).

Another extract on the same theme: strictly speaking, Christ, not God the Word, was born of Mary. Nestorius endeavours to support his careful phrasing by reference to Ambrose, Gregory of Nazianzus, and Athanasius.

(iv) From the fifteenth[2] roll (B. 282–284).

Another extract making clear that Christ is the proper description of God the Word during the period of His assumption of humanity. This again he defends by quotations from Athanasius and Gregory.

(v) From the twenty-seventh[3] roll (B. 284–289).

[1] This number is inserted in accordance with the numbering in Loofs, op. cit., p. 285, Mansi, op. cit., iv. 1197E, and Labbe, op. cit., iii. 522.

[2] Following Loofs, p. 248, Mansi, iv. 1200C, and Labbe, iii. 522.

[3] Following Loofs, p. 289, Mansi, iv. 1200D, and Labbe, iii. 522.

An extract illustrating common sense in the interpretation of terms. (Nestorius might well have applied the same principles when his opponents said 'God the Word' for 'Christ', and said God the Word was born or died!)

(vi) From the fifteenth roll (B. 290–303).

Another extract illustrating the difference in significance of the terms God the Word and Christ.

Near the beginning of B. 293 there is a translator's slip: the sentence "But hear also from us: He is not one thing and another; for he would be one thing and another if Christ were apart from God the Father" should read "But hear also from us: He is not one thing and another; for he would be one thing and another if Christ were apart from God the Word." (Noted to the author by Professor Driver.)

(vii) From the sixteenth roll (B. 303–309).

An extract to illustrate how Nestorius regarded the two natures as completely united (though not naturally): "God is not distinguished from him who is visible" (B. 303). His elaboration of this point is a valuable source for the systematization of his views, as may be seen by reference to pp. 171–173. He again quotes Athanasius, and also Gregory of Nyssa.

(viii) From the seventeenth roll (B. 309–314).

A quotation, not very happily worded, identifying God the Word with Christ. There are not two Sons. He quotes Gregory of Nazianzus as stating a similar view.

(ix) From the seventeenth[1] roll (B. 314–317).

Another unhappily worded quotation, which looks very like a statement of duality. Nestorius endeavours to defend himself by quoting Ambrose, Athanasius, and Gregory of Nazianzus, and emphasizes that the diversity is in ousia and nature, but there is oneness of prosôpon and one Christ.

(x) From the sixth roll (B. 317–319).

God, quickener of the passible temple, is Himself impassible. He supports his view by quoting Ambrose.

(xi) From the twenty-seventh roll (B. 320–325).

"The child and he that dwelleth in the child are the same" (B. 320). This means the same in prosôpon, though there

[1] Thus the Syriac, which Driver and Hodgson and Nau follow. But the Greek has 'fifteenth' (ιε'): Loofs, p. 249, Mansi, iv. 1201D, Labbe, iii. 523.

are the two ousias. He quotes Gregory (of Nazianzus) and Theophilus in support.

(xii) From the first roll (B. 326–328).[1]

The Trinity shows three prosôpa (or, in the special Trinitarian use, three hypostases), but one ousia and nature; Christ is one prosôpon (that of God the Word) with two natures (divinity and humanity). So say Gregory, Ambrose, Athanasius, and "all the Fathers" (B. 328).

(xiii) From the sixteenth roll (B. 328–335).

A very reasonable statement of some aspects of the union of the natures—Christ is not "God by himself" (B. 329).

B. 333: In this passage Nestorius confusingly involves his arguments by trying to attack his opponents on too many issues at once. If God the Word used a body and soul or even a complete man as an instrument, like a craftsman using a tool, that would not be an incarnation. (It would be a syntax, and of course a theophany.) On the other hand, natural union with a body and soul would be Arianism or Apollinarianism, and would impair the nature of God, involving passibility. These two errors—instrumental union (mere syntax) and natural union—are on opposite sides of the true solution (voluntary adoptive prosôpic union), and it is unhelpful to bring them into the same argument. Probably Nestorius brings the two ideas together for the following reason: Instrumental union (syntax) of a crafts-man and a tool involves the complete subordination of the tool to the craftsman; the powers and properties of the tool are within the powers of the nature of the craftsman, whereas the powers and properties of the craftsman are not trans-ferred in any way to the tool. (In more exact phraseology, the syntax is voluntary so far as the craftsman is concerned, but imposed so far as the tool is concerned; and the quasi-prosôpon of the syntax is identically the allogenous pro-sôpon of the craftsman, whose durative prosôpon includes the period during which he uses the tool.) Similarly, natural union of God and man (or something of man) involves the complete subordination of man to God; the powers and properties of man may become powers and properties (or limitations and modes of expression) of God, but God is

[1] Nau inadvertently omits this extract from his analysis, op. cit., p. 402.

not similarly subordinated to man. Instrumental (syntactic) and natural union as applied to God and man therefore have this in common: God is dominant and man subordinated. (Yet it must always be borne in mind that God cannot enter into natural unions—see p. 125. It is only in discussing an erroneous view that we can contemplate God entering natural union, continually bearing in mind that any such view is necessarily untenable.)

(xiv) From the third roll (B. 335–337).

The Trinity is one in ousia and nature, three in hypostases (i.e. in the special Trinitarian sense). Correspondingly, Christ is one prosôpon with two natures, the divinity and the humanity.

(xv) From the sixth roll (B. 337–344).

The human development of Christ illustrates the reality of the duality of the natures, though He was one prosôpon, one Christ. Nestorius supports his view from Gregory and Ambrose. The section is a valuable one for deducing the meaning of prosôpon and prosôpic union (see pp. 171–173).

B. 341–342: Here again there is an unfortunate bringing into parallel of the ideas of instrumental union and natural union. As pointed out above in the note on B. 333, instrumental (syntactic) union and natural union as applied to the union of God and man have this in common: in either case God is dominant and man subordinated, and neither provides for the reciprocity of the kind of union which Nestorius envisages, which must be mutually voluntary and prosôpic.

(xvi) From the seventh[1] roll (B. 344–351).

It was necessary that Christ should possess full and true humanity. Prosôpic union of the two natures is the satisfactory solution.

B. 350: "For the man, who, as not united, was not what he is by nature, namely man, is called God through that which is united." This sentence is perfectly comprehensible if taken in conjunction with the view of the genesis of Jesus Christ set out on pp. 154–157. 'The man', that is, the potenti-

[1] Thus the Syriac, which Driver and Hodgson and Nau follow. Loofs, op. cit., p. 240, confirms 'seventh', and in this case Mansi and Labbe, both of whom give 'seventeenth' (ιζ'), appear to be in error (op. cit., iv. 1205B and iii. 527).

ally separate man Jesus (for this usage see pp. 163–164), never existed otherwise than in union with God the Word; and, further, his nature was complete only so long as God the Word was supplying that which completed it into full manhood. Except as so united, 'the man' never existed nor ever could exist. This is surely a close approach to the idea of enhypostasia. (Driver and Hodgson are certainly to be followed in retaining the negative as in the Syriac text—'was not what he is by nature'. Nau, as a conjectural emendation, suggests omitting it to make obvious sense; but, as we have seen, the original text, though its meaning is less obvious, when understood confirms our interpretation of Nestorius' views.)

(xvii) From the fourth roll (B. 351–354).

Nestorius calls attention to the distinction drawn between Christ and His body, presumably as supporting the idea of two natures distinct yet in one prosôpon. He again quotes in support Gregory, Athanasius, Theophilus, and Ambrose.

(xviii) From the sixteenth roll (B. 355–363).

Yet again: 'God the Word' is the divinity only; Christ is God the Word in His humanity. "For the name of Christ or of Son or of Lord, which is taken for the only-begotten from the divine Scriptures, is indicative of two natures and indicates sometimes the divinity, but sometimes the humanity and sometimes both of them" (B. 355).

(xix) From the twenty-fourth[1] roll (B. 363–366).

Nestorius is quoted as having observed that the people (at Constantinople) had lacked exact instruction in the faith. Peter, chief secretary to the Council (see p. 454), distorted this into a confession by Nestorius that he had been teaching new doctrines. (As Driver and Hodgson indicate, we can only make sense of the Syriac text at the bottom of B. 363 if we supply from the Greek[2] some words which have either dropped out or were omitted by Nestorius himself. The words to be inserted, between "the exact faith." and "This man", are: "Peter, priest of Alexandria, and chief of the secretaries, said:".[3])

---

[1] Thus the Syriac, which Driver and Hodgson and Nau follow; but the Greek has 'twenty-third' (κγ'): Loofs, p. 283, Mansi, iv. 1208B, Labbe, iii. 530.
[2] See Loofs, Mansi, or Labbe, locis cit.
[3] Πέτρος πρεσβύτερος Ἀλεξανδρείας, καὶ πριμμικήριος νοταρίων εἶπεν·

Nestorius explains the obvious meaning of what he had said and declares his faithful adherence to the Creed of Nicæa.

(5) An account of the events from Nestorius' deposition and excommunication at the first session of the Council (June 22nd, 431) till the accord of John of Antioch and the Easterns with Cyril (433) (B. 366–403).[1]

B. 366–368: Nestorius complains that judgment was passed upon him with undue haste and without any cross-examination, the haste having been due to Cyril's desire to dispose of the matter before the arrival of the Easterns. Many of those who signed the condemnation did so with no clear ideas as to the issues involved, acting simply in blind obedience to Cyril. Only one—Acacius of Melitene—gave reasons, and his reasons were self-contradictory. (Note Nestorius' sarcasm at the expense of Acacius.) Cyril was getting his way by intimidation and violence.

B. 369–372: Then John bishop of Antioch and the other Eastern bishops arrived. They constituted themselves into a Council, degraded Cyril and Memnon, and anathematized those who had acted with them. John sent a detailed letter describing the situation to the Emperor.

B. 372–382: Thereupon Cyril stirred up the whole city, inflaming feeling against Nestorius and staging signs and portents. He finally arranged that Dalmatius, the aged archimandrite, should go to the Emperor in witness against Nestorius. Theodosius, after a long and well-reasoned reply to Dalmatius, finally yielded to his fanatical importunity, and allowed the condemnation of Nestorius to stand.

B. 382–391: This decision caused such foolish and disorderly demonstrations that the Emperor decreed the deprivation of all three: Nestorius, Cyril, and Memnon. He then appointed Count John to mediate, who sent Nestorius back to Antioch. Cyril was supposed to be kept in custody at Ephesus, but by bribery was able to effect his return in triumph to Alexandria. The section ends with a number of rhetorical questions addressed to Cyril.

---

[1] Nestorius' account, as might be expected, is heavily biassed in his own favour, and his order is not always chronological. As a corrective, and for general background, see Kidd, *A History of the Church*, iii. 242–262.

B. 391–398: After Nestorius had been sent back to Antioch, the Emperor ordered that seven bishops from each side should report to him at Chalcedon. He agreed with the statement of the Easterns, but allowed the Cyrillians to nominate the new bishop of Constantinople (Maximian). The section passes over into a complaint against the weakness of the Emperor and the iniquities of Cyril.

B. 398–403: To close the matter, the Emperor sent Aristolaus to enforce peace between the Easterns and Cyril. The condemnation of Nestorius was to be upheld, but Cyril's Twelve Anathematisms[1] were tacitly dropped. Nestorius makes much of this latter point, arguing that it represented his vindication.

(6) Nestorius quotes from the correspondence of Cyril with Acacius bishop of Melitene, who was anxious lest Cyril had compromised orthodoxy by coming to terms with the Easterns (B. 404–452).

Nestorius endeavours to show the metaphysical unsoundness of Cyril's position as reflected in these extracts. The arguments depend on Nestorius' rigid metaphysic of ousia and nature, and he certainly makes good his case from his own point of view. Cyril's letter to Acacius was not worded so circumspectly as the circumstances demanded, and Cyril thus presented Nestorius with an open target.

B. 404–406: After some further remarks on the implications of the agreement with the Easterns, still insisting that the tacit dropping of the Twelve Anathematisms was tantamount to a vindication of his own position that 'Mother of God' is acceptable only if understood aright, and that the idea of hypostatic union is untenable, Nestorius gives a number of extracts from the correspondence and makes his comments on them:

(i) B. 406–409. Cyril, quoting Nestorius, asserts that Nestorius' teaching implies "two Sons".

Nestorius goes over the familiar ground, the burdens being "There is of the divinity and of the humanity one Christ and one Lord and one Son; he was not born of

---

[1] See Migne, *Patrologia Græco-Latina*, lxxvii. 120–121, or Gieseler, *A Compendium of Ecclesiastical History* (Engl. trans.), i. 397–398.

woman in the divinity, but in the humanity" (B. 407); and "But there both exists and is named one Christ, the two of them being united, he who was born of the Father in the divinity, [and] of the holy virgin in the humanity, for there was a union of the two natures" (B. 408).

(ii) B. 409–412. The quotation from Cyril could quite well be interpreted in terms of Nestorius' metaphysic, but he supposes it to imply the union of ousias and natures in one ousia and nature, and attacks the extract on that basis. The arguments are the old familiar ones: "How then is it to be conceived that he is consubstantial with us ourselves in the humanity when he exists not in the *ousia* of the humanity? But how is he consubstantial with the Father, when he exists not in his *ousia*? Or how [is] the same in *ousia* of the *ousia* of God the Father and of our *ousia*? And [how] is it the same *ousia*? And [how] are two *ousias* alien one to another one, so that each one of the *ousias* both is and is conceived in one *ousia*? But if this is impossible, [it is] also inacceptable that it should be conceived in the word of truth" (B. 411).

(iii) B. 413–416. Cyril quotes words of Nestorius which might suggest a duality (though we know that by 'man' Nestorius meant 'potentially separate man'). Nestorius shows that such modes of expression are inevitable from the nature of the problem, and that Cyril himself uses expressions which could be taken to imply duality. But Nestorius asserts yet again that he teaches that "there exists of two natures, of divinity and humanity, Christ, one Son, one Lord; through the union of the divinity and of the humanity the same is Son and Lord and God" (B. 414–415).

(iv) B. 417–421. Cyril is here lacking in metaphysical coherence. Nestorius seizes the opportunity thus presented, and elaborates his own rigid metaphysic on the union of ousias and natures.

(v) B. 421–427. An unconvincing attempt on the part of Cyril to bring logic into his ascription of distinctly divine and human attributes to the one Christ. Nestorius, with his clear metaphysic, shows that the attributes of two distinct natures cannot be supposed to belong to one united nature. He puts his case against Cyril very concisely in these words:

"Thou speakest of the Son [as formed] of two natures unlike one another and further removest [one of them] from him and attributest one nature alone unto him" (B. 424). This section contains some very useful material for the deduction of Nestorius' views, as may be seen by reference to pp. 124–127.

(vi) B. 427–428. Cyril's statement is unexceptionable, so Nestorius contents himself with interpreting it in the light of his own metaphysic.

(vii) B. 428–434. Cyril asserts that Nestorius' teaching is a duality, though the quotation he gives from Nestorius hardly bears him out. Nestorius, quite rightly, starts by suggesting that if Cyril's case against him had been so clear as this, Cyril might well have waited and confuted him unanswerably before the whole Council. He proceeds to reveal the contradictions involved in Cyril's statement, and states what his views actually are.

(viii) B. 434–438. A rather confused statement, in which Cyril tries to indicate the degree to which the combined natures were to be regarded as distinct yet indistinguishable. Nestorius opens, perhaps with justification, "I indeed suppose that he does not even know what he says" (B. 434). He then proceeds to elaborate the contradictions involved in Cyril's statement.

(ix) B. 438–444. Cyril admits that some things stated concerning our Lord apply to Him as a unity, but others apply rather to His divinity or to His humanity as the case may be. Nestorius shows how this admission weakens Cyril's case, and shows how his own views completely fit the problem: "The common *prosôpon* of the two natures [is] Christ, the same *prosôpon* whereof the natures make use even likewise, that wherein and whereby both of them, the divinity and the humanity, are known in *ousia* without distinction and with distinction. Neither the divinity nor the humanity exists [by itself] in the common *prosôpon*, for it appertains to both the natures, so that therein and thereby both the natures are known" (B. 439).

(x) B. 444–446. After an irrelevant reference to Arianism, Cyril repeats that the Easterns have admitted when necessary the ascribing of some things to the divinity and others to the humanity, yet do not (like Nestorius) divide the Son. Nestorius, not very convincingly, tries to show that Cyril himself approaches Arianism by supposing one ousia with the natures of both God and man: "For the *ousia* of man, as thou hast said, is the *ousia* of God: 'He is God and man'. [He is] then alien to the Father in every way whatsoever and he is inferior in everything according to thy own imagination, since thou imaginest that he is man also in the one same *ousia*" (B. 445).

(xi) B. 446–451. Cyril says that he has been accused of tending towards Arianism and Apollinarianism. This he stoutly denies. But Nestorius emphasizes the illogicality of Cyril's position.

(xii) B. 451–452. A debating point of no consequence.

(xiii) B. 452. The last extract shows that Cyril could not have regarded the reconciliation with the Easterns as an unqualified victory for himself, and Nestorius presumably quotes it to confirm the position he sets out in B. 398–403 —that the enforced peace was to an extent a vindication of his own position, and that the Twelve Anathematisms had had to be tacitly dropped.

(7) After the enforced peace, Cyril continued to impose his will on all and to set himself up as the standard of orthodoxy, even against Fathers anciently accepted (B. 452–459).

Nestorius ends Book II, Part I, with a summary of the trend of events after the enforced peace between the East and Cyril. He would have been content to accept his personal defeat and deposition if it had led to real peace and settlement; but that had not happened (B. 452–453). On the other hand, Cyril had continued his crafty scheming for power, and in so doing had dared to set himself against those formerly accepted, such as Diodorus and Theodorus, and had even seemed to approve some things in Apollinarius (B. 453–456). If Diodorus had been a heretic, would not Basil and Gregory, his great contemporaries, have seen to the matter? Cyril was on the way to setting himself above Basil and Gregory, and even Athanasius and Ambrose! (B. 456–457.) Thus Cyril with his cunning and intimidation was bending everyone to his will, and setting himself up as the one standard of orthodoxy, dismissing even the anciently accepted doctors if they seemed to agree with Nestorius (B. 457–459).

This section prepares the way for Book II, Part II, in which Nestorius endeavours to show that events were trending towards the vindication of the positions for which he had contended.

(Cyril did not get his way quite so easily and so absolutely as Nestorius seems to suggest, as may be seen by following the course of events from the first mission of Aristolaus till the death of Cyril, e.g. in Kidd, *A History of the Church*, iii. 262–266, 275–280. Nestorius probably over-emphasizes the ease and completeness of Cyril's dominance in order to heighten by contrast the dramatic effect of the new trend which he is about to elaborate in Book II, Part II.)

Book II, Part II

This part mainly consists of a commentary on the events from the time of Flavian's consecration as bishop of Constantinople (446) until just before the Council of Chalcedon (October 451).[1] Nestorius' concern is to show that the struggle between Cyril and himself continued in the opposition of Eutyches and Dioscorus to Flavian and Leo; that although by intrigue and violence Dioscorus was at first in the ascendant, having the support of Theodosius and forcing his will on the Latrocinium (August 449), matters took a different turn after the death of Theodosius (July 450); that although Flavian had been done to death at the Latrocinium, that for which Flavian had stood, for which Leo was still standing, and which Nestorius identified with his own position, was in course of being vindicated and would surely triumph.

Nestorius must have died, or have ended his book, after it had become apparent that the triumph of Leo and the downfall of Dioscorus were certain, but before the Council of Chalcedon was actually held; for he shows no sign of knowing that it had condemned not only Eutyches but

---

[1] As Nestorius' account is selective and not always strictly chronological, the general background may conveniently be gathered from Kidd, *A History of the Church*, iii. 281–314.

himself as well. So perhaps Nestorius was at least "felix opportunitate mortis", in that he died believing that his views were at last to be understood and approved.

There is very little that throws any additional light on Christology in this part. It falls into the following main divisions:

B. 459–462: Soon after Flavian became bishop of Constantinople (446), Eutyches endeavoured to gain the ascendancy over him, advocating his own monophysite views and complaining that Nestorianism had not been thoroughly eradicated.

B. 462–466: As the result of a conversation between Eutyches and Eusebius, bishop of Dorylæum, the latter was led to doubt Eutyches' orthodoxy, and charged him before Flavian at a Council at Constantinople. This Council condemned Eutyches (November 448).

B. 466–470: This angered Theodosius, who made plans to restore the prestige of Eutyches and to humble Flavian. He secured the help of Dioscorus, bishop of Alexandria, but failed to win over Leo, bishop of Rome, who had already approved Flavian's condemnation of Eutyches. Fear of the Emperor, however, ensured that the great majority of bishops sided with him, Eutyches, and Dioscorus, and after many things had been done to humiliate and insult Flavian, Theodosius finally commanded that an Œcumenical Council should assemble at Ephesus to depose him. Flavian was not allowed to retire to a monastery, but was ordered to face his trial.

B. 470–496: The preliminaries and the Council itself (August 449) were carried through with force and violence, the Emperor, Dioscorus (who presided), and Eutyches gaining their way by the display and use of stark force. Leo was well justified in naming it the 'Latrocinium' ('band of robbers'). Flavian and Eusebius were condemned, Flavian dying shortly after the first session of the Council as a result of violent handling by the partisans of Dioscorus (see B. 493–495). (There is a digression (B. 478–481) concerning the mean behaviour of the Emperor towards Cyril over a money matter. The incident has little relevance at this point beyond illustrating the unscrupulousness of Theodosius.

The date of the incident is uncertain; it may have been as early as 432. In any case it was many years before the Latrocinium, for Cyril had died in 444.)

B. 497–506: Nestorius gives a list of disasters which he considered to be signs of the displeasure of God at the transgressions wrought by Cyril, Dioscorus and Theodosius against the true faith. These evils continued till the death of Theodosius (July 450). (There is an interesting reference to the Trisagion on B. 500–501. From the context it would appear that Nestorius ascribes the revelation of the Trisagion to some time in the period just before the death of Theodosius. This is not necessarily incompatible with the generally accepted statement that its first recorded use was at the Council of Chalcedon on October 8th, 451.)

B. 506–521: The concluding pages show how he identified his own case and cause with that of Flavian. There are two groups of thoughts: he believed that events had proved the rightness of his views (B. 513), that the righteous often have to suffer (B. 516–517), and that Councils are not invariably right (B. 517–518); but he also believed that events were moving towards the vindication, if not of himself personally, at least of the positions he had meant to defend and had held dear (B. 514). He evidently knew of the increasing influence of Leo since the death of Theodosius, and of the growing anxiety of Dioscorus (B. 514). Whether Nestorius knew that an Œcumenical Council was shortly to be called is uncertain. We can hardly suppose that he would have ended his book on a note of vague but confident hopefulness if he had known that his views had again been condemned. It seems likely, therefore, that when he finished his book he did not know of the proceedings of the fourth session of the Council (October 17th, 451), though he certainly knew of the turn which events had been taking since the death of Theodosius in July 450. 'The shape of things to come' was perhaps sufficiently clear by June 451, which we might provisionally regard as the end point in Nestorius' information. If Nestorius had known definitely that a Council was certainly to be called, he would probably have mentioned the fact.

The prophecy about the fall of Rome (B. 520) came all

too true in 455, when Gaiseric the Vandal captured Rome, carried away the sacred vessels which Titus had brought from the Temple at Jerusalem, and led away captive the Empress Eudoxia and her daughters Placidia and Eudocia. To have foretold the fall of Rome would merely have been intelligent anticipation, and the details would naturally be in accordance with the inevitable accompaniments of the fall of any great city—the looting of its most precious treasures and the taking of the most exalted captives. It may be, however, that the details were adjusted later by a copyist.

The book ends with the resignation of his body to the desert, that there it might rest until the day of resurrection.

BIBLIOGRAPHY

Andrade, E. N. da C.: *The Structure of the Atom.*
Anselm: *Proslogion.*
Assemani, J. S.: *Bibliotheca Orientalis.*
Aulén, G.: *Christus Victor* (English translation by A. G. Hebert).
Barnes, E. W.: *Scientific Theory and Religion.*
Bastian, H. C.: *The Nature and Origin of Living Matter.*
Baumstark, A.: *Oriens Christianus.*
Baur, F. C.: *Die christliche Lehre von der Dreieinigheit und Mensch-werdung Gottes in ihrer geschichtlichen Entwichlung.*
Bedjan, P.: *Nestorius: Le Livre d'Héraclide de Damas, édité par Paul Bedjan, avec plusieurs appendices.*
Bergson, H.: *L'Evolution Créatrice.*
Berguer, G.: *Some Aspects of the Life of Jesus* (English translation by E. S. Brooks and Van W. Brooks).
Bethune-Baker, J. F.: *An Introduction to the Early History of Christian Doctrine.*
Bethune-Baker, J. F.: *Nestorius and His Teaching.*
Bethune-Baker, J. F.: *The Meaning of Homoousios* (in *Texts and Studies*, edited by J. A. Robinson, vol. viii, no. 1).
Brasnett, B. R.: *The Infinity of God.*
Braun, O.: *Das Buch der Synados.*
Briggs, C. A.: *Theological Symbolics.*
Bright, W.: *Age of the Fathers.*
Brunner, E.: *The Mediator* (English translation by Olive Wyon).
Cave, S.: *The Christian Estimate of Man.*
Cave, S.: *The Doctrine of the Person of Christ.*
Doctrine in the Church of England (The Report of the Commission on Christian Doctrine appointed by the Archbishops of Canterbury and York in 1922).
Dorner, I. A.: *History of the Development of the Doctrine of the Person of Christ* (English translation by D. W. Simon).
Driver, G. R., and Hodgson, L.: *Nestorius: The Bazaar of Heracleides, newly translated from the Syriac and edited with an introduction, notes and appendices.*
Eddington, A. S.: *Space, Time and Gravitation.*
Eddington, A. S.: *The Mathematical Theory of Relativity.*
Eddington, A. S.: *The Nature of the Physical World.*
Edser, E.: *Light for Students.*
Einstein, A.: *Zur Einheitlichen Feldtheorie.*
Emmet, D. M.: *The Nature of Metaphysical Thinking.*
Encyclopædia Britannica: relevant articles.

Encyclopædia of Religion and Ethics (editor, J. Hastings): relevant articles.

Expository Times: relevant articles.

Farrer, A.: *Finite and Infinite.*

Fendt, L.: *Die Christologie des Nestorius.*

Fisher, G. P.: *History of Christian Doctrine.*

Foakes-Jackson, F. J.: *History of the Christian Church.*

Forsyth, P. T.: *The Person and Place of Jesus Christ.*

Fortescue, A.: *Lesser Eastern Churches.*

Garvie, A. E.: *The Christian Doctrine of the Godhead.*

Gieseler, J. C. L.: *A Compendium of Ecclesiastical History* (English translation by S. Davidson).

Gore, C.: *Belief in Christ.*

Gore, C.: *Belief in God.*

Goussen, H.: *Martyrius-Sahdona's Leben und Werke.*

Grensted, L. W.: *The Person of Christ.*

Grove, A. J., and Newell, G. E.: *Animal Biology.*

Gwatkin, H. M.: *Studies of Arianism* (Second Edition).

Gwatkin, H. M.: *The Arian Controversy.*

Harnack, A.: *Lehrbuch der Dogmengeschichte.*

Hefele, C. J. von: *Conciliengeschichte* (Second Edition). (Sometimes quoted, owing to changes in German orthography made towards the end of the nineteenth century, as 'Hefele, K. J. von: *Konziliengeschichte*'.) (English translation, Second Edition, by W. R. Clark, *A History of the Christian Councils*; French translation by Abbé Delarc, *Histoire des Conciles.*)

Hodgson, L.: *The Doctrine of the Trinity.* (See also Driver and Hodgson.)

Jeans, J.: *Physics and Philosophy.*

Jeans, J.: *The Mysterious Universe.*

Journal of Theological Studies: relevant articles.

Jugie, M.: *Nestorius et la controversie nestorienne.*

Kidd, B. J.: *A History of the Church to A.D.* 461.

Labbe, P.: *Sacrosancta concilia.*

Laird, J.: *Theism and Cosmology.*

Lampert, E.: *The Divine Realm.*

La Touche, E. D.: *The Person of Christ in Modern Thought.*

Libbey, H. C.: *Science looks at Jesus.*

Libbey, H. C.: *The Boy Jesus.*

Liddell, H. G., and Scott, R.: *A Greek-English Lexicon* (new edition, 1940, revised by H. S. Jones and R. McKenzie).

Loisy, A.: *La Naissance du Christianisme.*

Loisy, A.: *Les Origines du Nouveau Testament.*

Loofs, F.: *Nestoriana.*

Loofs, F.: *Nestorius*.

Luce, A. A.: *Monophysitism Past and Present*.

McDougall, W.: *Body and Mind*.

McDougall, W.: *The Riddle of Life*.

Mackintosh, H. R.: *The Doctrine of the Person of Jesus Christ* (Second Edition).

Maher, M.: *Psychology* (Ninth Edition).

Mansi, G. D.: *Sacrorum conciliorum nova et amplissima collectio* (based on Labbe's *Sacrosancta concilia*).

Margoliouth (Mrs.), J. P.: *Supplement to the Thesaurus Syriacus*. (See Smith, R. Payne.)

Mascall, E. L.: *Christ, the Christian and the Church*.

Mascall, E. L.: *He Who Is*.

Mason, A. J.: *The Conditions of our Lord's Life on Earth*.

Matthews, W. R.: *Studies in Christian Philosophy*.

Mellor, J. W.: *A Comprehensive Treatise on Inorganic Chemistry*.

Migne, J. P.: *Patrologia Græco-Latina*.

Mingana, A.: See Narses.

Moberly, R. C.: *Atonement and Personality*.

Moberly, R. C.: *The Incarnation as the Basis of Dogma*.

Morgan, C. L.: *Emergent Evolution*.

Mozley, J. K.: *The Impassibility of God*.

Narses: *Homilia et Carmina* (edited by A. Mingana).

Nau, F.: *Nestorius: Le Livre d'Héraclide de Damas, traduit en français par F. Nau*.

Neander, A.: *General History of the Christian Religion and Church* (English translation by J. Torrey).

Nestle, E.: *Syriac Grammar* (English translation by R. S. Kennedy).

Nestorius: *Sermons and other Writings*. See Loofs, *Nestoriana*.

Nestorius: *The Bazaar of Heracleides*. See Bedjan, Driver and Hodgson, and Nau.

Nöldeke, T.: *Compendious Syriac Grammar* (English translation by J. A. Crichton).

Nolloth, C. F.: *The Person of Our Lord and Recent Thought*.

Otto, R.: *The Kingdom of God and the Son of Man* (English translation by F. V. Filson and B. L. Woolf).

Pesch, C.: *Nestorius als Irrlehrer*.

Pesch, C.: *Zur neueren Literatur über Nestorius*.

Planck, M. K. E. L.: *The Universe in the Light of Modern Physics* (English translation by W. H. Johnston).

Prestige, G. L.: *God in Patristic Thought*.

Poynting, J. H., and Thompson, J. J.: *Electricity and Magnetism*.

Raven, C. E.: *Apollinarianism*.

GI

Rawlinson, A. E. J. (editor): *Essays on the Trinity and the Incarnation.*

Relton, H. M.: *A Study in Christology.*

Relton, H. M.: *Some Postulates of a Christian Philosophy.*

Robinson, T. H.: *Syriac Grammar.*

Rucker, I.: *Studien zum Concilium Ephesinum.*

Sanday, W.: *Christologies Ancient and Modern.*

Schrödinger, E.: *What is Life?*

Seeberg, R.: *Lehrbuch der Dogmengeschichte* (Third Edition).

Sellers, R. V.: *Two Ancient Christologies.*

Smith, J. D. M.: *Chemistry and Atomic Structure.*

Smith, R. Payne: *Thesaurus Syriacus.*

Smuts, J. C.: *Holism and Evolution.*

Socrates: *Historia Ecclesiastica.*

Sorley, W. R.: *Moral Values and the Idea of God.*

Strauss, D. F.: *Leben Jesu.*

Tixeront, J.: *Histoire des Dogmes* (Second Edition).

Webb, C. C. J.: *God and Personality.*

Weston, F.: *The One Christ.*

Weyl, H.: *Raum, Zeit, Materie.*

Whitehead, A. N.: *Process and Reality.*

Whitehead, A. N.: *Science and the Modern World.*

Whitehead, A. N.: *The Concept of Nature.*

GENERAL INDEX

INDEX TO PASSAGES IN THE BAZAAR

Comment on passages in the *Bazaar* should first be sought in the appropriate place in the Appendix (pp. 411–476). This index enables any other comment or reference to be traced. Reference is given in the form "B. 51...73, 144," which means: "Something on B. 51 is quoted or referred to on pp. 73 and 144 of this book."

INDEX TO PASSAGES OF SCRIPTURE